KĀLĪ'S CHILD

KĀLĪ'S CHILD

The Mystical and the Erotic in the Life and Teachings of Ramakrishna

JEFFREY J. KRIPAL

With a foreword by Wendy Doniger

THE UNIVERSITY OF CHICAGO PRESS
Chicago & London

Jeffrey J. Kripal is the Vira I. Heinz Assistant Professor of Religion at Westminster College in New Wilmington, Pennsylvania.

The University of Chicago Press, Chicago 60637
The University of Chicago Press, Ltd., London

Printed in the United States of America

04 03 02 01 00 99 98 97 96 95 1 2 3 4 5

ISBN: 0-226-45375-8 (cloth)
ISBN: 0-226-45376-6 (paper)

Portions of chapter 5 were originally published in "Kālī's Tongue and Ramakrishna: 'Biting the Tongue' of the Tantric Tradition," *History of Religions* 34, no. 2 (November 1994): 152–189, © 1994 by The University of Chicago.

Library of Congress Cataloging-in-Publication Data

Kripal, Jeffrey John, 1962–
Kali's child : the mystical and the erotic in the life and teachings of Ramakrishna / Jeffrey J. Kripal ; with a foreword by Wendy Doniger.
p. cm.
Includes bibliographical references and index.
1. Ramakrishna, 1836–1886. 2. Ramakrishna Mission—Biography. 3. Hindus—India—Biography. I. Title.
BL1280 292.R36K75 1995 94-48743
294.5′55′092—dc20 CIP

∞ The paper used in this publication meets the minimum requirements of the American National Standard for Information Sciences—Permanence of Paper for Printed Library Materials, ANSI Z39.48-1984.

For Julie,

নায়িকা সাধন, শুনহ লক্ষণ,
যেরূপে করিতে হয় ।
শুষ্ক কাষ্ঠের সম, আপনার দেহ
করিতে হয় ।।
ব্রহ্মাণ্ড ব্যাপিয়া আছয়ে যে জন
কেহ না দেখয়ে তারে ।
প্রেমের পীরিতি, যে জন জানয়ে,
সেই সে পাইতে পারে ।।

Chandidas

CONTENTS

FOREWORD

In its previous incarnation this was an extraordinary dissertation, and now it has been reborn as a wonderful book. As a dissertation it was unusual not merely in its scholarly qualities, which are considerable, but in its charm: it was full of sex and humor and playful writing, and I found myself smiling often and laughing almost as often as I read it—something that, to put it mildly, rarely happens when you read dissertations. (When I took chapters of it with me to the beach last summer, people offered to trade me their novels—mostly Susan Sontag and Norman Mailer—for a chance to read it, so evident was my pleasure in it. I was sorry that academic decorum forced me to deny them that pleasure, but now they can read the whole thing.) The work has lost none of its liveliness in crossing the great divide into bookhood, and as a book it will, I think, delight many readers, infuriate others, and generate a great deal of creative controversy.

Kālī's Child focuses on the gender reversals implicit in the writings about Ramakrishna and raises intimate and sensitive questions about the sexuality of a man whom many regard as a saint. It confronts the problem of reading the personality of a saint in a way that simultaneously respects and challenges the interpretation cherished by the native tradition. Further, it raises questions about the relationship between sanctity and insanity and about the status of historical data that have been filtered through a hagiographic tradition.

Kripal is fully aware of the intricacies of these questions and has developed his own personal, fair-minded formulation of possible answers. His study therefore tells us a great deal about a man who was a very important figure both in Indian religious history and in the history of India's impact on the West, and whose alleged/apparent sexual aberrations were problematic to him, to his contemporaries, and to those who guarded the subsequent hagiographic tradition. The book will therefore be of great interest not merely to Indologists and historians of religions but to students of cross-cultural psychology and of gender. It also offers a most-needed and welcome corrective to the studies of the goddess that are proliferating in religious studies, in feminist studies, and in the culture at large; Ramakrishna's goddess is someone whom one would think twice about worshiping, let alone marrying (or voting for as a U.S. senator).

The subject takes on the solidity of three dimensions, as Kripal views his subject through two lenses simultaneously. The first lens, the native lens, is the enormous corpus of textual evidence in Bengali and English about Ramakrishna. I cannot recall ever working with a student who knew the basic text so thoroughly at the beginning of the dissertation as Kripal knows the *Kathāmṛta,* the principle text dealing with the life of Ramakrishna. He knows the text inside and out, and has come almost to think with it, through it, when he tries to think through a problem in the life of his subject. The other lens, the Western lens, through which he views his subject is that of a particularly humanistic brand of psychoanalysis. Kripal has a well-balanced and well-informed grasp of the ways in which Western psychological theories, such as Freud's, are and are not useful in analyzing a Hindu mystic. He is anything but reductive or doctrinaire in this matter. He makes use of only the most basic and least controversial aspects of Freud's thought, such as the theory of the unconscious, of the censorship of the unconscious, and of the distortion of the latent material of the unconscious through such processes as displacement. He carefully avoids the more detailed and distorting aspects of Freud's theories, refusing to wield the Oedipus complex or the castration complex as a cookie cutter to slice up Hindu culture. He is also free of the biases against religion and against homosexuality that mar so much of the work of Freudians in the field of cultural studies. He is sensitive to the homophobia in the culture in which Ramakrishna lived, but he does not share it. He is simply concerned to ferret out hidden meanings below the surface of the man's behavior, meanings hidden by Ramakrishna's own conscious mind as well as by the protective instincts of his followers. His analyses are right on target.

I am very proud to have played a small part in this wonderful book.

Wendy Doniger

PREFACE: "A VISION OF EMPTINESS"

RAMAKRISHNA ONCE SAW the goddess in a vision. She emerged from the dark waters of the river, gave birth to a child before the saint's eyes, and then proceeded to eat it. As a terror-stricken Ramakrishna watched the horrible sight, he noticed that the child became "empty" as it entered the goddess's mouth. On the outside, as a creature, it was solid enough. Inside the goddess, however, it was merely a relative moment in a flurry of mystical "emptiness" (*śūnyatā*). Ramakrishna came out of the dreamlike vision and confidently advanced his own interpretation: "Everything is empty!"

Kālī's Child is meant to function in ways not unlike those of Ramakrishna's vision. The religious world that the book attempts first to recover and then to present and decipher may, much like the saint's vision, initially horrify some of its readers. Those readers who have given their lives to Ramakrishna, whether in personal devotion or in a formal commitment, might be particularly troubled. I can only hope that the book, like Ramakrishna's vision, is nuanced and sophisticated enough to carry them beyond their initial shame, disgust, and fear (and the anger such emotions might encourage) to a deeper understanding of what both this work and their own Master's visions are all about: Kālī and her mystically "empty" Tantric world. Certainly it is not my intent to offend or to anger. Rather, I am after something that might be better described as surprise, shock, or awe. Such reactions, of course, are ambivalent, for they carry within themselves the seeds of both revelation and rejection. I can only state here that for me such emotions have functioned more as revelations than as reasons for rejection. It is awe and wonder, certainly not malice, that have carried me through the years it took to see this work to completion.

Kālī's Child also shares something of the "empty" nature of the vision in that it is only a relative moment, a snapshot if you will, of a larger, ongoing project of inquiry. I thus ask that the book be read not as a definitive conclusion, which it is not, but as a tentative summary of where I stand now and, moreover, as a suggestion of where I would like to see the scholarship go from here. It is no exaggeration to say that Ramakrishna studies are still in their infancy. There are too many texts still to translate (and retranslate), too many personalities to research, and too many questions left unanswered (or even unasked) for us to draw any definitive conclusions. We are only at the beginning.

Further, this larger personal project, of which this book is only a part, must itself be contextualized, and so again relativized, within another equally complicated and halting process of energy and desire—my own life. In this sense too *Kālī's Child* is eminently "empty." The book, in other words, resembles Ramakrishna's vision, and more particularly the child of the vision, on a specifically autobiographical plane. On the surface the book might appear to be real enough, the product of an individual human being. In reality, however, "inside the goddess," if you will, it possesses no such distinct identity, for its genesis, content, and form are all products of a flurry of virtually infinite energies, presences, books, dreams, thoughts, hopes, and relationships. Although notes are a way to acknowledge some of the academic dimensions of this emptiness, prefatory acknowledgments seek to convey something of its existential meanings. In this spirit, I would like first to affirm here the biographical context of this study and then acknowledge at least a few of the relationships that have taught, challenged, encouraged, and loved this particular Child into being.

§ § §

AS AN AUTHOR who has spent the last six years trying to uncover the intimate details of another human being's life, I should say at least something about why I have done so. My original interests in erotic mysticism began while I was studying in a Benedictine seminary and considering the monastic life as a vocation. While living and studying there, I became fascinated with the relation between human sexuality and mystical experience, partly through my personal observations and partly through my reading of the great Spanish mystics John of the Cross and Teresa of Avila. Such interests eventually led me to Indian Tantra and its own systematization of the mystical and the erotic. I had heard that Tantra was especially popular in Bengal, so I took up Bengali in graduate school and soon found myself in Calcutta. As part of my tutoring, I began reading the Bengali texts about Ramakrishna and was immediately struck by their Tantric dimensions and the way these aspects had been covered up in the official translations of the tradition. I also eventually discovered that these same Tantric elements revealed all sorts of symbolic tensions and emotional conflicts that in turn fell into consistent patterns, most of them shaped by the saint's pronounced homosexual tendencies. I did not go looking for a homoerotic saint, nor were my research motives political in any advocative sense. From my own perspective, I was asking questions about erotic mysticism in the history of religions; as I focused on a particular historical manifestation of this phenomenon, however, I was confronted with further questions that I simply could not ignore, such as the role of homosexuality in this type of experience.

All of this implies that I have read Ramakrishna's life, at least partially, through the lens of my own. I knew, of course, that the cultural and personal curves of that lens would distort some aspects of his life and teachings, but I was also convinced that these same curves would bring other dimensions of his life into sharp, unmistakable focus. I am still convinced that what follows is more focused than false. Precisely what I have distorted and what I have clarified I leave to my colleagues and the historical record to decide.

I am not a Hindu. Nor do I consider the saint my guru. And yet I cannot help but think that Ramakrishna has deeply affected me. In my more imaginative and bolder moments, I also allow myself to think that if Ramakrishna were alive and could fully understand what follows, this work would deeply affect *him,* for he could then read his life through the lens of mine and see things he never saw before. Perhaps something here might clear up a particular vision or help him deal more adequately with some of his painful emotional reactions. Whatever objective basis such thoughts might have in our world of space and time, they are nevertheless very real for me and this book, for I wrote it from a perspective defined by just such an imaginal world. This world, if nothing else, has at least given me a genuinely human way of understanding Ramakrishna and, through him, myself. As such the book is an act, if not of love, certainly of friendship, sympathy, and a deep compassion.

§ § §

BUT THE BIOGRAPHICAL CONTEXT of the present book is by no means exhausted with such a personal *muthos,* for numerous other figures have graced this same story with their talents and time. I am above all indebted to Wendy Doniger. Her own voluminous work, in both its rhetorical style and its erotic content, provided me with a scholarly context, a genre if you will, in which I could write and defend my own ideas. Wendy, moreover, was always ready to read yet another draft or conclusion, went out of her way to write a foreword for the book, and, most important, laughed at all the right places (and then some). Clinton Seely and Bernard McGinn sat with Wendy on the dissertation committee that guided and counseled me through the early and middle stages of this project. Clint taught me Bengali, spent hours upon hours with me puzzling over arcane expressions, and allowed a banana in the story to dissolve his initial doubts about my psychoanalytic tendencies. In a different vein, Bernie's expertise in the study of Christian mysticism, theoretical sophistication, and truly Catholic interests served as an important model for me, since it was precisely out of these religious and philosophical traditions that my own questions were first born and articulated. Finally, I must also mention here the presence and learning of Edward Dimock Jr. It was Ed who first initiated me into things Bengali and Tantric and who told me strange stories about eight-armed visions and mysterious Tantric saints.

Aditi Sen and Hena Basu, both of Calcutta, also deserve to be acknowledged. Aditi's grace, charm, and literary tastes taught me much about Bengali culture and its rich language, and Hena's documentation services and professionalism have been invaluable to me as I tried to research a topic whose Calcutta sources I could not have possibly mined in the eight short months of my stay in that City of Kālī. I must also thank Swami Lokesvarananda of the Ramakrishna Mission Institute of Culture, who graciously put me up in the Institute's foreign scholars' wing for the extent of my stay in that remarkable city. Outside and inside Calcutta, a host of other colleagues have contributed to the book by agreeing to read the manuscript in one of its many incarnations. Stanley Kurtz offered his psychoanalytic and anthropological expertise in the form of numerous shared articles and books, lunch conversations, and phone calls. I thank him especially for his unique ability to create potent insights and new directions out of a mix of much-needed encouragement and healthy challenge. Narasingha "Ram" Sil of Western Oregon State also played an especially important role, offering criticisms, obscure texts, and his own brand of Bengali mischievousness along the way. I must also mention Narendra Nath Bhattacharyya of Calcutta University; Hal French of the University of South Carolina;

Carl Olson of Allegheny College; Bill Barnard of Southern Methodist University; and Norvin Hein, professor emeritus at Yale University. Rachel Fell McDermott also figures heavily in the text, both up front in the notes and behind the scenes in numerous conversations (many of them in bumpy Calcutta taxi rides) and conference projects. Finally, Sarah Caldwell pushed me at the very end of the project with troubling questions that I could only half answer and ask again.

The American Institute of Indian Studies supported me for eight months in Calcutta, and the Committee on South Asian Studies at the University of Chicago offered financial assistance for the final two years of the project's dissertation stage. Westminster College then picked up the project and offered me generous financial and institutional support in the form of a job and an endowed professorship. Finally, I must thank T. David Brent, senior editor at the University of Chicago Press, and the staff of the Press's various departments for transforming a very unwieldy manuscript into a more manageable and physically beautiful book. Here I would like to thank Robert Williams, assistant design manager, who designed the book, and Bimal Sen of Calcutta, a talented artist whose fiery Kālī graces the cover. Because this powerful image first appeared in a major Calcutta newspaper during Kālī-pūjā of 1989, while *Kālī's Child* was first being conceived, I cannot help associating it with those first few crucial months and the rituals and experiences that marked them as "auspicious." Bimal's Kālī has always struck me as an especially powerful, and lurid, image of the book's most basic ideas.

Finally, there are all of those particularly intimate relationships that define not so much what one does but who one is. I am quite sure that the present work (and perhaps its author) would never have taken form were it not for the Benedictine monks of Conception Abbey, who showed me the humanity of God and taught me to confront it. My parents, John and Idonna Kripal, have always supported me in my adventures, as much in the freedom they have silently bestowed as in the emotional and material gifts they have so actively showered upon me. I dedicate the work to my wife, Julie, an especially impressive manifestation of the goddess as both Mother and Lover. Finally, I would like to mention my two little daughters, Jenna and Jessica, whose giggles and attention ploys kept it all in perspective and without whom, as someone once put it so well, I would have finished this a lot sooner.

§ § §

SIGNIFICANT PORTIONS of three earlier articles appear strewn throughout the pages that follow in various revised forms: "Revealing and Concealing the Secret: A Textual History of Mahendranath Gupta's *Śrīśrīrāmakṛṣṇakathāmṛta*" (originally published in *Calcutta, Bangladesh, and Bengal Studies*, ed. Clinton B. Seely [Lansing: Michigan State University, 1992], 245–252); "Ramakrishna's Foot: Mystical Homoeroticism in the *Kathāmṛta*" (originally published in *Religion, Homosexuality and Literature*, ed. Michael L. Stemmeler and José Ignacio Cabezón, Gay Men's Issues in Religious Studies Series, vol. 3 [Las Colinas, Tex.: Monument Press, 1992], 31–74), quoted with permission of copyright holder and publisher; and "Kālī's Tongue and Ramakrishna: 'Biting the Tongue' of the Tantric Tradition" (originally published in *History of Religions* 34, no. 2 [November 1994]: 152–189).

A NOTE ON TRANSLITERATION

I HAVE ASKED MANY SCHOLARS who work with Bengali texts how we should be transliterating the Bengali script into roman characters. To my dismay, I have received a different answer every time. There simply is no standard transliteration scheme. One could, though, identify two broad camps. Some scholars, opting to be faithful to the Sanskritic derivation of many of the Bengali religiophilosophical terms, have chosen to use a transliteration scheme similar to that commonly used in transliterating *devanāgarī*. Others have chosen to stick more closely to the actual sound of the Bengali words and have created different transliteration schemes that carry over the "vernacular feel" of the texts. Whereas scholars from the former Sanskritic camp, for example, have written about "Śiva," even though Bengalis speak of a "Śib," scholars from the vernacular camp write only of this "Śib," despite the fact that it is a local Bengali variant of the "Śiva" of the Sanskrit tradition.

Both options are equally defensible. They are also both compromises. For my own part, I have chosen to write primarily, but by no means exclusively, out of the Sanskritic camp, partly because I sense that constantly referring to "Śib" and "*bed*" (instead of "Śiva" and "*veda*") artificially isolates the Bengali discourse from its broader historical context, but mostly because I am convinced that this Sanskritizing scheme more accurately reflects the self-representation of the tradition I am studying. After all, no one in the Ramakrishna tradition writes in English about "Bibekanando," "Bedanto," and "Ramkrishno"; rather, they write about "Vivekananda," "Vedanta," and "Ramakrishna," all Sanskritized transliterations of the Bengali words. I am aware that much of my work argues passionately against such a Sanskritizing of Ramakrishna's quintessentially vernacular character, but I prefer to present my case in terms that are not completely foreign either to the historical discourse of the tradition itself or to the Sanskritized ears of many of my readers.

Accordingly, Sanskrit terms, Bengali expressions or phrases, and all names of mythological figures will be Sanskritized and written with the proper *devanāgarī* diacritical marks. Names of historical figures and most place-names, however, will occur in their most popular transliterated forms, whether these preserve the "Bengali feel" of the language, for example, "Ramprasad" (instead of "Rāmaprasāda"), or Sanskritize the word, for example, "Ramakrishna" (not "Ramkrishno"). Along similar lines, I will italicize most Sanskrit and Bengali terms, but I will not italicize mythological figures or technical terms that are used extensively in the book (like "Vedānta" and "Tantra"). In short, because the culture itself rocks back and forth between Sanskritic and vernacular transliteration schemes, I too will alternate between the two options, trying as best I can to approximate the self-representation of the culture. This dualistic system will carry over into the bibliographic references as well, with authors, place-names, and presses recorded in approximate vernacular transliterations and book titles appearing in their Sanskritized forms with full *devanāgarī* diacritical marks.

Such a system no doubt will strike the linguistically sensitive reader as a confused mélange of broken rules and inconsistencies. I can only admit my compromises, note that they are at least partly a function of the culture's own history, and hope that they do not unduly draw attention away from the broader religious and cultural issues this book tries to address. *Kālī's Child,* after all, is not about diacritical marks or the technicalities of transliteration schemes. It is about a man who stuttered, spoke a delightfully crude form of village Bengali, knew only a few words of broken, mispronounced English, and liked to make fun of us "dry" boring scholars. I hope that what follows will be judged by what it has to say about him and not by whether there is a line over this or that *a*.

ABBREVIATIONS

GSR	*The Gospel of Sri Ramakrishna*
GM	*The Great Master*
JU	*Śrī Śrī Rāmakṛṣṇa Paramahaṁsa—Jīvana o Upadeśa*
JV(4)	*Śrīśrīrāmakṛṣṇa Paramahaṁsadever Jīvanavṛttānta,* 4th ed.
JV(5)	*Śrīśrīrāmakṛṣṇa Paramahaṁsadever Jīvanavṛttānta,* 5th ed.
JV(7)	*Śrīśrīrāmakṛṣṇa Paramahaṁsadever Jīvanavṛttānta,* 7th ed.
KA	*Śrīśrīrāmakṛṣṇa-Kathāmṛta*
KS	*Karpūrādistotram*
KT	*Kālī Tantra*
LP	*Śrīśrīrāmakṛṣṇa-Līlāprasaṅga*
PDU	*Paramahaṁsadever Ukti*
PRU	*Paramahaṁsa Rāmakṛṣṇer Ukti*
PU	*Paramahaṁser Ukti (Dvitīya Saṁkhyā) evaṁ Saṁkṣipta Jīvana*
RJR	*Rāmaprasāda: Jīvanī o Racanāsamagra*
RSG	*Rāmaprasāda Sener Granthāvalī*
SM	*Śāstra Mūlaka Bhārata Śaktisādhana*
SP	*Śākta Padāvalī*
TP	*Tattvaprakāśikā* (1891)
TS	*Tattvasāra*
YT	*Yoni Tantra*

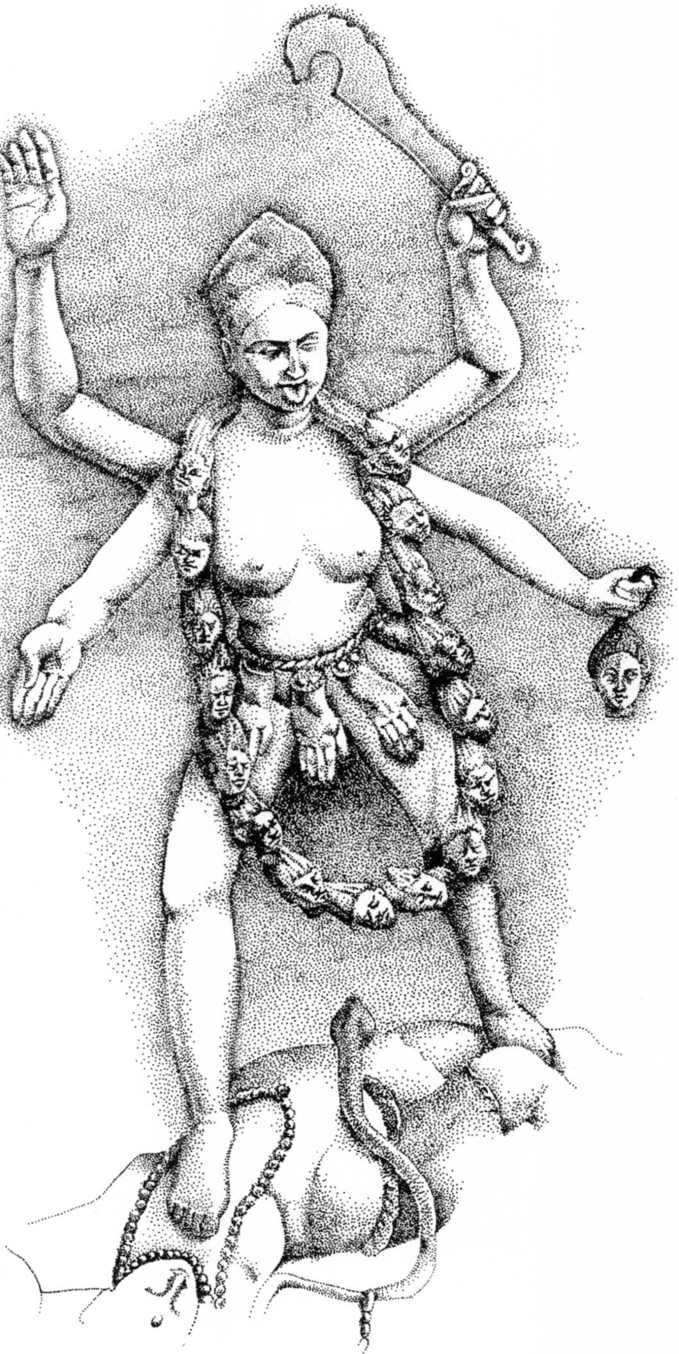

INTRODUCTION: APPROACHING THE SECRET

Now I'm telling you *something very secret.*

Ramakrishna in the *Kathāmṛta* 4.227

DEFINING THE STUDY: RECOVERING THE TEXT AND REVEALING THE SECRET

RAMAKRISHNA PARAMAHAṀSA [1] was a nineteenth-century Bengali mystic who experienced hundreds of ecstatic states and visions, experimented with different religious traditions, including something he called "the Jesus state," entertained the belief that he was the latest of the incarnations of God, and played a major role in the creation of modern Hinduism, both directly through his teachings and indirectly through the work and writing of his most famous disciple, Swami Vivekananda. It would be difficult to overestimate Ramakrishna's importance within the Hindu tradition. Countless books have been written about him. His famous face, reproduced on innumerable posters, calendars, and statues, grins over stall after stall in the markets and streets of Calcutta. In the West whole generations of aspiring scholars and faith-filled seekers have cut their Indological teeth on his teachings, especially as they appear in Swami Nikhilananda's *The Gospel of Sri Ramakrishna,* a "classic" if ever there was one. Ramakrishna is everywhere, and everyone seems to know him. And yet, I would argue, no one really does. Despite the books and the posters and *The Gospel,* and his towering place in both the modern Hindu tradition and Western images of India, Ramakrishna has remained to this day a strange, mysterious, inexplicable saint, a being to marvel at perhaps but certainly not to understand.

Take, for example, the curious habits of his foot. When Ramakrishna went into *samādhi,* a type of mystical absorption, he would sometimes place this foot "in the lap" (*kole*)—that is, on the genitals—of a young boy disciple. Observers were scandalized by this "sinful" foot and would angrily confront the saint when he eventually came down from his ecstatic state. Ramakrishna never denied the troubling actions of his foot, but neither did he have an answer for his critics. In the end, by his own confession, he simply could not explain it. Nor could his disciples. No one since then has tried. Books that are as historically naive as they are sincere, glossy pictures that hide as much as they show, translations that are not translations, and talk (and more talk) about Vivekananda have effectively buried that foot and its meanings beneath a mountain of pious ink, touched-up images, bowdlerized books, and wordy words. As a result, the once outrageous Ramakrishna has become simply quaint.

This book can be read as one long attempt to ignore that mountain and get back to that foot. In it, I will argue that Ramakrishna's mystical experiences, far from being examples of some simple *samādhi,* "without even the smell of lust" (KA 5.105),[2] were in actual fact *profoundly, provocatively, scandalously erotic.* To this end, I will offer a historically accurate, psychologically nuanced reading of the Hindu Tantra as it was practiced by Ramakrishna. More specifically, I will demonstrate that even though Tantra, *not* Vedānta, structured the saint's ecstasies, visions, and teachings, Ramakrishna was emotionally torn by the tradition and its heterosexual symbolism; he could not be forced to complete the Tantric ritual of *maithuna* or "sexual intercourse" with a woman, for example, *not* because he had somehow transcended sex (the traditional claim) but because the ritual's heterosexual assumptions seriously violated the structure of his own homosexual desires. His female Tantric guru and temple boss may have forced themselves and numerous prostitutes on the saint for both personal and Tantric reasons, but Ramakrishna remained, until the very end, a lover not of sexually aggressive women or even of older men but of young, beautiful boys, those "pure pots," as he called them, that could hold the "milk" of his divine love. Finally, I will show in some detail how the saint took this Tantra, these desires, these gurus and bosses of his personal history, and fashioned out of his experience of them an impressive "spirituality of secrets" that could speak, and yet not speak, about the pain of his past, affirm the joys of his present, and transmute it all into a life of ecstasy and vision that would enter the realm of legend and myth.

In short, I will argue that Ramakrishna was a conflicted, unwilling, homoerotic Tāntrika who was as skilled at refashioning and realizing the meanings of the Hindu Tantra as he was uncomfortable in its symbolic world. I will amply support this claim with an array of nineteenth- and early twentieth-century Bengali texts, many of which, having been threatened, denied, and systematically censored by Ramakrishna's monastic disciples, have remained untranslated to this day.

Recovering the Text

ONE OF THE PRIMARY OBJECTS of this censoring, and the source of much nervousness within the tradition, happens also to be both the central text of the tradition and the centerpiece of this study, Mahendranath Gupta's *Śrīśrīrāmakṛṣṇakathāmṛta,*[3] known to Bengalis simply as the *Kathāmṛta* and to English readers as *The Gospel of Sri Ramakrishna.* Gupta's *Kathāmṛta,* based on diary notes he took down while he was with the saint, records in five volumes—published in 1902, 1904, 1908, 1910, and 1932—conversations Ramakrishna had with his disciples from 1882, the year Gupta met Ramakrishna, to a few months before the saint died in 1886. These five volumes are arranged cyclically, that is, instead of a linear chronological sequence (with volume 1 starting in 1882 and volume 5 ending in 1886), we find that each volume begins anew with 1882[4] and ends again in 1886. Each successive volume, in other words, makes another pass through the entire corpus of Gupta's diary notes, picking up material that the former volumes missed in their earlier passes.

Although this curious feature of the volumes has been noted before,[5] no one has been able to offer a convincing reason why Gupta chose to structure his text the way he did. It is a basic thesis of this study that the volumes are so structured in order to conceal, however intentionally, a secret. The best way to demonstrate this is to analyze Ramakrishna's "secret talk" (*guhya kathā*)—eighteen passages dealing with visions and confessions Ramakrishna thought too troubling or important to reveal to any but his most intimate disciples, whom he called his "inner circle"—and its distribution throughout the five volumes. What we find is that this "secret talk" is held back in volume 1 (there is not a single occurrence), hinted at in volume 2 (the term is used once in a section heading), toyed with in volume 3 (a "transition volume" with six relatively innocuous occurrences), and finally revealed in volume 4 (with eight, often potentially scandalous, secret talk passages). By the time

Gupta got to volume 5 (1932), he had apparently exhausted his diaries. There was not much left to tell. Accordingly, this last volume is very short and contains only three such secret talk passages. The text thus spirals through Gupta's diaries, penetrating further and further into Ramakrishna's secret as it goes along. The result is a reluctant text structured around an attempt to present certain more culturally acceptable aspects of Ramakrishna "up front" in the earlier volumes (1902, 1904, and 1908) and to push the more "secret" dimensions of Ramakrishna into the background of volume 4 (1910). The text, in other words, simultaneously reveals and conceals Ramakrishna's secret.

But Gupta, whose very name means "the Hidden" and who preferred to hide even "the Hidden" and be called simply M, *did* reveal the contents of Ramakrishna's secret talk, if only in the later volumes.[6] In his English translation, *The Gospel of Sri Ramakrishna,* Swami Nikhilananda, on the other hand, systematically concealed the secret M had reluctantly revealed. Nikhilananda violated both the form and the content of M's *Kathāmṛta,* rearranging the scenes in a neat linear sequence and ingeniously mistranslating many of the secrets; those passages for which he could not find a suitably safe enough "translation," he simply omitted. Nikhilananda's claim, then, that "I have made a literal translation, omitting only a few pages of no particular interest to English-speaking readers" (GSR, vii) should not be taken seriously. Those "few pages of no particular interest" contain some of the most revealing and significant passages of the entire text.[7]

Revealing the Secret

HAVING GONE BACK to the original Bengali text and its secrets, I am convinced—and this is the basic thesis of the study—that *Ramakrishna's mystical experiences were constituted by mystico-erotic energies that he neither fully accepted nor understood.* This is the secret, uninterpreted and so unknown, that glimmers so provocatively behind Ramakrishna's secret talk. As I will demonstrate in the course of the study, in case after case the Paramahaṁsa's sexual and mystical energies manifest themselves simultaneously in visionary experience, in ecstatic acts, and in symbolic discourse. They are joined at the hips, if you will.

Now this secret, at least in its emphasis on the link between the mystical and the sexual, is a secret often proclaimed in the Hindu Tantra, a tradition famous (or infamous) for its insistence that human eroticism and religious experience are intimately related, even identical on some deep energetic level. In asserting this basic relationship between the mystical and the sexual, then, I am in effect proposing that Ramakrishna was a Tāntrika.

But such an assertion is problematic, for Ramakrishna, who was quite conversant though very uncomfortable with Tantra, often questioned or even denied this basic Tantric equation of the mystical and the erotic. When a disciple, for example, mouthed the Tantric dictum that "the same mystical energy [*śakti*] that results in the bliss of God also produces the pleasure of sensual experience," Ramakrishna retorted: "What is this? Can the power that produces children be the same power that results in the experience of God?" (KA 2.231). If Ramakrishna was a Tāntrika, it seems that either he was not willing to admit the fact to others (not an uncommon strategy among practicing Tāntrikas) or that he himself was not fully aware of his own Tantric identity. Although there is no doubt some truth in both of these explanations, I am of the opinion that the latter interpretation, what we might call the psychological explanation, is the more convincing one. Tantra for Ramakrishna was not some simple thing that one practiced in private and then intentionally denied in public; rather, it was a grave and ominous tradition of teachings and techniques that haunted him, that horrified him, and yet that somehow formed who he was. Tantra was Ramakrishna's secret.

The unconscious nature of this secret becomes particularly evident when one examines closely not just what the Paramahaṁsa said but also what he did. Consider again the controversial actions of Ramakrishna's foot. When scandalized observers would confront him after he had emerged from *samādhi,* Ramakrishna would sometimes defend himself by insisting that he had no control over his actions while he was in such a state. He neither denied the action nor attempted to interpret its meaning; he simply refused to acknowledge it as his own. The shocking connection between the mystical and the sexual that others saw in his foot he himself simply disowned. In other words, *Ramakrishna's secret was secret even to himself.* He neither fully accepted the energetic unity of the sexual and the mystical proclaimed in Tantra nor was he capable of interpreting his own visions and acts as symbolic manifestations of this Tantric truth. This, no doubt, was why Ramakrishna, puzzled by his own visions and behavior, consistently turned to others for commentary, explanation, and defense in the face of criticism.

Ramakrishna's secret, then, has been triply concealed: (1) from the saint himself in visionary symbolism and unconscious ecstatic acts and (2) from M's readers in a complex cyclical structure and (3) a bowdlerized translation. Consequently, to begin to reveal this secret, Nikhilananda's translation must first be rejected and the original Bengali text must be recovered. The Bengali text must then be approached as a text informed by a dual attempt to reveal and conceal a secret. But this is still not enough. Even once Ramakrishna's secret talk has been located and described through the methods of textual analysis and translation, Ramakrishna's secret has not yet been revealed. We still only have a series of visions, ecstatic gestures, and mystical experiences recorded in a particular text. Such experiences do not organize themselves into meaningful patterns. They do not speak of themselves, not even to Ramakrishna, who was the first to admit that he did not always understand their meanings. To reveal Ramakrishna's secret, then, these visions, gestures, and states must be related to one another in some sort of meaningful whole, that is, *they must be interpreted.*

In interpreting the mystico-erotic experiences of Ramakrishna, I will employ two hermeneutical strategies, two meaningful wholes in which to understand the seemingly disjointed pieces and parts of Ramakrishna's experiences. One of these wholes, the Hindu Tantra, is indigenous to Bengali culture. The other, psychoanalysis, is a product of my own cultural heritage. Whereas the Hindu Tantra proposes a dialectical relationship between the mystical and the sexual, psychoanalysis, at least in its more traditional forms, unabashedly reduces the mystical to the sexual, understood in its most materialistic sense. Both, it should be noted, are interpretations. With such a dual perspective, I intend to demonstrate the extent to which psychoanalysis can make sense out of some of the otherwise bizarre behavior of Ramakrishna, but also how Tantra, with its dialectical model and its refusal to reduce the mystical to the simply sexual, can help us in interpreting mystical eroticism. In short, cautiously and critically looking both ways, acknowledging both but accepting neither in toto, I want to offer a nonreductive, psychoanalytically informed reading of Ramakrishna's mystical eroticism.

The study's method or "approach" (*meta-hodos*) to its subject, then, is neither strictly phenomenological, concentrating on ahistorical patterns of meaning, nor strictly psychohistorical, approaching religious forms as psychic aggregates built up over time through social interaction and symbolic discourse. In its attempt to demonstrate that Ramakrishna's mystical experiences and teachings can best be interpreted within a Tantric symbolic world, the study is phenomenological, for it argues its point by identifying consistent patterns of meaning enfolded into the symbols and metaphors of Ramakrishna's visions and language.

But in doing so, history, in the form of biography, inevitably creeps in, for, as I try to show, these Tantric phenomena often need to be uncovered through the methods of translation and symbolic analysis and are themselves at least partly dependent on biographical events in the saint's life that stretch back to his early encounters with his female Tantric guru, and even further back, to his adolescence and early childhood. One might say, then, that the study's general phenomenological method is further enriched by psychoanalytic principles. As such, it seeks to understand, not only "that which appears" (*phenomenon*), but also "that which does not appear" or, perhaps better, "that which does not appear clearly." Unlike psychoanalysis, however, the study's method does not reduce these half-appearances to strictly historical, social, or psychological forces. Rather, it insists on bracketing such ontological questions and opts instead to operate sympathetically *within* Ramakrishna's Tantric world. Hence it takes on the body of the goddess herself, modeling each chapter after a particular feature of her iconographic form.

In the language of our texts, the present inquiry is a *study of secrets*, of secrets hinted at but never fully revealed. But it is also a study of the *history* of these secrets, for it attempts to show how these secrets were generated, interpreted, debated, transformed, and eventually appropriated by the larger culture. Two social typologies determined the details and eventual outcome of this history: the householder and the renouncer; and the inner and the outer circles. Since my own hermeneutical stance assumes a certain position in relation to these social groupings and their interpretive strategies, it is essential that I discuss each of them in turn.

The Conflict between the Householders and the Renouncers

THE HOUSEHOLDERS CONSISTED of Ramakrishna's older married disciples, who, among other things, provided much of the early financial support for the movement. The renouncers, on the other hand, consisted of Ramakrishna's much younger boy disciples, who, rather than marry, took vows of renunciation and eventually became the first monks of the Ramakrishna Order. As we have them in the *Kathāmṛta*, it is a bit anachronistic to call these teenagers renouncers. Most of them, after all, were still living at home with their parents at this period (1882–1886). But since we are interested not in the technical definition of what constitutes a renouncer but in the way such a socioreligious category helped to define the intent, the content, and the interpretation of Ramakrishna's teaching, it is important that we consider the boys to be renouncers. Ramakrishna certainly did and adjusted his teachings to them accordingly.

Now although these two groups of disciples, the householders and the renouncers, were bound together on numerous levels—familial, spiritual, and financial—they also fought a great deal, disagreeing on just about everything. Most likely, such a primordial split in the community of disciples had at least something to do with the personality of Ramakrishna himself, who was technically both a householder (he was married) and a renouncer (he took a vow of renunciation). And Ramakrishna's split vocation, no doubt, was at least partly generated by the basic conflict in Hindu culture between these two ways of being in the world.[8] The saint, split in himself and split by his culture, seems to have passed this vocational ambivalence on to his disciples through his ambiguous remarks about the householder life, his misogynous statements and often cruel treatment of his own wife, and his predilection for keeping the householders and the renouncers apart when he taught them. The cultural conflict that found no permanent resolution in the life of Ramakrishna was thus passed on and embodied anew in the community of disciples: "He [Ramakrishna] did not talk about the renouncer disciples in the presence of the householder disciples, and he did not talk about the householder disciples in the presence of the renouncer disciples. But sometimes he would criticize both groups when both were present. They would chastise one another. In this way, there was a certain feeling of hostility [*vairībhāva*] between these two groups" (JV[4], 149).

It would be difficult to underestimate the depth and intensity of this "hostility." Take, for example, the case of the two cousins, the householder Ram Chandra Datta (the author of the passage just quoted) and the renouncer Narendra Nath Datta, better known to the world as Swami Vivekananda. Whereas there is no figure more central than Narendra to the renouncer version of Ramakrishna's life (Swami Saradananda's *Līlāprasaṅga*[9] spends more than one hundred pages on Narendra's first meetings with Ramakrishna and the details of their complex relationship), Narendra's name does not even appear in Ram's pioneering biography of the saint, the *Jīvanavṛttānta*! Why? We are never told explicitly, but Ram does go out of his way to tell his readers that certain well-known disciples threatened to sue him if he included their names in his biography. (Narendra, I might add, was once a law student.) Ram stresses the absurdity of all this but does not hesitate to offer two theories: perhaps such disciples wanted to make themselves into saints in place of the Paramahaṁsa, he speculates, or perhaps they simply did not want the shame of their previous lives to be exposed before the public. Denying that he fears any legal action, Ram closes the matter by describing these unnamed disciples as troublemakers who do not deserve to have their names connected with Ramakrishna anyway (JV[5], 144). Perhaps it was passages such as these that elicited Narendra's anger and led him to refer to his cousin's book as nothing but *"bosh and rot."*[10] Certainly it was feelings and scenes such as these that inspired Ramakrishna to explain, with a grin I am sure, how the renouncers and the householders even pee differently. Whereas the renouncer's stream veers to the right, he calmly and confidently noted, that of the householders veers to the left. Obviously, we are dealing here with a very deep cultural split.

To begin to make some sense out of such a situation and the effects that it had on the appropriation of Ramakrishna, I must begin by defining two broad traditions of appropriation. I will call them, predictably enough, the householder tradition and the renouncer tradition. Although in their social marks these two traditions are easily distinguished (renouncers are not married, wear ochre robes, live in single-sex religious communities instead of extended families, etc.), they are by no means mutually exclusive in the way they appropriate and interpret their Master's teachings. The householders, for example, may assert with their Master that the householder state is a legitimate religious response, but there is always a certain ambivalence behind this assertion, as if the renouncer state was somehow more adequate, more true to the real. The householder M, for example, felt especially reticent and ambivalent, indeed *ashamed,* about his married state.[11] And likewise, despite their obvious preference for the life of renunciation and purity, the renouncers take a certain amount of pride in pointing out that Ramakrishna was also a householder. In the minds and hearts of the disciples, then, there is always something of a renouncer in the householder and something of a householder in the renouncer. Moreover, it should be pointed out that the two traditions actually agree on numerous points. Both traditions, for example, boldly assert that Ramakrishna was an incarnation of God. It should be made clear, however, that the householder tradition was the first to make this claim in a public setting in the person of its first and probably greatest spokesman, Ram Chandra Datta.

It is also worth noting that, in an unusual twist on things, sometimes the two traditions mirror one another in their reversals. The householder tradition, for example, has tended to downplay, if not outright deny, any sort of "social concern" in the teachings of Ramakrishna, whereas the renouncer tradition has built its very foundation on this assumed social ethic. For the householder tradition, Ramakrishna is primarily a mystic, a saint, a religious reality to be approached through prayer and meditation. The renouncer tradition does not deny such an understanding, but neither does it emphasize it, stressing instead its understanding of Ramakrishna as a social reformer, a protofeminist, the inspiration of Vivekananda's social programs. The householders, in other words, renounce the world in their reading while the renouncers enter and embrace it.

My polar typology, then, is just that—a typology, a *construct* to enable us to think about the issues surrounding the interpretation and appropriation of Ramakrishna's secrets. I do not intend it to be taken as a clear-cut distinction between two mutually exclusive traditions. The renouncer tradition and the householder tradition are constantly overlapping, responding to one another, fighting, agreeing, doubting, proclaiming, repressing. One cannot be understood without the other. If we are ever to begin to understand the history of Ramakrishna's secret, I believe that we must place ourselves somewhere in the middle of this debate. We belong, in other words, in the heart of a conflict. On a particular issue we can certainly side with the householder tradition or the renouncer tradition, and in many cases there are good reasons to do so, but when we step back and try to interpret the big picture, the entire movement of the religious form from its birth in the soul of Ramakrishna to its transformation and eventual deification in the hearts and minds of the Master and his disciples, it is essential that we hold in balance both visions of who Ramakrishna was and what his life meant. Only then will we be able to see how Ramakrishna's secret was fought over by the householders and the renouncers, how it was concealed, revealed, and eventually appropriated as a theological truth.

The Debate over the Inner and the Outer Circles

THIS HOUSEHOLDER/RENOUNCER DIVISION was not the only social grouping that defined the manner in which Ramakrishna's secret would be revealed, received, and interpreted. There was a second and in some ways more important division that cut across the householder/renouncer division, adding a new level of complexity to the manner in which Ramakrishna revealed himself to his disciples. In the language of the texts, there was an "inner circle" (*antaraṅga*) and an "outer circle" (*bahiraṅga*).[12] The inner circle, comprised of *both* householders and renouncers, constituted the select community of Ramakrishna and, as such, received his most intimate teachings and revelations. The outer circle, on the other hand, consisted of occasional visitors, guests, and the many women who sought the Master's company. (I am not aware of a single woman ever being described as a member of the inner circle.) Members of this outer circle received simple instructions on general religious topics. Eventually, Ramakrishna became tired of them and appointed a few of his householder disciples to teach them. Sometimes when he became downright annoyed with them, he would politely but insistently suggest that they "go look at the temples." This was an especially popular move when the guests happened to be women.[13]

There were two groups, then, that received very different sorts of treatment and teaching: the inner and the outer circles. Unlike the outer circle, the inner circle was by no means an easily defined, static sort of group. People moved in and out. Different passages thus give different accounts of who was in and who was out. Its membership clearly changed over time. Beloved boy disciples married and left the inner circle. The little boy Purna, for example, who was said to "complete" (*pūrṇa*) the inner circle with his arrival in the early months of 1885 (LP 5.9.1), is never mentioned in the later accounts. He had married and was gone. Not surprisingly, Ramakrishna himself never seems sure about the elite membership of his inner circle.

Nevertheless, it is essential that we attempt to place the disciples, and especially the writing disciples, in either the inner or the outer circle, for *the social place of a particular author determines in large part the nature of the teachings he received and the manner in which he interpreted them.* Take, for example, the crucial case of M, the author of the *Kathāmṛta.* Was he in or out of Ramakrishna's famous inner circle? And how did his status affect the nature of his writing? For his part, M clearly believed that he was part of this inner circle. Again and again, Ramakrishna reveals his secret talk to his most intimate disciples, to his inner circle, *and M is there.* M's belief, no doubt, was nourished and confirmed by Ramakrishna himself. In one passage, for example, the Paramahaṁsa reports that he had a vision of Caitanya (a sixteenth-century Bengali saint believed by his followers to be an incarnation of God) and his disciples. Ramakrishna explains to his listeners that he saw his own disciples among the elect number of Caitanya's disciples: Caitanya's disciples, the vision seems to say, have reincarnated again to become Ramakrishna's disciples. Ramakrishna then turns to M and tells him that he thinks he saw him among their number (KA 4.45).[14] In another passage, Ramakrishna describes two "levels" (*thāka*) of disciples and tells M that he belongs to the higher level, to the inner circle: "There are two types of devotees who come here. One type says 'O Lord, save me!' The other type, those who belong to the inner circle, don't say such things. If they know two things, they are content: first, Who am I? and second, Who are they in relation to me? You belong to this last group" (KA 4.99).[15] This is a significant passage. Methodologically speaking, that Ramakrishna understood M to belong to the inner circle is very important, since it establishes M's text as a unique record of the inner circle's discourse and the secrets that constituted its life and energy.

Renouncer interpreters of Ramakrishna, however, seeking to establish their own views of Ramakrishna, have sought to expel M from this inner circle, claiming that, since he was only a householder and never renounced the world, he could not have been in the inner circle. His *Kathāmṛta*, from this renouncer point of view, is little more than a collection of "Sunday notes."[16] This is a serious charge, but one rooted, I think, more in nervous polemics than a serious look at the social context of Ramakrishna's revelations and teachings. The renouncer criticism, after all, is based on a false conflation of the renouncer/householder typology with the inner/outer circle typology, for it assumes that being a householder is equivalent to being a member of the outer circle and that being a renouncer is equivalent to being a member of the inner circle. From this perspective, renouncer equals inner circle and householder equals outer circle. But these two social typologies are *not* the same, for they divide up the same disciples along different lines. True, if so-and-so is said to be a renouncer, he is almost always also in the inner circle, but if so-and-so is a householder, this does *not* mean that he necessarily belongs to the outer circle. On the contrary, many householders were consistently described, even by the renouncers, as intimate members of Ramakrishna's inner circle. The social typologies of the renouncer/householder and the inner/outer circle, then, must be kept distinct.

This rather simple sociological observation carries major methodological implications, since the intended audience of Ramakrishna's secret talk, the topic of the present study, was *not* the renouncers (as opposed to the householders) but rather the inner circle (as opposed to the outer circle). Ramakrishna may indeed have split his disciples into renouncers and householders for many reasons, but when he wanted to reveal his secret talk, he made no distinction between the renouncers and the householders. All that mattered was that the listener was part of his inner circle, that, in Ramakrishna's words, that he was "my own." And if at times Ramakrishna *did* regulate his secret talk along the renouncer/householder lines, the texts would suggest that he preferred to reveal his secrets to the older householders and not to the much younger renouncers. This might explain why the householder texts, especially those of M and Ram Chandra Datta, are so full of bawdy secrets and those of the renouncers are so utterly silent. Perhaps Ramakrishna sensed the erotic nature of his secret and felt that the older householders, much more familiar with the way of desire (*kāma*), could better handle the revelations. The boys, after all, were, in the words of Ramakrishna himself, still "pure," untouched by the stain of lust. Perhaps Ramakrishna wanted to keep them so. In any case, it was the inner/outer circle distinction that defined the audience of Ramakrishna's secret talk, *not* the renouncer/householder division. Accordingly, the renouncer charge that M, being a householder, received only the "Sunday notes" of the Master does not stand up to closer analysis.

The renouncer/householder division, however, does become important when we come to the textual reception of Ramakrishna's secret talk, for the texts, as I have already pointed out, are indeed split along the renouncer/householder axis, with the householders faithfully recording the saint's secret talk and the renouncers scrupulously omitting or bowdlerizing it. Such a pattern tends to support my earlier suggestion that Ramakrishna may in fact have intentionally held his secrets back from the boy renouncers. In any case, the textual history of the secret would suggest that the householders were relatively comfortable with the secret whereas the renouncers either never received such revelations or, if they did, never fully accepted them. Certainly the renouncers cannot be considered the sole legitimate interpreters of Ramakrishna's life, as they sometimes claim they are. In the case of Ramakrishna's secret talk, at least, they have functioned more as censors than as interpreters, more as concealers than as revealers. One could, I think, even reverse the tables on them and claim that, to the extent that M's *Kathāmṛta* records secret talk that never appears in Swami Saradananda's *Līlāprasaṅga*, it is Saradananda's renouncer text, certainly not M's householder text, that more resembles a collection of "Sunday notes."

I begin, then, by defining the study as an interpretation of a secret revealed and concealed in a text. I propose to approach this secret with a phenomenological method enriched by the analytical insights of psychoanalysis. Moreover, I locate the study and its positions within a broader conflict of interpretations defined by two Hindu social groups, the householders and the renouncers, and by two types of disciples, those of the inner circle and those of the outer circle. Finally, I am arguing that, despite the claims of the renouncers, M's *Kathāmṛta* is a legitimate and relatively accurate source for approaching and understanding the secret of Ramakrishna's life and teachings.

THE MYSTICAL AND THE EROTIC

IN M'S *KATHĀMṚTA*, we have a text that is capable of supplying us with an unusual amount of information about the secret life of Ramakrishna. We have a way into the inner circle of Ramakrishna's world. But how shall we approach this text? Once inside the inner circle, what then? Let us not forget that the members of Ramakrishna's inner circle disagreed profoundly over the meaning of the saint's visions and acts and that Ramakrishna himself confessed that he did not always understand their import. We are entering a conflict, then, and a debate. How shall we proceed? I begin with two major categories, what I call the mystical and the erotic. Since both terms have deep roots in Western religious and academic discourse and have been used in a multitude of different and sometimes contradictory ways, it is important that I define very carefully the manner in which I intend to use them. As will be my practice in the body of the study, I will order this theoretical discussion around an iconographic image, in this case, the image of Śiva and Śakti.

The Image of Śiva and Śakti and Contemporary Discourse on the Mystical

THE *KATHĀMṚTA* opens neither with a proclamation of Ramakrishna's divinity nor with a discourse on the nature of reality, but rather with a careful and loving description of the Dakshineshwar temple precincts. These opening pages are significant, for in a very real sense the sacred space of the temple grounds defined the contours of Ramakrishna's religiosity as well. Both were characterized by strong Vaiṣṇava and Śaiva presences. In spatial terms, there is a smaller (Vaiṣṇava) Rādhā-Kṛṣṇa temple to the north of the main Kālī temple and twelve (Śaiva) Śiva-*liṅgam* temples to the west of it. Ramakrishna often talked about Kṛṣṇa and Śiva. They were both important to his religious vision. But however important these Vaiṣṇava and Śaiva influences may have been, both the temple grounds and Ramakrishna's religiosity were ultimately defined by one central Śākta image, that of the goddess Kālī triumphantly astride her corpse-like husband, Śiva, in the central temple. However ecumenical things may have seemed to the observer (the temple grounds were inhabited by gods of numerous Hindu sects), the Tantric foundations of both the temple and the saint were always more basic, deeper, more secret. The temple itself, dedicated to "she who dwells in the cremation ground," was rooted quite literally in Tantric (and polemical) soil, built as it was on an abandoned Muslim graveyard.[17]

Kālī's image, then, dwelt at the center of both the temple and of Ramakrishna's mystical life. And so this study, like the text, begins with that image. M describes it in these words: "In the southern temple there is a beautiful stone image of Kālī! . . . On the altar there is a silver thousand-petaled lotus upon which lies Śiva. . . . The beautiful stone image of the three-eyed black goddess is standing on Śiva's breast. . . . On her neck she wears . . . a garland of heads made of gold. . . . The two left hands of the Three-Eyed One hold a human head and a sword, and her two right hands grant boons and bestow freedom from fear" (KA 1.9).[18] The image is a Tantric one in which the nature of mystical consciousness, and of the universe in general, is represented as a bipolar, dialectical reality that is at once static and dynamic, transcendent and immanent, conscious and erotic. Mythologically, this state of consciousness and the level of reality that it reflects is symbolized by the union of the quiescent Śiva, tranquil and unmoving in his pale transcendence, and the dynamic Śakti, vibrant and seductive in her black immanence. In the Dakshineshwar version of the pair, Śiva, the silent witness, looks up at Kālī standing on his breast. In other renditions of the image, Śiva's penis stands erect, aroused out of its quiescence by the goddess's erotic presence.

For the most part, contemporary academic discourse on the mystical has focused almost exclusively on what we might call the Śiva half of mystical experience, on that silent witness-like consciousness that lies prostrate beneath the goddess. Thus such things as "pure consciousness" and the possibility of a "common core" beneath the wild plethora of the world's mystical traditions have dominated a discussion carried on largely in philosophical and, more specifically, in epistemological terms. Steven Katz's philosophical attack on the epistemological assumptions of earlier common core theorists, for example, has defined the general tenor of many of the most recent works on mysticism. In his seminal 1978 article, "Language, Epistemology, and Mysticism," Katz argued against earlier common core theorists, who claimed that the apparent differences reported in the classical accounts are a result of doctrinal interpretations superimposed on an originally "pure" experience, with the (literally) bold thesis that "*There are NO pure (i.e. unmediated) experiences.*"[19] God, *nirvāṇa*, and *brahman* are not mere names arbitrarily applied to a common reality, but actual descriptions of different ontological structures corresponding to different doctrinal contexts.[20] Accordingly, there is no such thing as "mysticism" or "the mystical experience." There is only Buddhist mysticism, Christian mysticism, Hindu mysticism, and so on; even within a particular tradition, there are only mystical experiences, as each event is unique in itself, issuing from its own distinct epistemological context.

The advantages of Katz's program are legion. By demonstrating the complexity of the epistemological processes involved in mystical experience, Katz has convincingly shown the radical contextuality of mysticism and, by so doing, has pushed the academic study of mysticism to a new level of hermeneutical sophistication. But there are problems. Katz, for example, attacks, perhaps rightly, the assumptions of earlier theorists, but he has his own assumptions, which he does not always recognize as such. Katz's approach is basically Kantian. The real cannot be known in itself; all knowledge is mediated, refracted through incredibly complex sensory, emotional, and mental lenses before we come to know it as it appears to us. We only know an "appearance" (*phenomenon*), never the "real in itself" (*noumenon*). The mystic is no exception. He never knows reality in itself, as he claims. Rather, according to Katz, he knows it only as it appears to him through the doctrinal and linguistic screens of his own mind.

However useful such a position may be in approaching the texts, it is based on an assumption—an assumption, moreover, that in turn presumes a whole set of philosophical propositions about the structure of human experience that are often completely foreign to the mystical authors themselves. Most seriously, Katz's Kantian method presupposes an essentially dualistic model of experience—with a knowing subject, a known object, and an act of knowing—that many of the texts argue pointedly against. This, it seems to me, is a serious problem. How, after all, can we talk about the real being perceived by the mystic through mental screens when so many of the texts insist that the hidden heart of human consciousness is essentially nondual and inseparable from the "external" world? More specifically, how can we speak of three somethings (the knower, the known, and the mental screen) when the texts are talking about one or none?

Toward a Dialectical Approach to the Mystical: "Beyond Form and the Formless"

IF WE ARE EVER to understand mystical texts and the states that they seek to communicate, it is essential that we develop methodologies epistemologically sophisticated enough to enter, however tentatively, into *their* perspective. At present our methodologies, Katz's included, too often assume from the outset that human experience is essentially dual. That the texts themselves so often dismiss such an assumption as false may not give us sufficient reason to abandon our beliefs, but it should at least give us reason to pause and consider whether we have truly met the challenge that mystical states offer, not only to our clumsy categories and halting methodologies but to our most basic assumptions of what it means to be human.

A number of scholars, taking their cues from the mystical traditions themselves instead of from western epistemological theory, have taken just such a pause and come up with very different conclusions regarding the nature of mystical knowing and the possibility of a common experience across cultures. In so doing, they have broken new ground for what I would call a dialectical approach to the mystical. Frederick Streng, for example, has drawn on Buddhist Mādhyamika to critique the use of descriptive language and dualistic (i.e., nondialectical) categories in approaching mystical awareness: "The attempt to analyse the nature of mystical awareness (along with the reality of what it is aware) in terms of the descriptive function of language (concepts) has led to the attempt to locate the basic perceived reality either in a personal subjective experience or in a transconscious reality. Because this goes contrary to the claim of the unitive character of the mystical awareness between the experiencer and what is experienced, philosophers of mysticism are pressed to find a more adequate solution."[21] Streng cautions scholars not to fall into the very trap from which the texts (and his essay) are trying to free them. Instead of talking about an undifferentiated Absolute into which form is absorbed, Streng sees mystical language as a dialectical attempt to transcend the distinction between form and the formless altogether.

I find this dialectic particularly creative for the study of mysticism. Such an approach does not restrict mysticism to states of formless absorption and so is much more open to Christian, Islamic, and Jewish theistic traditions than some of the more strictly monistic definitions offered so far. At the same time it takes quite seriously the claims of a nonintentional, unconditioned state of consciousness advanced by many mystical traditions, something Katz's program does not. It also fits in quite impressively with those nonecstatic mystical accounts that are neither strictly monistic nor dualistic but both. I am thinking particularly of Zen's return to the marketplace of form, now completely transformed against a backdrop of "emptiness," of Eckhart's concrete living "without a why" after having gone into the "simple ground, into the quiet desert, into which distinction never gazed"[22] and, as we shall see shortly, of Ramakrishna's "mansion of fun," that paradoxical state consequent upon the realization that "She herself has become everything" in which the world's forms are enjoyed as the blissful play of the formless *brahman*. Finally, and perhaps most important, there is ample room within such a model for the scholar's contextualizing methods, for every conditioning—be it social, psychological, physiological, linguistic or doctrinal—falls within the dialectic and can thus be seen as integral to the experience. Context is not fluff or "superimposition" here. It is the diaphanous stuff of the mystical.

Such a methodology, moreover, informed by what Sells has called the "dialectic logic"[23] of apophatic language, has the advantage of accounting for both the rich diversity and the unity of humanity's mystical experience without either reifying the former into a plethora of solipsistic ontologies or delimiting the latter through a naive use of referential language. Context is not fluff, but neither is it everything. Sells is to the point:

> This account of mystical dialectic suggests a change in the focus of contemporary discussion of mysticism. One group has claimed that "what" the mystic experiences is the same in different traditions. In response, in a discussion of the experience of "nothingness," Steven Katz answers that "the difference between cases is a difference between *what* is experienced, not just *how* something is experienced." Notice how "nothing" has been made into "something"! Mystical dialectic criticizes such a use of "what." . . . While we might argue that the experience is contextually conditioned, or that it is common to mystics in differing traditions, at the apophatic level we must withdraw the "what." Such withdrawal allows an alternative either to delimiting a common

essence of religious traditions or denying the possibility of comparative understanding.[24]

It is just such an apophatic, dialectic approach to the mystical that I am taking in this present study. Accordingly, I will make no attempt, as some common core theorists have, to identify and describe the common essence or "what" of the world's religious traditions, but neither will I rule out the possibility that states of consciousness exist whose structures can be traced across time and the traditions.

As I apply it here, however, such a dialectical approach, although critically open to common states of consciousness, is *radically* focused on historical forms, to the extent that Ramakrishna's defecating habits receive as much attention as his famous ecstasies. In the language of Robert Forman, I practice what might be called an "incomplete constructivism,"[25] that is, I do not deny that there is something about certain forms of mystical experience that might transcend the conditionings of culture and time, but I would also assert that the manner in which even this "pure consciousness event" is experienced is profoundly influenced by numerous, often seemingly infinite, psychological, physical, social, and doctrinal conditionings. In this, my method is itself nondual, not in the sense that it seeks to absorb all that is particular and unique (and so interesting and important) into a common (and so safe) Oneness, but in the sense that it refuses to separate the specific forms of Ramakrishna's life, however seemingly bizarre, from the famous formlessness of his ecstasies. As I will demonstrate again and again, the contextual forms and the formless content of his states are in fact inseparable. "Form is emptiness, emptiness is form," the Buddhist *Prajñāpāramitāsūtra* states. So too with Ramakrishna, who knew the formless joys of *samādhi* while looking at the cocked hips of a beautiful English boy, experienced trance at the exact moment the "secret door" of his anus opened to defecate, and entered ecstatic states to escape the sexual advances of his boss. Certainly the formed contexts—the boy, the physical opening of the anus, the boss—and the formless content of these mystical states cannot be facilely equated, but neither can they be artificially separated: "Form is emptiness, emptiness is form." These, Ramakrishna would say, are states "beyond form and the formless." They are both, and they are neither.

I use the specific expression, *the mystical,* within this broader dialectical method and its contextually focused, nondual perspective. As such, it will refer to a *hidden dimension of human consciousness in which the dichotomies of normal awareness are transcended in an intense experience of unity or communion with a hidden reality or presence.* The definition can be briefly explicated in three parts.

A hidden dimension of human consciousness: The mystical is "hidden" in a historical, a psychological, and a linguistic sense. In the term's historical roots in ancient Greek religion, that which is "mystical" is literally that which is "hidden" or "secret" (*mustikos*). Thucydides thus calls the famous Greek mysteries, kept hidden from all but the initiated, "the secret things" (*ta mustika*) and the initiates "the secret ones" (*hoi mustikoi*). Taking up and developing this line of thought, the early Christian Fathers wrote of the great "secret" or *musterion*—that hidden presence of Christ discerned by faith in the sacred texts, in the eucharist, and in the soul of the believer—and referred to as "mystical" anything, from the eucharistic bread to an interpretation of scripture, that touched on this greatest of mysteries. It was a textual, ritual, and personal secret reserved, once again, for the initiated.[26] When we turn to India, we find a similar connection between secrecy and mysticism in the early roots of the tradition. The earliest mystical texts of Hinduism, the Upaniṣads, are those that contain the "secret doctrine" (*upaniṣad*)[27] of the ultimate unity of the human being and the cosmos in *brahman*, a truth variously described by later Indian commentators as "the secret" (*rahasyam*), "the highest secret" (*paramaṁ guhyam*), and "the most secret" (*guhyatamam*).[28] Similar secrets are strewn throughout Indian religious history. Ramakrishna's penchant for secret talk is simply a modern version of this ancient Indian love of secrecy and mysticism. In its historical roots, then, both in the West and in India, the mystical is that which is secret or hidden. But the mystical is also "hidden" in a psychological sense, for it lies in the depths of human consciousness in a psychic space that is not easily accessible and not commonly known. In most instances, we might say that the human being is "unconscious" of its reality and presence. Finally, the mystical is hidden in Sells's apophatic sense, that is, it is "hidden" from the intentionality and referential structure of ordinary language.[29] It is something that, by its very nature, cannot be defined or captured with the dualities of words. It cannot be spoken about, for such an act already implies a dualistic, referential state of consciousness that the mystical state has transcended.

In which the dichotomies of normal awareness are transcended: The social, religious, and cognitive systems within which human beings normally experience the world operate within intricate symbolic webs of meaning based upon, among other things, a series of oppositions or dichotomies: good and evil, pure and impure, God and the world, "I" and "you," form and the formless, male and female, and so on. Such dualities are the "stuff" of our quotidian experience, the categories out of which we fashion our values, our beliefs, our self-perceptions, even our physical experience. Mystical states are particularly interesting because they tend to jump over or transcend such oppositions. Thus, as we shall soon see, in the mystical states of Ramakrishna, *brahman* is "beyond good and evil," the impure becomes pure, God becomes the world, the "I" becomes "you," formlessness has form, and man becomes woman, who in turn unites with man. The dichotomies of normal awareness have been transcended.

In an intense experience of unity or communion with a hidden reality or presence: The mystical path is always a path toward unity, communion, or identity with some other reality or presence that, much like the mystical depths of the person's own soul, is "hidden." Different mystical traditions seek to commune or unite with this hidden reality or presence in different ways and to different degrees, for each symbolic world defines the nature of the human being, the sacred other, and the manner in which these two can and cannot be related in different ways. There are, in other words, multiple mysticisms that function through the myths, symbols, doctrines, ethical norms, and rituals of multiple religious worlds. But there is also a certain commonality among the traditions, for the emphasis is always on intensity, energy, and power and, most important, on some form of unity or communion, be it a "mystical union" or "cleaving" with a personal presence or a complete "absorption" or "annihilation" in an impersonal reality. Often, moreover, the mystical event is such that the very terms of this union are themselves realized as dichotomous and so as ultimately false. Experience has transcended itself.

This, then, is my working definition of "the mystical." I use the category, not as a thing or object for others to fixate on as if there was nothing else of importance here, but, in McGinn's apt phrase, as a "term of art"[30] that effectively locates for comparative discussion an important and essentially interesting phenomenon in the history of religions.

Śakti on Top of Śiva: Restoring the Dialectic

IF WE ARE TO OPERATE within the dialectic proposed above, we must acknowledge that the mystical cannot be understood as some simple formless state of consciousness cut off from the historical world of individual human beings. Here we might recall the Tantric image in the Kālī temple again and notice that there is a naked goddess standing on top of the god. In this present study, I will take this powerful image of Śiva and Śakti—and more precisely, of Śakti *on top of* Śiva—as a symbolic corrective to contemporary academic discourse on the mystical, which, I would suggest, has focused too exclusively on pale Śiva, that transcendent witness.

In a popular Tantric aphorism, it is said that, without Śakti, Śiva is just a *śava*, a "corpse," a dead abstraction devoid of the erotic energy that gives him life and being (SM, 345–348). So too, I would argue, with scholarship on the mystical—without a serious and prolonged meditation on the dynamic aspects of mystical experience, on what the Tāntrika calls Śakti, the modern study of mysticism threatens to turn its object of study into a corpse-like abstraction, devoid of the very life and power that renders the experience "religious" for the mystic. Śiva's erect penis, aroused by the goddess's frenzied dance on his breast, finds no significant place in the discourse on pure consciousness. I seek to give it one by putting the goddess back "on top" of the god, both in a mythological and in a sexual sense. I will accomplish this in part through a category I call "the erotic."

The Category of the Erotic

FOR RAMAKRISHNA, understanding his words required what might be called an erotic hermeneutics. "If one doesn't hold the seed," the saint warned his listeners, "he can't understand all this" (KA 4.89).[31] "Holding" (*dhāraṇa*) the semen and "understanding" (*dhāraṇa*) the teachings are linguistically identical acts. The proper interpretation of Ramakrishna's *kathā* or "talk," in other words, is fueled by the same energies that drive the sexual powers.[32] If we follow the logic of Ramakrishna's comment a bit further, we might come to a startling conclusion, namely, that the *Kathāmṛta*, as the record of Ramakrishna's words, is a homoerotic text in the sense that its interpretation is the proper object of a man's sexual energies. It records words that can only be understood by a man in total control of his sexual energies, who has directed his sexual fluids, not outward but inward toward Ramakrishna and his words.

Although it is perhaps too much to ask the male reader that he "hold the seed" in order to understand this text, it is essential that the religious world in which Ramakrishna could make such a claim be understood. It is also important that we have at our disposal categories refined enough to interpret such a world without utterly destroying it in the process. With this in mind, I want to introduce a category I call "the erotic," by which I mean *a dimension of human experience that is simultaneously related both to the physical and emotional experience of sexuality and to the deepest ontological levels of religious experience.* An experience must contain both sexual and sacred components for me to consider it erotic. If a particular phenomenological description refers to a sexual urge or act devoid of any explicit ontological or religious dimensions, I will call it sexual but not erotic. Likewise, if a particular description refers to an experience with religious dimensions but in which no sexual components are present or suggested, I will call it religious but not erotic.

I intend to invoke a particular history with the use of the term. Because of its ancient use in Platonic and Christian mystical discourse, *the erotic* is capable of carrying mystical connotations, similar to those Ramakrishna would understand and enthusiastically accept. But because of its common usage in contemporary American culture, it can also imply sexual fantasy and arousal, the stuff of psychoanalysis. In other words, it can be used *both* in an essentially mystical sense *and* in a psychoanalytically defined psycho-biological sense. *The erotic* is thus a third, specifically methodological category, where the horizons of religious experience and psychoanalysis can meet in the act of interpretation.

As a dialectical term refusing to separate the sexual and the mystical, the category of the erotic forms an integral part of my contextually focused method. As such, it also mirrors Ramakrishna's own religious world, and especially the Indian category of *śakti,* a term that can mean everything from the goddess herself to "magical power," to "physical force," to the feminine energy lying dormant at the base of the spine waiting to uncoil and wind her way up through the different centers—referred to as the Anus, the Phallus, the Navel, and such—until she can unite with her lover in the head. This whole, essentially Tantric, symbolism demands a wholistic understanding of human energies, capable of incorporating everything from sexual desire to formless mystical experience under one interpretive category. *The erotic* is the closest one can come in the English language, for it harbors hints of Freud's omnipresent *libido,* infinite in its magical transformations, as well as Pseudo-Dionysius's Divine Eros, enticed away from its transcendent dwelling place to dwell within all things and yet, by virtue of its supernatural and ecstatic capacity, remaining within itself, turning "from itself and through itself and upon itself and toward itself in an everlasting circle."[33]

Finally, the term's Platonic origins and connotations—*eros* as a homoerotic love of boys sublimated into a vision of the divine—is particularly appropriate when we come to Ramakrishna's unique use of his homoeroticism as the driving force of his mystical life. Ramakrishna's love for his boys was truly "Platonic," not in the sense in which it is used today—a love devoid of passion—but in the sense Plato used it in his *Phaedrus* and *Symposium*—a homoerotic infatuation harnessed and "winged" for ecstatic flight. As we shall shortly see, Ramakrishna's love was just such an "erotic" love, at once sexual and mystical.

§ § §

I WILL ARGUE, then, throughout the course of this study that, like the image of Śakti on top of Śiva, Ramakrishna's religious experiences were defined by a dialectical unity between the historical forms of the goddess's energies and the timeless, formless states of the god. Within this erotic dialectic, moreover, I will establish that it was the goddess, not the god, who was "on top." My method mirrors this iconographic dominance of the goddess by concentrating on the erotic Kālī-like aspects of Ramakrishna's visions and teachings. Consequently, I will approach Ramakrishna's religious experiences not as proofs for an alleged common core but as manifestations of Kālī's mystico-erotic *śakti,* a power that constitutes the phenomenal world in all of its physical, biological, psychological, social, and historical messiness. Without denying the importance of the Śiva half of mystical experience, I want to focus on what we might call the Śakti half, and by so doing, redress what I see as an imbalance in the modern study of mysticism.

RAMAKRISHNA'S TANTRIC WORLD

AT FIRST GLANCE, Ramakrishna may seem an odd person to pick to begin moving away from the common core debate and its often undialectical ways. After all, he is probably best known for his claims of a *philosophia perennis.* Consequently, it is often assumed that nowhere are the claims for the universality of mystical experience made so explicitly and so consistently as in Ramakrishna. But as with many assumptions made about Ramakrishna, this one is made too quickly and without a real understanding of the religious and historical context in which Ramakrishna's universalism developed. The truth of the matter is that, although Ramakrishna certainly preached a type of universalism, such concerns were at best peripheral to his deeper desires and in actual fact inspired few, if any, of his numerous visions and ecstasies. The technical term for the "synthesis of all religions," for example, occurs only in M's section headings and glosses,[34] never in Ramakrishna's mouth,[35] whereas Ramakrishna uses the word for "anxious desire" (*vyākulatā*) well over 150 times. *It was desire not a synthesis of doctrine that formed the center of Ramakrishna's teaching.* Or in Ramakrishna's own words: "This anxious desire, whatever path you take—be it Hindu, Muslim, Christian, Śākta or Brahmo—this anxious desire is the last word" (KA 5.204).[36] Indeed, if one has "passionate desire," it matters little whether or not one believes in incarnations (KA 1.122),[37] much less in a Vedantic-inspired universalism. Doctrine is subordinate to desire.

To put it a bit differently, it was Kālī of the Śākta tradition that was the focus of Ramakrishna's life, not the abstract *brahman* of Vedānta and the Brahmos. The center of his teaching was ecstatic love for a personal deity, not formless meditation on an impersonal Absolute. Or to be more precise, it was the dialectical relationship between the two that constituted and defined the metaphysical order within which he lived and preached. The whole debate, then, about whether Ramakrishna was a *bhakta*, devoted to a personal deity, or a Vedāntin, privileging the impersonal Absolute, misses the whole point of Ramakrishna's religious world—that, as a Śākta Tāntrika, he was something of *both*. Any attempt, then, to paint him as a sophisticated Vedāntin or as a simple *bhakta* fails to grasp the single most important interpretive key with which to unlock the secrets of his mystical and charismatic success—Tantra.

"If You Are Ashamed . . ."

THERE ARE GOOD HISTORICAL REASONS why Tantra has been overlooked for so long, not the least of which is Ramakrishna's own profound ambivalence toward the tradition. But ambivalent or no, Ramakrishna's feet were planted deep in Tantric soil. Often this Tantric world informed the nature of Ramakrishna's own self-understanding. Consider, for example, how the saint described his all-important relationship to the young Narendra: it was, he explained, as if his own inner essence was "female" and Narendra's was "male" (LP 3.2.46). This bipolar, sexually charged symbolism of Tantra erupts again and again into Ramakrishna's language. With Ramakrishna's death, however, this Tantric world begins to break down as Narendra's own brand of Advaita

Vedānta begins to overshadow the Śākta elements that once were so pronounced in Ramakrishna; Ramakrishna's "female" essence or Śakti gives way to the "male" essence of Śiva in the person of Narendra. Already in the last scenes of the *Kathāmṛta*, dated in the months of 1887 and staged as appendixes in the different volumes, we are well on our way to the appropriation of Ramakrishna as a Vedāntin and the suppression of his troubling Tantric dimensions.

Ramakrishna knew that Narendra did not accept Śakti (KA 4.121).[38] After Ramakrishna's death, this rejection of the goddess resulted in a radical transformation of the young movement. Changes are apparent everywhere. The sacred environment has changed. Dakshineshwar is no longer the locus of the young disciples' meetings. In the newly established Baranagore Monastery, a converted house rented by the generous Suresh for the young disciples, Kālī is now a distant presence. Instead, the meeting room of the young disciples is called the "room of Śiva's demons"[39] in order to stress the "manly states" that would be practiced there and to distance its occupants from those effeminate men whom Narendra disdained as the "girlfriend class" (LP 5.12.3.11). This change of buildings, in other words, constituted a profound change of attitudes to gender and the practice of religion. Knowing full well that Ramakrishna had described himself as having a woman's nature and went so far as to dress like one, Narendra now confesses that he never believed all that "Kṛṣṇa-fiṣṇa nonsense" (KA 3.269) and boldly admits that he despises effeminate men who take on the mood of women (LP 5.12.3.11). "Your Bhakti is sentimental nonsense, which makes one impotent," he growled.[40] One can imagine how upset poor Narendra must have been with Ramakrishna's desire to call him Kamalālakṣa, one of those effeminate Vaiṣṇava names meaning "Lotus Eyes."

Rejecting such feminine states, Narendra the Lion[41] begins to preach the virtues of spiritual manliness and renunciation. Ramakrishna's usual response to Narendra's Sanskrit hymns and Vedānta talk was emphatic: "It's all so boring!" (KA 3.253). Boring indeed: wearing such luxuries as slick varnished slippers and black-bordered clothes (KA 3.196–197),[42] Ramakrishna had described the world he lived in as a "mansion of fun." Narendra and his disciples, on the other hand, dressed in the ochre robes of renouncers (KA 3.276), now see the world only as something to reject. The "I only eat, drink, and make merry" chant of Ramakrishna is replaced by an almost desperate "Renounce!" (KA 3.271). The music also has changed. Narendra's songs of manly renunciation, of Śiva, and of Śaṅkara begin to replace those of Kālī and the milkmaids of Kṛṣṇa, once so dear to Ramakrishna. Ramakrishna once sung of Kālī triumphantly astride the pale Śiva. Now Narendra brags that, in the end, Śiva reclaimed his rightful dominance over Śakti and made her a servant, and that Kṛṣṇa left the women of Vrindavana to become a mighty king in a distant city (KA 4.296).

And finally, the texts have changed. Ramakrishna had prayed to Kālī to teach him the contents of "the Vedas, the Purāṇas, and the Tantras."[43] But now Narendra, as Swami Vivekananda, rejects this sacred trilogy for another: "the Vedas, the Gita, and the Upanishads." Ramakrishna's Tantras have been excised from the tradition. M records Vivekananda's categorical rejection of Tantra in an appendix in volume 5: "Give up this filthy Vamachara that is killing your country. . . . Those who come out in the day-time and preach most loudly about *achara* [right practice], it is they who carry on the most horrible debauchery at night, and are backed by the most dreadful books. You who are of Bengal know it. The Bengali Shastras are the Vamachara Tantras. They are published by the cartload, and you poison the minds of your children with them instead of teaching them your Shrutis. . . . If you are ashamed, take them away from your children, and let them read the true Shastras, the Vedas, the Gita, the Upanishads" (KA 5.181).

Śakti—in her image, gender, music, and scriptures—has been made submissive and obedient. Bengalis are encouraged to be ashamed of her and her Tantras. Śakti is no longer on top of Śiva. An abstract universal, Narendra's *brahman,* takes over, and Kālī's erotic play in the visions and mystical experiences of Ramakrishna is tucked away in the later volumes of the *Kathāmṛta* or simply effaced in bowdlerized translations. Kālī is domesticated, and she never quite recovers, neither in Ramakrishna's interpreters nor in the *Kathāmṛta*'s prudish translators.

Strangeness, Seediness, and Sex

RAMAKRISHNA'S WORLD, then, was a Tantric world. But what exactly does this mean? How are we to define Tantra? And once we have defined the tradition, how are we to get at its meanings and truths? The Hindu philosopher-saint, Gopinath Kaviraj, opens his two-volume work on Indian Tantra, *Tāntrika Sādhanā o Siddhānta,* by commenting on the inability of a historical method to get at the deepest meanings of Tantric culture. Kaviraj does not deny the historical development of Indian philosophical thought but simply believes that such progression is the "external subject of historical research" and not the concern of his own theological method, attuned more to that "reality" which is manifested in history than to "the order in which it is manifested." Accordingly, Kaviraj gratefully acknowledges the work of Mahatma Sivachandra Vidyarnava and his famous disciple, John Woodroffe, but insists that, although important, their work is "only philosophical." For Kaviraj, Tantric studies have remained "on the outside." They have failed to attain the one thing necessary for uncovering the "deep secrets" of Tantric culture—"the inner gnosis."[44]

Although my own method differs markedly from Kaviraj's, I agree with him that Tantric studies have remained focused for the most part on historical questions and philosophical expositions. Often this has been more a function of necessity than of any willed lack on the part of the scholarly community. Enormous textual work still needs to be done before we can ask the questions Kaviraj wants us to ask. And even when scholars are ready to enter the "inner gnosis" of a particular tradition, they are more often than not turned away by the obtuse nature of the texts or the closed-lip nature of the community. As scholars have pointed out, perhaps too often, Tantra is an esoteric culture, infamously difficult to study. This situation has resulted in a number of fine studies more or less restricted to the textually oriented and philosophically inclined Tantric schools, especially those of Kashmir Śaivism.[45]

Such geographical limitations have been compounded by a certain unspoken bias in Tantric studies, a bias toward the philosophical and the Sanskritic. Too often scholars have equated Tantra with a philosophical school enshrined in ancient Sanskrit texts and have ignored the popular connotations of the term *Tāntrika,* almost all of which revolve around notions of magical power, strangeness, seediness, and sex. Whereas, for example, towering philosophical figures such as Abhinavagupta have been the focus of numerous books, such characters as the Tāntrika who claimed to be able to make a human skull smoke a cigarette[46] hardly ever appear in the scholarly discourse.[47] Too few scholars seem to realize, or at least admit, that the adjective "Tantric," far from invoking some hoary Sanskrit tradition, is usually "more an accusation than a description."[48]

Scholarship on Tantra, in other words, despite its impressive advances, is often still working in the legacy of its founder, John Woodroffe, whose work was marked by profound philosophical, scientific, and moral biases and an apologetics designed to rid Tantra of everything that smacked of superstition, magic, or scandal. Writing within this same "Victorian" tradition, numerous scholars have attempted all sorts of mental gymnastics in a desperate effort to rescue the tradition from its stubbornly "impure" ways. So, for example, we are asked to believe that the word *penis* (*liṅgam*) in the texts does not mean penis (SM, 212–227), that all that is decadent in Tantra came from the Buddhists (LP 4.1.23–28), and that scholars who read sexual connotations into the literal meaning of the word *yoni* (vagina!) are being imperialistic (YT, 14). Tantra's radical moral, ontological, and ritual nondualism, which *intentionally* plays with the sexual meanings of words and *consciously* uses decadence as a spiritual technique, is thus reduced to the silliness of prudes, polemics, and politics.

My own approach to Ramakrishna's Tantra rejects these distorting strategies, all of which are essentially dualistic in their attempt to separate the sexual and the religious, and opts instead, again, for a radically nondual, contextually focused approach. Accordingly, I will refrain from judging recorded acts and events that strike my own socialized conscience as repulsive or immoral and instead attempt to present Ramakrishna's Tantra as it presents itself—as a "dirty path" to ontological truths that are as terrifying as they are profound. Moreover, as part of this same contextually focused method, instead of analyzing a Sanskrit text as representative of an entire school or system of thought, I will approach a vernacular work, the *Kathāmṛta,* as an attempt on the part of a single human being, named simply M,[49] to capture the presence and power of another human being, named Ramakrishna. Given the vernacular nature of my sources and the complex, highly ambivalent reactions of my subjects, I am naturally more interested in what Tantra *feels* like in Bengali than in what it thinks like in Sanskrit. In short, *I seek to present Tantra not in its ideal state but in its lived compromises and contradictions.*[50] Again, the emphasis will be placed on the black, frightening complexities of Kālī, not on the pale abstractions of Śiva. In this, the study has been conceived as an answer to Brooks's call for the study of individual Tantric mystics as a means "to reclaim Tantric studies . . . and to correct our understanding of Hinduism in general."[51]

Defining Tantra

WHEN WE ENTER THE INNER CIRCLE of M's text, we enter the world of Tantra. The *Kathāmṛta* is an unusually open door into this world. It is filled with Ramakrishna's teachings on the Tantric nature of the world. It is peppered with graphic Tantric visions and descriptions of seedy midnight rituals. An occasional visiting Tāntrika even appears here and there in the text, always ready to offer a sexy interpretation of a particular symbol or metaphor. Because so much of the present study is concerned with uncovering and ordering this Tantric universe, it is important that I spell out clearly how I am using the term *Tantra* and what I mean by it. Numerous scholars have defined the slippery category.[52] Since, however, I am interested primarily in Ramakrishna's own understanding of the tradition and, more important, in the idiosyncratic reactions that such an understanding eventually produced in him, I would like to stick as close as possible to Ramakrishna's own words and categories. Accordingly, when I use the terms *Tantra* or one of its English or Sanskrit cognates (*Tantric* or *Tāntrika*), I intend them to refer to an Indian mystical tradition defined by the six following characteristics, each of which I have summed up with a direct quote from the texts themselves.

(1) "*That about which in the Vedas and the Purāṇas it is said, 'Don't do this, this shouldn't be done,' in the Tantras is called good*" (KA 2.132).[53] Tantra is at once an anti-Vedic and a Vedic tradition, for although it intentionally and systematically reverses the orthodox Brahmanical tradition in its rituals and images, it nevertheless defines itself in relation to the Vedas and Brahmanical culture. Its ritual deconstruction of Brahmanical notions of purity and caste take on religious meaning and sacred power only within a cultural system that presupposes those very religious notions and social categories. In short, Tantra may reject "the Vedas and the Purāṇas," but it also needs them to generate its antimeanings and reversed energies.[54]

(2) "*They practice according to the views of the Tantras. They practice the Five M's*" (KA 3.50). Tantra accomplishes its reversal of Brahmanical culture by ritually employing impure substances and illicit acts to transgress and transcend the Hindu category of purity and to activate the subtle energies of the psycho-physical organism that will carry the aspirant to his or her desired end. These substances and acts are known as the "Five M's": *madya* (wine), *maṁsa* (meat), *matsya* (fish), *mūdra* (parched grain), and *maithuna* (sexual intercourse). Again, it should be pointed out that such things are "impure" or "illicit" only in relation to Brahmanical social categories. In themselves, they lack any definite meaning or significance. For example, acts and foods that implicate the Indian brahmin in situations charged with religiously useful feelings of shame, disgust, and fear might be relatively bland and meaningless to a non-Hindu. To put it crudely, the same substances that might signal the initial stages of a Tantric ritual experience for an initiated brahmin (fish, meat, and wine) might be just another surf and steak dinner for a secular American hoping to get lucky on a date. The Five M's, in other

words, rely on specific social and ritual contexts for much of their meaning and power.

(3) *"In the first state there is form, in the second state there is the formless, and, after that, there is the state beyond form and the formless"* (TP, no. 23). In their energizing or activating function, these Five M's grant *bhukti* or "pleasure" within the world. But in their transgressing function, they are capable of granting *mukti* or "liberation" from the world. The Tāntrika can "have it both ways" because Tantric ritual and experience operate within a dialectical ontology that intentionally plays on the relativity of immanence and transcendence, of "form" and "the formless." Each, after all, implies the other. In mythological terms, the universe is the actual embodiment of the starkly transcendent Śiva and the immanent Śakti. This transcendence and this immanence, moreover, are not simply related. They are graphically, intimately, sexually united. Everything that exists flows out of and *is* their union. Such a world is radically "nondual" in that it affirms *both* the pleasurable particulars of form *and* the liberating reality of the formless in a mystical dialectic that escapes the inherently dualistic categories of language. In Ramakrishna's own words, this Tantric world is "beyond form and the formless."

(4) *"Everything about a Tāntrika is secret"* (KA 4.166). It is a mark of the texts that whenever they discuss Tantra, they inevitably invoke the category of secrecy; indeed, terms like *in secret* (*gopane*), *secret* (*guhya*), *concealed* (*gupta*), *filled with secrets* (*rahasyamaya*), and *hidden* (*gūḍha*) seem to appear, as if from nowhere, whenever the tradition is addressed.[55] There are good reasons for this. Tāntrikas are a shady lot. Their practices are usually considered immoral, if not fantastically obscene. But they are also known to possess hidden truths and special secret powers, which they allegedly teach and practice in very secret places (like cremation grounds) and at equally secret times (like midnight). Secrecy is "everything" for the Tāntrika. It can hint at profound religious truths and hide questionable practices with the very same expression or word. It forms communities by controlling who can teach and who can be taught and how. It generates duplicity by splitting the Tantric self into separate midday and midnight personas. It creates the sacred texts that speak in complex sexual metaphors. It necessitates torturous hermeneutical strategies, both to decipher the original metaphors and, once deciphered, to cover them up again. It creates power for itself, for it hides practices and truths that boldly reverse the reigning social categories of the proper and the pure. Finally, it teasingly attracts

attention to itself—who does not want to hear whispered secrets?—and then pushes the uninitiated, or the unwanted, away. It is in control. It is everything for the Tāntrika. Without it, he would cease to be so interesting, so dangerous, so sexy. No doubt, he would also get caught.

(5) *"Shame, disgust, and fear—these three must not remain."*[56] But we would be gravely mistaken if we supposed that the power of Tantra was simply a function of its philosophical sophistication or of its transgressive nature, as if "power" were simply a matter of thought or could be realized through a mechanical manipulation of the binary codes of society. For Ramakrishna, at least, the experience of Tantra was intimately and uncomfortably bound up with *emotional* reactions, with "shame, disgust, and fear," that in turn were psychologically connected to troubling memories of his own vague past. Ramakrishna, in other words, was neither a philosopher nor a structuralist. He was a human being struggling with the horrors of his past and the challenges of his present through the rituals and symbolic states of Tantra. If he became a Child, it was at least partly because he *feared* women as embodiments of the Lover and sought to escape their supposed wiles in a childish innocence. If he brought Kālī's sword to his own throat, it was at least partly because he felt *shame* for phallic desires that his culture considered inappropriate. And if he consistently associated Tantra with the latrine, it was because he himself had experienced and was *disgusted* with the dark abusive side of the tradition. All these emotional reactions, and many more, made Tantra for Ramakrishna a thing of almost limitless, and so terrifying, power.

(6) *"The Śāktas follow the views of the Tantras"* (KA 4.166). Finally, Tantra, as understood by Ramakrishna, is a tradition whose followers are called Śāktas or "worshipers of the Power." That is to say, the particular Tantric tradition with which Ramakrishna is the most familiar is a Śākta form of Tantra, whose myth, ritual, and doctrine focus on the worship and propitiation of Śakti in the form of the goddess Kālī. What I have to say about Tantra, then, should be understood as applying only strictly to Bengali Śākta Tantra, that is, to the tradition of Ramakrishna.

As for my use of the terms themselves, *Tantra* can refer either to the tradition in general ("Tantra") or to a text or group of texts belonging to that tradition ("a Tantra" or "the Tantras"). I should point out, however, that my use of the expression *Tantra* to refer to the tradition is, technically at least, a departure from Ramakrishna's own language. Ramakrishna speaks often of "the view of the Tantras" (*tantramata*), but he never actually uses the expression *Tantra* to refer to the tradition as a whole. Finally, *Tantric,* which does occur in Ramakrishna's discourse, is used as an adjective for anything expressing a quality or characteristic of Tantra, and *Tāntrika* or *Śākta,* both of which are also common, are used to describe a practitioner or follower of Tantra.

THE STUDY'S SYMBOLIC STRUCTURE: KĀLĪ'S CHILD

THE STUDY ITSELF is structured around the iconography of Kālī, for Ramakrishna's initial mystico-erotic crisis (chapter 1), his relationship to women as Mother and Lover (chapter 2), the dialectical nature of his Tantric world (chapter 3), his descent back into the human world and the energies this generated (chapter 4), and his profound ambivalence over his own Tantric world (chapter 5) all were derived on some level from his daily preoccupation with the goddess, in worship, in meditation, in song, and in vision. The study's chapter divisions are symbolically informed by the iconography of Kālī in an attempt to recreate and respect the culture's own indigenous, primarily symbolic, understanding of the mystical and the erotic. The motif analyzed in each chapter, then, is represented in the respective chapter heading by a particular iconographic aspect of the goddess. For example, chapter 3, which discusses the ontological dominance of Tantra over Vedānta in Ramakrishna's world, is symbolically summed up by Kālī's erotic play on top of her corpse-like husband, Śiva.

Each chapter, moreover, is divided into three parts: an initial study of a particular iconographic feature of the goddess; a biographical study of a specific period in Ramakrishna's life; and an extended analysis of how the iconographic theme of the chapter defined the doctrinal teachings and mystical experiences of the saint. Iconography, biography, and doctrine are thus the three focal points of each chapter. Because each of these three sections seeks to accomplish a different task, each requires a different set of texts.

The first part of each chapter, the iconographic study, draws on a select group of Sanskrit Tantras and a corpus of Bengali devotional songs to focus and to give shape, indeed almost a body, to both the theme of the respective chapter and to the book as a whole. Although fairly brief, these opening sections are important since they provide us with the images and symbolic connections through which we can enter Ramakrishna's Tantric world and re-imagine its meanings and secrets; in Ricoeur's memorable phrase, these iconographic studies provide us with the symbols that "give rise to thought."[57] Since these opening sections are primarily introductions, their focusing function is more important than their actual substance; they in no way pretend to be exhaustive studies of the few Tantras, commentaries, and Śākta songs upon which they are largely based. I must stress this point: this is *not* a book about the Tantras or the Śākta songs. It can, however, be read as a sustained analysis of a genuine Tantric oral tradition, for although such texts as the *Kathāmṛta* and the *Jīvanavṛttānta* are definitely not Tantras, they most certainly are the written products of an oral Tantric tradition, embodied anew in Ramakrishna, whose power and significance in Bengali culture should not be underestimated.

The second part of each chapter, the biographical study, engages a very different group of texts. Two major Bengali biographies of the saint are particularly important here: Ram Chandra Datta's householder text, the *Jīvanavṛttānta;* and Swami Saradananda's renouncer text, the *Līlāprasaṅga.* To provide the book with a "story," I have treated the different periods of Ramakrishna's life in roughly chronological order, at least as that "order" is commonly understood in the tradition. I have not, however, accepted the traditional narrative uncritically, for, as I demonstrate in numerous places, the "order" of Ramakrishna's life is often more a product of the saint's interpreters and their philosophical and cultural agendas than it is of Ramakrishna's own lived experience as recorded, however fallibly, in the historical record.

Finally, the third part of each chapter, the analysis of the iconographic theme in the teachings, visions, and ecstasies of Ramakrishna, concentrates primarily on the centerpiece of the study, M's *Kathāmṛta.* If the iconographic studies give the book its form and focus and the biographical studies provide it with its basic narrative or story, these doctrinal analyses provide the book's arguments with their textual depth and coherence.

Culture and Psyche

BY FOCUSING ON THE ICONOGRAPHY of Kālī as the organizing image of the chapters, I have tried to unite the form of the study with its function or thesis. With such a symbolic structure, I hope to explicate the relationship between the cultural symbols and the deep motivations structuring Ramakrishna's personal appropriation and experience of them. Here I have employed Obeyesekere's notion of the "personal symbol" as a creative interface between public culture and private fantasy, between mythology and mystical experience. "Personal symbols" for Obeyesekere are "cultural symbols that are related to individual motivation and make sense only in relation to the life history of the individual."[58] As a personal symbol carries public, communicable meanings, it makes sense to the culture at large, but it remains undeciphered until we relate it to the individual life history in which it occurs and reveal its uniquely personal dimensions, its secrets. Accordingly, in each chapter, after analyzing the cultural connotations of a particular aspect of Kālī's iconography (her sword, her feet, her tongue, etc.) as they are worked out in the Tantras and the songs of the Śākta poets, I will then proceed to explicate the manner in which Ramakrishna made personal use of the iconographic detail and how it fits into the larger patterns of his mystical life. My method, then, seeks to be both contextual, sensitive to cultural and historical detail, and psychological, open to the deeply personal, even unconscious, aspects of Ramakrishna's life.

By structuring the study around the iconography of Kālī, Ramakrishna's "desired deity" (*iṣṭadevatā*) and "personal symbol," I seek both to explicate what Ramakrishna achieved in his personal life and that public, specifically Hindu reality that defined the nature of his mystical experiences—Ramakrishna's Tantric world. As I will demonstrate below, these two dimensions—the public and the private, the cultural and the psychological, the mythological and the mystical—cannot be easily separated. *Culture* and *psyche* are by no means synonymous terms. If they were, communication across cultural boundaries would be impossible, translation could only be a sham, and interpretation would become pure projection. But neither can they be facilely distinguished from one another. The degree to which culture forms the psyche, even on its most unconscious levels, is indeed profound. Accordingly, I have adopted a method and a specific structural form that respect culture and psyche as two separate and yet mutually interactive forms.

Looking Out, Looking In

THE STUDY'S STRUCTURE is also intended as another less analytical, more symbolic way of revealing Ramakrishna's secret. As I have pointed out already, Ramakrishna's secret was a Tantric secret. As such, it was intimately connected with Kālī, *the* Tantric goddess in Bengal, but connected in a very special way. In her iconography, Kālī, with her full breasts, garland of heads, and skimpy skirt of human hands, appears to be an extremely daunting Lover, the very embodiment of eroticism and violence. She is the Lover of the Tāntrika, that Hero who dares engage her in sexual intercourse, be it in a midnight ritual with a human partner or in the timeless realm of the imagination in meditation.

Distrustful of such heroes and what they represent, Ramakrishna claimed that Kālī's daunting iconographic form is only an external appearance and that, deep down, Kālī is a gentle Mother. Ramakrishna's Kālī, in other words, was a Mother, not a Lover. Here we might recall Gopinath Kaviraj's charge that scholars of Tantra have remained "on the outside," or more literally, with their "faces looking out" (*bahirmukha*). Ramakrishna would most certainly agree. And both the pundit and the mystic would have us turn our "faces inward" (*antarmukha*) to the deeper, less obvious truths of the tradition. Kaviraj and Ramakrishna, no doubt, might see different truths "looking in," but they would surely agree that the person "looking out" is doomed to come to the wrong conclusions. There is, then, a radical disjuncture between what Kālī's iconography seems to suggest to the person "looking out" and what it means to the mystic or pious scholar "looking in." In the case of Ramakrishna, at least, we have *two* Kālī's, that of her public iconography and that of her devotee, Ramakrishna—Kālī the Lover of the Tantric Hero and Kālī the Mother of the devoted Child.

In a similar fashion, we can identify two Ramakrishnas, that which Ramakrishna himself affirmed and acknowledged as his own, and that which appeared in his visions and unconscious states. The former Ramakrishna we know from his photographs and self-descriptions—sweet, smiling, frail, the Paramahaṁsa compared to a boy of five. The latter Ramakrishna we know from his secret visions and ecstatic acts—strangely erotic, his hair standing on end, his tongue licking visionary lotuses shaped like vaginas, his foot extended into the genitals of young boys. The contrast is a radical one: Ramakrishna the devoted Child and Ramakrishna the Tantric Hero. In their relationship, then, Ramakrishna and Kālī are reversed images of one another's hidden or secret self. *That relationship (the devoted Child to the goddess as Mother) which is revealed in Ramakrishna is concealed in the iconography of Kālī, and that relationship (the Tantric Hero to the goddess as Lover) which is revealed in the iconography of Kālī is concealed or "secret" in Ramakrishna.*

Because of this revealing/concealing or "looking out"/"looking in" pattern, by structuring the study around the revealed or external iconography of Kālī, the Tantric goddess, I will be able to reveal the concealed or "secret" side of Ramakrishna. I will be able to show that within Ramakrishna the devoted Child there lived another unconscious Ramakrishna, the Tantric Hero, whose visions and unconscious acts bore an uncanny resemblance to the iconography of Kālī, powerfully erotic, her tongue sticking out, her feet on the breast and lap of Śiva. I thus will be able to demonstrate how Ramakrishna's seemingly undecipherable visions and ecstatic acts find their meaning and coherence in the iconographic details of Kālī.

The study's general methodology, then, informed on all its levels by Tantra and its symbolism, seeks to demonstrate that Ramakrishna was "Kālī's Child," that within the child-like demeanor and innocent charm of Ramakrishna there lived a being who saw striking Tantric visions and spoke secrets too controversial to be revealed. Ramakrishna was Kālī's *Child*, innocent in his charm and delightful in his antics, but he was also *Kālī's* Child, vulgar in his speech and scandalous in his Tantric secrets.

THE HINDU UNCONSCIOUS

ALL OF THIS, of course, implies something very close to the psychological construct of the unconscious. Can we posit such a "Western" construct in an Indian figure like Ramakrishna? It is a complicated question, but one absolutely central to this study. It is essential, then, that the parameters of the question be dealt with in some detail immediately. I define those parameters primarily in terms of ontology rather than structure. That is to say, I am not interested here in the structure or dynamics of the Hindu unconscious, namely, the manner in which it is related to Indian social forms, whether there is such a thing as an Indian Oedipus complex, and so on. Despite the inherent interest and importance of such questions, I cannot go into the details and complexities of such debates here. I can only say that I place myself somewhere in the middle, holding neither to a rigid Freudianism nor to a radical relativism. Put simply, I believe that the human mind possesses certain characteristics—a common biological base, a symbolizing function, defense and censoring strategies such as repression, displacement, and projection, a tendency to imagine in the language of the body and its shapes, and so forth—that give its functioning a certain universal character. This basic psychic or biological unity, however, is profoundly differentiated by such cultural forms as child-rearing practices, social organization, and religious doctrines, all of which differ radically from culture to culture. Human psychology, then, is relatively consistent across cultures. If it were not, such disciplines as anthropology and the history of religions would be impossible. But human psychology is *also* variable, and radically so. If it were not, anthropology and the history of religions might be possible, but they would also be unnecessary, not to mention uninteresting. Within this *via media*, I would assert that psychoanalysis, despite its birth in Western culture, *can* be used to interpret non-Western cultures, but I would add immediately, following the pioneering work of Stanley Kurtz, that it first must be "reshaped" to fit each and every cultural context in which it is applied.[59]

Although these issues of a general universal psychic structure and its specific cultural reshaping are always in the background, defining some of the basic assumptions of my writing, the history and complexities of this debate will not concern me here. On the contrary, my use of psychoanalysis is fairly light, restricted as it is to the Freud of *The Interpretation of Dreams* and to the writings of some of his modern disciples, especially Gananath Obeyesekere and Sudhir Kakar. Because I am convinced with Eliade that the historian of religions who adopts the methods of a discipline such as psychology too often ends up simply doing bad psychology,[60] I have avoided overburdening what is basically a phenomenological study with psychological categories and terms. Moreover, committed as I am both to respecting the truth of Ramakrishna's Tantric world and to the usefulness of psychoanalysis in uncovering some of the hidden patterns of that world, I have attempted to use psychoanalytic categories, but only *within* Ramakrishna's Tantric world. I would argue that within such a world psychoanalysis is indeed helpful, because it allows one to identify certain patterns and to ask interesting questions, questions one could not ask with the indigenous categories of Tantra. It is unlikely, for example, that I would have located the castration themes of chapter 1 or the virgin-whore split of chapter 2 without the cultural benefit of Freud's psychoanalytic insights. Nor is it likely that I would have been able to make any sense out of Ramakrishna's eating and defecation practices, as I try to do in chapter 5. My interpretations of Ramakrishna's visions, moreover, owe a great deal to psychoanalytic approaches to the dream. In Spiro's terms, it is psychoanalysis that has provided me with an analytic scheme capable of conceptually integrating a set of seemingly disparate images, myths, and teachings.[61] Having said that, however, I would also insist that such a use of psychoanalytic insights need not entail a wholesale acceptance of the early twentieth-century materialism that Freud happened to espouse. Nor does it require an a priori rejection of the ontology of Indian Tantra. As I will demonstrate in the course of this study, the Hindu Tantra operates with an energy symbolism that is quite capable of incorporating much of psychoanalysis without surrendering its own mystical worldview.

It is this energy symbolism and its structuring of the "Hindu unconscious" that I seek to uncover and explicate here. More specifically, I am interested in defining the *ontological status* of the Hindu unconscious and its energies and in exploring how this ontology might affect a psychological method such as my own. After establishing, then, that Indian culture itself identifies something that might be called the "Hindu unconscious," I will turn immediately to the specifically religious or sacred dimensions of this unconscious and ask, not how the hidden depths of the Hindu soul work or how they are shaped by Hindu social practices, but rather how these other worlds are defined and understood by Ramakrishna and his tradition.

The Reality of the Hindu Unconscious: Indigenous Understandings

OBEYESEKERE HAS NOTED that "in Southern Asia we are dealing with societies that have already dethroned consciousness in preference to realities which are achievable through states of trance where 'unconscious thought' prevails."[62] Certainly such an insight is born out in the texts that focus the present study. The *Kathāmṛta* is replete with hundreds of instances of Ramakrishna *bhāvāviṣṭha* or "established in ecstasy" and *samādhistha* or "established in union."[63] M again and again lovingly describes the strange features of the Paramahaṁsa absorbed in such states: his eyes frozen in ecstasy, his limbs stiffened in a corpse-like posture, a divine smile on his lips. Ramakrishna's secret visions appear to him in the brilliant darkness of these "unconscious" states, his songs sing of their joys, and his teachings explicate their ontological meanings.

Ramakrishna and his disciples, in other words, operated with cultural and religious assumptions about the hidden or secret dimensions of the human being that are, at least on the surface, similar to Western notions of the unconscious. Consider, for example, the following passage from Saradananda's *Līlāprasaṅga,* in which the pious biographer attributes special, almost psychoanalytic, powers to Ramakrishna: "We always saw shining in him a power to grasp the hidden states and past conditionings of people's minds" (LP 5.11.8). In another passage, Saradananda becomes the analyst and Ramakrishna the analysand. The subject is Ramakrishna's penis, which had the curious habit of retracting "like a tortoise" in the presence of sexy women. Saradananda reads such behavior as as an "outer manifestation of the purest mental states" (LP 4.APP.8). For him, the retracting penis is an external sign of Ramakrishna's total conquest of that darkest of human forces, lust. And this is an accomplishment that in turn helps establish Ramakrishna's status as an incarnation of God—only such an incarnation could achieve such a total conquest of the sexual powers. The retracting penis, in other words, points not to a conflicted sexual wish or fear but to a theological state and the reality of God. For others in the texts, however, it does indeed point to a sexual conflict, for it is a perfect example of Ramakrishna's "destroyed masculinity" (JV[5], 36).

The indigenous voices, then, agree on the reality of hidden or unconscious levels of the human being but disagree about the nature of those levels. They are arguing, in other words, not about whether human beings are multi-leveled—everyone seems to agree on that—but about what those levels *mean*, what they point to, what they *are*.

Kakar and the Mystics of Psychoanalysis

SUCH QUESTIONS are more religious than psychological, but, if taken seriously, they could have profound implications for the method of a psychological study. The present study at least will be carried through in a manner that respects not only these indigenous questions but also at least some of the indigenous *answers*. Here I take my inspiration from the work of the Indian psychoanalyst, Sudhir Kakar, who has begun what one might call an "ontological critique" of traditional psychoanalytic categories. In his recent *The Analyst and the Mystic*, Kakar notes that theoretical uncertainties in contemporary psychoanalysis "threaten its basic paradigm" and render its "earlier equation of the mystical state with a devalued, if not pathological regression" questionable. Psychoanalysis, Kakar believes, is "ripe for radical revision."[64] To demonstrate his thesis Kakar turns to, among all people, Ramakrishna.

Kakar, in a traditional psychoanalytic vein, boldly asserts that both the genesis of Ramakrishna's religious identity as a child of the goddess and his proclivity for dualistic devotion over monistic absorption were deeply influenced by emotional trajectories set in the saint's childhood.[65] Yet he then turns around and, in a decidedly untraditional psychoanalytic vein, refuses to reduce Ramakrishna's mystical states to "nothing but" the pitiful nostalgia of a child longing for its mother, or even worse, the primal yearning of a fetus for its womb. In fact, he does the exact opposite, "reducing" human desire and emotion to a specifically mystical dimension of reality. Invoking one of "the mystics of psychoanalysis,"[66] Jacques Lacan, Kakar refers to a "primordial state of affairs" Lacan called *"the Real."* Human beings, exiled from *the Real,* live with a fundamental feeling of incompletion, a lack that is translated on the emotional level as desire: "the human venture is a history of desire as it ceaselessly loses and discovers itself in (what Lacan calls) The Imaginary and, with the advent of language, in The symbolic order."[67] All objects of desire merely interrupt the search for *the Real.* And so Kakar quotes the Barandes on how all human desires, to the extent that they are mere detours on the way back to the Real, are "inexorably perverse." Kakar then draws a striking conclusion, turning the classical psychoanalytic paradigm on its head: "If we are all fundamentally perverse in the play of our desire, then the mystic is the only one who seeks to go beyond the illusion of The Imaginary and yes, also the *maya* [illusion] of The Symbolic register."[68] The mystic becomes the only healthy person, the only one truly attuned to reality. Everyone else is "perverse," lost in the labyrinth of fundamentally illusory desires. Kakar thus begins the "radical revision," the ontological critique of psychoanalytic categories that he promised in his opening pages.

Romain Rolland, some sixty years earlier, had suggested that a "mystic psycho-analysis" might benefit from studying the ecstatic states of Ramakrishna and his disciples.[69] It is only with Kakar and his unique use of those "mystics of psychoanalysis" that such an enterprise has begun. Here I would like to take up Rolland's suggestion and Kakar's program and advance a similar ontological critique. Applied to the present study, such an approach will ask not so much "How does the Hindu unconscious operate?" but "How should the historian of religions understand the ontological nature of the Hindu unconscious and its powers?" Is it some biological storehouse of memory and instinct? Or is it the mind of God, the silent witness behind all of the mind's functionings? Are its powers merely "libidinal energies," devoid of any cosmic significance? Or are they manifestations of *śakti,* literal embodiments of some divine cosmic energy? And what about its products? Are they "delusions," the result of repressed traumata? Or are they "visions," revelations of the sacred? Finally, and most important, was Ramakrishna's *eros* pure metaphor, expressive of a totally transcendent experience, as some of his interpreters have wanted to suggest? Or was it literal truth, witnessing to the simply sexual roots of his religious experience, as his detractors have argued over the last century? What *are* we to make of Ramakrishna's foot, so provocatively placed in the genitals of a young boy?

"There Are Two in Here"

IT SHOULD BE pointed out immediately that these questions and their clashing answers are not something that we need to impose on these particular texts. Their conflict is a conflict *internal* to the texts and the world they represent. Consider, for example, the following passage in the *Līlāprasaṅga:*

> From time to time Narendra became anxious to explain to the Master, with various examples, all the investigations and researches of Western physical science on subjective visions and how such things have been proven to be false. When the mind of the Master was established in a high state, he was very pleased with Narendra and considered such boyish efforts to be nothing more than indications of Narendra's dedication to truth. But at the times when he was established in a normal state, all the sharp arguments of Narendra overwhelmed the Master's simple, naturally boyish mind and caused him sometimes to be very anxious. (LP 5.6.1.17)

A hermeneutics based on a psychological reductionism convinced Ramakrishna himself, at least enough to get him thinking, to make him "very anxious" from time to time. At other times, however, when the saint was established "in a high state," such a hermeneutics fell far short, for it left untouched the specifically mystical states he knew so well. Ramakrishna was a *homo duplex,* a Man of Two, at once bothered and untouched by "the investigations and researches of Western physical science." Sometimes he would express this duality in terms of an incarnational theology: "There are two in here," he would say simply: "There is she [the goddess], and there is [her] devotee" (KA 3.251). While the devotee, Ramakrishna pointed out, suffered, broke his arm, and wept in pain, "she" simply watched, untouched by the physical and psychological drama of the devotee's life. There are two worlds, then, two levels of truth, two planes of being, each of which demands a hermeneutics specific to its nature. I have tried to hold these two planes in balance by adopting a method that is both psychologically searching with respect to the "Master's simple, naturally boyish mind" and ontologically sensitive to the "she" that dwelt mysteriously in him.

Such a dual approach to Ramakrishna, the Man of Two, carries serious consequences for my psychologically informed method. Most obviously, it relegates any psychological findings to only one side of this

Two. In the end, although its expressions and manifestations are open to psychological interpretation, the "she" of which Ramakrishna speaks is not something (or someone) my psychological method can approach. This needs to be stated clearly in the beginning.

This dual approach also assumes a certain ontological openness to what I have called "the Hindu unconscious." Saradananda, Ramakrishna's faithful biographer, once railed against Western scientists and philosophers for their hate-filled characterization of *samādhi* as a pathological form of unconsciousness. He was particularly incensed by their ontological blinders; their refusal to accept any dimension other than the material seemed to him to be simply "a demonstration of their own ignorance and stubbornness" (LP 5.12.2.20). There is more than a grain of truth in the biographer's angry words. He, at least, saw clearly that there is an entire, essentially foreign metaphysics enfolded into the meanings and connotations of psychological terms.

I take such criticisms very seriously. Consequently, when I use the expression *the unconscious* or *unconscious,* I refer simply to *a secret dimension or dimensions of the human person of which he or she is not aware.* As I will demonstrate, some of these dimensions clearly witness to repressed memories and childhood conflicts. Others, however, speak of godlike states of consciousness, patterns of divine energy, unions with the cosmos, and ecstatic flights of the soul. Pathology finds its roots in this unconscious, but so also does the mystical, for it too is "that which is secret" (*mustikos*). If we are to understand the Hindu unconscious, then, we must decipher it, not only with the tools of depth psychology, but also with the researches and categories of the history of religions. The Hindu unconscious, blossoming with multiple energies, identified with the deepest levels of the cosmos, and inhabited by mythological beings, is as much a religious reality as it is a psychological dimension. "There are two in here."

"Freud Only Got to the Third Cakra"

Ramakrishna often spoke of this multi-leveled "Hindu unconscious" in terms of the *cakras* or "circles," those lotus-like patterns of energy that constitute the subtle body of Tantric yoga. There are seven such petaled circles or centers, all located along the *suṣumnā* or "central channel" that runs along the spine. The lower three *cakras,* dubbed by Ramakrishna the "Anus" (or lit. "Secret"), the "Phallus," and the "Navel," control the powers of evacuation, sexuality, and digestion. The states and experiences of most people are restricted to the realms of these three lowest *cakras* (LP 4.APP.9). Such mental states are defined by their fixation on what Ramakrishna called lover-and-gold,[70] that worldly dimension of human experience defined by the energies of sexual desire and greed. For Ramakrishna, moreover, these first three centers were the place of "shame, disgust, and fear," those powerful emotional bonds that must be broken if one is to finally realize God. Above these three lower centers of energy bloom four others, located in the heart, the throat, between the eyes in the forehead, and in the skull. According to the Paramahaṁsa, mystical love awakens in the heart of the fourth, a still-speaking ecstasy is triggered in the throat of the fifth (KA 1.115), all words cease in the near-absorptive state that is the sixth, and "complete absorption" (*samādhi*) in the mystico-erotic union of Śiva and Śakti (KA 4.116) defines the experience of that "very secret place" (KA 2.149–150), the thousand-petaled lotus in the head. Much of Tantric religious practice involves "awakening"[71] the goddess in the lowest of the *cakras,* where she sleeps like a "coiled" (*kuṇḍalinī*) snake, and leading her up through the different centers until she erotically unites with her lover, Śiva, in the seventh and final *cakra* at the top of the head.

The implications of such a symbolic system are seldom drawn out in the texts that focus this study, but they are nevertheless fairly obvious. Ontologically speaking, the energy that constitutes the mundane experiences of the lower *cakras* is the same energy that drives the ecstasies of the upper *cakras.* Energy and consciousness may move in and out of these multi-petaled dimensions, blossoming here into this state of consciousness and there into this experience of the body and the world, but it is all one life force. In symbolic language, the number of the *cakra* petals may range from two to a thousand, but in the end all the states do possess petals; they are *all* likened to the lotus, that mystical flower that blossoms in the pure light of consciousness and yet draws its life, sustenance, and beauty from the dark, muddy bottom of the world and the body.

If handled properly, with an awareness that we are dealing here with a symbolism and not a science, this energetic unity of the Indian *cakra* system can enable the interpreter to identify and acknowledge both the "shameful" and the sublime of human religious experience. The energies that control defecation and mystical union, after all, are not two ontologically distinct realities. Rather, they are simply two different "wavelengths" of the same energetic spectrum, two differently petaled lotuses. So too with the energies of mystical union and sexual experience. Consequently, it is one thing to uncover the sexual dimensions of Ramakrishna's mystical experiences, to point out that he saw himself licking vagina-shaped lotuses and once worshiped the penises of young boys. It is quite another to conclude from this that his religious experiences were "nothing but" the expressions of a sexually frustrated man. Everything depends upon one's hermeneutical stance and, in this particular case, how seriously one takes Ramakrishna's Tantric world and its own way of dealing with the relationship between the mystical and the sexual. A Tantric interpretation would have no problem with all the vaginas and penises of Ramakrishna's religious discourse, since within its *cakra* system a mystico-erotic energy called *śakti* constitutes both human sexuality and mystical experience. Indeed, to the extent that human sexuality is considered to be ontologically grounded in *śakti*, a Tantric inspired method would *expect* such language. But this is not "reduction" in the sense that a classical psychoanalytic method entails. Indeed, in the dialectical world of Tantra reducing one form of *śakti*, the mystical, to another, the sexual, is a logically meaningless enterprise. Mystical experience is not "reduced" to sexuality. Sexuality, as a potent expression of *śakti*, is realized as essentially mystical. Tantra, in other words, while resembling psychoanalysis on the surface, actually turns it on its head and does this in a way that, given Tantra's ontological assumptions, is logically consistent. We are closer here to Kakar and his "mystics of psychoanalysis" than we are to Freud.

Freud knew that the shameful and the sublime were related, that somehow sexual forces were "sublimated" into profound works of art and culture, but, committed as he was to an ontology in which libidinal energies never quite escape their strictly materialistic origins, the Viennese master failed to explain how this process worked. As a result, his category of sublimation or "making sublime" remained undeveloped in his thought,[72] a silent acknowledgment that something was amiss. Perhaps the Tāntrika put it best when he quipped, "Freud only got to the third *cakra*." With an energy symbolism restricted by his materialistic, strictly physical notion of *libido*, how could he get any further? Kakar adds his own perspective on the problem when he notes that "much of the misunderstanding between psychoanalysis and yoga is due to different visions of reality."[73] For psychoanalysis to declare Indian yogic experiences pathological, Kakar argues, "is to confuse a vision of reality with *the* reality and thus remain unaware of its relativity."[74] We are back to the *cakras* and the *libido* and their conflicting symbolisms. Psychoanalysis may see within the penises and vaginas of Tantric symbolism a flurry of repressed libidinal energies finally taking their symbolic revenge, but Tantra in turn relativizes psychoanalysis by locating its discourse within the lowest of its energy centers. In the end, which interpretation one takes depends on which world one chooses to live in and on how many *cakras* one accepts as real. I am assuming here that there are more, many more, than three.

CHAPTER ONE

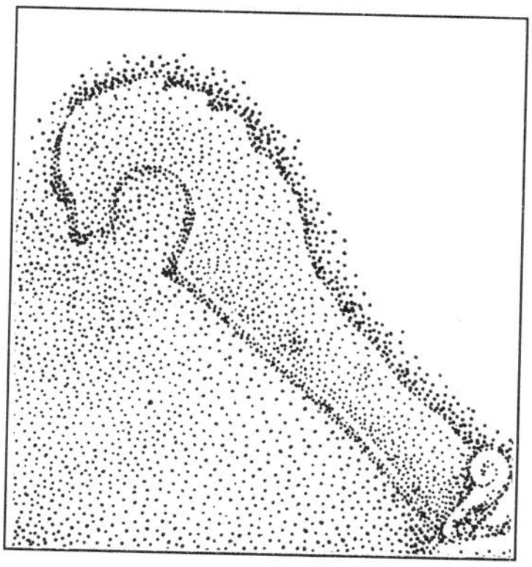

Kālī's Sword: Anxious Longing and the First Vision

This Dark Kṛṣṇa is this Dark Kālī in the form of a woman.
Wipe out the forms and think of her sword as his flute.

Ramprasad

THE PRESENT STUDY of Ramakrishna's mystical experiences begins with his first vision of Kālī at the age of twenty. But to understand this event in its biographical context we must first look at the saint's childhood and adolescence, for his initial encounter with the goddess can be understood adequately only as a dramatic climax of character traits and cultural patterns already in place and active in his earliest years. There is a great deal of truth in Isherwood's observation that much of Ramakrishna's developed personality is defined by "the sublimation of the village child he once was."[1] Indeed, many of the metaphors and figures that the Paramahaṁsa used to teach his disciples—from fish-traps and rice mortars to boys killing snakes in the fields—were drawn directly from his early experiences "in that country," as he used to say. The psychic patterns that resulted in his encounter with Kālī's sword are no exception; they stem directly from patterns that were already in place in the village. After an initial study of Kālī's sword, then, I will turn to the extant biographies in order to tell the story of Gadadhar (Ramakrishna's childhood name), the village boy. This will take us up to the young adolescent's move to Calcutta at the age of seventeen and his near fatal encounter with Kālī's sword at twenty.

KĀLĪ'S SWORD

KĀLĪ'S SWORD FIGURES prominently in the iconography and mythology of the goddess. The sword is a function of Kālī's left side, her "sinister" half connected with death, asceticism, and mystical eroticism. As in many cultures, right and left take on symbolic value in Indian culture. Generally speaking, that which is "right" is modeled after the established order of *dharma:* it is pure, filled with light, socially acceptable, a model to emulate. That which is "left" is characterized as *adharma,* that which does not conform to the socioreligious order: it is impure, dark, antisocial, evil, in constant need of control. Right and left taken together, then, represent those dualities of somatic, moral, and social experience—nourishment and destruction, purity and impurity, good and evil—that constitute the complexity and richness of human life.

Kālī both embodies these dualities of the right and the left and transcends them. She is all that is in the physical and social worlds. The physical universe vibrates with her conscious energies: "She herself has become everything," Ramakrishna often declared. She, moreover, is the energy of every human emotion, the connection constituting every engendered relation:

> Ma dwells in every house.
> Shall I reveal this secret to all?
> With a male Tāntrika she is a female Tāntrika,
> with a baby she is a young girl. . . .
> She is mother, daughter, wife, sister, and so many others.
> (RSG, no. 15)

Bengali Śākta culture delights in this secret—in seeing the goddess in the most common of human relations. Noting this motif in the Śākta songs of Bengal, Shashibushan Dasgupta has written of what he calls the "humanization" of mythology in the songs.[2] This same humanization of mythology also finds its way into language, legend, and vision. The word *mā,* for example, is an affectionate term used to address one's biological mother, one's divine mother (the goddess), and one's daughter. This linguistic union of the human and the divine manifests itself in the legends of the goddess (*mā*) appearing as the little daughter (*mā*) of the poet or mystic. Ramakrishna, for example, told the story of a zamindar, who through his ascetic practices gained the goddess' presence as his own daughter only to lose her when he lost his patience with her seemingly infinite questions: *Oṭa ki? Oṭa ki?* "What is that, Daddy?

Daddy, what is that?" Put off by his impatience, the goddess entered the local pond never to return (KA 4.213). In a similar fashion, it is said that Ramprasad was visited by Kālī in the form of his daughter to help him mend a fence. The poet sings of this realization of the divine in the daughter: "He is a rich man in whose house the Mother lives. Saying this, Ramprasad lays her down in her small bed, fast asleep."[3]

But Kālī also manifests herself in the cremation ground, beyond the physical and social worlds, for she is that order of reality realized in Tantra's "left-handed" antinomian ritual, that brilliant blackness that negates all dualities, relations, and forms. Because she "dwells in every house," in every human social bond, Kālī supports her children like a mother. But because her nondual divine nature excludes every human relation in its mystical blackness,[4] she also destroys like a ghoulish demoness.

Kālī's four arms, then, embodying in their symmetrical quaternity these two poles of religious experience, seem to constitute the ultimate double message. Her upper right hand, assuring safety, dispels fear. Her upper left hand, bearing a sword, instills it. Her lower right hand, offering boons, grants life. Her lower left hand, holding a lopped-off head by the hair, takes it away. It is a striking image of total affirmation and total negation, representing a bold coincidence of opposites attained briefly in mystical experience but realized permanently only in a divine mythological being, in Kālī.

An Instrument of Death

AS AN INSTRUMENT of Kālī's left side, Kālī's sword is above all an instrument of the dark forces in human experience, foremost among them, death. In battle her sword slays the demons and "cuts down evil."[5] But even off the battlefield, no one is safe from her sword, not even the reader or listener, for Kālī's sword swings out of the text or song and threatens to end the life of any who dares read or listen: "She is my Ma, Kālī with a garland of heads. Today she'll cut off yours!" (RJR, no. 81). Often, however, the sword is not so much feared as it is invoked. Hence the poet prays that the sword that decapitates the sacrificial goat now be turned on himself: "My worship is over," Ramprasad sings. "Now, O Ma, bring down your sword" (SP, no. 189).

Sometimes this symbolic act of self-decapitation is performed by Kālī's name, which is often associated with her sword and connected to the removal of "sin" (*pāpa*): "Where is sin with Kālī's name? Without a head one can't have a headache" (SP, no. 332). But more often this ritual violence is connected to a specifically mystical form of knowledge or experience. "That which is right [*dharma*] and that which is wrong [*adharma*] are the two goats," the poet sings. Both must be bound to the sacrificial stake and beheaded with the "sword of gnosis" (SP, 257). As the sword of gnosis, Kālī's sword cuts the bonds of *māyā* embedded in the "good" and "bad" of society and so releases the devotee from the dualities of ignorance. As such, Kālī's sword is an instrument of the goddess's grace, ushering in through its violence a reality untainted by the distinctions and divisions of language and society. As the goat head falls to the ground, so too does the mystic's, and with it, the polarities of human thought.

Related to this symbolism of death by decapitation or severing, Kālī's sword is also portrayed as an instrument of renunciation or asceticism. To renounce is to die, or more specifically, to be cut off by Kālī's sword. Accordingly, Kālī's skirt of human hands is said to represent the goddess's destruction of the bonds of action or *karma*. Hands that once acted to entangle their owners in the sufferings of the world are now but tinkling ornaments dangling around her sexy waist (RJS, no. 307).

So the head is cut off in mythic battles, in ritual sacrifice, in devotion, in remorse, in mystical experience, in ascetical practices, even in the act of reading or listening. Death in some form is always involved. Kālī's sword is a deadly thing, a weapon that cuts off.

The Corpse, the Head, and "The Secret of the Sword and the Flute"

But even something as cold and lifeless as a corpse comes to life with the touch of Kālī's lotus feet and the mystico-erotic *śakti* that they generate. Śiva's pale penis stands erect. The mystical body is thus the ithyphallic corpse, absolutely dead to the world but paradoxically aroused by the goddess. The state of the corpse becomes the state of Śiva, the erotic ascetic, and death becomes the locus of the ultimate erotic experience—union with Kālī.

All three dimensions of this ithyphallic corpse—eroticism, asceticism, and death—meet in Kālī's sword. Although clearly the sword's erotic function is not nearly as obvious as its martial and ascetic functions, numerous erotic connotations can be found in Kālī's sword. Simply by its location in the left hand of the goddess, for example, Kālī's sword is connected with the erotic aspects of the goddess, with the "left-handed" rituals involving alcohol, intoxicants, and sexual intercourse that form one of the defining features of Tantra. Accordingly, even Kālī's most macabre characteristics, those usually connected with her sword, are described in erotic terms. Streams of blood, for example, let loose no doubt by her sword, flow ceaselessly down her round sexy thighs (RJS, no. 277). And her garland of heads and skirt of human hands, both the handiwork of her bloody sword, are placed "just so" by the potter. One only has to walk through Komartoli, the "Potter's Village" of Calcutta, where most Kālī images are made each autumn, to see how the hands of Kālī's skirt are strategically, almost seductively, placed over the goddess's buttocks and sexual organs, creating a "bikini"[6] of human hands that reveal as much as they conceal and conceal only to seduce.

We also must remember that the head, the usual object of Kālī's sword, often takes on a phallic function as the ultimate storehouse of semen in Tantric physiology and as the proper focus of one's mystico-erotic energies in *kuṇḍalinī yoga*. Even when the head is that of a sacrificial goat, the symbolic connection between the head and the phallus remain: both are "cut off" by Kālī's sword and offered to the goddess, either literally in the goat sacrifice or metaphorically in sexual abstinence. Accordingly, Ramakrishna compares sexual abstinence to the act of sacrificing a spotless black goat to Kālī (KA 4.96), symbolically connecting the goat's decapitation with the "cutting off" of the sexual powers embodied in the penis. Those suspicious of such "Western" speculations should consider well Ramakrishna's reported technique for conquering the powers of lust: he would stand before a naked prostitute with a noose hung around his neck and tighten the rope when he became sexually excited,[7] a curious practice indeed if the head is not recognized as a symbolic phallus. The head, then—as the storehouse of semen, as the focus of one's mystico-erotic energies, and as the phallic object of Kālī's sacrificial sword—is an organ at once mystical and sexual. As the most common target of Kālī's sword, it is loaded with complex and provocative connotations.

Finally, Kālī's sword is connected to the erotic dimensions of human religious experience by its symbolic transformation into Kṛṣṇa's flute. The sword that once slew demons and sacrificial goats becomes the flute that seduces the voluptuous milkmaids of Vrindavana:

> O Ma Kālī! In the guise of the greatest of dancers you have become Kṛṣṇa in Vrindavana. . . .
> Your loins were exposed. Now you wear a yellow robe. Your hair was all dishevelled. Now you wear a crown and hold a flute.

> Your flirting glances once charmed Śiva. Now your dark shapely body and suggestive eyes charm the women of Vrindavana.
>
> (SP, no. 144)

Kālī, a resident of cremation grounds, now dwells in the romantic pastures of Vrindavana. Kālī and Kṛṣṇa have become one. And so Ramprasad sings: "This Dark Kṛṣṇa is this Dark Kālī in the form of a woman. Wipe out the forms and think of [her] sword as [his] flute" (RJS, no. 122). Ramakrishna would take up this same theme and sing with Ramprasad: "Dance again, O Dark One! Throw down the sword and take up the flute. . . . Dance, O Dark One!"[8]

Ramprasad called this realization of the ultimate unity of Kālī and Kṛṣṇa "the secret of the sword and the flute."[9] Although it certainly speaks of a need felt by the poet to reconcile the seemingly contradictory Vaiṣṇava and Śākta strands in his culture, I would agree with Dasgupta that Ramprasad's secret is more than simply a political strategy to synthesize two hostile traditions. The secret is first and foremost a product of Ramprasad's religious experiences, in which the dark goddess and the dark god disappeared in the black light of mystical experience,[10] for in the religious experience and poetic imagination of the poet, "black" (*kālo*) became "light" (*ālo*),[11] and this brilliant blackness is equated with the shining formlessness of that same secret: "Kṛṣṇa-Kālī with the garland of wild flowers has abandoned the flute and taken up the sword. . . . Prasad says, 'With the knowledge of nondifference, black forms blend together'" (RJS, no. 148).[12]

This "secret of the sword and the flute," then, is a complex secret, witnessing at once to a socioreligious conflict within Bengali culture and to a specific type of religious experience. As a secret setting up symbolic connections between Kālī's sword and Kṛṣṇa's flute, it is also an erotic secret. Kṛṣṇa's flute, after all, does not slay. It seduces. If Kālī's sword is Kṛṣṇa's flute, as the poets insist, then it is, at least potentially, an erotic instrument. Moreover, when the individual in question is male, the secret becomes a homoerotic secret, an unspoken desire on the part of the male aspirant to transform his vengeful, if divine, mother into an equally divine male lover: "Throw down the sword and take up the flute. . . Dance, O Dark One!" The aspirant moves away from the deadly abyss of maternal absorption into the joys of homoerotic love.

Death, asceticism, and eroticism, then, all meet in Kālī's left side, and more specifically, in her sword. The symbolic connections outlined above may seem too speculative at this point, but all of these details worked out in the mythology, iconography, poetry, and physiology of Śākta culture will become essential as I turn to Ramakrishna's first intense encounter with Kālī, the black goddess whose two left hands hold a head and a sword.

FROM THE VILLAGE TO THE TEMPLE, 1836–1856

MAX MÜLLER, recalling his attempts to reconstruct the life of Ramakrishna, complained as early as 1898, just twelve years after the saint's death, that the accounts of Ramakrishna's life were "so strangely exaggerated, nay so contradictory, that it seemed almost hopeless to form a correct and true idea of his earthly career and his character."[13] Rolland, on the other hand, writing thirty years after Müller, reveled in this same problem, seeing in the legend of Ramakrishna's birth and childhood a "subjective reality of living impressions" far more interesting and meaningful than "the objective reality of facts": "I have become simply the voice of the legend, the flute under the fingers of Krishna," he warned his European readers.[14] Sudhir Kakar, rejecting both the historical agnosticism of Müller and the epic genre of Rolland, has recently taken what seems to be a more balanced view of things: "Though we can never know what *really* happened in his or anyone else's infancy and childhood, the former forever beyond the reach of memory, I have no hesitation in extending a qualified belief to Ramakrishna's own version of his life story."[15] As long as one remembers that "Ramakrishna's own version of his life story" in fact does not exist, that Ramakrishna wrote nothing down, that *everything* we know about the man has been filtered through the religious, intellectual, and social lenses of his disciples, one can take Kakar's "qualified belief" as a healthy *via media* between the Scylla of historical agnosticism and the Charbydis of naive belief, be it religious or historical. This qualified belief is the position that I take as I turn to tell the story of Ramakrishna. Without such a "belief," we could never tell a story; to stop and lose ourselves in every historical question that comes along, few of which have conclusive answers, would only serve to kill the life we are out to understand. But I also must stress that my own belief in the events that follow is seriously qualified by the conviction, born out of years of research, that the historical record is at best ambiguous and at worst impossibly distorting. I tell *a* story, then, and acknowledge from the beginning that any particular event in this story, and especially the sequence or dating of the event, is at best a tentative reconstruction and may well be revised with further historical research. *Everything* is open to discussion, debate, and challenge.

With such qualifications, I turn to the story of Gadadhar, the village boy who became a god. The story opens, as most great stories do, with a strange and marvelous birth.

A Scandalous Conception, Birth, and Early Childhood

KSHUDIRAM CHATTERJEE[16] was a pious man from an established brahmin family of Derey, a village in the district of Hooghly. Because he refused to bear false witness against a fellow farmer for the local landlord, Kshudiram lost all of his ancestral land in Derey and had to move to the village of Kamarpukur, where a friend gave him a small plot of land. Kshudiram worshiped the god Raghuvīra, a form of Viṣṇu. He had auspicious dreams and saw visions.[17] Most of the family seems to have been open to such experiences. Kshudiram's sister was said to be possessed by a ghost, and his aunt suffered from cataleptic fits.[18]

Kshudiram's wife, Chandramani (or Chandra, as she was called), was known for her worldly incompetence, her simplicity, and her visions. We hear little about her before Gadadhar's birth and even less about her after the boy's move to Calcutta. But in her old age, when she moved to Dakshineshwar to live with her son, she enters the texts again, this time as a senile but beloved old woman who had a penchant for weaving myth and the work-a-day-world into humorous scenes. As a pious widow, for example, she refused to eat her lunch before Viṣṇu ate his in heaven, an event signaled, she thought, by a mysterious conch shell that blew each day around noon. Although commendable, such piety could also be problematic, especially when the divine conch shell (the whistle from a nearby jute mill) did not blow on the weekends and the old woman refused to eat. But all of this would come much later.

In 1835 Kshudiram, now sixty, went on a pilgrimage to Gaya where Viṣṇu appeared to him in a dream with the awesome message that he was about to be born as his son. The dream apparently became public knowledge, for Ramakrishna still remembered it almost fifty years later: "My father knew him who is within this body. In a dream at Gaya, my father saw Raghuvīra, who said to him, 'I will be born as your son'" (KA 4.240).[19] It was a dream that must have had profound consequences, both for the parents' perception of their son and for the son's own self-perception. What, after all, would it mean to believe that you were born a god?

While Kshudiram was at Gaya, seeing Viṣṇu in a dream, Chandra, now forty-five, was back at the village having her own nocturnal encounters: "Look here, one night while you were away in Gaya," she told her husband, "I saw a strange dream. It was as if a luminous god entered my bed and lay down" (LP 1.4.7). She wondered to herself whether a god ever appears to a human in this way and finally concluded that it must have been some wicked man who had entered her room "for some evil purpose." Her friends warned Chandra to keep silent about her visitor lest she cause a scandal: it would take quite a dream, after all, to lead to such a physically palpable conclusion. Then one day, her husband still away, the nocturnal visitor abandoned her dreams and entered her waking life: "On another day while I was talking to Dhani in front of the Śiva temple of the Yogis, I saw a divine light come out of the great limb of Śiva, fill the temple, and rush towards me in waves like the wind. Marvelling at the sight, I was telling Dhani about it when suddenly it was as if it covered me and entered into me with great force. Frozen with fear and wonder, I at one point fainted and fell to the ground. . . . Since then, I have thought that it is as if this light entered [me] and dwells in my womb and that I am in the early stages of pregnancy" (LP 1.4.8).[20] She was already showing when Kshudiram returned. The villagers noticed her great beauty, but concluded from it that she was about to die (JV[5], 2, n.). Others just thought she was crazy.

It is a strange story—a virginal conception that invoked derision. A being, human or divine, visits Chandra in her bed threatening an act that would cause scandal in the village. Then Śiva, known for his erotic exploits, impregnates the aging woman as she walks by his "great limb," most likely a reference to the Śiva-*liṅgam* enshrined in the temple. The scandal of her nocturnal encounter becomes the derision of her diurnal rape. And all this while another deity, Viṣṇu, announces to Kshudiram that he will be born as his son. No one has noted the obvious, that both Viṣṇu and Śiva are identified in the story as the divine source of Ramakrishna's conception. It does not seem to matter. This conflict over Ramakrishna's divine paternity is an example of that uneasy symbiosis of Vaiṣṇava, Śaiva, and Śākta strands in the Bengali Hindu religious imagination. "Every Bengali is half Vaiṣṇava and half Śākta," goes the saying. So too with Ramakrishna and his virginal conception: Viṣṇu, the god of the pious Vaiṣnava father, appears in the dream, but Śiva, the consort of Śakti, impregnates Chandra. This dual conception, defined by Kshudiram's Vaiṣṇava piety and Chandra's erotic encounters with divine beings, will carry over as a general pattern into Ramakrishna's later visions and religious practices. Thus the story of Ramakrishna's conception, whether a legend with no basis in the "historical facts" or an accurate representation of the "subjective realities" of dream and vision, is an important one. Indeed, as a marker of symbolic and mythological patterns evident in Ramakrishna's life and religious experiences, this dual conception will prove to be central.

Kshudiram was in the habit of naming his sons after pilgrimages: earlier, he had named his second son Rameshwar, in honor of his pilgrimage to southern India (LP 1.3.13). So the infant was named Shambhuchandra or Ramakrishna[21] but was called Gadadhar, "the Bearer of the Mace," in honor of his father's dream at Gaya (Viṣṇu is "the Bearer of the Mace"). With his birth, the family prospered, leading some to speculate that a god had been born in their midst. Kshudiram heard such rumors and warned his family: "Do not speak to anyone of these things which have happened" (JV[5], 3, n.). From the beginning, the boy's life was shrouded in a secret.

Gadadhar grew up to become a willful, mischievous village boy. Kshudiram was never harsh with him. One might say that he spoiled him.[22] The boy disliked math, but loved the artistic disciplines of sculpture, painting, acting, and storytelling (KA 5.46). Accordingly, while others turned their energies to school and their training for a profession, Gadadhar spent all of his time and attention on the heroes and deities of the local myths. He memorized their exploits and could act them out in great detail. Later, he would skip school to form a dramatic troupe in the village mango grove (LP 1.8.16), where he and his friends acted out the erotic exploits of Kṛṣṇa and the milkmaids in Vrindavana. He also loved to paint and sculpt figures of the gods and goddesses. His was a world ruled by the hero, the deity, the story, the form, the image, and the vision. The abstract number he hated. Later in his life he would paint two scenes on the sides of his bedroom door—a steamship on the left and a flock of parrots feasting on a custard-apple tree on the right. His preferences definitely lay "on the right," with the beautiful birds and their sweet fruit. He enjoyed rides on the steamship (KA 4.136), the embodiment of Western science and technology that floated by the temple every day, but he rejected the intellectual abstractions and mechanistic worldview that created it. As a result, he could not bear to listen to M describe Western logic or the principles behind the tides (KA 5.31). Nor could he look into a microscope, another instrument of

Western learning. He much preferred instead to fall into an ecstatic trance (LP 4.4.5), that realm of the colorful parrots and the tasty apples.

A Father's Death, a Mother's Worries, and the Beginning of the States

KSHUDIRAM DIED when Gadadhar was only seven. By most accounts,[23] his death created major repercussions in the psychic landscape of the little boy. Now Gadadhar felt especially drawn to his mother.[24] He helped her around the house with the chores and with the worship of the family deity. Jensen notes here a pattern developing in which the boy seeks to replace his "paternal loss" with a "maternal gain." It was a strategy that, according to Jensen, Ramakrishna would invoke again and again to deal with the tragic losses that punctured his life.[25] Whatever the reason, a great change now came over Gadadhar's mind. He became more solemn and began to spend time alone in the cremation ground and the mango grove. His preoccupation with molding the images of gods and listening to religious stories became even stronger. And he began to spend time with the wandering holy men who stopped in Kamarpukur on their way to Puri, a famous pilgrimage site. Indeed, he spent so much time with them that the villagers began to notice it. Chandra began to worry about such visits, especially when the boy returned home with his clothes torn into a simple loin-cloth and his nearly naked body covered with ashes, but Gadadhar assured her that nothing was wrong (LP 1.7.5).

But something *was* wrong. Strange experiences began to occur that his mother—quite reasonably, it seems—took for sickness but that others, especially the women of the village, interpreted as signs of the boy's precocious religious abilities. He began, for example, to fall into troubling trances. The most famous case occurred sometime around Kshudiram's death. Gadadhar was walking through a rice paddy munching on puffed rice when he looked up into the sky and saw a flock of white egrets flying in front of a bank of dark storm clouds. The beauty of the contrasting forms sent the boy into an ecstatic trance. His relatives had to carry him home to a very anxious mother.[26] Strangely enough, Ramakrishna never mentions this famous scene in the *Kathāmṛta*. Instead, he identifies another occasion—a trip to see the goddess Viśālakṣī—as the first occurrence of "this state": "When I was ten, I was walking through a field on the way to see Viśālakṣī when this state first occurred. Ah, what I saw! I was completely unconscious of the external world!" (KA 4.283).[27] Another passage referring to an ecstatic state at the age of ten, again minus the egrets and storm clouds of the more classical account,[28] suggests that the egret and storm cloud vision may be apocryphal.

Wherever one decides to place Gadadhar's first ecstatic experiences, two things are quite clear: (1) the tradition connects them, chronologically at least, to the death of his father; and (2) the boy's mother consistently interpreted them as signs of some serious illness. Chandra, in other words, was suspicious. And why should she not have been? Boys do not fall into trances for no particular reason, and her little Gadadhar was even entering such states in quite public places. Many of the biographers, for example, record a scene in which the boy went into a trance while taking the role of Śiva in a play.[29] Jensen and Sil have noted one possible reason for the persistency of the trances: they were consistently rewarded by the women of the village.[30] The texts agree. According to Saradananda, the women of the village, and at least one elderly man,[31] were so impressed with the boy and his trances that they worshiped him as Kṛṣṇa, giving Chandra even more reason to worry. To make things even worse, while some of the older women of the village mothered Gadadhar as Gopāla, the child Kṛṣṇa (a practice that Ramakrishna would later bitterly criticize as a religious disguise for sexual intentions), the younger women looked upon him as Kṛṣṇa, their divine lover, a troubling practice indeed considering the fact that Gadadhar was only a boy.[32] Gadadhar, it seems, entered his trances at least partially to escape these women and their worship. The women, in other words, not only rewarded the trances: they *caused* them. Certainly the neighbors were suspicious, despite the women's insistence that no harm was done.[33] Sil has recently re-echoed this suspicion in a tone undoubtedly similar to that of the village neighbors: "Indeed what the women of Kāmarkpukur did with the ecstatic boy . . . is anybody's guess."[34]

The biographers give their own, rather forced reasons for Gadadhar's association with the village women. According to them, the boy actively sought the company of the pious women of the village because they reminded him of the milkmaids of Vrindavana, who had realized Kṛṣṇa as their husband and had experienced the bliss and pleasure of his love.[35] The boy, in other words, sought out the women because he desired to become one of them. But if the boy desired to be a woman—and all the evidence suggests that he did—then why was he letting them worship him as a male lover? The mother and the neighbors perhaps had a right to be suspicious.

Gadadhar's own fantasy life certainly did not support the intentions of the village women. He, after all, wished that, if he were born again, he might be born as a child widow in a brahmin family. This widow would have a spinning wheel, a single cow, a simple hut, and a small plot of land to grow vegetables. She would make sweets for her beloved Kṛṣṇa from the milk of her cow and sing love songs to him in the evening as she spun her wheel. As the sun set, Kṛṣṇa would steal into her hut and take her sweets.[36] As we shall see, it is a fantasy that would enter deeply into the patterns of Ramakrishna's relationships.

The Move to Calcutta and Another Death

With the loss of his father at the age of seven, Gadadhar's oldest brother, Ramkumar, became the boy's second father. Ramkumar was a Śākta known for his occult powers. He could predict the deaths of patients, complete strangers, even his own wife, who died giving birth to their first child.[37] When Gadadhar was just thirteen, he left for Calcutta to find work so that he could support the seriously struggling family. With Ramkumar's move to Calcutta, Gadadhar lost his second paternal figure. He had been abandoned again.

Once again Gadadhar turned to worshiping the family deity and helping his mother with the housework. In Jensen's reading, he again sought to replace his paternal loss with a maternal gain.[38] These paternal losses and maternal gains at some point began to manifest themselves in the boy's behavior. He began, for example, to show signs that he was not completely comfortable with his apparent gender. He would dress up like the women of the village and mimic their mannerisms, their walk, their conversational habits, their vanities. Much later in his life he would describe in great detail how women walk with their left foot first (LP 2.14.9), how they gossip at the pond and the bathing ghat, and how they weep for their dead husbands (KA 4.272). All this he learned by close observation and, sometimes, by participation. His boyhood exploits in the guise of a woman became famous. Once he dressed up as a woman to sneak into the purdah of one of the village aristocrats, who had bragged to the young boy that no man would ever see his inner apartments. Gadadhar's effeminate nature and womanly ways did not go unnoticed by the villagers. Observing the boy's friendship with Ram Mallik, a seventeen-year-old teenager, the villagers used to say that, if Gadadhar were a woman, the two of them would be married (KA 3.184).

Despite the boy's rejection of school and the whole work ethic that it supported—"I have no use for the art of bundling rice and bananas, and I won't learn it" (LP 4.4.26 et al.)—Ramkumar eventually managed to convince his little brother, now seventeen, to move to Calcutta with him, where he had set up a Sanskrit school as a means to support the financially struggling family back in the village. Gadadhar most likely followed his brother to the city because he respected him as his second father.[39] He could not bear another loss. To help Ramkumar get by, Gadadhar took up priestly duties for a number of respected families in Calcutta, but he continued to neglect his studies. Jensen sees Gadadhar's rejection of his studies as a rejection of adulthood. The village boy refused to grow up and assume the responsibilities of a traditional householder. Instead, he would eventually opt for values he had learned in the village as a child—artistry, play, and vision.[40]

Ramkumar's school did not do well and the financial situation of the two brothers and their dependent family worsened. It was another dream, this time of a complete stranger, that determined their fate. Rani Rasmani, a wealthy woman of a local fishing caste, was planning to travel to Benares on a pilgrimage to see her chosen deity, the goddess Kālī. But the goddess had other plans. Kālī appeared to the Rani (lit. "the queen") in a dream and instructed her to forego her pilgrimage and, instead, build a temple in her honor. If the Rani would do this, the goddess promised that she would manifest herself in the installed image. Accordingly, the Rani purchased an auspicious piece of land for the temple (an old Muslim graveyard) and began to turn her dream into reality. As the consecration day neared, however, the Rani realized that, since she was a low-caste shudra, no brahmin would serve in her temple. Her plans were in grave danger. She consulted different experts in the law, but the opinions were not in her favor.

At this point, Ramkumar sent her a letter and suggested that, if the temple were given to a brahmin, a brahmin priest could be procured without breaking the ancient customs. The Rani took Ramkumar's unconventional[41] advice and invited Ramkumar to serve in the main Kālī temple. When Ramkumar accepted the invitation, Gadadhar objected on the grounds that no brahmin should accept a gift from a shudra, much less serve in a shudra's temple. Their pious father would have never accepted such an offer, Gadadhar argued. In the end, Ramkumar managed to convince his scrupulous brother only by using a *dharmapatra* or "leaf of right," an augury technique, but the boy still refused to eat any food served in the temple, preferring instead to cook his own.

Mathur, the son-in-law of the Rani and manager of the temple estate, was immediately attracted to Gadadhar: "the good-looks of the Master, his tender nature, his piety, and his youth caught the eye of Mathur." "At first sight," Saradananda tells us, seemingly completely unaware of the homosexual dimensions of his own description, a "sudden loving attraction" arose in the mind and heart of the temple boss (LP 2.5.1). Almost immediately, Mathur tried to convince the young priest to take a position in the temple, but Gadadhar refused, allegedly on the grounds that such a position would involve him too deeply in the concerns and cares of the world. When Gadadhar's cousin, Hriday, arrived looking for work and offered to handle the costly ornaments of the temple, something Gadadhar was particularly averse to, Gadadhar finally agreed to accept a position.

Sometime in the summer of 1856, Ramkumar died, but not before he had had Gadadhar initiated into the cult of Kālī by a certain Kenaram. The boy was now a Śākta. With Ramkumar now gone, Gadadhar, known as "the little Chatterjee," was appointed as head priest of the main Kālī temple. From what she had seen already, the Rani believed that the precocious abilities of her young priest would "awaken" at last the goddess asleep in the stone image. Gadadhar, now twenty, had lost two fathers. The Rani was hopeful. The stage was set for the young man's encounter with Kālī's sword. The image was about to come alive.

"Anxious Desire and the First Vision"

WITH THE DEATH of Ramkumar, the young Ramakrishna lost his second father figure. His mother and friends were far away in the village. He was alone again. Jensen, counting Ramkumar's initial move to Calcutta as the boy's second paternal loss, describes Ramkumar's death as Gadadhar's "third death," yet another paternal loss, which he would soon replace with yet another maternal gain, this time in a most dramatic fashion. For it was at this time that Ramakrishna turned to Kālī, the divine Mother, and sought her "vision" (*darśana*). He could not eat. He could not sleep. He could not even blink (JV[5], 9). He could barely breathe so great was his desire.[42] He began to spend his nights meditating naked in the cremation ground. But Gadadhar saw nothing. He rolled in the dust, crying for his divine Mother. So pathetic were his attempts to win his Mother's succor that people would come just to watch. According to Datta, this is what they saw:

> Crying, "Ma! Show yourself to me!" he would fall down suddenly as if he were mad. His face and eyes were bloody red,

> his eyes were rolled up back into his head. His chest was ceaselessly wettened by such a stream of tears that the ground below him on which he sat looked like it had been rained on. . . . If someone would raise some food to his mouth, he would eat it. He would defecate and urinate unconsciously, and yet he was only able to say "Ma," and saying it, he would weep. . . . His state at this time was like that of a boy nursing at its mother's breasts. When one looked at Ramakrishna, one immediately thought of an infant who cannot see its mother and so cries "Ma! Ma!" and will not be consoled. (JV[5], 9–10)[43]

Having been denied a father, he now sought to return to infancy, when he nursed at his mother's breasts, ate from her hand, and soiled his clothes at will. And yet still, there was no vision, no Mother.

On one of these awful days, tormented by desire but frustrated by his unsuccessful attempts and at the point of despair, Ramakrishna's eyes fell on the sacrificial sword hanging on the temple wall. He reached for it and was about to decapitate[44] himself before Kālī when the goddess intervened:

> Just then I suddenly attained a strange vision of Ma and fell down unconscious! After that, I knew nothing of what happened in the external world anywhere for the rest of that day and the next. But within me flowed a new intensely concentrated stream of bliss as I realized a direct vision of Ma. (LP 2.6.13)

In what seems to be another version of the same event, Saradananda has Ramakrishna describing the event as follows:

> It was as if the room, the door, the temple itself, everything vanished—as if there was nothing anywhere! And what was it that I saw? A boundless, endless, conscious ocean of light! Wherever and however far I looked, from all four directions its brilliant rows of waves were roaring towards me with great speed, ready to devour me. And as I watched, the waves fell upon me and all at once pushed me to the bottom. Gasping and thrashing, I fell unconscious! (LP 2.6.13)

As this experience was the culmination of Ramakrishna's initial search for Kālī and as such represents the beginning of his mystical life, the event is absolutely central to all the classical accounts of Ramakrishna's life.[45] What the commentators have often failed to note, however, is that there are numerous variants of the story and that, even in Saradananda's famous *Līlāprasaṅga* (by far the most often-quoted variant), there are in fact two separate accounts. No one, moreover, seems to have noticed that these two accounts possess all the linguistic sophistication of the learned Saradananda and almost none of the simple "village talk" (*grāmya bhāṣya*)[46] of Ramakrishna, so impressively preserved, if only erratically, in the *Kathāmṛta*. The second, more extended version is especially sophisticated. It is most likely Saradananda's own gloss on the first, much simpler version. Indeed, in some of its features (waves of light rushing toward the visionary culminating in an engulfment and an unconscious state), the passage bears a striking similarity to Chandra's recorded experience before the Śiva-*liṅgam*. We must also keep in mind that there is no such ocean of light in the much earlier accounts of Datta and Mitra; indeed, in Mitra's biography, Ramakrishna uses *darkness* as the major metaphor to describe the "black *bhāva*" of his Kālī-vision as an eminently Tantric state whose dark depths taught him the identity of Kṛṣṇa and Kālī and the meaning of the goddess's union with Śiva (JU, 48–49).[47] Are the visions of the mother and the son, of Chandra and Ramakrishna, then, simply the products of Saradananda's pen and stylized rhetoric, the stuff of hagiography? Or are they psychologically accurate descriptions of historical experiences?

A Textual Study of Ramakrishna's "Anxious Desire": Discerning a Vocabulary of Desire

WE WILL NEVER KNOW. Text and experience have become synonymous. Given this basic uncertainty, I want to begin by focusing, not on the presumed structure or origin of the famous First Vision account, but on the term Saradananda uses to describe Ramakrishna's mental state at the time the experience occurred: *vyākulatā*, "anxious longing," a desire that torments. A close study of this unquestionably real emotion will in turn lead us into a whole vocabulary of desire that the texts develop to give a more definite shape and form to the saint's original, seemingly amorphous "drowning desire."

Vyākulatā: Drowning in Desire

VYĀKULATĀ: THE WORD sums up Ramakrishna's feeling at this time and in fact forms the title of the chapter in which Saradananda's classical account occurs: "Anxious Desire and the First Vision." The term is even more important to the *Kathāmṛta*, where it appears as a category absolutely central to Ramakrishna's teaching. Indeed, it occurs well over 150 times in the text. While we cannot be sure of the precise details of Ramakrishna's First Vision, then, we can be absolutely certain that the "anxious desire" that generated it was especially real and important for the saint. It thus seems a good place to start.

A closer look at Ramakrishna's teaching on this anxious desire is revealing. Ramakrishna is portrayed traditionally as likening it to the gasping urgency one feels when someone holds one's head under the water for too long: "A disciple asked his teacher, 'How can I attain the Lord?' The teacher responded, 'Come with me.' Saying this, the teacher took the disciple to a pond and held his head under the water. A little while later, he pulled him out of the water and asked, 'What was it like under the water?' The disciple answered, 'I was gasping [*āṭuvāṭu*] for breath, as if I were about to die!' The teacher said, 'Look, if you gasp for the Lord like this, then you will attain him'" (KA 3.110).[48] Here we might recall that in Saradananda's account of Ramakrishna's First Vision, the saint was engulfed by an ocean of light and "pushed" to the bottom, gulping and thrashing all the way. The sound of Ramakrishna's thrashing arms and frantic bubbles can almost be heard in the onomatopoeia of the Bengali. As he is pushed to the bottom, Ramakrishna is said to "eat" the mystical waters with the sound *hābudubu* (LP 2.6.13). *Vyākulatā,* then, is like a drowning man's frantic gasp for air. Even in its alliterative associations, it bobs up and down in the water: *āṭuvāṭu* and *hābudubu.*

On a more mundane level, the term *vyākulatā* is used to describe a state of emotional conflict, anxiety, or impatient desire. M, for example, experiences *vyākulatā* when he tries to reconcile his Western education with Ramakrishna's traditional notion of "discrimination between the real and the unreal" (KA 2.11), and Ramakrishna likens *vyākulatā* to the emotional state of a family member frantic for a sick relative or to a young man's anxious quest for a job, or again, in a less serious note, to a child's insistent pleading for a few pennies (KA 5.4). *Vyākulatā,* moreover, is a desire that pushes one on to act. It is the very essence of the religious life. Without it, reason is impotent (KA 2.162), books and scholarship are useless,[49] doctrine is superficial,[50] and social work is just a distraction (KA 5.204).[51] It is dialectically related to sensual desire and pleasure, for it begins only when the senses and their drives have been exhausted.[52]

But most important for our purposes is the fact that Ramakrishna often identifies *vyākulatā* with the Vaiṣṇava notion of *anurāga,* that intense passion for Kṛṣṇa that constitutes the mystical lives of Rādhā and the milkmaids of Vrindavana.[53] The aspirant must identify completely with these feminine lovers of God. He must experience a love so great that it is capable of transforming his physical gender over time. Only then will he truly be able to love Kṛṣṇa. Desire for God, in other words, can turn a man into a woman: "Do you know who the milkmaids are? Rāmacandra was traveling through the forest when he came upon sixty thousand sages sitting in the forest. He lovingly glanced at them just once and they anxiously desired (*vyākula*) to see him! In some Purāṇa or another it is said that it was these sages who became the milkmaids" (KA 2.213).[54] Ramakrishna's childhood fantasy of being born in a brahmin family as a child-widow and lover of Kṛṣṇa appears again. A childish wish has grown into a profound desire, a specifically mystical reality capable of determining the course of external events and transforming the corporal body.

Related to his psychological desire to become a woman and this theological necessity for a female body is the fact that Ramakrishna's anxious desire often was directed to his young male disciples. Ramakrishna, for example, not unlike the forest sages, describes how, after seeing Narendra for the first time, his "anxious desire" to see Narendra again increased so much that he could hardly breathe (again, recall the drowning metaphors used to describe Ramakrishna's First Vision and the dunking quality of *vyākulatā*). The same longing that was once directed to Kālī and her sword is now directed to Narendra and his sweet singing voice. Clearly troubled by the experience, he asks another (much older) disciple why he feels this way for such a boy. The disciple replies that, after emerging from *samādhi,* a pure soul can stand only the company of other pure souls, for they alone can calm his spiritualized soul. Hearing this, Ramakrishna's mind was eased a bit, but he nevertheless continued to cry for Narendra.[55] Again, troubled by his desire for the boys, Ramakrishna asks M, "Why do I feel so anxious for them?" M can give no answer before an upset Ramakrishna breaks in, "Why don't you say something?" (KA 3.126). In another passage, we are told that Ramakrishna loves Naran, a boy of seventeen with beautiful fair skin. He sits down and cries, so "anxious" is he to see and feed him (KA 1.192). *Vyākulatā,* then, can refer equally well to both mystical longing and Ramakrishna's desire to be with his male disciples.

Uddīpana: Exciting the Erotic Memory

A WHOLE VOCABULARY of desire is developed in the *Kathāmṛta* around this dual longing for mystical experience and young male disciples. Take, for example, the term *uddīpana.* The word literally means "enkindling" or "lighting up" but often can be translated best as "reminded." Sometimes it is used in a mundane context, for example, Ramakrishna is "reminded" of a childhood friend in the course of a conversation (KA 5.48), or he explains how a wax custard-apple can remind one of the real thing.[56] But more often, the object of this remembering is a mythical or religious figure. Ramakrishna, for example, sees a tree and is "reminded" of the ascetic hermitages of the forest sages (KA 2.159). Or again, watching minnows dart for puffed rice in a pond, he is "reminded" of what it is like to swim in the ocean of Saccidānanda (KA 2.58).

Ramakrishna might be described as hyperassociative. Almost anything he saw or heard could awaken powerful forces that often overwhelmed him. When one is in love, he explained, "even the littlest thing can ecstatically remind one [of the beloved]" (KA 3.93).[57] In one particularly humorous scene, some disciples decide to take Ramakrishna to the zoo. The first animal they see is a lion, which, unfortunately for those who wanted to see the rest of the zoo, happens to be the auspicious mount of the goddess Durgā. Ramakrishna is "reminded" immediately of the goddess and falls over unconscious. The party has to return home (KA 4.74). Ramakrishna, it seems, was like poor Rādhā, for whom everything—from the dark blue clouds to the deep blue neck of the peacock—reminded her of her blue Kṛṣṇa and made her "anxious" for his love (KA 4.17).

Often this mythic remembrance is triggered within a context that might be construed as erotic. Ramakrishna, for example, describes how he was reminded of the Mother while worshiping a fourteen-year-old girl, and at another time, a virgin. Again, when Ramakrishna sees a prostitute dressed in blue sitting under a tree, he becomes "completely enkindled" and is "reminded of Sītā" (KA 2.49). Sometimes this mythic remembrance possesses a homoerotic dimension. For example, when Ramakrishna sees an English boy leaning up against a tree, he is "reminded of Kṛṣṇa," who, like the English boy, is thrice-bent in a seductive pose. Stunned by the cocked hips of the boy, Ramakrishna falls into *samādhi.*[58] Again, he looks at the boy Rakhal and becomes "all excited" (*uddīpana*). Why? Because Rakhal reminds him of Gopāla, the child Kṛṣṇa (KA 4.5). In still another passage, he looks at the boy Kedar and is reminded of Kṛṣṇa's sexual exploits with the milkmaids (KA 4.7).[59] All of this leads M to ask himself troubling questions. In one such passage, Ramakrishna's body hairs all stand on end when he looks at little

Naren. M recalls one of his Master's teachings and asks himself a question: "Where lust is not, there the Lord is present. . . . Was the Master all excited about the Lord?" (KA 3.263).

Often the mythic referent is absent, leaving the homoerotic element even more obvious. When it comes time for the disciples to leave one evening, Ramakrishna turns to the youth Bhabanath and says: "Please don't leave today. When I look at you, I get all excited [*uddīpana*]!" (KA 2.24). Again, when a boy of fifteen walks into a theater box to see Ramakrishna, M tells us that the saint stroked the young boy with his hand and asked him to sit down: "With you here, I get all excited." When the boy left, Ramakrishna told M that the boy's physical signs were very good and that "if he would have stayed a little longer, I would have stood up" (KA 2.121).[60]

If this all seems merely suggestive, consider Ramakrishna's comments on the excitement he feels when looking at pictures of holy men: "When I look at pictures of holy men I become aroused [*uddīpana*] . . . just as when a man looks at a young woman and is reminded [*uddīpana*] of [sexual] pleasure" (KA 5.108).[61] Ramakrishna's *uddīpana* was at once religious "enlightenment," mythical "remembrance," and sexual "excitement." It was the erotic that "lit up" the memory and sparked Ramakrishna's mystical states. Accordingly, he spoke of a "memory nerve" (*medhā nāṛī*) that grew when the semen was held for seven years (KA 4.85).[62] The erotic gives access to the unconscious. This mystical enlightenment, this mythical remembrance, this homoerotic excitement—they cannot be separated in Ramakrishna, nor can one somehow be reduced to the other.

Ṭāna: Charismatic Attraction

Alongside *vyākulatā* and *uddīpana*, Ramakrishna also used *ṭāna*, "attraction" or "dragging," to express his dual desire for God and male disciples. According to Ramakrishna, the human being is caught in desire. One is passively pulled or "dragged" in a thousand directions. The trick is to accept these attractions as indestructible realities and then try to "turn them around the corner" until they find their proper ends in God (KA 1.215). For example, instead of lusting after a woman, one must turn this lust "around the corner" and lust after the Absolute: "Have sex with Saccidānanda," Ramakrishna counseled (KA 1.215).[63] There is, in other words, a certain passivity that marks all human attraction for Ramakrishna. The human being is attracted, is pulled, is dragged.[64] Accordingly, religious practice consists more in trying to redirect forces that are already in place and dangerously active than in instituting new ones. There are exceptions to this passivity in the language and teachings of Ramakrishna—Ramakrishna, for example, "drags" Kālī to him (KA 4.62) and "pulls" Saccidānanda with the cord of desire (KA 4.119)—but they are rare. Ramakrishna's belief in the complete inability of the human being to initiate action was total. Human agency is a pernicious illusion.

This radical passivity is evident in the way Ramakrishna is powerfully attracted to different boy disciples and the manner in which they in turn are attracted to him. "Their natures are very pure," Ramakrishna declares, "and so when they sing they attract me!"[65] As passive experiences of forces that overcome his own powers of control and understanding, these attractions often elicited doubt and confusion from Ramakrishna: "Why am I so attracted to them?" he often asked in a troubled tone (KA 5.145). Passivity implies a lack of control, an incomplete understanding of one's own depths. To be attracted, after all, is to be overcome.

But if one does not act, does not attract, then who does? For Ramakrishna, the answer was obvious—Kālī. It is Kālī's *śakti* that attracts the boys to Ramakrishna and "drags" them to him. "O Ma, drag him here!" he often prayed.[66] The erotic nature of this magical attraction and its origin in the goddess are both evident in the following passage. Ramakrishna is talking to M about the coming of his disciples: "Lately I've been saying to Ma, 'I'm done talking.' And I'm saying, 'O Ma, if you touch them but once, their consciousness will be awakened.' Such is the greatness of the Magical Power (*yogamāyā*)—she is able to cast a spell. In the play of Vrindavana the Magical Power cast a spell. By means of her, Subola united Kṛṣṇa and Rādhā. The Magical Power—she who is the Primordial Power—she has an attracting power. I have assumed this power" (KA 3.121–122).[67] In this complicated passage, Ramakrishna claims that he has assumed the same "attracting power" (*ākarṣaṇī śakti*) that once joined Kṛṣṇa and Rādhā in an erotic union. This power is part of the goddess's nature as the Primordial Power (*ādyāśakti*). Through such a power and its incarnation in Ramakrishna, the goddess can awaken the souls of others with a mere touch. Moreover, by assuming such a power, the now "attractive" Ramakrishna can unite the boy disciples to himself, just as Subola once united the famous lovers, Kṛṣṇa and Rādhā. So effective are these attracting energies that they are likened to a magical spell or a trick.

In another series of passages, Ramakrishna links this magico-erotic attraction to his status as a divine incarnation: "Look here, that all these boys are coming, and that all you are coming—what is the meaning of this? Within this (i.e., within me) there is a certain something. If there were not, how could there be such a pull [*ṭāna*]—why would there be such an attraction [*ākarṣaṇa*]?" On a more philosophical level, Ramakrishna believed that the disciples somehow shared the same essence with him. "Attraction" (*ṭāna*) and desire flowed naturally from this essential union or ontological identity (*sattā*) (KA 2.166). Like attracts like. Such a deep union can be detected in a dream. In one scene, for example, a young boy comes to Ramakrishna and reveals to the Paramahaṁsa that he has seen him in his dreams, just sitting there saying nothing. An excited Ramakrishna breaks in: "That's very good! . . . You're attracted to me, isn't this so?" There is silence, followed by Ramakrishna's request that the boy come again. But he will make no promises, for his family objects (KA 4.149). Ramakrishna's power over the boys and the disciples is mysterious, inexplicable, controversial. It is not even Ramakrishna's. It is divine, a function of Kālī's spell-like *śakti.* It unites the human and the divine in the persons of Rādhā and Kṛṣṇa, it unites Ramakrishna and the disciples, it is discerned in a dream, and it is rejected by the social world as dangerous.

"Wrung Like a Wet Towel"

FINALLY, consider the expression, "wrung like a wet towel." The expression is best known as it is used in the *Līlāprasaṅga* to describe the state of desire that preceded Ramakrishna's First Vision of Kālī: "It felt like someone was squeezing my heart like a person forcibly wrings and wrings a towel dry!" (LP 2.6.13). Like Ramakrishna's "anxious desire," the expression reveals its homoerotic dimensions only when it is used in contexts other than the famous First Vision. In one such passage, Ramakrishna describes his great desire to meet his inner circle of boy disciples: "Then such a desire to see you all would arise in my heart that on account of this wringing-like pain I would get shaky and fall down!"[68] In another passage, Ramakrishna describes his desire to see Narendra in the exact terms that Saradananda used to describe Ramakrishna's "anxious desire" to see Kālī: "If he should delay a few days, my heart would feel as if it were being wrung like a towel" (LP 4.5.5). Psychologically speaking, then, the First Vision and Ramakrishna's tortured "wrung" desire to see Narendra are very close, if not identical.

As the passages pile up, a pattern is revealed: in nearly every occurrence[69] of the expression "wrung like a wet towel" in the *Līlāprasaṅga* other than the famous First Vision, and probably even there, the phrase refers to Ramakrishna's anxious desire to establish intimate contacts with young males. In one passage, Ramakrishna even describes this "wringing" in specifically erotic terms: "My heart throbbed with such an anxious desire [*vyākulatā*]—never have I heard of such a desire to be united, even among girlfriends or two lovers" (LP 2.21.12). Like Ramakrishna's "anxious desire," "enkindling," and "attraction," then, his heart "wrung like a wet towel" can express both his desire to see God and his longing "to be united" with his boy disciples.

Having established this dual desire in the terms *vyākulatā, uddīpana, ṭāna,* and "wrung like a wet towel," let us turn now to some possible textual variants of Ramakrishna's "Anxious Desire and First Vision," this time in the *Kathāmṛta,* and see what they might reveal to us when placed beside this study of Ramakrishna's vocabulary of desire.

"I'll Cut My Throat with a Knife!"

Interestingly enough, there are numerous textual variants of Ramakrishna's attempted suicide with Kālī's sword in the *Kathāmṛta.* Indeed, Ramakrishna's habit of threatening to cut his throat with a knife[70] was so common and so well-known that, after he was dead, at least one disciple made fun of him by imitating his *vyākulatā* and faking his dramatic gestures: "O my! I'll cut my throat with this knife! There is nothing left to do! I can't stand the pain anymore!" Narendra watches the performance and then corrects the disciple's mimic in a serious tone: "You need to stick out your arm here more." Everyone laughs (KA 2.248). Ramakrishna apparently was a melodramatic figure, a show to laugh at.

The phrase itself, "to cut the throat with a knife," seems to have been a general expression of exaggeration, a rather immature way of forcing one's demands. The phrase, for example, appears in a story Ramakrishna tells about a son trying to force his father to give him his inheritance before the appointed time (KA 4.65). As a general expression of demand or exaggeration, there is little evidence to suggest that it was meant to be taken literally. Perhaps even Ramakrishna himself intended it more as a dramatic gesture, a form of symbolic prayer, rather than as a serious attempt to kill himself.

There are four separate occurrences of the expression in the *Kathāmṛta* that seem to be based on actual events in the life of Ramakrishna. It is possible that they all refer to the famous First Vision, but it would be difficult if not impossible to establish this with any degree of certainty. As with so much else concerning the saint, the evidence is more suggestive than probative. All four occurrences do refer to incidents very early in Ramakrishna's career, during his early periods of madness and his first experiments with Tantra. This would suggest that they refer to an early crisis much like the one Saradananda relates as the saint's "Anxious Desire and First Vision." Saradananda places this initial crisis *before* Ramakrishna's Tantric practices, but if we do not privilege Saradananda's account as somehow more original or accurate than that of the *Kathāmṛta,* then there is no reason that Ramakrishna's comments in the *Kathāmṛta* might in fact be referring to the same event. As I will demonstrate below in chapter 2, Ramakrishna's "Tantric" practices cannot be bracketed and subordinated to a particular period in Ramakrishna's religious practices, as Saradananda wants to do; rather, they were omnipresent, defining virtually every point along Ramakrishna's religious development. Finally, it is perfectly possible, indeed likely, that Ramakrishna was working from a fallible memory and simply did not remember the exact order of events: this would explain the chronological confusion apparent in the different accounts of the saint's early crisis. Both the *Kathāmṛta* and the *Līlāprasaṅga* ultimately depend on Ramakrishna's memories, which, we must never forget, he related to his followers in a most haphazard fashion at a distance of twenty to thirty years. These memories, moreover, at least as we have them in the texts, are usually ambiguous, sometimes contradictory, and often vague. The confusion of the texts, then, might very well reflect the confusion of Ramakrishna himself.

With all of this in mind, let us turn to the four accounts recorded in the *Kathāmṛta* and see what they might reveal to us when placed beside the famous account recorded in the *Līlāprasaṅga.* The first passage[71] is simple and short. It occurs in volume 4. Ramakrishna has just told the story of a son forcing his demands on his father by threatening to cut his throat with a knife. He then, almost casually, adds: "I used to do this when I called on Ma" (KA 4.65). The details are so close—calling on Kālī by threatening suicide with a knife—that it is likely that he is referring to the First Vision here, or at least to the same general period and its troubled states.

In our second passage, this time in volume 5, Ramakrishna is talking about how his madness reached such a state that, again, he was going to cut his throat with a knife. It was then that he realized that he could do nothing of himself, that he was the "machine" (*yantra*) and Kālī the "operator" (*yantrī*) (KA 5.23). Again, the emotional conflict and pain is great, great enough to end in death. But here Ramakrishna adds that this crisis led to the realization that he was controlled by external forces, that he was not in control, an ambiguous sign warning of madness but also promising divine possession.

In our third passage, this time in volume 3, Ramakrishna clearly associates the act with a specifically Tantric approach to Kālī: "There is such a thing as dark [*tāmasika*] mystical practice—practice which relies on the dark aspects of human nature. '*Victory to Kālī!* What? You'll not show yourself to me! If you don't show yourself, I'll cut my throat with a knife.' In this type of mystical practice, as in Tantric practice, there's no concern for purity" (KA 3.138). Again, the similarities are impressive. We note the same threatened suicide designed in order to attain a vision of Kālī. Although Ramakrishna does not specify that he is talking about an actual event from his past, the passage is most likely autobiographical. His assimilation of the act into a Tantric framework in which the concern for purity is systematically rejected is interesting but unclear. Exactly what the "dark aspects of human nature" that Ramakrishna is relying on are not specified. It is likely, however, that he is hinting at the sexual nature of his mystical practices, for in another text he explicitly associates this same dark devotion with "obscene" dancing and singing (PU, 21–22). It is certainly no accident that in the *Kathāmṛta* passage Ramakrishna immediately associates this "dark mystical practice" with Tantra. Another text associates this same "darkness" with all that is most troubling in Tantra: the ritual violence of Kālī-pūjā, a "beastly" attitude toward women, the consumption of wine and meat, and ritual intercourse (TS, 96–99).

The fourth and final passage involving the phrase "I'll cut my throat with a knife" is in many ways the most interesting. It occurs in volume 3. Ramakrishna is talking to his disciples about how he conquered "lust" (*kāma*): "Even in my case, after six months I felt a strange sensation in the breast. Then I sat down beneath the tree and began to cry. I said, 'O Ma! If this continues, I'll cut my throat with a knife!'" (KA 3.131). Once again, the passage is much less ornate than Saradananda's account of Ramakrishna's attempted suicide. Spatial differences now are added to chronological differences: we are no longer in the temple of the saint's first Vision but under the trees of Ramakrishna's early mystical practices. Nevertheless, because there are important similarities between the two accounts—foremost among them, a knife and a threatened suicide—the passage may hint at a secret dimension to

Ramakrishna's anxious longing and First Vision not at all apparent in Saradananda's more classical account. Indeed, if we read Saradananda's passage alongside these other four, we might speculate that the threat announced under the tree was carried out in the temple and that Ramakrishna's threatened suicide was understood by the saint to be "Tantric" in the sense that it involved that "darkest" of the human passions—lust.

Can we establish such a reading with the evidence at hand? We have four different passages dealing with a knife and a threatened suicide. Perhaps all four refer to separate events. Or perhaps they all refer to the same event or, more probable, to the same general period. One thing is nevertheless fairly obvious: however chronologically distinct these four accounts might be, they are, psychologically speaking, indistinct, virtually identical. All four are explicitly connected to Kālī. All four are defined by a profound sense of anxiety or emotional pain. The last two go further and hint at the source of this anxious desire and pain: the dark forces of sexual desire.

Having looked at these four accounts in the *Kathāmṛta,* I want to pursue now the textual strands of the fourth passage and their place in the warp and woof of the text and see whether any patterns can be detected that might, in turn, fit into the larger patterns that I have identified already in Ramakrishna's vocabulary of desire. Only then will I return to my tentative reading of Ramakrishna's First Vision as some sort of erotic crisis and try to define it more precisely.

The "Strange Sensation"

FROM THE CONTEXT of the fourth passage, I conclude that Ramakrishna's "strange sensation" had something to do with a form of sexual desire, with "lust," but the precise nature of the "strange sensation" that led him to threaten suicide is still not clear. The fact that the expression "a strange sensation in the breast" (*buka ki kare*) is used more commonly by women than by men suggests much but proves little. The use of the expression in a song sung by a male (Caitanya) addressing another male (Nitai) is equally suggestive and equally inconclusive: "Hold me Nitai! Today my heart feels a strange sensation!" (LP 5.11.14). However, when we find a variant of the same phrase used again in the *Kathāmṛta,* the nature of Ramakrishna's early temptation becomes a bit more clear. Ramakrishna's early erotic crisis is now some twenty years behind him. Now in his late forties, he is talking to M about Purna, a boy of fourteen who figures prominently in the saint's secret talk: "If I see Purna one more time, then my anxious desire might lessen! How clever he is! He feels a very great attraction for me. He says, 'I also feel a strange sensation to see you.' (to M) They've taken him from your school. Will this cause you any trouble?" (KA 3.182). Purna and Ramakrishna confess that they feel "a strange sensation" for one another. For a similar feeling years before, Ramakrishna had threatened to cut his throat. Now he seems to be quite comfortable with the feeling, which he relates to his "anxious desire" (*vyākulatā*) for the boy Purna and to Purna's great "attraction" (*ṭāna*) for him. But even here, the nature of this "anxious desire," "great attraction," and "strange sensation" is still not fully revealed. We are told that it has resulted in a situation that might cause M, the schoolteacher, trouble at school, but that is all.

Similarly, other passages tease us with what they do not say and leave us reading between the lines. M, for example, tells us that Ramakrishna was "anxious" (*vyākula*) for Purna. In another passage, Ramakrishna explains that Purna possesses the "divine essence" of a god: "If you put a garland on his neck and sandalpaste on his body and then burn incense, he goes into *samādhi*!" (KA 4.212).[72] In yet another passage, M tells us that Ramakrishna was so "anxious" to see Purna that he showed up at M's house late one night and asked M to fetch the boy, which M did (KA 3.224).[73] Again, a stray comment that Ramakrishna did not visit Purna at his home is explained a bit later when M tells us that Purna was afraid to visit Ramakrishna lest the saint praise him in public and his relatives hear, for Purna's family objected to the boy visiting Ramakrishna (KA 3.127). In yet another scene, M gets nervous when Purna scoots closer to Ramakrishna—will the boy's family hear about this visit too (KA 3.149)?[74] Finally, Ramakrishna brags that even in his illness he is not deluded by *māyā*. To prove his point, he notes that his mind no longer dwells on his wife or his home. Now he thinks only of Purna, the boy (KA 4.286).

The nature of this anxious infatuation with Purna becomes even more evident when we turn to another passage, again in M's *Kathāmṛta*, that record of secrets, where Ramakrishna clearly reveals the secret dimension of his "anxious desire" and "strange sensation" for Purna to M:

> The Master is talking to M about Purna—
>
> Sri Ramakrishna—"What I'm telling you—all this is not for others to hear—I want to kiss and embrace man (God) as a woman." (KA 4.271)[75]

Ramakrishna reveals to M a secret that is "not for others to hear": he is in love with Purna. He wants to kiss and embrace Purna as if he were a woman and Purna a man. M, troubled by this revelation, adds in parentheses after the word "man" the gloss "(God)." Ramakrishna was clear. M is clear but obviously troubled: a flimsy set of parentheses is invoked to hide a glaring secret. Nikhilananda is more successful. He adopts M's parenthetical gloss as the meaning of the sentence, completely neglecting the fact that M specifically says that Ramakrishna was talking about Purna. Ramakrishna's homoerotic infatuation with Purna is thus concealed completely in Nikhilananda's English translation between Sanskrit abstractions and the swami's bowdlerizing agenda: "The devotee looking on himself as Prakriti likes to embrace and kiss God, whom he regards as the Purusha" (GSR, 895). The boy Purna, the object of Ramakrishna's erotic desire, is nowhere to be found. Only the context of the quote—Ramakrishna is talking to M about Purna—preserves a glimmer of the once glaring scandal.

An Interpretation of Kālī's Sword

I BEGAN with Ramakrishna anxiously longing to see Kālī in a passage made famous by nearly all of Ramakrishna's biographers. I analyzed the "anxious desire" (*vyākulatā*) that led to this First Vision and showed how it is structured around a dual desire for mystical experience and intimate contact with male disciples. I added two other terms in the *Kathāmṛta*'s vocabulary of desire (*uddīpana* and *ṭāna*) structured around the same dual desire. I then turned again to the *Līlāprasaṅga* account of the First Vision and analyzed another expression used to describe Ramakrishna's emotional state at that time, "wrung like a wet towel." Again, the expression was discovered to be structured around Ramakrishna's dual longing for ecstatic vision and boy disciples: "wrung like a wet towel" for a vision of Kālī and "wrung like a wet towel" for boy disciples are indistinguishable in the *Līlāprasaṅga*. Then, noting that Ramakrishna's "anxious desire" preceded an attempted suicide with a knife, I turned to four other "knife passages," never quoted by the biographers, and demonstrated that Ramakrishna associated the same act with: (1) his early longings for Kālī, (2) madness and the illusion of human agency, (3) Tantra and the "dark" forces of human nature, and (4) a "strange sensation in the breast." I speculated that the four passages might be related to the famous "Anxious Desire and First Vision" account of the *Līlāprasaṅga*. I then focused in on the fourth passage dealing with Ramakrishna's attempts to conquer an unspecified "strange sensation" and demonstrated how this "strange sensation" was used in other passages to describe Ramakrishna's "anxious" feelings for Purna, a boy of fourteen whom Ramakrishna secretly confessed he wanted to embrace and kiss as an erotic object.

In the end, we are left with five expressions—"anxious desire," "enkindling," "attraction," "wrung like a wet towel," and "a strange sensation"—*all* of which are used to refer both to Ramakrishna's anxious desire for mystical experience and his homoerotic longing to see, even to embrace and kiss, his boy disciples. Two of the terms ("anxious desire" and "wrung like a wet towel") are specifically connected with Ramakrishna's encounter with Kālī's sword. A third expression ("a strange sensation") seems to be related to a similar, if not the same, event. The last two terms ("enkindling" and "attraction") hook up to the First Vision account through a common referential structure and through numerous textual associations.

From such an analysis, I would suggest that Ramakrishna's attempted decapitation, which led to the saint's first full-blown mystical experience, was triggered by homoerotic longings Ramakrishna was at that time rejecting as illegitimate: the pattern created by Ramakrishna's vocabulary of desire—and especially the three terms "anxious longing," "a strange sensation," and "wrung like a wet towel"—suggests as much, as *all three terms are explicitly connected with Ramakrishna's threatened self-decapitation and all three terms are consistently used to describe Ramakrishna's attraction for his boy disciples.* By employing a culturally meaningful act—offering one's head to Kālī—Ramakrishna attempted to end his erotic torment (*vyākulatā*) and the shame attached to it by symbolically castrating himself, the head being in the mystical physiology of yoga and Tantra the ultimate goal of one's semen and so an appropriate symbol for the phallus.[76]

Kālī's sword thus became a "personal symbol" for Ramakrishna in the sense that Obeyesekere has defined it, a symbol that carries communicable cultural meanings but is properly interpreted only in reference to the deep motivations of a particular life history, in this case, Ramakrishna's.[77] Ramakrishna's attempted suicide and consequent experience of Kālī, in other words, can be understood *both* as a genuinely religious experience driven by mystical longing (the culturally accepted interpretation advanced by Saradananda in his *Līlāprasaṅga*) *and* as a desperate attempt to put an end to his tormenting shame fueled by homoerotic longing (as hinted at in psychologically analogous passages recorded in the *Kathāmṛta*). The latter, it seems, somehow triggered the former—*an erotic crisis led to a mystical experience.*

RAMAKRISHNA'S "ANXIOUS DESIRE" IN THE EYES OF HIS CONTEMPORARIES

IT MIGHT BE OBJECTED that such a reading of Ramakrishna's early encounter with Kālī's sword is excessively speculative, that it is more an imposition of Western categories on a non-Western figure than an accurate portrayal of a specifically Indian experience. But a close look at the texts suggests quite the opposite. Indeed, if one listens carefully to Ramakrishna's contemporaries who appear in the texts, it becomes apparent that my reading of Ramakrishna's "Anxious Desire and First Vision," although certainly distinct in its categories and interpretive conclusions, finds much support from many of the figures who knew and observed Ramakrishna personally.

Getting the Tantric Joke: The Goat's Banana

IS THE CASTRATION THEME, for example, really there? I have made the argument that it is through a study of the texts and their symbolism. The burden of proof that I am wrong now rests on the skeptic, who must offer a better explanation of numerous texts that powerfully support a castration theme. Never mind Ramakrishna's comment that sexual abstinence is like the act of sacrificing (i.e., decapitating) a spotless, black goat to Kālī or his reported habit of slipping a noose around his neck to control the reactions of his penis. There are other passages even more explicit in their suggestions. Consider, for example, a passage that occurs in Datta's *Jīvanavṛttānta*. Datta has just told his readers that he has heard things about the Brāhmaṇī (Ramakrishna's female Tantric guru, also referred to as the Bhairavī) that he cannot tell the public. He must keep secrets. But then in the very next paragraph, as if he could not bear to keep *this* secret, he relates, almost mischievously, the following scene: "One day a goat was being sacrificed to Kālī for some special purpose. When the plate of its blood was presented to the goddess, the Brāhmaṇī began to drink it. With an expressionless, though bloody, face she ate *this* newly cut off banana smeared with blood and some sweets. The Paramahaṁsa watched all of this and grinned" (JV[5], 33). The goat's head is cut off with Kālī's sacrificial sword. The Brāhmaṇī, taking on the identity of the goddess, consumes the offerings: a plate of blood, a bloody "banana," and some sweets. Given that (1) bananas do not bleed, that (2) the phrase "newly cut off" refers more properly to a limb than a piece of fruit, that (3) the word for "banana" used here (*rambā*) is a relatively uncommon one, and that (4) Datta seems particularly amazed with "*this* . . . banana" (the emphasis is his), I would argue that Datta is dropping as many hints as he can without revealing the secret: that the Brāhmaṇī was eating the goat's penis. And even if she was only eating a bloody banana, it is likely that Ramakrishna was quite aware of the act's symbolic meaning. He grins in acknowledgment. He is aware of the secret meaning of her action. He gets the joke.

The Brāhmaṇī, no doubt, would side with my reading of the texts, for her consumption of the goat penis, whether literal or symbolic, makes explicit what is hidden or "secret" in Kālī's sword, namely, that it is aimed at the phallus as well as the head, that the head in Tantric symbolism *is* the phallus. The Brāhmaṇī enacts one of the meanings of Kālī's sword for us within the text. We would be wise to listen to her. A simple offended frown or worn-out trope against "Western" psychoanalysis will not do. A bemused grin, like that of Ramakrishna, seems much better. He at least got the joke. He at least could laugh.

Sex as a Cure

THE IDEA, moreover, that Ramakrishna's religious states were somehow driven by suppressed sexual energies is by no means a "Western" insight imposed upon an innocent Bengali mystic. Indeed, the idea was central to the understandings of Ramakrishna's superiors and family members at the time of his early periods of madness. Mathur, the proprietor of the temple, for example, assumed that Ramakrishna's madness was due to his celibate lifestyle and hired prostitutes to cure his young priest (KA 1.244). Ramakrishna's strategy of avoiding sex by considering every woman to be his mother and, by so doing, equating intercourse with "raping the mother" (*mātṛharaṇa*) evoked outrage and scandal from the community: "He's completely crazy," the people said (JV[5], 26). Datta tells us what happened when the scandal grew: "When it was decided that the cause of his madness was the fact that he did not sleep with a woman, Hriday Mukherjee began to instruct him about many things concerning this in secret [*gopane*], but he could not change his mind with such talk" (JV[5], 26). This refusal on Ramakrishna's part resulted in a whole series of sexual temptation scenes, orchestrated by everyone from Ramakrishna's cousin to the temple proprietors, all of which were designed to "cure" Ramakrishna of his madness. In still other scenes, Ramakrishna's family, hearing of the strange behavior of their son, proposed their own remedy—marriage, again with the unspoken assumption that the young man's madness was somehow connected to his unsocialized sexuality. In all of these instances, Ramakrishna's contemporaries assumed that his madness was connected to his sexual continence. Far from being "Western," this is an idea *internal* to the culture and the texts.

The Problem and the Scandal of Ramakrishna

WHILE RAMAKRISHNA'S SUPERIORS and family sought sexual remedies for his early periods of madness, Ramakrishna's critics would have an opposite reaction to his, much later, adult antics. They were angered by his unusual ability to tempt their sons away from their schoolwork and future family lives and shocked by his eroticized language and actions. In short, from the perspective of the public, Ramakrishna's ability to "steal" the boys constituted a *problem*, and his sexual behavior mounted to a *scandal*. The words of an anonymous boatman capture both aspects of the public reaction: "What a sham this is! He eats well, lounges on cushions, and under the guise of religion ruins so many school boys!" (LP 5.7.20).

He "ruins so many school boys" (lit. "eats the heads of so many school boys"). The phrase carries both a sexual scandal and a social problem. Homosexual behavior was considered improper by Bengali society and, no doubt, carried a certain social stigma. Sarkar's characterization of homosexuality in nineteenth-century Bengali culture as "rigorously repressed" is certainly not far off the mark,[78] although there was much in the culture, and especially in its religious symbolism, that in fact nurtured and idealized homosexual tendencies.[79] In any case, heterosexual acts were considered to be more natural. Ramakrishna himself suggests as much: "A woman very naturally [*svabhāvataḥi*] loves a man. A man very naturally loves a woman" (KA 2.97). But even given the scandal of Ramakrishna's homosexual behavior, it was the social problem that was more basic, more troubling. The parents were primarily concerned about their boys' studies, which they feared were being neglected. And not without reason: Narendra would give up his study of law to follow Ramakrishna, and Sarat (Saradananda) would have to be imprisoned in his own home to prevent him from seeing the Paramahaṁsa and abandoning his studies.

Parents do not like to lose their sons to saints. Such a fear could turn particularly tragic when the family had pinned their hopes on the eldest son (and on a Western education) to deliver them from their poverty.

In such a context, renunciation meant religious salvation but also a great deal of pain for everyone involved, including the son. Ramakrishna was quite aware that he had brought such pain to numerous families. In one telling scene, he asks Sarat about his little brother, "Should I attract him too?" Sarat replies in the affirmative, but Ramakrishna hesitates and then decides against it: "No, enough. I've taken one, and if I take another, your parents will be greatly pained, especially your mother. I've enraged many Śaktis [women] in my life. There's no more need of it now" (LP 5.7.7). One son locked in his room was enough.

This problem of the boy-stealing saint and this scandal of the erotic mystic weave themselves through the texts in complicated and often confusing ways. Sometimes, for example, we are told nothing more than that "a certain person is slandering" Ramakrishna (KA 4.190). Or M describes "a critic" who walks into the room only to receive the whispered giggles of some of the boy disciples (KA 4.215). Sometimes, however, the nature of the criticism is more specific. We are told, for example, that Narendra's relatives did not like the fact that Narendra was seeing Ramakrishna, and that Narendra's aunt scolded the older Surendra for paying Narendra's carriage fee to Dakshineshwar (KA 2.65).[80]

At other times, the nature of the problem and the scandal are more apparent, their results more severe. Surendra, for example, warned Ramakrishna that Rakhal's father could sue him, for Rakhal was a minor (KA 4.143). Narayan was actually beat up by his family when he returned home from visiting Ramakrishna on more than one occasion;[81] Ramakrishna jokingly suggested that he buy a leather jacket to absorb the blows (KA 2.157–158). In another scene Narayan has to flee to his friend's house in order to escape his family's wrath (KA 3.100). In yet another passage, a piqued Ramakrishna scolds little Naren for abandoning his studies to visit him: "Your father will hurt you" (KA 3.196). It was not an unreasonable fear: at one point, Naren stays three nights at Dakshineshwar, apparently to escape his father's anger. Ramakrishna was also afraid of Naren's father. In one passage he relates how he went to see Naren but then turned back in fear of Naren's father. Everyone laughs (KA 3.182). Paltu is also in trouble for seeing Ramakrishna (KA 3.129), as are Tarak (KA 3.124–125) and Dvija.[82] The families object to an unspecified crime. M fears for himself (KA 3.149). Ramakrishna reacts by alternating between fits of fear and anger: "A mother who says 'Don't go to Dakshineshwar' is no mother" (KA 3.125). And again: "You should be very devoted to your father and mother, but if they block your path to God, then grit your teeth and say, 'That son-of-a-bitch of a father!'" (KA 3.152). Perhaps this is what the saint was thinking as he turned back in fear from visiting Paltu.

Finally, sometimes the sexual scandal dominates the social problem and takes over a scene or a passage. Hazra, for example, did not approve of Ramakrishna's "anxious desire" for the boys (KA 4.172)[83] and accused him of loving only rich and beautiful boys (KA 4.230). Bholanath considered Ramakrishna's love of Narendra to be "improper" (KA 4.163), as did the "Fat Brahmin" (KA 4.164), and another man accused Ramakrishna of inordinately "loving the boys" (KA 4.190).[84] Ramakrishna asks M if he could go to M's school to look for boys. M suggests that instead Ramakrishna wait at his house and that he bring the boys to him (KA 3.101). But the parents catch on to M's tricks, and M is in trouble (KA 1.192). This sort of maneuvering won M the title of "the kidnapping teacher," a title jokingly bestowed by the boys and accepted by Ramakrishna as appropriate (LP 5.7.29). And finally, Girish Ghosh once confessed that seeing Ramakrishna playing with a young boy reminded him of a "terrible canard" that he had once heard about the saint.[85] The charge is transparent enough to anyone willing to look.

Even M was not immune to serious doubt. Watching Ramakrishna mother Narendra, M asks himself: "Why does he caress the body and feet of Narendra so? Is he serving Narendra as Narāyāṇa? Or is he infusing Narendra with his mystical power [*śakti*]?" (KA 1.204). Ramakrishna sings of Rādhā, "maddened for love of Kṛṣṇa." Narendra responds with another song, and Ramakrishna falls into ecstasy again. This whole scene invokes serious reflection on M's part (most of which is omitted by Nikhilananda). M thinks to himself: "What love! He is crazy for Narendra and cries for Narāyāṇa! He says, 'These and the other boys—Rakhal, Bhabanath, Purna, Bhaburam, and the others—they are Lord Narāyāṇa himself. They have taken a body for me!' . . . He cries to bathe them, to lay them down, and to see them. He runs all over Calcutta to see them. He flatters and sweet talks people into bringing them from Calcutta to him in their carriages. . . . Is this worldly affection? Or is it the pure love of God?" M tries to answer his own questions concerning Ramakrishna's embarrassingly obvious infatuation with Narendra and, in the process, reveals his own awareness of the physical dimension of Ramakrishna's attraction for the young man: "Looking at Narendra, he forgets the external world and gradually forgets even the embodied Narendra. He forgets the 'Apparent man' and begins to see the 'Real man.' His mind dissolves in the unbroken Saccidānanda. . . . Exclaiming, 'Narendra! Narendra!' he becomes mad!" (KA 1.207). M thus puts the scandal in its starkest binary terms—"Is this worldly affection? Or is it the pure love of God?"—and then attempts to transcend his own simple categories with a more dialectical, almost Platonic, answer. From the apparent to the real, Ramakrishna dissolves into the Absolute, maddened with love for the boy.

Pure Pots for the Milk of Love

RAMAKRISHNA WAS ACUTELY AWARE of his critics and their charges. At first, he turned to others for defense and support but then gradually began to develop his own, specifically mystical, argument for why he loved the boys so much. God, he taught, is manifest in all things, but God is especially "apparent" in human beings (KA 2.74). But among human beings, God is more manifest in some than others. Just as water is water, but only some water is appropriate for drinking and washing, so some people are more spiritually fit, more mystically "powerful" (*śakti*) than others—all men are *not* created equal (KA 3.181). Boys are particularly lucent bearers of God's light and power, for their breasts have not yet been covered over by the feces of worldly concerns[86] and that most damaging of worldly realities—a job. Nor have they fallen into the clutches of lover-and-gold, that abyss from which the best one can hope is to return "sooty," still alive but defiled.[87] Ramakrishna's most common answer to why he loved the boys so much was that this lover-and-gold or "worldliness" had not yet entered their pure souls.[88] They were still like the new clay pots that it was safe to keep pure milk in. Other used pots would surely spoil the milk.[89] In another passage he explains why he is so "excited" (*uddīpana*) in the presence of the boys: unlike the common man, they contain the sweet pudding of devotion (KA 2.50). For Ramakrishna, boys alone are fit containers for the milky sweet substance of love.[90] Even in defending himself against his critics, Ramakrishna's language remains powerfully, if still symbolically, erotic.

Haramohan was a good example of what happened when one of these pure pots went bad. Ramakrishna once "anxiously desired" to see Haramohan, but when the boy married, he quit coming as often, and when he did come, he brought his wife along, the two of them sitting together apart from Ramakrishna. Peeved at this new development, Ramakrishna told Haramohan to leave, explaining, "How can my body touch yours?" (KA 4.109).[91] The pot had gone bad, its pure milk wasted on a mere woman.

Summing up, we might say that the culture recognized the same two dimensions of Ramakrishna's mystical experiences that I have outlined above: the public, socially acceptable side advanced by Saradananda (Ramakrishna was experiencing the deepest sources of existence); and the private, "secret" dimension revealed in the *Kathāmṛta* (Ramakrishna was using, however legitimately, his own homoerotic tendencies as religious forces). Granted, both dimensions were evaluated differently by different groups, but there is clear evidence that both dimensions *were* recognized from the earliest date. This should not surprise us. As Obeyesekere has pointed out, there is no "native viewpoint" on a subject, only conflicting views that spar and fight in the "debate" that characterizes any culture and its act of self-interpretation.[92] What Isherwood has called "the phenomenon"[93] of Ramakrishna was certainly no exception—some worshiped him as a veritable incarnation of God; others beat their children who dared to visit him, leather-jacket or no.

"Her Sword as His Flute"

"Wipe out the forms and think of her sword as his flute," Ramprasad sang. Ramakrishna began his mystical career with Kālī's sword in an erotic crisis. Over a period of some thirty years, he was able to turn Kālī's sword into Kṛṣṇa's flute. No longer a source of threatening shame or tormenting crisis, Ramakrishna's homoeroticism eventually became a mystical technique with which he could induce mystical states almost at will. Ramakrishna no longer threatened suicide with "her sword." Now he listened ecstatically to "his flute" in the Vaiṣṇava songs of Narendra and sang back to Narendra as Rādhā to her beloved Kṛṣṇa. Like a dry match, his mystical passions now were "enkindled" by the merest brush of bodies, by a glance of the eyes, or by a seductive bend in an English boy's hips. Feelings that once took the form of Kālī's deadly sword and ended in suicidal gestures now took the shape of Kṛṣṇa's seductive flute and ended in mystical states.

It could be said, then, that Ramakrishna's mystical career began with Kālī's sword and ended with Kṛṣṇa's flute. And yet the beginning and the end, this sword and this flute, are mysteriously, secretly connected. The very last line of the *Kathāmṛta* still echoes with the "anxious desire" of Ramakrishna's first tortured encounter with Kālī's sword, and yet the high-pitched seduction of Kṛṣṇa's flute also can be heard, vibrating impressively alongside that distant echo. Past and present blend together in their harmony. The scene is a familiar one: the Paramahaṁsa's heart is anxiously wrung in homoerotic desire. But now Ramakrishna, although dying from throat cancer, does not reach for a knife in shame or despair. He dances in joy: "Because my heart was so anxious, I wanted to embrace Harish. When the medicinal oil was applied I felt better, and then again I began to dance" (KA 5.153).

Truly, her sword had become his flute.

CHAPTER TWO

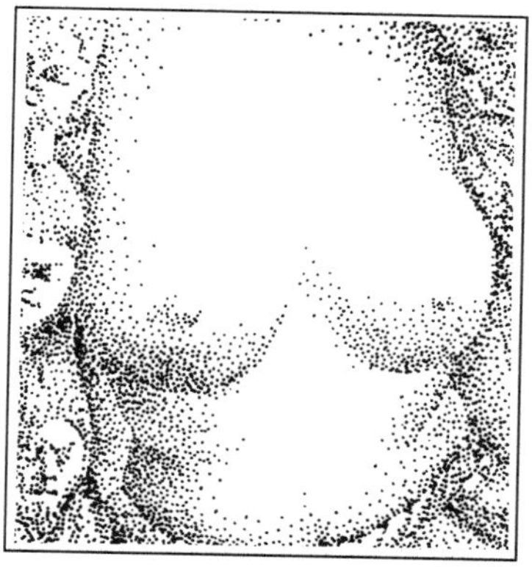

Kālī as Mother and Lover: Interpreting Ramakrishna's Tantric Practices

This is the meaning of Tantric ritual. The Mother is the Lover.
Dr. Sarkar in the *Kathāmṛta* 3.230

KĀLĪ'S SWORD had become Kṛṣṇa's flute. But how was this mythological transformation effected in the soul of Ramakrishna? How did the saint learn to transform his originally suspect sexual desires into the driving force of his mystical life? How did what I have called the erotic become the central focus of Ramakrishna's life and teachings? The importance of Tantra cannot be overestimated in attempting to answer such questions. One even could go so far as to suggest that Ramakrishna's entire life be summed up by the Tantric dictum: "One must rise by that by which one falls." In Ramakrishna's case, Kālī's deadly sword, by which he sought to end the tormenting desire of his early crisis, became Kṛṣṇa's delightful flute, by which his passions were forever being aroused into mystical heights. Like a true Tāntrika, Ramakrishna learned to rise by that by which he once fell.

To understand this transformation we must go back to the years immediately following Ramakrishna's initial crisis and First Vision, the years of Ramakrishna's *sādhana* ("religious practice" or "striving"). Many of Ramakrishna's reminiscences in the *Kathāmṛta* concerning this early period of his religious practices are preceded by the heading *pūrvakathā,* "talk about the past," and are introduced by the phrase *se samaye,* "at that time."[1] Most important for the purposes of this study is the fact that this "talk about the past" is often haunted by Tantric themes of uncanny power, depth, and sometimes horror. Ramakrishna's memories continually return to these days. His secret visions speak in their troubling forms. His secret talk anxiously stutters as it struggles to reveal their truths, truths of which even Ramakrishna is not yet fully aware. Cloudy memories, symbolic visionary forms that speak only in undeciphered images, and the troubled stutter of Ramakrishna's tongue: all witness to the profoundly meaningful and yet unconscious truths of these years. All give witness to the secret.

These early years, then, especially those which involved Ramakrishna's Tantric practices, are "prior" (*pūrva*), certainly in a chronological sense, and, I would argue, in a developmental one as well. They constituted the very foundation—structurally, doctrinally, and mystically—of the rest of his career. Here I am building on the thesis of Walter G. Neevel, who in his seminal essay, "The Transformation of Śrī Rāmakrishna," argues that Ramakrishna's Tantric *sādhana* and the categories it generated are the best starting point for interpreting the saint's teachings: "We will suggest that his Tantric *sādhana* was much more than casual or formal, and that in interpreting his teachings we can understand them more adequately in the categories of Tantric thought and practice than in the concepts of Saradananda's *advaita* which the biographers primarily employ."[2] In Neevel's opinion, it was Ramakrishna's acceptance of Tantric categories that enabled him to see the whole world as a manifestation of divine *śakti* and come to the realization that "the whole world was filled with God alone." Neevel believes that it was this, basically Tantric, realization that healed the young despairing priest and transformed him into the charismatic teacher of a "life-affirming Śākta Tantric worldview."[3] For Neevel, M's *Kathāmṛta* is the most accurate rendering of this transformation and its doctrinal foundation. Accordingly, the *Kathāmṛta* should be read through Tantric eyes: "Not only did this Tantric realization affect the state of his mental and physical well-being, but, in my opinion, it also determined the basic framework in which he viewed the significance of all his experiences and in which he set all of his teachings as they appear in M's diary."[4] I could not agree more. And although much of the present study will demonstrate how Neevel's basic thesis needs to be qualified by numerous passages expressive of Ramakrishna's profound ambivalence toward Tantra and its radical acceptance of the phenomenal world, I am in basic agreement with Neevel's original insights. Tantra is *the* hermeneutical key to interpreting the religious teachings and experiences of Ramakrishna.

But there is one serious obstacle in establishing and extending Neevel's thesis—we know very little about the approximately twelve years of Ramakrishna's experimentation with different religious forms. Because of this, I have dubbed these years of Ramakrishna's *sādhanas* "the secret years." Ramakrishna once explained that the blackness of midnight is enjoined in the Tantras as the most appropriate time for meditation, when the Dark Mother, "naked and black, shines in the lotus of the heart" (KA 5.136). In another passage, the saint adds a specifically erotic dimension to this brilliant blackness by associating it with the love-play of Kālī and Śiva (KA 2.25). These secret years of Ramakrishna's mystical strivings are shrouded in a similar erotic darkness. What I hope to show is that the blackness of these early years, like Kālī herself, lit up the later secret visions of Ramakrishna with forms that were at once troubling and enchanting. For his part, Ramakrishna found the meaning of these forms extremely powerful but ultimately undecipherable. As "secret" visions, they spoke of a past that he did not, could not remember.[5]

To begin to remember these lost years and to interpret their troubling forms I will turn again to Kālī, this time to her dual roles as gentle Mother and uncontrolled Lover. As in chapter 1, I first will analyze these roles in the Tantras and the songs of the Śākta poets. I then will turn to the *Kathāmṛta* and the biographies and demonstrate how Ramakrishna's Tantric practices were structured around these same two roles.

Kālī as Mother and Lover

In the course of a conversation with a dying Ramakrishna, Mahendralal Sarkar, the saint's doctor, made a fascinating observation: "This is the meaning of Tantric ritual. The Mother is the Lover" (KA 3.230).[6] Sarkar's word for *mother* is *jananī,* literally, "she who gives birth." His word for *lover* is *ramaṇī,* literally, "she who makes love." Both words can mean simply "woman." I translate them literally as "mother" and "lover" and capitalize them to make a theoretical point: in Tantric culture, the goddess is understood to be a gentle, consoling Mother *and* a wild, uncontrollable Lover. Sometimes a particular song or Tantra will emphasize only one of these roles. Sometimes both roles will fuse in metaphor or symbol. They can never be permanently separated, but neither can they be completely fused. A certain tension or ambivalence always remains, giving Tantric symbolism its power, depth, and psychological efficacy. The Tāntrika is thus fascinated and yet repelled, mesmerized and yet horrified. For this study, this ambivalent union of the goddess's two roles as Mother and Lover defines the basic structure of Tantric symbolism and practice. In other words, I agree with the doctor. "The Mother is the Lover." This *is* one of the most basic meanings of Tantric ritual.

Not surprisingly, whereas the initiate sees this coincidence of the motherly and the erotic, of the gentle and the violent as an accurate revelation of reality, the uninitiated too often sees only a blatant contradiction. The outsider looks at the black naked woman with her garland of heads and skirt of human hands and asks how anyone, believer or not, could address such a form as "mother." It is not an unreasonable question. Indeed, it is an obvious question, one that the tradition has asked itself in the form of an amusing song:

> O Kālī, why do you walk about naked?
> Shame! Shame! Aren't you the least bit embarrassed? . . . .
> O Ma! Is this your family's way, to stand on your husband?
> You're naked. Your husband is naked. And you both roam
> about from cremation ground to cremation ground!
> O Ma! We could all just die! Now, woman, put on your
> clothes!
>
> RJS, no. 99

Anyone who has witnessed recently the annual Kālī-pūjā or "Worship of Kālī" in Calcutta knows that, if Kālī has turned a deaf ear to the poet's request, her children have forced their demand anyway and dressed her in more proper attire, covering her full breasts and shapely hips with strategically placed garlands and long flowing garments. If Kālī feels no shame for exposing her naked form, her children most certainly do.

The Sexy Mother

THE TĀNTRIKAS AND THE POETS, like the modern-day potters who construct the pūjā images in Calcutta, imagine "Ma Kālī" as a nude voluptuous woman of sixteen. Motherly and erotic qualities alternate freely in the descriptions of the goddess. By far, Kālī's most common epithet is a simple "mama" or "ma" (*mā*). But this familiar Ma is also a lovely lady whom the poets and Tantras describe in frankly erotic terms. Indeed, the *Kālīhṛdayam* describes the goddess as the very "form of erotic desire" (KS, p. 1).[7] Her body forms the perfect erotic object, resulting in an iconographic form that reveals the sacred in the sexually graphic. She is nude, "clothed with the sky" (KS, v. 7). Her breasts are described as high and full (KS, v. 6).[8] Indeed, they are so full that they weigh heavily on her stomach, creating three sexy wrinkles that look like serpents biting her lotus-like navel.[9] Her shapely thighs are compared to round banana tree trunks.[10] Her buttocks, adorned by her flimsy skirt of human hands, are said to be beautiful (KS, v. 7). She is seductively posed just so, erotically bent in three places like Kṛṣṇa.[11] She is young, a girl of sixteen.[12] Even her *mantra* vibrates with erotic energies. The first term of Kālī's famous twenty-one syllable *mantra* is made up of *k-r-ī-ṁ*, the first three letters of which are known as "lust" (*kāma*), "fire" (*vahni*), and "sexual desire" (*rati*).[13]

"Like the Mother's Vagina"

SO SOMETIMES KĀLĪ is addressed as a gentle Mother, and sometimes she is addressed as a Lover. But often it is difficult to decide *which* Kālī the poet is addressing. The numerous examples of her full breasts and large hips are good examples of this ambiguity. Woodroffe claims that such expressions are "emblematic of Her great Motherhood,"[14] but they could just as easily be taken as emblematic of what the texts call her "erotic form" (KS, p. 1).[15] It seems more likely that these full breasts and shapely hips, like so much else about the goddess, represent *both* motherly *and* erotic features, and that, interestingly enough, what makes a good mother is also what makes a sexually attractive partner.

A goddess who is both Mother and Lover often evokes feelings from her devotees that might strike the Western reader as profoundly oedipal. Consider, for example, the following verse from the *Karpūrādistotram:* "He who delights in his own sexual partner while he meditates on you with a steady mind, you who delight in waves of passion on top of Śiva . . . he, O Mother, becomes Śiva himself, the destroyer of the god of love (KS, v. 18)." In the midst of sexual intercourse with his own ritual partner, the *sādhaka* or "striver" thinks of his divine Mother erotically astride his divine Father, Śiva. Everything about the enjoined ritual is designed to reproduce this iconographic scene of Kālī atop Śiva. The *sādhaka*'s female ritual partner, for example, is assimilated to his Mother Kālī. Often, they are described in *exactly* the same terms: the same full breasts, the same heavy hips, the same youthful appearance, the same naked form (KS, v. 10). Moreover, the ritual act takes place in the same sacred space of Kālī and Śiva's mystico-erotic union—the cremation ground (KS, vv. 15, 16), and the *sādhaka*'s partner is on top of him, just as Kālī is on top of Śiva (KS, v. 11). The ritual act thus seeks to reproduce the archetypal act of the aspirant's divine Mother and Father.

By means of it, the *sādhaka* is united, not only to his own human *śakti*, but to Kālī herself, his divine Mother and mystical Lover. As the verse states, he has become "Śiva himself, the destroyer of the god of love." He has taken the place of Śiva, his divine Father.

Sometimes this erotic desire for the Mother makes its way into a more literal but still symbolic form. Consider, for example, Woodroffe's aphoristic footnote on how the left-handed rituals of Tantra are kept secret: "Mātriyonivat, as it is said." [16] This footnote about Tantric secrecy itself contains a secret Woodroffe refuses to translate: *Mātṛyonivat*, "like the mother's vagina." The secret, like one's mother's vagina, must be kept from the public, lest it be violated. Only the Tāntrika skilled in the left-handed rituals has access to it. If one followed the symbolism of comparing the ritual secret to the mother's vagina, one might arrive at the conclusion that the secret of the *vīrācāra* ritual, in which the Tāntrika unites with his ritual partner in sexual intercourse, is symbolically equivalent to a possession of "the Mother's vagina," a form of mystical incest.

So Kālī is a pure, gentle Mother whom the devotee addresses in song, prayer, and worship, and Kālī is a naked voluptuous Lover, with whom the Tāntrika ritually unites. As we turn to the details of Ramakrishna's mystical practices, this Tantric vision of the goddess as Mother and Lover will appear again, this time in the public teachings and secret visions of the saint.

THE SECRET YEARS: TEXTUAL CONSIDERATIONS

RAMAKRISHNA'S *SĀDHANAS* are traditionally said to have lasted twelve years, from around 1856, when, after encountering the goddess in the famous "First Vision," the young Ramakrishna set out to realize Kālī's maternal presence permanently, to around 1867, after which Ramakrishna's interests gradually turned outward, to a pilgrimage, to visits with Calcutta's cultural elite, and eventually to teaching. There are at least three important accounts of this approximately twelve-year period. The first appears in Datta's *Jīvanavṛttānta* (1890), the first major biography of the saint. A second account can be reconstructed by piecing together a series of references scattered randomly throughout the *Kathāmṛta* (1902–1932), both in M's section headings and in the body of the text. The third account, by far the most famous, appears in Saradananda's *Līlāprasaṅga* (1911–1918). It is usually considered to be the most authoritative account of Ramakrishna's mystical practices, but, as we will see, many of its claims dissolve when analyzed in the light of textual comparison.

But before I turn to the fantastic forms of Ramakrishna's secret years, I need to demonstrate that the texts must be approached, not as objective reports of simple events, but as records of fuzzy memories, troubling dreams, and powerful cultural agendas that are as obfuscating as they are suggestive. I will accomplish this through textual analyses of each of the three major biographical sources listed above. Such a textual comparison will demonstrate that the texts, like dreams, never reveal certain aspects of their subject without at the same time concealing others. I will approach the three accounts in order of their complexity. M's *Kathāmṛta* version is by far the simplest. It will be studied first. Datta's account in his *Jīvanavṛttānta* is more complex but still shows signs of a certain innocence, especially in its numerous accounts of Ramakrishna's sexual exploits and in its disjointed, unordered account of Ramakrishna's *sādhanas*. In Datta's text there is still no attempt to order Ramakrishna's "strivings" into any purposeful sequence. Saradananda's *Līlāprasaṅga,* on the other hand, shows clear signs of a high degree of interpretation, to the extent that the content and even order of Ramakrishna's *sādhanas* become subordinated to Saradananda's philosophical agenda. It will be treated last, then, for it builds on and transforms the two earlier and simpler accounts of Datta and M.

The Kathāmṛta Version: The Purāṇas, the Tantras, and the Vedas

RAMAKRISHNA'S OWN ORDERING of his mystical practices in the *Kathāmṛta* is structured around texts (the Purāṇas, the Tantras, and the Vedas) and places (the Panchavati or "Place of Five Trees," the bel tree, and the temple portico). In the fourth volume, he relates the following "talk about the past":

> She performed *sādhanas* of many types in me. First according to the Purāṇas, then according to the Tantras, and then according to the Vedas. First I used to perform *sādhanas* in the Panchavati. A tulsi tree grove grew up there—I used to sit in it and meditate. Sometimes I would become very anxious [*vyākula*] and would cry, "Ma! Ma!" Or I would cry, "Rāma! Rāma!"
>
> When I used to cry "Rāma! Rāma!" I would wear a tail and sit down in the mood of Hanumān. I was mad. At that time, while I performed the worship, I would wear silk gar-

> ments [like a woman] and would experience such bliss—the bliss of worship!
>
> *Sādhana* according to the Tantras took place under the bel tree. Then it seemed to me that the sacred tulsi tree and the stem of the horse-radish were one!
>
> In that state I would eat the left-overs of jackals—all night they would lie there—whether a snake ate them, I wasn't sure—this was my left-over food.
>
> I used to follow a dog around and hand-feed him bread, and I myself would eat with him. "The whole world is made of Viṣṇu"—I washed my mouth out with the water that would gather in the mud. I took this water from the pond in this field and washed my mouth out with it.
>
> If one does not destroy ignorance, nothing will happen. That's why I became a tiger—as a tiger, I ate ignorance!
>
> At the time when I practiced *sādhana* according to the Vedas, I became a renouncer. Then I would lie down in the portico—I would say to Hriday,—"I've become a renouncer, I'll eat my rice in the portico!" (KA 4.175)

The passage requires some commentary. In other passages, Ramakrishna provides us with a few glosses. In one such passage, he associates his textual categories (the Purāṇas, the Tantras, and the Vedas) with specific religious traditions. The Vaiṣṇavas follow the views of the Purāṇas, he tells us, and the Śāktas follow the views of the Tantras (KA 4.166). As he associates "the Vedas" elsewhere with the Vedāntins (KA 2.66), one can safely assume that Ramakrishna understood the Vedas as belonging to the Vedāntins.

So we have a sequential pattern defined by three broadly conceived religious traditions: the Vaiṣṇava tradition, Tantra, and Vedānta. Ramakrishna's claim that his Purāṇic *sādhana* occurred first and that it combined Vaiṣṇava and Śākta elements is interesting. The fact that during these practices "according to the Purāṇas" he cried to both Rāma and Kālī suggests that this was a transitional period in which the young priest, still very much rooted in his family traditions (directed toward the Vaiṣṇava deity Raghuvīra), was only gradually moving into the Śākta world of the goddess at Dakshineshwar. The Vaiṣṇava *sādhana* of which Ramakrishna speaks in the passage above, then, refers primarily to his family traditions, not to his later visions of Rādhā and Kṛṣṇa. Granted, he does refer to this period as one in which he dressed up as a woman, but there is no attempt to associate this cross-dressing with one of the Vaiṣṇava *bhāvas* ("moods" or "states"). Most likely, the "bliss of worship" of which he speaks refers to his dressing up as a female attendant of Kālī and his famous worship of the Mother when he lived with the women of Mathur's household. This distinction may seem a minor one, but it is in fact a very important one, for it supports my thesis, advanced below, that Ramakrishna's adoption of the handmaid state and the Rādhā state were not *sādhanas* in the same sense as were his practice of Tantra and Vedānta. Rather, as I have suggested already and will demonstrate below, they were something much more than temporary experiments with passing religious forms: they were symbolic transformations by which Ramakrishna tried to deal with the changing circumstances of his sexual experiences.

The dominant theme of Ramakrishna's practices "according to the Tantras" is Tantra's systematic violation of Hindu social customs and notions of purity. For Ramakrishna, who we must remember was a high-caste brahmin, eating with jackals and dogs and washing his mouth out with muddy water were acts that bordered on social and psychic destruction. They threatened to destroy the very foundations of his symbolic world. Ramakrishna's Sanskrit aphorism—"The whole world is made of Viṣṇu"—is most likely a very early form of what would become a much more vernacular and Śākta chant—"She herself has become everything." It was just such a theistic monism that provided the metaphysical base both for Ramakrishna's destruction of the dividing lines of his social categories and for his eventual reintegration back into the phenomenal world.

The only significant thing about Ramakrishna's account of his practices "according to the Vedas" is the fact that it is not significant. Ramakrishna does not see it as the pinnacle or natural end of his religious experiments. Rather, it is just one more experiment. There is an almost childish ring to his account of it, as if he saw it as more of a game, complete with treats, than as an awesome metaphysical journey: "I would say to Hriday,—'I've become a renouncer, I'll eat my rice in the portico!'" Where he was and what he ate seem far more important to Ramakrishna than the content of the teachings that he received "according to the Vedas."

When we turn to another account of Ramakrishna's *sādhanas*, this time in volume 2, we see again many of the same themes:

> In the Vedas and the Purāṇas there are practices called pure practices. In the Vedas and the Purāṇas it is said—"Don't do this. It would be improper." But in the Tantras just such an act is called good.

> What a state came about! I used to extend my mouth to the heavens and to the underworld and cry "Ma!" It was as if I were going to seize Ma, like a fisherman throwing out his net and quickly dragging in the fish. . . . The state that came about was like madness. This is anxious desire [*vyākulatā*]. (KA 2.132–133)

Here one can see the same triple ordering (the Purāṇas, the Tantras, and the Vedas), the same stress on Tantra's violation of the laws of purity, and the same mystical hunger (the tiger eating ignorance has been replaced by Ramakrishna's desire to eat Kālī). And once again, Ramakrishna describes a state similar to madness and associates it with his early cries for the Mother.[17]

The *Kathāmṛta,* then, is consistent enough to warrant speaking of "a *Kathāmṛta* version" of Ramakrishna's *sādhanas.* Such a version is defined by a set of three textual traditions (the Purāṇas, the Tantras, and the Vedas), which are in turn associated with three types of practitioners (the Vaiṣṇavas, the Śāktas, and the Vedāntins) and with three places (the Panchavati, the bel tree, and the portico). Whereas madness is consistently associated with the first Purāṇic/Vaiṣṇava period, the violation of social customs regarding purity characterizes the Tantric/Śākta period. The Vedic/Vedāntic period is associated with little, except the fact that Ramakrishna became a renouncer and ate his rice in the portico. Ramakrishna gives no dates for any of these events, although M attempts to do so in some of his section headings.

Ram Chandra Datta's Jīvanavṛttānta: States in a Tantric World

Datta begins his *Jīvanavṛttānta* with a bit of historical agnosticism and two fascinating theological claims. The biographer points out that some of what he has written is based on what he has seen with his own eyes or heard directly from the mouth of Ramakrishna. The events of the biography, he seems to be saying, are, for the most part, reliable. Their particular sequence, however, can only be a guess, since no one in the temple or back in Ramakrishna's home village seemed to know the particular days, months, or years of the events described in the biography.[18] The order of Ramakrishna's mystical practices are particularly difficult to determine, Datta tells us, for Ramakrishna himself forgot "what happened when" (JV[5], 21).[19] Datta, in other words, is guessing, and he tells us that he is guessing. But even given such historical limitations, Datta is convinced that his text is profoundly meaningful. Indeed, he goes so far as to claim that his text, if approached properly, is capable of transforming the reader's unconscious "conditionings" (*saṁskāra*), just as his meetings with the Paramahaṁsa once transformed his own deepest thoughts about the nature of reality.[20] The *Jīvanavṛttānta*, in other words, is Datta's attempt to make real for the reader the charismatic influence and mystical power of the Ramakrishna he knew and loved. The text embodies *Datta's* Ramakrishna.

And Datta's Ramakrishna possesses many secrets. The biographer tells his readers that it is a terrible fault to hold anything back in telling the story of Ramakrishna: "Because of this, we have revealed many secret things [*guhya kathā*]."[21] Datta's fascination with the "secret things" or "secret talk" of Ramakrishna's life, especially as they relate to the saint's mystical practices, bears a remarkable similarity to M's use of the very same expression in his *Kathāmṛta*. This is probably no accident. Perhaps M got the term from Datta. Datta's use of it is certainly the first textual occurrence of the term that we have in the Ramakrishna corpus. Given the memorable nature of so many of these "secret things," however, it is just as likely that both writers, having no trouble recalling such striking revelations, remembered the exact expression that Ramakrishna himself used to announce them. Such "secret things" and "secret talk," recorded so impressively in the writings of Datta and Gupta, constitute one of the main rhetorical strategies of what I have called the householder tradition, that alternate, often censored tradition of interpretation and appropriation represented in the writings of Ramakrishna's householder disciples.

One of the most interesting sections of Datta's biography is the section on Ramakrishna's *sādhanas:* chapters 4 ("Praying for a Vision of Ma-Kālī") through 16 ("The Worship of the Sixteen-Year-Old Girl"). For Datta, the *sādhanas* did not begin until after Ramakrishna's famous vision of Kālī and the six-month period of madness that constituted the vision's psychic context. This six-month period of madness (chapter 4), the fascination with fecal matter that followed (chapters 5 and 6), and Ramakrishna's practices in the Panchavati (chapter 7) all fit nicely into what Ramakrishna calls in the *Kathāmṛta* his practices "according to the Purāṇas." The two texts are in general agreement. Likewise, Datta's chapter 8 on "Union with the Brāhmaṇī" and chapter 9 on "Testing the Senses" (a euphemism for a series of sexual temptation scenes) easily could be read as fitting into what Ramakrishna calls his practices "according to the Tantras." The two accounts, again, are very close.

But not quite the same. While Ramakrishna's practices "according to the Purāṇas" and his practices "according to the Tantras," as portrayed in the *Kathāmṛta*, find close counterparts in the chapter divisions and ordering of the *Jīvanavṛttānta*, his practices "according to the Vedas" are more difficult, but perhaps not impossible, to fit into Datta's account of things. Datta includes Ramakrishna's initiation into Vedānta with Tota Puri very early in his discussion of this period, in chapter 7 on the practices that took place in the Panchavati. We might recall that, while Ramakrishna places his practices in the Panchavati first, he relates his practices "according to the Vedas" as the last of his *sādhana* periods. We have, then, a discrepancy. But perhaps a false one. Datta, after all, never claims that Ramakrishna's practices with Tota Puri occurred early in the *sādhana* period. Rather, he only says that it took place in the Panchavati, which in fact it did. Datta's account, then, especially given his avowed doubt concerning the temporal order of the *sādhanas*, might have been more spatially than temporally ordered. For Datta, *where* Ramakrishna performed a particular practice was more important, and more historically available, than *when* Ramakrishna performed it. Accordingly, paying too much attention to the page or chapter in which Datta discusses Ramakrishna's practices "according to the Vedas" is most likely a mistake. Datta, like Ramakrishna, is much more interested, and certain, about trees than times. History is always a guess and much too abstract, but a tree is always a tree. Its roots reach down deep into the memory. It is always there.

One of the primary organizing principles of Datta's account is a general Śākta framework in which he interprets Ramakrishna's experiences. For example, the handmaid state is interpreted by Datta as a metaphysical symbol for the psychic forces that aid Rādhā, in the form of the *kuṇḍalinī*, on her way to the thousand-petaled lotus in the head, where Kṛṣṇa waits for her arrival (JV[5], 51). Datta's interpretation of Islam is similar in its emphasis on the mystical and the erotic. "From a metaphysical perspective" (*tattvapakṣe*), Datta tells us, Muhammad's promise of heavenly maidens to the man who kills a heretic constitutes a promise of "intellectual sex" (*vidyār sahavāsa*) with the "energy of wisdom" (*vidyāśakti*) to the man who can kill the emotional and mental enemies within (JV[5], 55). For Datta, Ramakrishna lived in a Śākta world. His numerous experiments with different religious forms were understood to be Śākta states. They spoke of erotic unions in the subtle body and mystical sex with the powers of metaphysical knowledge.

Saradananda's Līlāprasaṅga: Stages on the Way to Vedānta

SARADANANDA'S ACCOUNT of this same period is very different. He divides the period of Ramakrishna's *sādhanas* into three neat four-year periods: (1) the four years following the First Vision up to the coming of the Bhairavī; (2) the four years of Ramakrishna's Tantric practices under the tutelage of the Bhairavī; and (3) the last four years of *sādhana*, including his Vaiṣṇava experiments, that culminated in Ramakrishna's Vedantic realization under his naked guru, Tota Puri. Saradananda sees theological meaning in this particular order of Ramakrishna's mystical practices. For him, Ramakrishna's "states" (*bhāvas*) were not just states. They were also *stages* on the way to ultimate truth. They led to Vedānta. For Saradananda, the dualistic states all end in a nondual *brahman* (LP 2.13.3–5).[22] Saradananda thus locates Ramakrishna's different mystical practices along a developmental line that leads straight to the biographer's understanding of this nonduality, that is, to Vedānta. Tantric states preceded Vaiṣṇava states, which in turn eventually led to a Vedāntic realization. Islam and Christianity are tacked on the end with no real place in Saradananda's scheme, or as variations on the dualistic theism of his Vaiṣṇava stage. To sum up, *for Saradananda, Ramakrishna's "states" are also stages.*

But as Neevel has pointed out, Saradananda's attempt to arrange the years of Ramakrishna's *sādhanas* into an ordered progression—beginning with the primitive rites of Tantra, moving through the semi-enlightened theism of his Vaiṣṇava *bhāvas*, and culminating in the Vedantic heights of *nirvikalpa samādhi*—is based more on Saradananda's apologetic concerns than on the biographical evidence. Taken as a whole, the textual evidence supports neither the sequential order nor the theological teleology of Saradananda's account. Take, for example, the placing and interpretation of Ramakrishna's Vaiṣṇava practices. The closest one can get to any sort of Vaiṣṇava "stage" in Datta's *Jīvanavṛttānta* is a discussion of the handmaid state. But Datta clearly states that it happened twice—once, as a "girl of eight," worshiping the goddess with Mathur's household, and once on a pilgrimage that occurred after the *sādhana* period (in 1868). Since the first scene happened toward the very beginning of the *sādhana* period and the second scene occurred well after the period was over, it is impossible to fit either event into Saradananda's developmental scheme. The *Kathāmṛta* version is equally at odds with Saradananda. In it Ramakrishna clearly states that his Vaiṣṇava practices "according to the Purāṇas" occurred *before* his Tantric practices, not after as Saradananda would have it. Finally, perhaps the most damaging argument against Saradananda's stage-theory is his own alternative account of the same events. In the fourth book of his *Līlāprasaṅga*, the biographer states in passing, perhaps not noticing it himself, that Ramakrishna's Vaiṣṇava practices preceded his Tantric practices, which in turn preceded his Vedantic practices (LP 4.2.24). This clearly contradicts his own more developed account earlier in the work. However, it is in perfect agreement with what I have called "the *Kathāmṛta* version" of things. Given all of this—and I could go on—it is almost impossible to understand Ramakrishna's Vaiṣṇava experiments as a "stage" after Tantra and before Vedānta. Such a theory simply does not stand up to the textual evidence.

As for a Vedantic teleology behind Ramakrishna's *sādhanas,* neither the *Jīvanavṛttānta* nor the *Kathāmṛta* even hints at such a thing. The numbers alone argue powerfully against any Vedantic meaning behind Ramakrishna's practices. As Neevel has pointed out, the first eight years, fully two-thirds of the traditional twelve years of Ramakrishna's mystical practices, were dominated by the presence of Kālī and defined by Śākta categories and practices. If one adds to these numbers the fact that the Bhairavī may have been with Ramakrishna for as many as twelve years (LP 3.8.3), including the few months he practiced Vaiṣṇava and Vedantic disciplines, one can begin to see just how central Tantra was to these early years of Ramakrishna's religious formation.

Saradananda reads the fact that Ramakrishna practiced Vedānta last as indicative of Vedānta's ultimate truth. For Saradananda *last* means "ultimate," "summation," or "natural end." But the other texts suggest something quite different. For them, *last* means "least," as in "least interesting" or "least important." The few months Ramakrishna spent with his Vedantic guru, Tota Puri, barely make it into the other accounts. Consider, for example, Datta's *Jīvanavṛttānta:* whereas Ramakrishna's "Union with the Brāhmaṇī" (chapter 8) and the dialectical nature of *brahma-śakti* (chapter 21)—both Śākta topics—are given page after page, *Ramakrishna's Vedantic tutelage under Tota Puri receives only a single paragraph, and then in a chapter dealing with Ramakrishna's early periods of madness!* (JV[5], 21–22). Not only are there no stages leading up to Vedānta in Datta's account, then, there is almost no Vedānta! The *Kathāmṛta* is even less enthusiastic than the *Jīvanavṛttānta.* Ramakrishna refers to the period as the time when he "fell into the clutches" of a knower, who "made him listen" to Vedānta for eleven months (KA 3.173). Such comments hardly constitute a warm memory, much less the pinnacle of his religious life. Finally, even in Saradananda's account of things, the saint agreed to Tota Puri's instructions only after he had received permission from Kālī. Ramakrishna, in other words, understood his Vedantic practices within his Śākta world, not vice versa.

All Ramakrishna seems to have cherished about his Vedantic practices was the fact that he ate his rice outside and took *sannyāsa* or a "vow of renunciation." But even this act of renunciation is open to interpretation. I have noted already that Ramakrishna seems to have approached it more like a child's game than as a serious adult commitment. That it was performed in secret, and then only after Tota Puri promised not to tell Ramakrishna's elderly mother about it, leaves one doubting the depth of the saint's ascetic "grit."[23] He, in fact, had very little. The truth of the matter is that Ramakrishna never could bring himself to reject the world. How could he? As he eventually came to understand, it was the very body of the goddess. From the beginning, it was Kālī and Kṛṣṇa, not Saradananda's brand of neo-Vedānta, that provided the saint with his primary categories of understanding.[24]

Except for Saradananda's *Līlāprasaṅga*, then, there is little textual evidence to suggest that Ramakrishna was moving from Tantra to Vedānta through the Vaiṣṇava *bhāvas*, and even the *Līlāprasaṅga* contradicts itself here. Datta's portrayal of a Tantric world in which Ramakrishna experimented with different religious forms, *but always through and with Śākta categories*, seems much more reasonable. One must remember that Datta's *Jīvanavṛttānta* appeared over twenty years before Saradananda's *Līlāprasaṅga*. When one compares the two biographies with this in mind, it becomes apparent that Saradananda followed Datta's biography very closely but rearranged some events and supplemented others in order to present an impression that everything was leading up to Ramakrishna's Vedantic *nirvikalpa-samādhi*. He in effect transformed a Śākta account of Ramakrishna's religious *states* into an ordered set of *stages* with a specific theological lesson—Vedānta is the highest truth.

Given all this, it seems evident that how one tells the story of Ramakrishna's mystical practices is just as much a function of what one wants to prove as what might have happened. The conflict evident in the writings of Datta, M, and Saradananda over the life and teachings of Ramakrishna is nevertheless historically important, not because it ends in historical certainty on any particular topic, but because it suggests that Ramakrishna's life became a cultural myth around which different parties argued for their particular religious worldviews. Datta argued for a Śākta world defined by the dialectical categories of Tantra. The Ramakrishna of the *Kathāmṛta* seems to have agreed. Saradananda, on the other hand, presented his Ramakrishna in order to argue for a Vedantic world defined largely by the neo-Vedantic philosophy of Vivekananda.

I will return to this hermeneutical fight over the primacy of Tantra or Vedānta in chapter 3, when I study the doctrinal structure of Ramakrishna's religious world. For now it is sufficient to point out that, when Ramakrishna's Tantric practices have not been selectively forgotten, they have been artificially relativized, subordinated to a doctrinal scheme foreign to Ramakrishna's Tantric world. The interpreter, then, is faced with a double challenge. Not only must one analyze secret visionary forms that Ramakrishna himself found too painful to remember and too scandalous to interpret; one must also tell Ramakrishna's story in order to remember a secret that the tradition itself has concealed through intentional neglect and obfuscating forms of interpretation. Here I will try to "remember" Ramakrishna's secret by means of three methodological paths: first, I will employ Datta's *Jīvanavṛttānta* as a primary text alongside Saradananda's more canonical and well-known *Līlāprasaṅga;* second, I will analyze Ramakrishna's stray comments in the *Kathāmṛta* about his early practices; and third, and most significant, I will read Ramakrishna's secret visions recorded in the *Kathāmṛta* as dreamlike memories of how Ramakrishna experienced the events of those secret years. Taken separately, each path could be criticized as overly speculative, especially the last path through the unconscious, but taken together, the three paths tend to support one another in their respective views of the fields and valleys of Ramakrishna's inner life.

And here I must stress the word *inner,* for such a method, so deeply informed by psychological principles, can never hope to arrive finally at historical certainty, at "what really happened" (although perhaps it can bring us a bit closer than we currently are). Rather, such a method's true objective is uncovering *meaning,* that is, how Ramakrishna experienced the events of his life and how others interpreted the meaning and significance of those same events for their own lives. We probably will never know what Ramakrishna did with the Bhairavī for all those years, but by following the three paths outlined above we can form a fairly good idea of how Ramakrishna remembered those events and what he thought about them. This, in a nutshell, is my goal as I turn to the troubling forms and ambivalent meanings of Ramakrishna's "secret years."

Following Ramakrishna's "three trees and three times" account in the *Kathāmṛta*, I divide the years of *sādhana* into three periods: (1) the early years before the coming of the Bhairavī, when Ramakrishna cried to Kālī and Rāma "according to the Purāṇas" and experienced different "states of madness"; (2) the years of Ramakrishna's Tantric practices with the Bhairavī "according to the Tantras"; and (3) the few months he spent with Tota Puri learning the practices "according to the Vedas." Although I date each period, given the fluid nature of such periods and the manner in which they tended to flow in and out of one another (especially at their temporal boundaries), such dates should be taken only as rough approximations. I will treat the first two periods in the present chapter. The last, Vedantic period I will study in chapter 3.

THE SECRET YEARS: THE PRACTICES ACCORDING TO THE PURĀṆAS, 1856–1861

RAMAKRISHNA'S ENCOUNTER with Kālī's sword occurred sometime around 1856, shortly after the temple's consecration in 1855. For the next four years, Ramakrishna would see lights and experience strange burning sensations in his body as he walked the thin line between religious enlightenment and madness. Saradananda tells us that "at this time an inner anxious desire to obtain the Lord was his only support" (LP 2.8.3). But such desire without discipline is always dangerous, and Ramakrishna was now alone, without a guide. As a result, it was not long before the young priest's body and mind were shattered. Ramakrishna kept falling back into unconsciousness. Datta tells us that when Ramakrishna remained in such "unconscious states" (*ajñānāvasthā*), Hriday had to feed him and wash the "slimy mud" off his body, probably a reference to Ramakrishna's uncontrollable bowel movements during this period of his life (JV[5], 22).[25] Ramakrishna could not wear clothes at this time. A single coarse scarf covered his entire body. Unconsciousness, uncontrolled bowel movements, and nudity: something was wrong.

Datta locates the beginning of Ramakrishna's *sādhanas* at the time when these "states of madness" began to stabilize and Ramakrishna returned to normal consciousness (JV[5], 11). Saradananda tells us that after the First Vision the Master could not work for some time, and that his cousin, Hriday, thought that the young priest had become insane (LP 2.7.1). In both biographies, then, a period of madness follows upon the First Vision and continues into the period of Ramakrishna's *sādhanas*. It was a particularly painful period for the saint, partly because he had no way of telling whether his strange experiences were genuine (LP 2.7.2). The public, like Hriday, considered him mad. Perhaps because of this social rejection, Ramakrishna often resorted to a technique of social divination to establish his legitimacy. "If the rich landlords respect me," he would say to himself, "then my experiences must be true" (KA 2.47).[26]

The visions gradually increased. Moreover, he no longer saw just a foot or a hand of the goddess. Now the full iconographic form came alive for the young visionary (LP 2.7.4). Before, he had seen the stone image animated by a living presence. Now he saw the Mother herself in "the form of congealed consciousness . . . with hands that offered boons and freedom from fear" (LP 2.7.4). Ramakrishna placed his fingers over the nostrils of the stone image and claimed that he felt it breathing. He also noticed that the image, like a divine being, cast no shadow. During the day, the young priest treated the image as a living being, laughing, singing, and dancing in a drunken state as he tended to the Mother's needs (LP 2.7.5). At night, he could hear the goddess's anklets jingling as she walked up the porch stairs "like a happy girl" (LP 2.7.5). On one such night, he came out to see the goddess and found her looking out over Calcutta from the porch, her dishevelled hair blowing in the night breeze. The Rani's dream had come true: the image had been awakened. But only half of it. Ramakrishna saw the goddess "with hands that offered boons and freedom from fear." The "left-handed" Kālī, with her sword and erotic "left-handed" rituals, is nowhere to be found. For Ramakrishna, Kālī was a Mother who consoles or an innocent little girl who skips up the stairs, not an erotic ritual partner. In his earliest visions, the Mother is affirmed, the Lover denied . . . at least for now.

To aid himself in his practices Ramakrishna planted a new Panchavati, a sacred "Place of Five Trees" where he could perform his meditations and rituals in secret. Datta tells us that as long as he stayed in these trees, no one knew what he was doing: "The Paramahaṁsa performed each of his practices in secret. No one from the temple knew of them."[27] Later, he would bow to this place when he passed it. It was here, in the shady secrecy of the Panchavati, that he became mad, wept, saw visions, longed for God, recited the names of the Lord, and performed the practices "according to the Purāṇas." I will discuss four events that most likely occurred during this period: the Hanumān state, the handmaid state, the worship of the goddess in the cat, and Ramakrishna's marriage to Sharada.

Ramakrishna the Monkey

ONE OF THE FIRST PRACTICES that Ramakrishna associates with this period and these five trees is his imitation of Hanumān, the monkey god and faithful servant of Rāma. Imitating the monkey god, Ramakrishna tied his cloth around his waist so that it looked like a tail. He ate nothing but unpeeled fruits and roots. It is said that his coccyx even lengthened an inch to resemble that of a monkey![28] Despite Ramakrishna's association of this state with madness (KA 4.175), Saradananda sees Ramakrishna's monkey-like antics as an example of what the Vaiṣṇavas call the servant state (*dāsyabhāva*), that religious mode of being in which the devotee looks on the divine as his or her Master. There is some textual evidence for Saradananda's version of Ramakrishna's noble servant state. Ramakrishna, for example, does talk about Hanumān as an example of the devotee who considers himself a "servant" and looks on God as his "Lord" (KA 4.211 et al.), but he never explicitly associates his early monkey antics with this devotional servant state. For Ramakrishna, the state was always associated with madness: "I was mad," he states simply (KA 4.175).

Haladhari, a cousin of Ramakrishna's, offers another view of this state, one very different from that of Saradananda but much closer to Ramakrishna's version of things. Haladhari refuses to ennoble Ramakrishna's madness by comparing it to a classical *bhāva*. Rather, he sees only his crazy cousin peeing from the trees of the Panchavati (LP 2.8.14). For Haladhari, wearing a cloth tail, jumping around on all fours, and peeing from trees has nothing to do with devotion. It is madness, pure and simple.

Mathur's Handmaid

OTHER THAN MADNESS and his Hanumān state, the Ramakrishna of the *Kathāmṛta* associates his practices "according to the Purāṇas" with cross-dressing and a particular form of worship: "At that time, while I performed the worship, I would wear silk garments and experience such bliss—the bliss of worship!" (KA 4.175). Here he is most likely referring to the period in which he lived with Mathur's household and fanned the image of the goddess as a woman with the other women of Mathur's house. Datta deals with this "handmaid state" (*sakhībhāva*) and its related experiences in chapters 11 and 12, where he states that it happened twice, once as an "eight-year-old girl" fanning the goddess in worship, and once in Vrindavana as the "girlfriend" of the elderly woman, Gangamata (JV[5], 43).[29]

The *Kathāmṛta* version of things is not all that different than the two-times account of Datta's *Jīvanavṛttānta*, for the Ramakrishna of the *Kathāmṛta* likewise places this handmaid state both very early in his career, during his practices "according to the Purāṇas" (see the passage quoted above), and again, sometime later, during the eight months he had to spend with Sharada, his young wife. Both the *Jīvanavṛttānta* and the *Kathāmṛta*, then, locate two separate occurrences of the handmaid state and even agree (roughly) about when they took place. The two texts, however, differ on the location and meaning of the second occurrence. The *Kathāmṛta* version of this second occurrence reads thus: "I was in the state of the Handmaid for a long time. I used to dress in women's clothes and wear jewelry and a scarf. With a scarf over my body I would perform the worship! If I didn't do this, how could've I brought my wife and lived with her for eight months? The two of us were Handmaids of the Mother!" (KA 2.154–155).[30] Here we see the same worship context and the same silken clothes, but here Ramakrishna becomes a "Handmaid of the Mother," not to live with Mathur and his household but to conquer his sexual desires for his wife back at the temple (KA 5.140). Perhaps Ramakrishna is referring simultaneously to his practices with Mathur's household and his practice with Sharada. He does, after all, say that he was in the state "for a long time."

We have, then, at least three separate occurrences of the handmaid state: the "bliss of worship" scene with Mathur's household; the eight-month "trial" with Sharada; and the Vrindavana scene with Gangamata during the pilgrimage of 1868. As I will deal with the Vrindavana incident in the next chapter and the scene with Sharada later in this chapter, I will concentrate here on the worship scene. In all three accounts, one thing will become clear: *where* and *with whom* Ramakrishna became a Handmaid is much more important than *when* he became a Handmaid.

Certainly one of the most suggestive aspects of Ramakrishna's handmaid state is the manner in which the biographers consistently relate it to the temple proprietor. For Datta, this period in Ramakrishna's life is intimately related, both geographically and psychologically, to Mathur. Thus many of the scenes related in Datta's two chapters on the handmaid state occur at Janbajar, the family residence of Mathur, and involve unusually intimate contact with Mathur and his family. Mathur, Datta tells us, could not bear to be away from Ramakrishna at this time. He would dress Ramakrishna with his own hands and buy expensive shawls, women's clothes, and jewelry for him.[31] Sometimes such gifts would induce ecstasy and vision in the young priest: Ramakrishna's handmaid-like vision of Rādhā, for example, is said to have occurred immediately after Mathur gave Ramakrishna some feminine ornaments and garments to wear (JV[5], 44). Saradananda also notes that Mathur provided Ramakrishna with his feminine garments and jewelry, and then adds that Mathur's gifts and Ramakrishna's consequent cross-dressing caused some to advance "scandalous" interpretations of the Master's "austere renunciation" (LP 2.14.6). Datta and Saradananda also both note that during this time Ramakrishna lived with the women of Mathur's household.[32] Saradananda stops there. Datta goes on.

Mathur, Datta tells us, often took Ramakrishna away from the temple precincts to his home in the Janbajar district. Previously, "Mathur Babu became greatly agitated if he could not see Ramakrishna," but now, Datta tells us, "his dejection disappeared" (JV[5], 48). An interesting fantasy of Ramakrishna's stems back to this period: "One day Mathur Babu was returning to Jan Bazar in his deluxe phaeton and was bringing Sri Ramakrishna with him. When the carriage reached Chitpore Road, the Master had a wonderful vision. He felt that he had become Sita and that Ravana was kidnapping him. Seized by this idea he merged into samadhi."[33] Sītā was the faithful wife of the god Rāma, whose exploits are recounted in the *Rāmāyaṇa,* one of the two great Hindu epics. Abducted by the demon-king Rāvaṇa, Sītā was eventually rescued after a long and involved battle but then ultimately rejected by Rāma on the grounds that she may have been unfaithful with the demon. With Rādhā,[34] who appeared to the saint immediately after Mathur dressed him in women's clothes, Sītā would be one of the first, indeed the very first, figure to appear in the spontaneous visions of the saint: "Such a vision had never occurred before in this way, without thinking or meditating. Perhaps because I first saw Sītā, who suffered from her birth, I have suffered like her all my life!" (LP 2.8.9). *I have suffered like her all my life!*—the phrase is significant, for the "sufferings of Sītā" involved a sexual abduction, a series of attempted seductions, and a final rejection by her divine husband on the grounds that she had in fact given in to her devilish captor. Since this first Sītā vision was actually of both Sītā and Hanumān, it fits in well to this early period of

Ramakrishna's practices "according to the Purāṇas," when he cried to Rāma, behaved like Hanumān, became Sītā, and was "abducted" by the Rāvaṇa-like Mathur. To make some sense out of his sufferings, Ramakrishna understood them, indeed literally "saw" them, within the myths of his own cultural epic.

Another version of the Sītā vision, this time in the *Kathāmṛta*, suggests that Ramakrishna was at once pained and sexually delighted by Mathur's demonic abduction. As is usual, the *Kathāmṛta* version of the experience adds a specifically erotic dimension to Saradananda's rather enemic description of the same vision; not surprisingly, it occurs in volume 4. Ramakrishna has just explained how Gauri, one of his many Tantric friends, taught him that "if one is to know the Man [*puruṣa*], one must take the state of the Woman [*prakṛtibhāva*]—as a Female Friend, as a Handmaid, or as a Mother." He then goes on to describe such a Woman: "I had a vision of Sītā's image. I saw that her whole mind dwelt only on Rāma. She paid no attention to her vagina, hands, feet, dress, or ornaments. It was as if her life was filled with Rāma—if Rāma were not, if she could not have Rāma, she would die!" (KA 4.36).[35] The vision, or at least Ramakrishna's description of it, plays on a pun: the expression *rāmamaya* can be translated either as "filled with Rāma" or "filled with sexual pleasure."[36] The imprisoned Sītā, in other words, is at once pained at being separated from the god Rāma and yet filled with the pleasure of *rāma* or "sexual delight." So intolerable are her external circumstances that she tries to forget her physical self. We can thus reasonably place this second textual occurrence of Ramakrishna's Sītā vision within the same painful context of the first and again relate it to the myth of Sītā's abduction. The textual context of this second vision, however, adds a completely new dimension to the "sufferings of Sītā," for here in the *Kathāmṛta* Ramakrishna speaks of his Sītā vision immediately after suggesting that one must become a woman, a Handmaid, for example, "to know the Man." Indeed, he explicitly identifies Sītā as one of the figures who, driven by a passionate love to "know" God in man, practiced asceticism to win a female body. A suffering Sītā, a demonic abduction, and the gender transformation of the handmaid state: such a vision of Sītā "according to the Purāṇas" impressively reflects the biographical details of these early scenes with the temple boss.

So Mathur as Rāvaṇa the demon-king kidnapped Ramakrishna as the pure and faithful Sītā. It was an event of mythological proportions for Ramakrishna, a painful yet pleasurable abduction that induced both fantasy and vision in the young priest. And this fantasy: it could both deal with the traumatic event and somehow preserve the innocence and purity of the abducted. Mathur, after all, was the demon, not Ramakrishna. Ramakrishna remained, at least in the fantasy, the ever pure Sītā. Almost. In another vision, Ramakrishna would see this very same Sītā, with whose sexual sufferings he seems to have so deeply identified, in a prostitute (KA 2.49).

Datta describes Sītā's sufferings at Mathur's Janbajar home in some detail. We are told, for example, that Mathur's daughters would bathe Ramakrishna and rub his body with oils. Sometimes, when the young priest would enter into unconscious ecstatic states, his clothes would fall off. "But in this," Datta assures us, "no one was corrupted" (JV[5], 49).[37] When Ramakrishna awoke, the women would dress him. M records a similar scene: "I was almost always unconscious. Mathur would take me to Janbajar and keep me there for days. I began to see that I had actually become the Female Servant of the Mother. The women of the house would feel no shame in regards to etiquette, as one feels no shame when looking at a small boy or girl. With Mathur's wife I used to lay Mathur's girls down near him" (KA 2.49–50).[38] *I was almost always unconscious . . . Mathur would take me to Janbajar and keep me there for days . . . I began to see that I had actually become the Female Servant of the Mother.* Why? Datta records for us an unusually explicit scene that might suggest an answer. In it, Ramakrishna enters Mathur's bedroom at an inopportune time, angering Mathur and his wife and leading them to exclaim: "Father! Now that you've watched us, why are you leaving? Do you have something else in mind?" (JV[5], 49).[39] Datta then immediately relates another scene, perhaps to hint at the nature of this "something else." In this next scene, after "a certain kind of mood" comes upon Mathur, he asks Ramakrishna to lie down next to him. Ramakrishna makes no objections to his boss's request (JV[5], 49).[40] Perhaps it was scenes such as these that Datta regarded as "secret," too controversial for "the public"[41] to learn of and yet too engaging for Datta not to tell. Certainly such scenes help explain what Ramakrishna meant by becoming a Handmaid "to know the Man."

The Ramakrishna of M's *Kathāmṛta* also states clearly that he slept in the same room with Mathur and his wife but is silent on whether he "lay down" with Mathur. Instead, a humorous note is introduced. Ramakrishna, who could never tell a lie and always offered information to all who asked, was a valuable informant for Mathur's prying wife, who would ask Ramakrishna about Mathur's adulterous affairs. Ramakrishna always offered her plenty of information, angering Mathur and winning for himself the reputation of a fink (KA 4.72). How, we might ask, would have Ramakrishna known about Mathur's affairs? Were these affairs homosexual in nature? And was Ramakrishna involved or at least present?

Mitra's brief description of Ramakrishna's Handmaid state in his *Jīvana o Upadeśa* is in basic agreement with the texts of Datta and M but adds its own revealing perspective. After connecting the state with Mathur's household, the rubbing oil, and the saint's boyishness, Mitra comes right out and tells his readers that Ramakrishna appeared quite sexy in his "woman's state," for his was that ideal feminine beauty that "completely infatuates" men. To demonstrate the power of such a state Mitra then goes on to describe an elaborate flirtation scene between a wife and a husband, with the husband refusing food and sweets and the wife playing shy and looking beautiful. As if speaking from experience, Mitra concludes: "Once one has seen this strange woman's state, one never forgets it" (JU, 154–155). For this biographer, at least, the homoerotic dimensions of Ramakrishna's feminine states are as unmistakably clear as the meanings of a wife's flirtatious advances and the hunger of a husband who refuses food.

Saradananda certainly never told such secrets or saw such a sexiness. Granted, he notes that Mathur was struck by the exceptional beauty of one of the women who performed the worship of the goddess (a reference to the cross-dressed Ramakrishna engaged in the "bliss of worship") (LP 3.7.7),[42] but he seems completely innocent of any homosexual dimension to such an attraction. For this biographer, there are no mythical abductions, no bedroom scenes with Mathur, no sexy Ramakrishnas, no scandalous secrets behind the saint's handmaid state. There was only more Vedānta. Ramakrishna's cross-dressing, Saradananda claims, was a spiritual technique that enabled the Master to realize the conditioned status of gender (and the Vaiṣṇava states that rely on it) (LP 2.13.26). It helped Ramakrishna to learn an important Vedantic lesson: gender, and everything else about the body and the mind, is conditioned, plastic, and so ultimately impermanent, false. For Saradananda, in other words, Ramakrishna's handmaiden gender finds its meaning, not in Ramakrishna's anxious attempt to deal with Mathur's mythical abduction or the troubling presence of his young wife, but in the nonconditioned truth of Vedānta, in the state of nonduality beyond every state and gender (LP 2.14.17).

But this simply will not do. Ramakrishna nowhere even hints at such an understanding. Much more significant than Saradananda's Vedantic hermeneutics are the persons of Sharada and Mathur, whose presences figure prominently in almost every scene involving the handmaid state. Datta, for example, entitles an entire section, "Living in the Handmaid State" (JV[5], 49); and in Datta's account, "Living in the Handmaid State" is equivalent to "Living with Mathur," for every scene dealt with in the section is associated with Mathur or his household. These feminine states, then, did not constitute some Vaiṣṇava "stage" on the way to Vedānta, nor did they constitute a lesson in the conditioned status of gender. Rather, they were the symbolic means by which Ramakrishna dealt with the troubling presence of his wife and the traumatic treatment he received from Mathur. Much later in Ramakrishna's life, when Sharada had been effectively rejected and Mathur was long dead, these same feminine states would enable the saint to transform his homoerotic desires into the mystical states that defined and legitimated his charisma. As such, they were permanent forms in the repertoire of Ramakrishna's mythical and symbolic artistry. These feminine states, in other words, were absolutely central, not only to Ramakrishna's ability to deal with the sexual advances of his wife (whom he could resist) and superior (whom he could not resist), but also to his success as a religious teacher, for they defined the mythical lines of his charismatic "attraction" (*ṭāna*).

The Goddess in a Cat

THE THIRD SCENE of this period that I want to look at is Ramakrishna's worship of the goddess in a cat. Saradananda and Datta only mention it.[43] The *Kathāmṛta*, on the other hand, records at least four accounts of the incident.[44] M even has a title for the experience, "The Vision of Everything Filled with Consciousness" (KA 4.35). The fullest account occurs in volume 4:

> Ma showed me in the Kālī Temple that Ma herself has become everything. She showed me that everything was made of consciousness [*cinmaya*]!—The image was made of consciousness!—The altar was made of consciousness!—The water pot and ladle were made of consciousness!—The door frame was made of consciousness!—The marble floor was made of consciousness!—Everything was made of consciousness! I looked into the temple—It was as if everything was soaked in syrup [*rasa*], in the syrup of Saccidānanda! I saw

> an evil man in front of the Kālī Temple, but in him also I saw her power blazing! That's why I fed the offerings of the worship to a cat. I saw that Ma herself had become everything—even the cat. (KA 4.35)

In another passage, Ramakrishna relates this same incident, describing how, like one mad, he began to worship everything with flowers. This then reminds him of another time when, just as he was about to worship the Śiva-*liṅgam,* he was shown that "this universe is the very form of Śiva," that is, he was shown that the entire cosmos was a Śiva-*liṅgam* (KA 3.68). The phallic dimensions of this experience are significant. Indeed, they are cosmic. Again, while picking flowers for worship, he was shown that the trees were like bouquets themselves, and so already offered to the divine (KA 3.68). He could not even cut a lemon without invoking the violence of Kālī: "Victory to Kālī!" he would shout, as he cut the living fruit (KA 2.192). The universe, like the Kālī Temple, is made of consciousness. It blazes with the goddess's *śakti* and exists in and as the syrup of Saccidānanda. It reveals itself as a cosmic phallus. All of this fits in well to this first period of Ramakrishna's practices "according to the Purāṇas," for "in the view of the Purāṇas he himself has become everything" (KA 5.51). For Ramakrishna, such a monistic theism defines the Purāṇas.

These visions and ecstatic states eventually reached such proportions that it became impossible for Ramakrishna to carry out his priestly duties. The very metaphysical underpinnings of worship began to dissolve. The universe revealed itself as a Śiva-*liṅgam.* The trees offered their own natural worship. Cats looked divine. And Ramakrishna himself began to identify so closely with the goddess that he would decorate his own body with the flowers and leaves meant for the goddess (LP 4.4.27). He, in effect, ceased to worship the image and began to worship himself as the goddess incarnate, according to the Tantric dictum that, "Having become the goddess, one should worship the goddess."[45] But scriptural or no, the temple workers and general public were not at all impressed. They were angry and scandalized. Datta tells us that the temple workers were so put off by the saint's seemingly arrogant actions that they prevented Ramakrishna from entering the temple. The temple doorkeeper went so far as to hit Ramakrishna when he tried to enter (JV[5], 39).[46] Many years later Ramakrishna would still remember proudly how Mathur defended him against his detractors by writing a letter to the temple employees and commanding them not to say anything about Ramakrishna's actions (KA 4.35).

Village Rest and Marriage

News of Ramakrishna's madness soon drifted back to Kamarpukur. As a result, Ramakrishna's mother became very anxious for the health of her son and sent for him. Bowing to the pressure, or perhaps relieved, Ramakrishna went home to his village for a rest sometime toward the end of 1858. The idea of a rest in the village to cure Ramakrishna of his madness seems to have worked quite well. True, strange happenings still marked the march of events. Ramakrishna, for example, was visited by a ghost, who warned him not to chew betel-nut lest it increase his lust, and at night Ramakrishna would visit the local cremation grounds with potfuls of sweets to feed the jackals and demons (LP 2.9.4). But despite such occurrences, back home in his village, the saint's illness abated somewhat (LP 2.9.6).

To heal him permanently of his maladies the family decided to arrange a marriage, to which, strangely enough, Ramakrishna made no objections. Instead, he seemed delighted, in a childlike way, with the proposition (LP 2.9.7). But since everyone seemed to know of Ramakrishna's madness and eccentric ways—one could imagine how difficult it would have been to keep Ramakrishna's habit of feeding jackals and demons out of the village gossip—a wife was, to say the least, difficult to procure. Family after family refused the offer until Ramakrishna himself reputedly entered an ecstatic state and discerned the identity of his future bride in a vision: "The bride, marked with a straw, is kept in the house of Ram Chandra Mukherjee in the village of Jayrambati" (LP 2.9.8). Marked or not, Ramakrishna's family had to pay a fee of three hundred rupees to convince the Mukherjees to marry their daughter off to such a character. Having done so, Ramakrishna was finally married to the five-year-old daughter of Ram Mukherjee, a little girl named Sharadamani. Hints of conflict, however, remained. Sharada's uncle, for example, came and took the girl back home when he learned that the ornaments with which Ramakrishna's family adorned the young bride were borrowed and had already been returned. Ramakrishna was married, but barely.

As we might expect, the fact that Ramakrishna married at all is something of a problem for Saradananda and the renouncer tradition. In his *Līlāprasaṅga*, Saradananda spends a number of pages struggling with the question (LP 3.4.7–11). After rejecting various solutions to the problem, from family pressure to *karma* theory to Ramakrishna's own humorous but honest answer ("I needed a cook"), Saradananda finally offers his own solution: Ramakrishna married to teach a spineless India, "converted by the doctrine of Western materialism," that renunciation is the true aim of life. According to Saradananda, it is doubtful whether there has ever been so much sexual indulgence in marriage as there is now in India. "The Master, as teacher, was married in order to destroy this beastliness of modern Indian men and women."[47] Ramakrishna married, in other words, to teach married Indians to be more continent!

Whether it was for *karma*, a cook, or the good of India, Ramakrishna did marry, probably in the year 1859.[48] According to Saradananda, he stayed in the village for another year and a half, then left his young bride and returned to the temple against the pleadings of his mother, who feared that he would relapse back into madness (LP 2.9.11). The mother's fears seem to have been justified, for, in Rolland's words, "Kālī was waiting for him."[49] So, no doubt, was Mathur. As a result, soon the same reddish chest, the same burning sensations, the same sleepless nights returned, but they were not so bad this time (LP 2.9.12). Ramakrishna was back. His practices "according to the Purāṇas" had ended. His practices "according to the Tantras" were about to begin.

THE SECRET YEARS: THE PRACTICES ACCORDING TO THE TANTRAS, 1861–1865

IN 1861 THE RANI DIED. Jackals could be heard howling auspiciously in the distance as her body was consigned to the flames and its ashes were thrown into the Ganges. Mathur, her son-in-law, was now the sole proprietor of the temple. Saradananda goes out of his way to note that Mathur's new-found position of authority and power enabled him to help Ramakrishna in his Tantric practices (LP 2.10.6). There are numerous other personalities in the texts who no doubt also aided the young Tāntrika in their own ways. Indeed, there are so many that the list amounts to a who's who of the temple's religious life. Even those who appeared to object to Tantric forms of worship often practiced the tradition in secret. Haladhari, for example, who objected to sacrificing goats to Kālī, secretly practiced the *parakīyā* path of Vaiṣṇava Tantra, whereby one engages in ritual intercourse with "someone else's wife" (*parakīyā*) in imitation of Kṛṣṇa and the milkmaids, who left their husbands to tryst with Kṛṣṇa in the fields and streams of Vrindavana (LP 2.8.12). Hriday, Ramakrishna's nephew, paid an especially heavy price for his Tantric practices. He was expelled from the temple for worshiping the feet of Mathur's young granddaughter in some unspecified immoral way (LP 2.APP.26). Haladhari and Hriday were by no means alone in their secret practices. Indeed, as Saradananda points out, numerous learned scholars of the local Vaiṣṇava communities often practiced "secret *sādhanas*" (LP 4.1.29). Even the austere heights of Vedānta were not immune from this Bengali penchant for Tantra. Padmalochan, for example, a local scholar of Vedānta, practiced the tradition as well (LP 4.2.48). And the list could be greatly expanded. Regardless of their traditional allegiances during the day, almost everyone, including Ramakrishna's own wife (LP 5.11.9),[50] seems to have led secret midnight lives. Dakshineshwar was a very secret place.

"Union with the Brāhmaṇī"

A few months after the Rani died, a strange woman appeared at the temple river landing. An attractive—one text describes her as "extraordinarily sexy" (JU, 72)—middle-aged brahmin woman (or "*brāhmaṇī*"), she was dressed in the red robes of a Bhairavī and carried a bundle of books in her hand. Her hair was dishevelled, like that of Kālī (JV[5], 28). She claimed that she had found two out of the three great souls that had been revealed to her by the goddess. She was now seeking the third. To Hriday's amazement—Ramakrishna had refused to associate with women up to this point (JV[5], 28)—Ramakrishna immediately entrusted himself to her wisdom, relating to her all his visions and strange experiences, "like a child" (LP 2.10.10). The Bhairavī assured the troubled priest that he was not mad by using her books to prove that the same things had happened to Rādhā, the lover of Kṛṣṇa, and Caitanya, the sixteenth-century saint of Bengal: "Who calls you mad, father? You are not mad. You are in the great ecstasy" (LP 2.10.10).[51] Probably at the Bhairavī's prodding, Mathur brought in a local Tantric scholar named Vaishnavacharan, whom the Bhairavi seems to have known (LP 4.1.18), to establish the Bhairavī's conclusions that Ramakrishna's seemingly pathological behavior was in fact a sign of his unprecedented religious status. The young priest was relieved when Vaishnavacharan's diagnosis matched the Bhairavī's: "I'm glad to know it's not a disease" (LP 4.1.18–20). A similar discussion, staged again by Mathur shortly after the arrival of Gauri, yet another Tantric scholar, would conclude that Ramakrishna was a veritable incarnation of God (LP 4.1.134–136). Mathur, the Bhairavī, and their Tantric friends were clearly in control of things.

The precise nature of Ramakrishna's relationship with the Bhairavī, like almost everything else about the saint, is something of a secret. In the *Kathāmṛta* we are told that after seeing Ramakrishna eat, Gauri used to ask Ramakrishna whether he took the Bhairavī for his *sādhana,* that is, whether he engaged in ritual intercourse with her (KA 5.73). Ramakrishna made no reply to Gauri's question, or if he did, M refuses to record it. The reader is left with a similar silence in the *Jīvanavṛttānta.* Datta uses an ambiguous section heading for these initial scenes with the Bhairavī, a heading which constitutes, like Gauri's curiosity, a question and, like Ramakrishna's reply, a refusal to answer. The phrase Datta uses is *brāhmaṇīr sahita milana.* It could mean either "union with the Brāhmaṇī" or "meeting with the Brāhmaṇī," depending on how one wants to take the verbal noun, *milana.* The term is commonly used to mean sexual union. When Ramakrishna, for example, uses the term, it usually refers either to the sexual pleasure a wife and husband experience in their conjugal relations (KA 5.118) or to a mystical form of sexual union: "Saccidānanda Śiva is in the thousand-petaled lotus—he unites with Śakti. The union (*milana*) of Śiva and Śakti!" (KA 4.116).[52] It is also used in the texts to refer to the physical joining of the sexual organs (TP, no. 201) and to Tantric ritual intercourse (TS, 99). The term, however, can also mean simply "meeting." But even here, it should be pointed out that, for Ramakrishna, a "meeting" of this type possesses unmistakable sexual dimensions: "Sitting down or visiting with a woman for a long time, that too is called sexual intercourse [*ramaṇa*]" (KA 5.141). Accordingly, in the last volume of the *Kathāmṛta,* the Paramahaṁsa, quoting the Tantras, lists "the eight types of sexual intercourse" (*maithunamaṣṭāṅga*) that a renunciant must avoid: "There are eight kinds of sexual intercourse. That bliss one experiences when one listens to talk about women, that is a kind of sexual intercourse. Talking about women (praising them) is also a kind of sexual intercourse. Whispering in private with women, that too is a kind of sexual intercourse. Keeping anything of a woman's close to you and deriving bliss from it, that too is a kind of sexual intercourse. Touching is a kind of sexual intercourse" (KA 5.141).[53] For Ramakrishna, as for the Tantras, *any* kind of social intercourse with a woman is always just that: intercourse. Human interaction, at least between the sexes, is charged with sexual powers, acknowledged or not.

Datta's use of the expression "Union with the Brāhmaṇī," then, is at best ambiguous. He never explicity describes a scene in which Ramakrishna actually engages in ritual intercourse with the Bhairavī,[54] but in the end he leaves the door open to just such a possibility by his acknowledgment that he is keeping secrets: "We have heard of various happenings concerning the Brāhmaṇī, but on this topic we hesitate to reveal all of them to the public" (JV[5], 33). Like Ramakrishna in the *Kathāmṛta,* then, Datta refuses to answer Gauri's question concerning the precise nature of Ramakrishna's "intercourse" with the Bhairavī.

This secret silence surrounding the Bhairavī and the ambivalence that her presence seemed to invoke from practically everyone carries over into almost every scene involving her. Mathur, of all people, immediately distrusted her. Suspicious of both her physical charms and her traveling habits (she traveled alone), he is said to have one day asked her mockingly, "Where is your Bhairava [male Tāntrika], O Bhairavī?" She cleverly pointed to Śiva lying beneath the feet of the goddess in the Kālī temple. "But that Bhairava doesn't move," Mathur replied. "Why have I become a Bhairavī if I cannot arouse the unmoving?" she snapped back. Mathur shut up (LP 2.8.6).

Two other early scenes involving the Bhairavī are especially revealing in light of my analysis of Kālī as Mother and Lover. In the first, the Bhairavī is meditating on her chosen god, Raghuvīra (the same deity of Ramakrishna's family), in the Panchavati and is about to offer him food and drink when the sight of a "strange vision" plunges her into *samādhi:*

> At this same time, the Master felt drawn [to that place] and in a half-conscious state showed up there. Completely possessed by a divine power, he began to eat all of the ritual food offered by the Brāhmaṇī. After a while, the Brāhmaṇī regained consciousness, opened her eyes, and saw that such actions of the Master, merged in an ecstatic state, corresponded to her own vision. She was filled with bliss as the hairs of her body stood on end. After a while, the Master regained normal consciousness and was disturbed about what he had done. He said to the Brāhmaṇī: "Who knows, mother, why I lose control of myself and do such things!" (LP 2.10.11)

The Bhairavī, convinced now that her chosen deity dwelt in the body of Ramakrishna, immersed her image of Raghuvīra in the river, for she had obtained "the concrete and abiding presence of Raghuvīra in the body and mind of the Master." Ramakrishna in effect had replaced the image.

It is important to note here the terms with which Ramakrishna commonly addressed the Bhairavī—"Mother"—and with which the Bhairavī addressed Ramakrishna—"Child." It was a relationship that Ramakrishna felt quite comfortable with, despite the hints of something improper or scandalous in his behavior. But sometimes the Bhairavī attempted to initiate a quite different relationship, one to which Ramakrishna objected. Saradananda, for example, relates how the early encounters of Ramakrishna and the Bhairavī were filled with tension as each tried to define the relationship in his or her own terms: "We heard from Hriday that at this time the Brāhmaṇī now and then would enter into the mood of the milkmaids of Vraja and begin to sing songs filled with erotic sweetness. The Master would say that he did not like this mood and would ask her to stop and instead sing songs addressing the divine as Mother" (LP 2.14.3). A disciple's bitter comment is pertinent here: he saw no use for such songs expressing this "lovey-dovey stuff" (*prema-ṭrema*) unless one wanted to get married (KA 4.287). The disciple saw the Vaiṣṇava songs as a thinly veiled attempt to woo a human lover. Ramakrishna most likely saw the Bhairavī's attempts in a similar light. For his part, while Ramakrishna did not hesitate to sing such songs to his young disciples, he found it very disturbing when a woman sung them to him. The Bhairavī would then "change her tune" and sing songs to the goddess as one of her handmaids, or to the child Kṛṣṇa as his mother, Yaśoda. Ramakrishna, no doubt, was relieved. The Mother had eclipsed the Lover.

But despite these initial squabbles and symbolic posturings, Ramakrishna and the Bhairavī eventually did begin a series of extensive Tantric practices that would last three to four years (LP 2.11.17). As I have noted already, Datta believed that it was impossible to reconstruct the precise order of the events of these years. Saradananda also admits that Ramakrishna never made clear the specific order of the events of these years (LP 2.11.17). Because of these limitations, the sequence or order of my own account of them, like both Saradananda's and Datta's, must remain chronologically arbitrary.

The Five M's: Transgressing and Transcending the Pure

BUT THOUGH CHRONOLOGY must remain arbitrary, the *structure* of Ramakrishna's Tantric practices is very consistent. I have already quoted one of Ramakrishna's memories in which he associates this period of his life, immediately before or during his Tantric practices, with a radical dissolution of the categories regarding the pure and the impure: "Then it seemed to me that the sacred tulsi tree and the stem of the horseradish were one! . . . I used to follow a dog around and feed him bread, and I myself would eat with him. 'The whole world is made of Viṣṇu'— I washed my mouth out with the water that gathered in the mud" (KA 4.175). For Ramakrishna, Tantra dissolved what society and its binary categories constructed. In the social world, the tulsi tree was sacred and muddy water impure. In a Tantric world, on the other hand, where "everything is made of Viṣṇu," the lowly radish is as sacred as the tulsi tree and Ramakrishna can wash his mouth out with "impure" muddy water. This dissolution of social and religious categories, more than anything else, defined Ramakrishna's understanding of Tantra.

The Bhairavī, we are told, encouraged Ramakrishna to follow the path of the Tantras so that he could see that his own experiences agreed with those of the Tantric mystics, the *sādhakas* (LP 2.11.2). The Bhairavī, in other words, was attempting to show Ramakrishna that his mystical experiences were structured around Tantric themes. From the viewpoint of the Bhairavī, Ramakrishna, whether he realized it or not, was a Tāntrika even before he began his Tantric practices. One might disagree with the Bhairavī at this point in time, but once she had almost four years to form her disciple, the issue becomes a moot one, for even if his mystical experiences were not structured around Tantra before the Bhairavī's coming (and in many ways they were), after four years of sometimes "bizarre" and "grave" (KA 3.24) rituals with her, Ramakrishna's religious experiences, whether he liked the fact or not, were indeed profoundly "Tantric" in that they consistently transgressed and transcended the social and religious category of the pure.

Having been encouraged by the Bhairavī, Ramakrishna asked Kālī's permission to take up the Tantric path and, upon receiving it (LP 2.11.5), set out with the Bhairavī to perform his practices "according to the Tantras." The details we have of these rituals are unusually rich, if incomplete. The biographers compile a list that amounts to a rough equivalent of left-handed Tantra's "Five M's" (*maṁsa, matsya, madya, mūdra,* and *maithuna*), which, in Doniger's mischievously anticlimactic translation, became "the Five F's": "flesh, fish, fermented grapes, frumentum, and fornication."[55] The irreverent or "sinful" quality of Doniger's translation is not inappropriate, as these Five M's are specifically designed to transgress the boundaries that society and religion have set up. *They are intentionally, purposefully scandalous.* This is what Tantra is all about to the figures who people the texts. Indeed, in the *Kathāmṛta,* the Five M's are equated with "the Tantric view" (*tantramata*) (KA 3.50), which in turn is usually associated with Tantra's most infamous rite, "taking a woman" in ritual intercourse (KA 2.8). These Five M's as literal acts are the unmistakable marks of the "left-handed practitioner" (*vāmācārī*) (KA 2.141). Their practice is Tantra *par excellence.*

Many Indian commentators and Western scholars have tried to read these Five M's metaphorically. Ramakrishna's interpreters also have been very slow to acknowledge the radical nature of Ramakrishna's left-handed practices. Saradananda, for example, goes so far as to claim that by refusing to participate in the Tantric left-handed rituals as a Hero, Ramakrishna the Child purified the Tantric tradition of its corruption and demonstrated its true meaning: that the divine should be approached as a Mother, not as a Lover. Saradananda sees this as Ramakrishna's "advancing" (*pravṛtta*) of Tantra to its purer, truer, more original form. This, for Saradananda, is the "hidden purpose" (*gūḍha abhiprāya*) of Ramakrishna's Tantric practices (LP 2.11.14). The pure Devoted Child conquers the decadent Tantric Hero, *bhakti* takes over Tantra, and Tantra is "advanced" by a profound reversal, its erotic base denied for a sexless, childlike state of devotion.

It is interesting to compare Datta's understanding of Tantra to that of Saradananda. Writing some twenty years before Saradananda, Datta had rejected such an "advancing" as a serious misrepresentation of both the Tantric tradition and Ramakrishna's place in it. For Datta, such interpretations are the *exact reverse* of Tantra's unabashedly horrific core: "The practices of Tantra are by nature horrific. The results of the practices cannot be attained without the Five M's. Even though many people want to reverse the literal meaning of the M's by demonstrating their 'deeper' mood or meaning, that is not the purpose of this book" (JV[5], 31).[56] After rejecting a metaphorical interpretation of Tantra, Datta then goes on to describe a certain text called the *Urddhvamukha-Tantra,* claiming that the rituals described in this Tantra are so horrific that they cannot be introduced to the public. He argues that, although such secret rites are filled with obscenities, the *sādhaka* is untouched by them. According to Datta, Ramakrishna was just such a *sādhaka:* he easily performed all of these obscene and horrific rites with the Bhairavī (JV[5], 31–32).

The *Kathāmṛta* version of things acknowledges the same horrific nature of the rites but differs with Datta on the subject of Ramakrishna completing them with ease. In the *Kathāmṛta,* Ramakrishna tells his disciples that the Bhairavī "forced" him to undergo the "bizarre" rites of the Tantras.[57] Ramakrishna does not always specify the precise nature of these rituals, but he does consistently display an unusual familiarity with things Tantric, a familiarity that may be rooted in his actual experiences with the Bhairavī. Unfortunately, we have no reliable historical evidence concerning the actual order of these rituals and experiences. Given such limitations, I have organized what follows around the Five

M's of left-handed Tantra. By so doing, I seek, not only to acknowledge the gaps and ambiguities of the historical record, but also to replicate something of the Tantric ritual itself (or at least the indigenous talk about the ritual), which, like this study, tends to move quickly through the first M's—flesh, fish, wine, grain—to the last and most exemplary M, ritual intercourse with a woman.

The first M is *maṁsa,* "meat" or "flesh." Normally, *maṁsa* is understood to mean animal flesh, as in our "meat," but in Ramakrishna's case Doniger's translation of "flesh" is more appropriate since a piece of rotten human flesh was used (LP 2.11.9). The act, in other words, amounted to a form of cannibalism, most likely in imitation of Kālī. Ramakrishna's comment that at this time he enjoyed "the sweet smell of burning corpses" is pertinent here, because it again establishes connections between the consumption of corpses and Ramakrishna's Tantric practices (KA 2.131). The human corpse is central to the Tantras. Kālī stands on it. Kālī has intercourse with it. The *sādhaka* meditates on it. The *sādhaka* breathes into its mouth in an attempt to magically awaken it back to life. And, as we have seen, the *sādhaka* consumes it. Often, moreover, the corpse and its cremation ground are associated with human sexuality. The cremation ground, for example, is both the place of erotic ritual and the place where all desires are burnt away with the body. This textual connection between corpses and desire carries over into Ramakrishna's teachings, where the corpse pit is often associated with sexual desire.[58] All of these themes meet in Ramakrishna's consumption of the corpse flesh. By forcing him to eat human flesh, the Bhairavī tried to push Ramakrishna beyond the fear, the shame, and the impurity that his culture attached to *maṁsa,* the bearer of sexuality and the abode of death.

Saradananda also tells us that Ramakrishna ate a piece of fish cooked in the skull of a dead body. The act constituted Ramakrishna's fulfillment of the second M, *matsya* (LP 2.11.8). Eating fish is not a particularly troublesome thing in Bengal. Bengalis in fact are known for their love of fish. Accordingly, Ramakrishna often compared his religious eclecticism to the Bengali mother who knows how to curry fish five different ways, thus pleasing everyone in her family.[59] Fish is thus central to the culture. It certainly is not a sinful substance. But fish cooked in the skull of a dead body is another matter. The Bhairavī, it seems, was adopting the traditional M, but since it had lost its scandalous status in Bengali culture, she supplemented its normality with a profoundly abnormal, illicit form of preparation: cooking it in a skull.

The third M, *madya* or "wine," figures heavily in the texts, mostly because Ramakrishna had a great deal of trouble with it. There was something sacred about this eminently Tantric liquid for Ramakrishna. The very sound of the word *kāraṇa* or "wine," we are often told, sent Ramakrishna into *samādhi* (LP 4.2.21). Wine (*kāraṇa*) is sacred, then, a sacrament to remind the adept of the bliss of the "cause of the universe" (*karaṇa*). But there was also something scandalous about it. Ramakrishna, for example, often noted with a certain disgust that Achalananda, a local Tāntrika, drank too much (KA 5.180).[60] He also liked to tell the story about a group of Tāntrikas he was with in Benares: much to Ramakrishna's dismay, they broke their circle of meditation to drink wine and to dance on the bank of the river.[61] This ambivalence toward wine is especially evident in Ramakrishna's inability to drink it (KA 2.143). Indeed, he could not even touch a bottle of the substance (KA 2.131). All he could manage to do was touch his tongue with a drop of it, smell it, or rub it on his forehead, lest he offend Kālī.[62] Wine, then, is an eminently Tantric fluid for Ramakrishna, powerfully sacred and yet troublingly impure.

The fourth M, *mūdra* or "parched grain," does not appear explicitly[63] in the texts, but this should not surprise us, since very few commentators seem to agree about what is meant by "parched grain."[64]

The fifth and most important M, *maithuna* or "sexual intercourse," however, is everywhere, and everyone is quite clear about what is meant by the term. I will discuss it under three categories: ritual intercourse, temptation scenes, and erotic visionary experience.

The Bhairavī clearly tried to employ sexual intercourse as one of her means to teach Ramakrishna Tantric truths. Consider, for example, the following scene. Night has fallen. The Bhairavī calls into the darkness and a beautiful young woman appears. The Bhairavī sits her down on the "seat of the goddess," strips her naked, and instructs Ramakrishna to worship her as the goddess: "Father, repeat your *mantra* as you sit in her lap with your thoughts filled with the knowledge that she is the Mother of the Universe herself!" Ramakrishna weeps and cries to his divine Mother, but the Bhairavī does not relent. Ramakrishna begins to repeat his *mantra*, sits in the woman's lap, and immediately falls into *samādhi*. He has to be brought back to consciousness by the Bhairavī (LP 2.11.8).

Here again, one can see a Tantric ritual designed around profoundly oedipal themes: Ramakrishna is instructed to sit in a naked woman's lap "with the knowledge that she is the Mother of the Universe herself." But Ramakrishna cannot perform the incestuous act. Once again, he cannot relate to woman as Lover, even in the secret confines of a Tantric ritual. Unlike the Tantric Hero, "who delights in his own sexual partner" as he meditates on Kālī "delighting in waves of passion" on top of Śiva (KS, v. 18), all poor Ramakrishna can do is cry to his Mother and retreat into a state that looks as much like a defensive trance as a mystical state. For Ramakrishna, the goddess is a consoling Mother who protects her child from the adult dangers of sexuality and not, as for the Hero, a Lover who grants the striving aspirant the bliss of union.

"Testing the Senses"

THE BHAIRAVĪ, then, had a very difficult time trying to get Ramakrishna to perform the fifth M. Perhaps she failed altogether. She certainly was not the first to fail, and she probably was not the last. Many people living with Ramakrishna believed that the saint's madness stemmed from his sexual continence. Some prescribed oils and medicines, others aphrodisiacs. Some were even more forthright, suggesting "sleeping with a woman" as a cure. Ramakrishna did his best to resist all of these "cures." At some point, Datta tells us, Hriday took the young priest aside and talked to his cousin about the matter "in secret," but his mind could not be changed (JV[5], 26). Something had to be done. What followed was a whole series of sexual temptations, orchestrated by everyone from Hriday to the superiors of the temple to the Bhairavī. Datta records a number of these bawdy scenes for us in his *Jīvanavṛttānta* under the euphemistic heading, "Testing the Senses." Most of these "tests" seem to have been designed by Hriday, Mathur, and the Rani before the Bhairavī arrived. At least one of them, however, involved the participation of a Tantric group active around Dakshineshwar at that time. As such, it may represent yet another of the Bhairavī's attempts to break the will of her stubborn student, to push him beyond the three social bonds of "shame, disgust, and fear" to which he seems to have been so tightly bound.

Datta records the first scene as taking place well before the coming of the Bhairavī, during Ramakrishna's "practices in the Panchavati," or what Ramakrishna referred to as his practices "according to the Purāṇas." The scene is a short one. Hriday, Datta tells us, employed a middle-aged servant woman of the temple behind Ramakrishna's back to bring a young sexy woman to Ramakrishna's bedroom. Upon seeing her, Ramakrishna became very upset and scolded Hriday for his ploy. The plan failed.

In the next scene Hriday is scheming again. After talking his plan over with Mathur and the Rani, he sets out to try again, this time with the help of a certain Lachmibai, the owner of a brothel in a red-light district of Calcutta. Hriday takes Ramakrishna to the brothel, where Mathur is hiding. Datta, probably to set up what follows, tells us that at this time Ramakrishna wore almost no clothes. When he arrived at the brothel, the half-naked Ramakrishna saw that he was surrounded by a whole retinue of equally naked "fully developed" fifteen- and sixteen-year-old prostitutes, whose "beauty, shapeliness, and lovely eyes could disturb even the mind of a desireless castrated sage" (JV[5], 31). The scene, it seems, was more than Ramakrishna could take. Crying "O Ma so full of bliss! O Ma so full of bliss!" he fell into *samādhi*. The prostitutes became afraid, brought him back to consciousness, and begged his forgiveness. Mathur was extremely embarrassed by the whole incident and from then on became even more devoted to Ramakrishna. Poor Hriday had failed again, miserably.

But not everyone had the same reaction as Mathur. In the eyes of some, the brothel incident provoked not devotion but ridicule. People were genuinely troubled by Ramakrishna's behavior. Some went so far as to claim that the young priest was imperfect, that his "masculinity had been destroyed" (*puruṣatvahāni*) by a "nervous disease" (*snāyavīya rogavaśataḥ*). After all, he seemed incapable of "going to a woman." Unlike Datta and Mathur, they were not at all impressed. The Rani heard of these rumblings. Perhaps fearing that Ramakrishna's demise could only hurt her temple, she decided that yet another test was necessary. And so Datta quotes Ramakrishna as describing a third scene in which Mathur's wife sent two women to one of the bedrooms of Mathur's house, where Ramakrishna was resting (his bedroom was in Mathur's mansion). The two women entered the bedroom and grabbed Ramakrishna with intentions that Datta refuses to describe, "for the sake of courtesy" (JV[5], 36). Ramakrishna jumped up in dismay and then fell down unconscious. Once again, he awoke to find the women weeping for forgiveness as they held his feet in remorse. Ramakrishna, reverently addressing the two women as "Ma so full of bliss," quickly pulled his feet away. He had passed another test.

Datta records a final temptation scene, this one orchestrated by Vaishnavacharan, a local scholar and friend of the Bhairavī. Vaishnavacharan, who had clear connections with different Tantric sects in the area, especially the Kartābhajās,[65] took Ramakrishna to a place called Kachibagan, where a Tantric sect called the Navarasikas gathered. Upon arriving, a group of women immediately surrounded Ramakrishna and sat on the floor. Datta tells his readers that these women were not prostitutes, "but," he adds, "their way of life is of a kind so repugnant that I am unable to reveal it to the public" (JV[5], 37).[66] He will reveal a little, however, for he tells us that the group followed a Tantric form of Vaiṣṇava practice in which the women engaged in ritual intercourse with the men (LP 4.1.39). Datta records what happened that day in an obscure passage: "Having gotten the Paramahaṁsa, a certain young woman of the Navarasikas immediately stuck her big toe in her mouth. Then a second young woman acted out a very obscene gesture" (JV[5], 37). The sexual intentions implied in the first woman's act of sucking her big toe were no doubt as transparent then as they are now. For the Navarasikas, and probably for Ramakrishna as well, the meaning of the act was quite clear. For anyone who could not read the meaning of the first woman's oral act, the second woman added her own, much more literal gloss on the scene. The second woman, in other words, made explicit what was perhaps only implicit in the first woman's act. Together, the two women acted out the nature of Tantric symbolism with its constant use of the sexual and the "very obscene" behind almost every act and symbol. Whatever the two women intended by their symbolic (and not so symbolic) gestures, Ramakrishna did not like it. He scolded Vaishnavacharan for plotting against him and left. He had passed yet another test.

But had he? There are two traditional interpretations of Ramakrishna's reactions to the Kartābhajā community, which, if we take into account how much the saint knows about it and how often he speaks of it, he seems to have visited quite often. The first, coming out of what I have called the householder tradition, might be described as the Tantric view of the visits. Not surprisingly, it is recorded only in M's *Kathāmṛta*, a householder text. Such a Tantric reading sees Ramakrishna's refusal to engage the two women in some sort of sexual act as a sign of the saint's arrested development. According to this view, Ramakrishna did not pass any test. He failed to live up to a challenge and so proved that he was just a "beginner" (*pravartaka*). The fullest account of this interpretation occurs in the second volume of the *Kathāmṛta*. Ramakrishna is speaking:

> There is one opinion that holds that one should take a woman in one's mystical practice. Once someone took me into a group of Kartābhajā bitches. They all came and sat down near me. When I began to address them all as "Ma," they began to talk among themselves, "This one is just a beginner, he's still not aware of his own shortcomings." According to their view, the undeveloped state is called the beginner; after that comes the striver; and after that the perfect of the perfect.[67]
>
> A young woman sat down near *Vaishnavacharan*. At her asking, Vaishnavacharan said, "His is the nature of a little girl!"
>
> In the state of the Lover one quickly falls. *The state of the Child is the pure state.* (KA 2.89)[68]

The passage is consistent with the temptation scenes discussed above. As in the temptation scenes, Ramakrishna reacts to the implied sexual challenge of the women by attempting to desexualize them: he calls them "Ma." Unlike in the previous temptation scenes, however, here the women do not give up. They neither weep in remorse for their actions nor beg for forgiveness for their thoughts. Instead, they begin to "talk among themselves" about the unenlightened state of the man before them: "He's still not aware of his own shortcomings." In the eyes of these women, Ramakrishna is no enlightened saint. On the contrary, he is "just a beginner," unaware of his own arrested development on the path of the mystical and the erotic. Vaishnavacharan, no doubt agreeing with the women's reading, adds his own twist on things by noting Ramakrishna's famous effeminate nature and by hooking it up to the arrested development theme in an exclamation that could be read in a number of ways: "His is the nature of a little girl!" The passage ends with Ramakrishna rejecting the Kartābhajā challenge but then, "still not aware," ironically confirming the truth of that very challenge by reasserting his own preference for the pure state of the Child.

This unconscious defense that was so astutely identified by the women, or "bitches" as Ramakrishna liked to call them, is later picked up by Saradananda and the renouncer tradition and developed into a tortured reading of Ramakrishna's Tantric practices that, not unlike Ramakrishna himself, completely misses the whole point of Tantra and ignores both the intentions and genuine insights of the whispering women. In this "renouncer" reading of the event, exemplified in the writings of Saradananda, Ramakrishna's refusal to engage the Kartābhajā women is seen as a sign not of failure and arrested development but of renunciation and purity. Such a reading is possible because the renouncer tradition (incorrectly) sees Tantra not as a ritual inversion and transgression of the laws of purity aimed at an experience beyond all such categories, but as a mixture of "immoral ideas" and the "pure path" (LP 4.1.27). The renouncers, probably "still not aware," are thus bound by the very polarity that Tantra seeks to transcend.

Bizarrely, this same renouncer tradition takes up the Kartābhajā title of "the unbroken one" to describe such an eminently untantric state. For the Kartābhajās, the unbroken one must: "Be a cook, distribute the curry but don't touch the pot, make the frog dance in the snake's mouth but don't let the snake swallow it, bathe in the sea of nectar but don't get your hair wet" (LP 4.1.28). These are hardly images of renunciation and purity. Rather, they speak of spicy cooking, dancing frogs, and sensuous bathing. The pot, the snake's mouth, and the sea of nectar, moreover, can all function as sexual images, as can the talented frog. The unbroken one, in other words, is not a simple renouncer. Rather, he is someone who actively engages in the food and sex of Tantric ritual and comes out unburned, unswallowed, and dry. He wallows in impurity and conquers it like a striving Hero. He does not run from it like a Child. Ramakrishna may have been many things, but he most definitely was not such an unbroken one.

Ramakrishna's experiences with the Kartābhajā women, then, elicited two widely different interpretations. What I have called the householder tradition, peopled largely by Tāntrikas, saw in the event a simple failure and pointed to this failure as a sign of the saint's unconsciousness and immaturity: "His is the state of a little girl!" The other interpretation, advanced largely (but not exclusively) by Saradananda and his successors within the renouncer tradition, saw in Ramakrishna's protest and assumption of the child state more proof for the genuineness and purity of his renunciation. Ramakrishna had not failed to meet a challenge. He had passed a test. The two readings remain enshrined in the texts to this day, still in conflict, still unreconciled.

Finally, related to these numerous temptation scenes, there was Ramakrishna's secret vision of "the man of sin." In volume 3 of the *Kathāmṛta,* Ramakrishna describes it in this way:

> At the time of my *sādhana,* how many things I used to see while meditating! I was meditating under the bel tree when the man of sin came and began to show me different kinds

> of enticements. He took the form of an English soldier. Money, fame, sexual pleasure—all these different kinds of power [*śakti*] he wanted to give to me. I began to call to Ma. This is very secret talk. Ma showed herself, and I said: "O Ma, cut him in two!" I remember Ma's form, that world-bewitching form, the form of Krishnamayi! . . . and yet the world seemed to move by her glance! (KA 3.140–141)

Saradananda tells us that Ramakrishna meditated on this form "according to scriptural prescription" (LP 2.7.10), perhaps a reference to the *Mahānirvāṇa-Tantra* where a similar "man of sin" is described in some detail. The presence of the bel tree also suggests Tantra, for it was "under the bel tree" that the saint practiced "according to the Tantras" (KA 4.175). The fact that Ramakrishna saw the man of sin in the form of an English soldier is interesting, not only because of its implicit connection between the English and evil, but also because of its homosexual dimensions (a male is offering Ramakrishna "sexual pleasure"). Once again, one can see Ramakrishna confronted with his homoerotic desires and, once again, one can see him invoke Kālī's sword to resolve the crisis. Krishnamayi was the daughter of one of Ramakrishna's householder disciples. Kālī thus appeared as a little frail girl to slay the mighty English soldier. Here one can see the beginning of Kālī's political life. Soon after Ramakrishna, she will be wedded to the militant causes of Bengal's political insurgents, who will see in her violence a religious justification for their own terrorist tactics. All of this, of course, is not present in Ramakrishna's vision, but one can see its beginnings in the little girl who slays the English soldier. To sum up, we might say that dimensions that are moral (the man of sin), homosexual (the English soldier offers sex), familial (Kālī appears as the daughter of a disciple), and political (Kālī slays the English soldier) are all woven tightly together in this secret vision. It is a vision, moreover, that is experienced in the present but whose roots sink deeply into Ramakrishna's past and whose images will be taken up by the culture for new "revolutionary" purposes. Past, present, and future all meet in its symbolism.

Licking the Lotuses: The Cunnilingus Vision

IN THE END, the man of sin was cut in two, the temptation scenes all failed, and Ramakrishna consistently fell into a trance when he was pushed into ritual intercourse. The Bhairavī, it seems, failed to take Ramakrishna through the fifth M. But it is possible that she was successful in other, more roundabout ways. Another of Ramakrishna's secret visions might provide us with some clues about how she went about doing this. In volume 4, the saint relates the following secret talk:

> This is very secret talk! I saw a boy of twenty-three exactly like me, going up the subtle channel, erotically playing with the vagina-shaped lotuses with his tongue! First the Anus [*guhya*], then the Phallus, then the Navel, the four-petaled, the six-petaled, the ten-petaled—they were all drooping—now they became aroused! When he got to the heart—I remember it well—after he made love to it with his tongue, the drooping twelve-petaled lotus became aroused—and blossomed forth! After that, the sixteen-petaled lotus in the throat and the two-petaled lotus in the forehead [became aroused]. Finally, the thousand-petaled lotus blossomed forth! *Ever since then I have been in this state.* (KA 4.238)[69]

From the fact that Ramakrishna appeared as "a boy of twenty-three," I conclude that the vision occurred when Ramakrishna was in his early twenties, that is, about the same time he was practicing under the Bhairavī. That the Ramakrishna-*homunculus* is using his tongue and not his penis to arouse the lotuses is particularly striking. While acts of sexual intercourse, both actual and symbolic, are quite common in the history of mystical literature, cunnilingus is extremely rare. How are we to account for it showing up here? Granted, the fact that Ramakrishna was horrified at the thought of actual intercourse, indeed, that he seemed incapable of it (his penis was said to pull back up into its sheath, like the limbs of a tortoise, at the touch of a sexy woman [LP 4.APP]),[70] goes a long way in explaining Ramakrishna's preference for visionary cunnilingus over intercourse. But not far enough. After all, despite his secret vision in which he saw God dwelling in the vagina of a bitch in the heat of intercourse,[71] Ramakrishna once compared men attached to lover-and-gold to the jackals and dogs who "wet their faces" in their mates' behinds (KA 5.215),[72] not a particularly positive assessment of oral contact with the vagina.

And where would he have gotten the image of himself licking vagina-shaped (*yonirūpa*) lotuses? The association between the vagina and flowers is common enough in Indian culture. The *Kālī Tantra*, for example, secretly[73] refers to the woman's menstrual fluids as "the woman's flower" (KT 3.1) and describes a menstruating woman as "the flowered one." In the absence of an actual vagina, the *Bṛhadyonitantra* counsels the practitioner to worship the *aparājitā* flower instead, since it possesses "the shape of the vagina" (*yonirūpa*).[74] The *Yonitantra* likewise prescribes a ritual anointment of the "cave of the vagina" with sandal-paste so that it might look like a "seductive flower" (YT 1.15).[75] The *Kathāmṛta* is just as rich in symbolic equations between the vagina and flowers.[76] In it, Ramakrishna compares the Kartābhajā practice of *coitus reservatus* with the bee who sits on the flower without sipping the honey. Other figures in the text are more explicit. A Tāntrika, for example, one day visited Ramakrishna and pointed out that the "stem" and "lotuses" of *kuṇḍalinī* yoga represents Śiva's phallus (*liṅgam*) and the goddess "in the form of a vagina" (*yonirūpa*) (KA 5.103),[77] establishing the very same symbolic equation that Ramakrishna's secret vision had established twenty-five years earlier. For the Tāntrika, the secret was evident, the latent was manifest. For Nikhilananda, on the other hand, such a meaning was *too* manifest. He thus omitted the Tāntrika's interpretation from his translation, concealing once again the secret that Ramakrishna had seen and the Tāntrika had revealed (GSR, 374).

It is likely, then, that Ramakrishna's vagina-shaped lotuses are of Tantric origin. But what about the act of licking or penetrating them? His stray comments that the Bhairavī "forced" him into "bizarre" rituals may be of significance here (KA 2.22).[78] Given that Ramakrishna invariably went into a trance every time he was placed in his ritual partner's lap, effectively making ritual intercourse redundant,[79] one could speculate that the Bhairavī attempted to engage her disciple in the fifth M through a ritualized form of cunnilingus or through the oral consumption of sexual fluids. The practice of licking the Bhairavī's vagina has been described in the ethnographic literature on Bengal,[80] and the ritual drinking of menstrual blood, sometimes mixed with wine (YT 2.24), is quite common in the Tantras and was known by Ramakrishna (KA 3.51). Although I am speculating here, I think that there is good reason to take such a possibility seriously. The type and number of adjectives used in the texts to describe (or refuse to describe) Ramakrishna's Tantric practices suggest as much: "horrific," "obscene," "improper," and "bizarre" all resonate quite well with Ramakrishna's jackals wetting their faces in their mates' disgusting behinds.

One also could speculate that Ramakrishna's tongue has something to do with the "cosmic vagina" (*brahmayoni*), "lolling" like Kālī's tongue, that Ramakrishna saw under the banyan tree in one of his secret visions (KA 4.232). The shape of the tongue and the vagina seem to be homologized here in their common act of lolling. Another lolling tongue, this time of fire, once came out of Ramakrishna in a vision and tasted all things—feces, urine, cooked food—with its fiery licks, proving for Ramakrishna that "everything is one, undivided" (KA 3.46). The tongue, then, associated in Ramakrishna's visions with oral sex, with tongue-like lolling vaginas, and with the basic unity and purity of all things, is an eminently Tantric organ, establishing by what it does (ritual sex is an integral part of Tantric practice), by its shape (the vagina is worshiped in Tantric ritual), and by what it tastes (otherwise unlawful substances are consumed in Tantric ritual) that "everything is one, undivided," even something as impure and defiled as that "place of disgust," the vagina (KA 3.51). By licking lotuses shaped like vaginas, the Ramakrishna-*homunculus* thus establishes a basic Tantric dictum: *everything* is pure.

Whatever the origin of the vision's material, one thing is unmistakably clear: the experience that Ramakrishna identified as the beginning of his more or less permanent mystical state was an experience symbolically loaded with erotic connotations: the Ramakrishna-*homunculus* was not "communing" with innocent lotuses, as Nikhilananda would have us believe (GSR, 830),[81] but engaging in a mystical form of oral sex, arousing vagina-shaped lotuses into ecstatic blossoms with a playful Tantric tongue. The secret vision thus accomplishes in its obscene, if still symbolic, form what Ramakrishna could not accomplish in his Tantric practices with the Bhairavī, namely, the breaking of the bonds of "shame, disgust, and fear" and the transcendence of society's notions regarding purity that they represent. The unconscious vision was necessary because Ramakrishna could not consciously make it through the Five M's. Indeed, the only M he seems to have truly conquered was *matsya* or fish, but this was the very M his culture had accepted already as a legitimate food. This victory, in other words, was not much of a victory. He did consume a piece of "rotten flesh," fulfilling the first M, *maṁsa* or "meat," but every other M gave Ramakrishna serious problems. *Madya* or "wine" and *maithuna* or "sexual intercourse" were particularly difficult for him. He simply could not bring himself to drink wine and could only fall into trances when presented with the challenge of the fifth and most important M, sexual intercourse. Moreover, when these two M's were combined—for example, in the ritual of drinking wine mixed with menstrual blood—the saint showed only ridicule and disgust. Ramakrishna, in other words, was a failed Tāntrika. But only in his external life with the Bhairavī. In his inner life, in his secret visions, he conquered like a true Tantric Hero that which he so feared and hated in his waking life. True, it was an unconscious victory, one accomplished quite despite Ramakrishna himself, but it was a victory nonetheless. Ramakrishna, it seems, was an unwilling, unconscious Tāntrika, profoundly uncomfortable in his Tantric world. This is why his unconscious visions are filled with Tantric images. This is why his secret talk vibrates with a nervous stutter and ends in excited exclamation points. This is one of the meanings of what I have called Ramakrishna's secret.

The Hero and the Child

One of the ways in which Ramakrishna dealt with his troublingly Tantric self was by splitting it into two separate identities, that of the Hero and that of the Child. He then could consciously identify with the safer half, with the Child, and reject the darker heroic half as illegitimate and dangerous. But however much Ramakrishna sought to distinguish these two roles in his life and teachings, they remained profoundly related in their symbolic and psychological natures, for each was defined by how it related to the same goddess. "The goddess as Primordial Power must be worshiped," Ramakrishna taught, "She must be pleased" (KA 5.140). Since she takes the form of women,[82] she must be pleased as a woman, either as a Mother or as a Lover. The Child pleases her with the gifts of childlike surrender, devotion, and purity, thus Ramakrishna referred to this identity as "the state relating to the Mother" (*mātṛ-bhāva*) or simply as "the child state" (*santāna-bhāva*). The Hero, on the other hand, pleases her with "sexual pleasure" (*ramaṇa*).[83] Ramakrishna referred to this identity as "the state of the Hero" (*vīra-bhāva*). Since Ramakrishna often defined the Child by contrasting it with the Hero, and vice versa,[84] it is difficult, if not impossible, to separate these two identities artificially. In reality, since both states are defined in a symbolic world informed by the same Tantric principles, the Child is related to the Hero whether he knows it or not.

The Hero: Faithful or Fallen Husband

For Ramakrishna, the Tantric Hero is associated with a particular stage in the Hindu life cycle, that of the householder. It is thus as much a social or psychological category as a religious one. It certainly is not a sectarian notion. Like Tantra itself, the Hero transcends sectarian religious boundaries in Bengal: there are heroic states among the Vaiṣṇavas, the Śāktas, and the Bauls, Ramakrishna pointed out (KA 5.105). As a householder, the Hero is the husband who takes the goddess in the form of a woman in order to cut the bonds of illusion (KA 3.24). Almost all of Ramakrishna's references to the Hero, then, imply the married state and the family. It is a religious identity intimately bound up with the complexities of social involvement, financial gain, and mature human sexuality. He is a man deeply involved in both the family and the world, two virtually synonymous realities carried by a single word, *saṁsāra*.

"If the Bhairava and the Bhairavī are husband and wife," Ramakrishna teaches, "this path is very honorable" (KA 2.143). But is it? In another passage, the saint reverses himself and describes the Hero who enjoys both worldly pleasure (*bhoga*) and mystical experience (*yoga*)—the stated goal of Tantric discipline—as a virtual demon. Such a Hero shares the nature of Rāvaṇa, who took both demonic and heavenly women for his pleasure (KA 2.199). So for Ramakrishna, sex, even legitimized by marriage, is still sex, a demonic, duplicitous sort of thing. It almost always leads to a fall.[85] The Hero's marital path is "very difficult,"[86] "hard" (KA 5.105), "dirty," and "dangerous" (KA 2.143). Like the gradual slope one travels on the way to the Calcutta Memorial, the worldly man's path is a slippery slope down which he unknowingly slides to his ultimate demise (KA 2.61–62). Accordingly, Ramakrishna counsels the married man to move beyond his animal-like existence (*paśu-bhāva*) and arrive at that "divine-state" (*divya-bhāva*) in which sex is transcended. Here other men's wives are treated "like one's own mother" and one's own wife becomes a friendly companion or a sister[87] on the path of religion and right conduct.[88] The Hero's *sādhana* ends when he can live with his sexy spouse and yet refrain from sex (KA 4.134). Now the husband only talks to his wife about God.[89] Religious discourse has replaced sexual intercourse.

Or so it is supposed to go. The actual state of affairs was much different, and Ramakrishna knew it. After all, it was the Paramahaṁsa himself who prayed to the goddess as both the wife of the family and the prostitute of the brothel: "O Ma! . . . You are the wife of the household, and you are the prostitute of the red-light district. O Ma! In both of these forms you are my Mother. I am your son" (JV[5], 36). Kālī seems to have listened closely to this prayer, for she appeared to the saint as a prostitute as often as a mother. In both his visions and his public discourse, then, Ramakrishna knew that Kālī's forces could not be domesticated. He knew perfectly well that her infamous children, the flesh-and-blood Tāntrikas of the neighborhood, cared little for his moralizing agendas.

And it bothered him. When asked about the local Tantric sects (he seemed to be the right person to ask), Ramakrishna often would change the subject by dancing and singing: "He did not reply to that," M tells us (KA 2.141). Sometimes he was more aggressive, ridiculing and making fun of their Tantric views and practices. Ironically, such criticisms and attacks often betray an impressive and unexplained familiarity with things Tantric. They engage in sinful pleasures in the name of religion, he would growl (KA 2.141–142). To back up his claims, Ramakrishna often would talk about the village women and their male ritual partners, their "passionate Kṛṣṇas" (*rāgakṛṣṇa*). "Have you attained [a] Kṛṣṇa?" their guru would ask them. "Yes, I have attained," they would answer, uniting religious achievement and sexual pleasure in a single ambivalent phrase (KA 4.164). Ramakrishna related how one such woman became scandalously pregnant by means of such passion (KA 3.52). We also are told that another Tāntrika, this time a local man whom M refuses to identify, was engaging in secret relations with his brother's wife, performing the Five M's "under the guise of religion" (KA 3.50).[90] Instead of succumbing to such temptations, the true Hero should curse the "naughty woman" for trying to destroy his ideals: "I'll cleave your body in two, you bitch!" he should yell (KA 3.86). In a more playful note, the saint referred to the Tāntrika's forehead ritual mark as proof that he was notoriously "branded" (KA 1.134). Such "thieves" do not listen to religious aphorisms, he quipped with a grin (KA 3.52).

The childlike Paramahaṁsa was particularly upset with Achalananda,[91] yet another Tāntrika whom he seems to have known quite well. Besides the fact that the man drank too much, Ramakrishna was particularly upset with him for not supporting his children and for engaging in weird rituals in order to win a lawsuit. It was Achalananda who claimed to have drank wine mixed with menstrual blood (KA 3.51). For his part, Achalananda responded to Ramakrishna's attacks by noting that his behavior was legitimated by Śiva himself: "Why don't you accept the practices of the Hero who takes a woman? Don't you honor the writings of Śiva? Śiva wrote the Tantras. In them are all the different states, including the state of the Hero." Ramakrishna had no answer for Achalananda. He could only frankly confess: "Who knows, Sir, why I don't like all these things—my state is that of a Child" (KA 3.50). Here we should take the Paramahaṁsa at his word. He simply did not know. As the whispering Kartābhajā women saw, he was "unaware," unconscious of the forces that defined his childlike demeanor.

"Every Woman's Vagina Is Mother's Vagina"

Even when Ramakrishna looked like a Hero, he remained in fact a Child. Consider, for example, the famous scene that is said to have ended Ramakrishna's *sādhana* period, his worship of his wife as the goddess.[92] There are few scenes in Ramakrishna's life over which the texts are as conflicted as they are concerning this "worship of the sixteen-year-old girl" (*ṣoḍaśī-pūjā*). The *Jīvanavṛttānta* and the *Līlāprasaṅga* are particularly at odds. Whereas the *Jīvanavṛttānta* sees the scene as an emotionally tragic and yet theologically profound event that elicited outrage and sorrow in little Sharada's village household, the *Līlāprasaṅga* sees it as the dramatic conclusion of Ramakrishna's one-year "test" of his sexual control and his Vedantic realization that gender is illusory! The *Līlāprasaṅga* version[93] is by far the more famous of the two (as far as I can tell, Datta's version is virtually unknown). I will treat it first.

According to Saradananda, Sharada became an object of pity and contempt in her village for being married to a madman. Sometime in 1872 she decided to visit her husband and see for herself if the words of her tormentors were true. When she and her father finally arrived (they had to walk the entire distance), Sharada was carrying a fever. Ramakrishna put her up in his own room instead of his mother's, "since the cold might make the fever worse," and then, when she got well, moved her back into the chilly music tower with his elderly mother.[94] He nevertheless gave her permission to sleep with him at night (LP 2.20.12). This went on for eight months[95] as Ramakrishna "tested" himself before his sleeping spouse and fell continuously into the depths of ecstatic states. When these death-like conditions finally got to poor Sharada and began to interrupt the nocturnal slumber of the temple (Sharada would wake Hriday to help bring her husband back), Ramakrishna moved Sharada back into the music tower with his mother (LP 2.20.21). Once again, ecstasy and seeming unconsciousness had saved him from the Lover.

According to Saradananda, after all of these "tests" and fears, the saint was finally convinced that he had reached the "divine state" (*divya-bhāva*)—a technical term in Tantra for the transcendence of carnal desire—and decided, under the influence of the goddess, to worship Sharada as the goddess herself (LP 2.20.17). Accordingly, on a night sacred to the goddess, he had the proper preparations gathered together in his own room, invited his young wife, sat her on the sacred seat, and began to worship her in a half-conscious state. She too soon entered an altered state of consciousness. Deep in the night both of them were "united" (*milita*) and "made one" (*ekībhūta*) in a common ecstasy (LP 2.20.20). According to Saradananda, this worship of the goddess in the body of a woman was the culmination of the Master's *sādhana*. His worship of the divine had now received its final oblation. The fire that burned behind all of his strivings now ceased to rage (LP 2.21.1). At last, it was over.

For Saradananda this "test" was carried out to set an example of continence and control for the householder disciples. Of course, Ramakrishna knew that no disciple could ever match such a feat—"If I piss standing, you sons-of-a-bitches will do it spinning around"—but at least they could accomplish "one-sixteenth" of it (LP 3.4.21),[96] at least they could try and by their efforts bear children of strong memory and mind (LP 3.4.23). For Saradananda, Ramakrishna is thus the model householder, the ideal husband who enacted "a strange, never-before-seen play of love"[97] with his wife and yet never engaged, not even once, in that "wretched physical union."[98] By such austerities, this unique incarnation cast a radically new "mold" for married life.[99]

Datta's version of things is, to say the least, different. According to Datta, it was Ramakrishna who visited Sharada back in her village, not Sharada who visited Ramakrishna at the temple. Moreover, according to Datta, this "worship of the sixteen-year-old girl" was orchestrated by none other than Mathur,[100] who, having heard of Sharada's desire to see her husband, decided that it was time to send Ramakrishna to the village to worship his now sixteen-year-old wife "according to the Tantras." In the *Jīvanavṛttānta* account, then, Ramakrishna is not visited. He is sent, and sent with a mission conceived by another. He is not inspired by the goddess to perform the worship. He is commanded by his boss.

When Ramakrishna arrives in Sharada's village in Datta's text, neither his wife nor his mother-in-law recognize him. Sharada sees him first and runs back to her mother: "Ma, Look! Look! Some crazy man has come!" Eventually, when the mother realizes who the strange visitor is, she becomes hopeful. But the saint soon dashes all of these hopes with his worship of the sixteen-year-old girl. Sharada's mother, furious at Ramakrishna's interpretation of the act, hurls "bitter reproaches" at Ramakrishna, for he has "reversed" (*viparīta*) everything. Instead of addressing young Sharada as "wife" (*strī*), he makes her sit in the "place of the Mother" and worships her. "Seeing her daughter in such a pitiful state, how could a mother's heart be consoled?" Datta asks. Seeing everything destroyed for her daughter, everything seemed empty now to Sharada's mother. They may talk and chat, but "there was no relation between the daughter and the son-in-law." Sorrow would now be the mother's only companion. For her part, Sharada, still a naive sixteen-year-old virgin, innocent "in this subject," did not realize what was happening. But she would, Datta points out, for some day she would become the "mother" of thousands of sons and daughters, that is, she would become the Mother of Ramakrishna's disciples. Datta thus ends the tragic scene by finding in it theological meaning.[101]

The *Kathāmṛta* version of the event is much less developed. It does, however, add a more personal, psychological element to the scene, as if it were closer to Ramakrishna's own subjective experience of the event than either of the more distant and refined accounts of Saradananda and Datta. Certainly it knows nothing of the extravagant interpretations of Saradananda. We have already seen that the Ramakrishna of the *Kathāmṛta* understood his eight months of room sharing with Sharada as a trial and took on the female servant state to deal with it: "The two of us were Handmaids of the Mother!" (KA 2.154–155). The worship of the sixteen-year-old girl seems to have fulfilled a similar function. Toward the very end of the very last volume of the *Kathāmṛta*, Ramakrishna describes what it all meant to him:

> The Child is a very pure state. In the Tantras there is talk about the left-handed practice with a woman, but this is not good. It leads to a fall. *As long as there is pleasure, there is fear*[102]. . . . I performed the worship of the sixteen-year-old girl in the child state. I saw that her breasts were Mother's breasts, that her vagina was Mother's vagina.
>
> This is the child state—*the last word in mystical practice*—"You are my Mother, I am your son." This is the last word.[103]

Here the Child state takes its psychological form in front of Ramakrishna's wife and all that she represents. *It is born in fear.* Other passages speak of this same scared Child: "If I am alone and a woman enters the room, I become a boy and call her Ma" (KA 2.232).[104] Unlike the Tantric Hero, who engages the fear by entering the pleasures that woman as Lover represents, Ramakrishna the Child turns from it and seeks to go back to an earlier stage in the life cycle, when a woman's breasts signaled not sex but food, and even further back, when a woman's genitals, encompassing his fetal form, offered no threat. Such a passage suggests that Ramakrishna's child state, far from being an independent religious state free from any contact with the realities of the adult world, was in fact defined by its opposition to the identities of that very world, namely, the Hero and the husband.

Other passages in the *Kathāmṛta* flesh out this fear with numerous scattered observations and teachings that can be read as glosses on the worship scene. In one such passage, Ramakrishna describes a state in which one no longer looks at women "with a worldly eye" (KA 1.114). Now one's divine eye sees what women *really are*—forms of the divine Mother.[105] In such a state, one need not fear women (KA 1.73). Now one can worship them "as if they were mothers."[106] Women and fear go together for Ramakrishna, since fear is a result of gender and adult sexuality.[107]

In a slightly different vein, the saint spoke of the knowledge that *brahman* is everything,[108] a type of gnosis in which one realizes that the unqualified Godhead alone exists and all particular manifestations of it, like women, are illusory. They are not (KA 3.156). This too leads to a freedom from fear: how can one fear what does not exist? This "knowledge of *brahman*" made it possible for the saint to deal with people he otherwise could not tolerate. Now armed with this knowledge, for example, he can bear the company of worldly men, those "crow-pecked mangos" and "bony fish" who are unfit to be offered to God (KA 3.176). In a particularly striking passage that may stem back to his worship of his own sixteen-year-old wife, Ramakrishna explains how such knowledge enabled him to worship a "shitting, pissing girl" and still see the pure goddess in her (KA 2.97).[109] Finally, in yet another passage, the saint explains how this same knowledge of *brahman* enables him not to "hate" (*ghṛṇā*) women. With such knowledge he sees that God has become everything and that "every vagina is Mother's vagina" (KA 2.200).

With his worship of the sixteen-year-old girl, then, Ramakrishna sought to transform his young wife, whom he feared, into his divine Mother, whom he worshiped. More specifically, he sought to transform the sexual organ of the Lover into the maternal womb of the Mother. By so doing, he changed the Tantric dictum, "Abandoning the mother's vagina, one should delight in every other vagina,"[110] into its exact opposite: "Every woman's vagina is Mother's vagina." He thus reversed the Tantric tradition, standing it on its head.[111]

In the Womb, in the Lap, at the Breast

RAMAKRISHNA REJECTED the adult Hero in order to remain a Child. But what kind of Child? The saint's behavior and discourse travel back and forth along the Hindu life cycle: sometimes he is a boy (*bālya*), hiding his sweets from other children in the room (KA 4.2) and playing with flower petals (KA 2.236); sometimes he is an adolescent of twelve or thirteen (*paugaṇḍa*), joking with his boy disciples (KA 4.203); sometimes he is a bold teenager (*yuvā*), offering his teachings to all who will listen; and finally, at certain points in his actions and teachings he goes back to the very beginnings of the life cycle, to the womb, to the lap, and to the breast.

The womb appears only occasionally in Ramakrishna's discourse. In one such passage, Ramakrishna cites a Bengali proverb: *Garbhe chilām yoge chilām*, "When I was in the womb, I was in union." With birth, this union is severed and the newborn falls to the earth crying. In the infant's heart-rending wail (*Kāhā e! Kāhā e!*), Ramakrishna hears the tragedy of every birth: "*E kothāe elum?* Where have I come? I was meditating at the lotus feet of the Lord, and now I have come to this place again!" (KA 1.173).[112] For Ramakrishna, then, the womb is the locus of mystical union, and the fetus is in fact a yogī. But Ramakrishna was not after this fetal union. Unlike the newborn of his proverb, Ramakrishna delighted in the fact of being alive in the world. He did not seek to return to the womb. He did, however, seek to return to the breasts and to the lap. Kakar's description of the saint's child state is both eloquent and precise: "The unity then Ramakrishna aimed for is not the merger-like states of the infant at the breast, though these too prefigured his trances, but the ending of separation striven for by the toddler. It is a state in which both mother and child have boundaries in relation to each other while another boundary encloses their 'double unity' from the rest of the world. Here the enjoyment of the mother's presence is deeply sensuous, almost ecstatic, and informs Ramakrishna's selection of words, images and metaphors that describe his experiences."[113] Let us look briefly at some of these words, images, and metaphors.

Breasts are common in Ramakrishna's *kathā* or "talk." For example, he liked to tell the story about the young renouncer who was so innocent of sexuality that he mistook a visiting woman's breasts for huge sores (KA 4.143). But this was only a story. For his part, Ramakrishna knew very well what a woman's breasts were for: food and sex. On the Mother, they provided food. On the Lover, they offered the promise of sex. But as we have seen already, Ramakrishna rejected the Lover and insisted instead on approaching every woman as Mother: "I saw that her breasts were Mother's breasts." Consequently, when his discourse concentrates on woman as Lover, he ridicules their breasts as embodied symbols of excessive lust. They are a "bad sign." And he frankly confesses that he is terrified of women, that they remind him of female demons with their huge vaginal and mammary "holes" (*chidra*) (KA 4.201).[114]

In stark contrast, when he speaks of woman as Mother, his images of breasts become warm, loving, and nostalgic. For Ramakrishna, the infant at the mother's breast experiences "only bliss" (KA 2.35). It laughs and plays as it sucks. It experiences sheer delight. Ramakrishna often contrasts this bliss at the breast with social and intellectual activity. In numerous places, for example, Ramakrishna slams his disciples' desires to build "hospitals and dispensaries"[115] and found communities[116] as so many pacifiers (i.e., fake breasts), mere distractions that offer no real nourishment or joy. The toys and dolls of society are fine until the Child becomes really hungry, throws down its pacifier, and begins to cry. Then such ephemeral concerns lose all their importance. "I'll go to Ma," the Child finally says (KA 5.35). In a similar vein, Ramakrishna's metaphors equate "analytic reason" (*vicāra*) with the Child's cry. When the Mother comes and offers her breasts, that too will stop (KA 2.35). Unlike the Mother's breast, reason is "dry" (*śuṣka*) (KA 5.131).

The lap also functions significantly in Ramakrishna's discourse, and it too is "split" by the Paramahaṁsa into the Mother and the Lover. As with her breasts, the lap of the Lover is consistently rejected, both in Ramakrishna's Tantric rituals and, later, in his teachings and metaphors. The young priest, as we have seen already, simply could not approach this "seat of bliss" (KA 5.25) without becoming unconscious. As a Tantric reality, the Lover's lap was a "place of disgust" (KA 3.51) that sent the saint into ecstatic retreat. And when it did appear in his visions, it purified itself by appearing as the beautiful lotus (KA 4.238), that pure flower to which even water cannot stick.

The Mother's lap, on the other hand, is a place of refuge, a place to which one flees from the world: "In childhood one fears the world. One only thinks of how to get close to Ma" (KA 2.21). For Ramakrishna, this maternal intimacy is likened to the attainment of God. Unlike that "place of disgust," then, this lap is a place of "affectionate love" and protection. Trailokya, a friend of Ramakrishna, sings of this lap of refuge: "I've hidden myself in your lap, O Ma, and I'll stay there. Keep me.

Hold me to your breasts. With affectionate love, hide me under your skirt, O Ma!" (KA 3.65).

Ramakrishna, then, sought to return, at least symbolically, to the lap and to the breasts, and sometimes, to the womb. But only to the *Mother's* lap, to the *Mother's* breasts, and to the *Mother's* womb. Each of these feminine organs, so deeply informed by maternal and sexual qualities, were profoundly ambivalent realities for the saint. To deal with them he first had to split them into their motherly and sexual forms and then reject the sexual for the motherly. He could thus effectively transform the dangerous and threatening Lover into the consoling and nourishing Mother: "I saw that her breasts were Mother's breasts, that her vagina was Mother's vagina."

The Paradoxical Child: The Worldly Family and the Sexual Mother

THE PRESOCIAL DIMENSIONS of Ramakrishna's metaphors should not be read as proof of some simple regression. The texts are much more complicated than that. In the saint's mind, the issue was not who was acting like a child or an infant. Everyone was. After all, the scholars and the social workers had their own dolls and pacifiers. The issue rather was who had the *real* breasts. Ramakrishna was convinced that social and intellectual activity are nothing more than painted red pacifiers, paltry imitations of the real thing. The issue, then, was not who was regressing but how to evaluate the social in relation to the mystical. Is the divine reality known in mystical experience socialized? Or does it transcend and precede the socialization process? Ramakrishna's stance is clear: the mystical precedes and transcends society. Society, in all of its familial, sexual, financial, and professional complexities, distorts what was once a pristine, perfectly plastic nature. The socialization process is seen as a tragedy, a "souring" of the milk of the mystical Child. As a result of this basic rejection of normal human development, many of Ramakrishna's metaphors for the mystical life and for God himself[117] draw on the years of infancy and early childhood, that short span of time just before the social process takes its all too heavy toll.

There are, however, at least two paradoxes involved in Ramakrishna's insistence on the presocial nature of the Child's mystical condition. Both involve the family. One deals with its social dynamics, the other with its sexual dimensions.

Socially speaking, the child, despite its relatively unconditioned nature, is nevertheless a social being that thrives, indeed exists, only within particular human relationships. A child, after all, in turn implies a mother, a father, and the whole social, sexual, and economic network that the saint so feared. Ramakrishna the Child may have rejected the householder's life as too scary, dangerous, and dirty, but the emotional tone of his language, metaphors, and mystical states all implied the householder's family life. In short, the symbolic and emotional structure of Ramakrishna's religious world implicated the very social order that the saint tried so hard to renounce.[118] This is the first paradox of Ramakrishna's child state, what we might call its social dimension.

The second paradox of Ramakrishna's child state involves a particularly controversial, but nevertheless persistent, theme in studies of Indian child-rearing practices: the sexually aggressive mother.[119] As we have seen, Ramakrishna believed that by becoming a Child he could render the goddess harmless. But because the goddess did not always cooperate, Ramakrishna the Child had to resort to other means of coercion. No longer able to win her over with childlike love and devotion, he sometimes had to embarrass her: "My state is that of the Child. When the goddess of illusion sees this state, she becomes embarrassed and steps aside to let one pass" (KA 5.105).[120] Perhaps the saint was referring here to the numerous times he successfully embarrassed prostitutes and potential lovers by shouting "Ma! Ma!" and falling into unconscious states. The prostitutes, once embodiments of the goddess of illusion (i.e., the Lover), found themselves transformed into mothers, and as mothers they could only be ashamed of trying to seduce their own child. They could only "step aside." But whatever the biographical roots of this passage might be, it clearly hints at another unresolved conflict in Ramakrishna's child state, namely, the possibility that even the relationship between the Mother and the Child might become sexualized.

This troubling possibility seemed to be a particularly pressing issue in Ramakrishna's dealings with a number of local Vaiṣṇava women, who liked to take on "the mother state" of Yaśoda (Kṛṣṇa's mother) and approach the local boys as manifestations of Gopāla, the child Kṛṣṇa. Ramakrishna often warned his young disciples about these women: "Beware of the Gopāla state!" he would shout (KA 2.154). Haripad seemed particularly susceptible to their wiles:

> Haripad has fallen into the clutches of a bitch from the Ghoshpara sect. She won't let him go. She tells him to sit in her lap and then feeds him. And she calls this the Gopāla state! I've warned him many times about what is called the mother's state. From such maternal affection [*vātsalya*] comes deception [*tācchalya*]. Do you know what? If you are to attain

> the Lord, you have to stay very far away from *women. . . . They steal one's essence. . . .* The Gopāla state! Don't listen to all this stuff. Woman consumes the three worlds. Many women look at handsome boys, see that they look good, and set new traps of illusion. *This* is the Gopāla state! (KA 2.154) [121]

"Haripad and the boys know nothing," Ramakrishna complained (KA 4.164). They lie down in women's laps and eat from their hands. They just do not see the trick.

One could speculate about how Ramakrishna learned of such a trick. His boyhood experiences of the young village woman worshiping him as their divine lover, Kṛṣṇa, is suggestive but by no means conclusive. With the Bhairavī, who often fed the young saint in her lap, we are on firmer historical ground; her songs and tricks no doubt contributed to the saint's distrust of this Gopāla state. Certainly the Paramahaṁsa's general disgust with women, those eaters of the three worlds who steal a man's essence, was also a function of his frustrated efforts to turn the goddess, in the form of the Bhairavī and the Ghoshpara "bitches," into a pure and sexless Mother. We simply do not know how he fared with the village women. He may have succeeded with his wife. He most certainly failed with the Bhairavī and the women of Vaishnavacharan's group. It seems his boy disciples fared no better with the women of the local Tantric sects. The goddess was simply not embarrassed. Even as a Mother, she insisted on remaining a Lover.

A further irony of all this is that, despite all of his vociferous protests against the sexual mother, *Ramakrishna was himself an erotic Mother.* Ramakrishna, M tells his readers, was the very "image of motherly love for the devotees" (KA 4.178). M supplies us with numerous passages to justify such a description. "As if playing," Ramakrishna lays Rakhal's head in his lap, M notes with an exclamation point. He sees Gopāla in the boy (KA 2.47). In another scene, the saint, like a worried mother, counsels a sick Rakhal to eat lots of ice and warns him not to go out into the sun: "I will put you in my lap and feed you," he adds (KA 5.118). Again, the motherly Paramahaṁsa puts the boy in his lap and tries to nurse him with his strangely full breasts (KA 5.31). Looking at this same Rakhal, Ramakrishna often got goosebumps all over his body and fell into *samādhi* (KA 1.83).[122] This motherly state was a "strange" mood, M confesses as he uses the adjective three separate times (KA 1.83).

Whether as a Child or as a Mother, then, Ramakrishna found it impossible to desexualize the mother-child relationship. Just as he could not escape the social world, he could not escape the dangers of adult sexuality. The goddess incarnate in women, be she a prostitute, the Bhairavī, the Ghoshpara women, or Ramakrishna himself, was always manifesting herself as a Lover. Kālī's dual nature as Mother and Lover thus remained troublingly intact, despite the angry protests and impressive efforts of her most famous Child.

CLEAVING THE BITCH IN TWO

"THIS IS THE MEANING of Tantric ritual. The Mother is the Lover." Dr. Sarkar's insight, focused through the curved surface of my own cultural lenses, has functioned as the thesis of the present chapter. As I have tried to show, the symbolism of Ramakrishna's Tantric practices was formed, much to the dismay of Ramakrishna himself, around this Tantric understanding of the goddess as Mother and Lover. By rejecting this cultural synthesis of the feminine, Ramakrishna rejected Tantra and the existential situation that its symbolism implies, the life of the householder. If a man is to become a householder, that is, if he is to marry, procreate, and carry on the *dharma* of the social and religious orders, he must move beyond what Ramakrishna called the state of the Child. As a Tantric Hero, as a husband, he *must* unite the Mother and the Lover in the person of his wife. But Ramakrishna failed to do this. He could only see the Mother in his wife's breasts and genitals. From the perspective of the Tāntrika, then, the childlike Paramahaṁsa failed: he could not abandon his Mother's vagina and *viharet sarvayoniṣu,* "delight in all vaginas." On the contrary, he insisted, to the utter horror of those around him, that, since the goddess incarnates in every woman, sex with *any* woman is a "raping of the mother," an act of incest. "Every woman is my Mother," he taught. A whole series of arguments, temptation scenes, and Tantric rituals followed, all designed to free Ramakrishna of these mad notions and the impossible developmental quandaries into which their logic inevitably led. His family, his superiors, his Tantric guru, all tried their best to help him see with Dr. Sarkar that "the Mother is the Lover."

But they all failed. Ramakrishna the Child remained a child. As he had counselled his tempted disciples to do, the saint had successfully "cleaved" the goddess in two: "You bitch! You're going to ruin my ideals! I'll cleave your body in two!" (KA 3.86). In his own soul, the saint had split the goddess into a pure sexless Mother and a despised Lover bitch. For this profound act of violence toward the symbolic order, the social world, and women in general, the goddess, who is angered when any woman is despised or injured, took her revenge. She turned her own cleaving sword on the saint and split *him* in two. Now there were two Ramakrishnas: the public Child and the secret Hero. On the outside, in the external world, now all Ramakrishna would see was the goddess as a Mother: her breasts, her genitals, her pure and gentle form in every woman. But on the inside, in the depths of his own soul, now he would see the goddess as a Lover. Licking her lotus-like genitals, he would arouse the goddess's energies into a thousand-petaled excitement and ever-new blossoming forms. Licking her lotuses, he would become a great mystic, and eventually, a god: "The four-petaled, the six-petaled, the ten-petaled—they were all drooping—now they became aroused! . . . Finally, the thousand-petaled lotus blossomed forth! *Ever since then I have been in this state*" (KA 4.238).

CHAPTER THREE

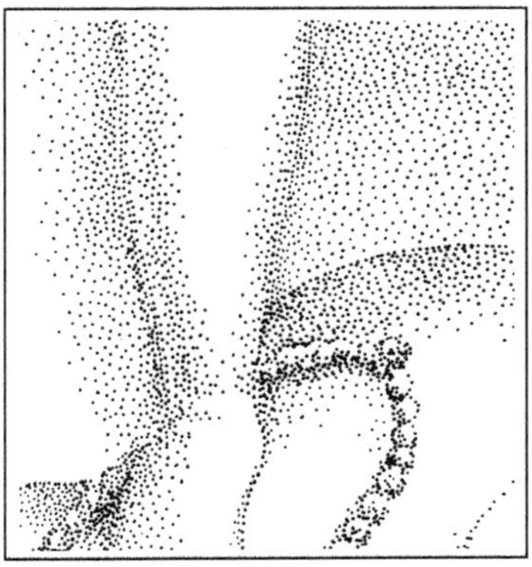

Kālī on Top of Śiva: Tantra and Vedānta in Ramakrishna's Teachings and Mystical Experiences

> She is immersed in sexual delight on top of her lover. He trembles
> as he tries to hold the weight of her feet.
> Both seem mad. They know no fear, they know no shame.
>
> *Kathāmṛta* 1.196

EARLY IN HIS LIFE, Ramakrishna turned Kālī's sword on himself in a crisis defined by his homoerotic tendencies. It was this initial crisis that led to the saint's first full-blown mystical experience, the famous First Vision in the ocean of light. In his early Tantric practices and later in his teachings about the Child and the Hero, Ramakrishna turned this same sword on the goddess herself and cleaved her form in two, splitting her into two separate identities. It was a radical, violent sort of cleaving, a clear cut down the middle. Henceforth, Ramakrishna's relations with women, those incarnations of the goddess, would be marked by a profound ambivalence: he would worship them as Mothers and fear them as Lovers. His emotions followed exactly along the cut of his symbolic sword.

In this chapter, we will see Ramakrishna take up his sword once again to cut the goddess in two, this time in order to realize the truths of Vedānta in the last months of his mystical practices. Since Vedānta relegates the phenomenal world of *śakti* to the level of a pure illusion, it was necessary that Ramakrishna transcend the goddess and her form in order to practice Vedānta with the monk Tota Puri. But he could not.

As much as he tried to empty his mind of all forms and thoughts, the goddess's form kept appearing to him, floating in his psychic sky to challenge the legitimacy of Vedānta's attempt to split human experience asunder. As long as she appeared, the saint could not practice the foreign path. He could not deny the goddess and her energetic world. And so to practice Vedānta, Ramakrishna had to take up his sword and cleave the goddess in two. He had to split his world yet again, this time into an unreal illusion (*māyā*) and a real Absolute (*brahman*): "Then again, determined, I sat down to meditate, and just as the blessed form of the Mother of the Universe rose up in the mind as before, I imagined that gnosis was a sword and with it cut this form in two in the mind. Then no kind of distorting functions remained in the mind; all at once it rose blazing above the realm of all name and form, and I merged in *samādhi*" (LP 2.15.17). This, according to most traditional interpreters, was the pinnacle of Ramakrishna's religious life, the final goal.

But if this was the goal, it was a goal that the saint rejected, for *this* splitting of the goddess would prove to be only a fleeting experiment, and an experiment with a half-truth at that. For although the goddess indeed remained split in the saint's emotional and personal life—Ramakrishna would shun the Lover until the very end—she remained quite whole in his metaphysical teachings, for those teachings preserved the dialectic that defined the goddess and her erotic union with Śiva, the Absolute. In his ontological understanding of the world, if not in his emotional and moral counsels, the goddess remained united to Śiva. Consequently, after Ramakrishna's brief experience of Vedānta's formless *samādhi*, the young saint returned to teach his Vedantic guru the truth of *śakti*. *Brahman* and *śakti* cannot be separated, the Paramahaṁsa taught his teacher, for they are "nondifferent" (*abheda*). The world of name and form cannot be separated from the Absolute. It cannot be cut in two for the sake of the formless. In more abstract terms, he would later teach his disciples that there is always a both-and, a dialectic beyond the one and the two of a simple monism or dualism. Moreover, within this dialectic, the goddess of the Many always is given preference over the god of the One. Psychologically speaking, she is always more important. Thus she stands atop the quiescent Śiva, that silent Absolute of Vedānta. In the end, her truths are more ultimate, more psychologically true, more mystically satisfying than those of Śiva's Vedānta. It is she who erotically dominates the god. It is this dialectic and this erotic dominance of the goddess over the god that will focus the present chapter.

WHY IS KĀLĪ ON TOP OF ŚIVA?

TO BEGIN I want to concentrate on a single Bengali commentary on the *Kālī Tantra,* that of Nityananda Smrititirtha. In the course of Nityananda's discussion on the first chapter of the Tantra, he quotes another Tantra in order to ask a common question regarding the iconography of Kālī: "Why is Kālī standing on a corpse?" As this question will concern us in one way or another for the rest of this study, it is important that we have some idea, not only of the different ways that the question has been answered in India, but also of why it is asked at all. It is a question, after all, that often arises from a feeling of horror or embarrassment. Kālī's form, in other words, is not just a *question* for the art historian and the curious. It is also a *problem* for the faithful. This present chapter will concern itself more with the question and the different ways it has been answered in India. Chapters 4 and 5, on the other hand, will concern themselves with the indigenous questioning of the question, with the *problem* of Kālī on top of Śiva and what amounts to an offended rejection of the image itself as shameful or embarrassing. Chapter 3, in other words, is about why Kālī is on top of Śiva, while chapter 4 and especially chapter 5 will be about why Kālī should *not* be on top of Śiva. But here I am getting ahead of myself. In this present section, I will treat some of the more traditional answers to our question under three broad categories or genres—myth, philosophy, and ritual.

The Early Myths: To Destroy the World and Conquer the Demons

NITYANANDA, WHO FIRST ASKED our question for us, begins to address the issue by advancing one of the most common and most ancient answers: Kālī is standing on Śiva to destroy the world. To prove his point, the commentator quotes the *Toṛala Tantra:* "O goddess! . . . when Śiva, the destroyer of the world, becomes Kālī in the form of destruction, then quickly, O goddess, the Eternal Śiva takes the form of a corpse, and at that moment the goddess stands on the corpse."[1] Śiva is commonly understood to be that aspect of the three-formed deity (*trimūrti*) that destroys the world. While Brahmā is the Creator and Viṣṇu the Preserver, Śiva is the Destroyer. Here Śiva becomes the goddess Kālī to fulfill his cosmic function. His destructive powers now embodied in the goddess, Śiva quickly becomes a corpse for Kālī to stand on. The precise meaning of this act is unclear, but it seems to have something to do with destruction and death, the original purpose of Kālī's creation. Śiva as Kālī stands on top of a corpse to destroy, to kill.

Our commentator identified the corpse beneath Kālī's feet as Śiva. But in some of the Śākta songs, the corpse is just a corpse, or a pile of corpses, a pile of slain demons killed in the cosmic battle.[2] Quoting such songs, Dasgupta speculates that the body below the goddess was originally simply a demon, a corpse (*śava*) pure and simple. At some point, however, with the help of a wordplay, this *śava* became Śiva. Kālī "mounted on a corpse" (*śavārūḍhā*) thus became Kālī "mounted on Śiva" (*śivārūḍhā*). Dasgupta sees hints of this history in one of Ramprasad's songs:

> It's not Śiva under Ma's feet. This is false, people say.
> A demon fellow fell to the ground, and Ma stood on him.
> At the touch of Ma's feet the body of the demon
> Took the form of Śiva on the battlefield.[3]

For Dasgupta, it is history as much as "the touch of Ma's feet" that has turned the demon corpse into a god.

Philosophical Roots: Sāṁkhya

DASGUPTA SPECULATES that the philosophical system called Sāṁkhya had something to do with this transformation of the *śava* into Śiva. Sāṁkhya is an ancient "philosophical vision" (*darśana*) in India that posited two distinct but related aspects of reality, an inactive transcendent male principle called *puruṣa* and an active immanent principle called *prakṛti*. According to Sāṁkhya, *prakṛti* constitutes the matter of the physical and mental worlds, everything that comes into the purview of our normal experience. *Puruṣa*, on the other hand, is transcendent, cut off from the conditionings of *prakṛti*. But despite this transcendence, this independence, it is only in the light of *puruṣa*'s witness-like gaze that *prakṛti* "dances the world dance."[4] So the two are related, and yet they are not. Unlike the *māyā* of classical Vedānta, the Sāṁkhya *prakṛti* truly exists. Reality is two. The stated goal of Sāṁkhya reflects this ultimate duality. Spiritual discipline consists of an attempt to split off the *puruṣa* from the workings of *prakṛti* and establish it in its own completely independent eternity or "separation" (*kaivalya*).

Tantra took this vision of things and adopted it for its own purposes. It acknowledged the twoness of reality and agreed that the phenomenal world truly exists. It also, again much like Sāṁkhya, identified the feminine principle as the active agent, the great Actress of the world, and asserted that the masculine principle was passive, an inactive Witness ultimately aloof from the workings of the world. Perhaps, as Dasgupta suggests, it was such borrowings that helped Tantra to imagine a wild Kālī poised on top of a slumbering (or dead) Śiva. But the borrowings stopped there, for Tantra differed from Sāṁkhya on the relationship between these two ontological genders. Rather than seeking to permanently split this twoness asunder for the sake of an eternal separation, Tantra instead sought to reunite it. For Tantra, a male spirit cut off from its feminine counterpart is no goal, no grand *kaivalya.* It is a corpse: "When he is joined to Śakti, he is in the form of Śiva. When he is without Śakti, he is a corpse."[5] In Tantra, Śiva is only completely himself when he is "joined to Śakti." The tradition thus seeks to arouse, to harness, to identify with this feminine energy until it climaxes in the erotic joys of mystical experience. For Sāṁkhya, the goal is separation. For Tantra, the goal is union. Clearly, Tantra borrowed from Sāṁkhya, but it did not follow it into separation and eternal transcendence.

Tantric Ritual: Reversed Sex in a Cremation Ground

WE HAVE SEEN our commentator advance two different interpretations of why Kālī is standing on Śiva: to destroy the world and the demons and to energize or enliven Śiva. One has its roots in ancient Indian mythology, the other in Sāṁkhya philosophy. Appropriately, both are backed up with long Sanskrit quotes from a Tantra. They are "up front," so to speak, both in the commentator's mind and in his text.

But another interpretation lurks in the background. The commentator takes it up and then hesitates. There are no long Sanskrit quotes here, just a quick phrase, a fleeting interpretation, and a parenthetical note that amounts to a concealment. It all begins with a very common phrase in the Tantras: "and she delights in reversed sexual intercourse with Śiva." The commentator is comfortable with the cosmogonic implications of such a symbolism: without the union of Śiva and Śakti, he tells us, the world would not exist. Their union creates the world. We are back to Sāṁkhya. He even acknowledges that for such an act they must both be "clothed with the sky," that is, naked. But as he feels himself too close to a Tantric abyss, he hesitates and resorts to parentheses: "(The special meaning of this [phrase] as advanced by the way of the Hero will not be mentioned here any more)."[6]

What is the commentator hiding? What is the Hero's "special meaning"? Here we might recall that in Tantric ritual the Hero employs sexual intercourse to unite with the goddess. By engaging in ritual intercourse with a woman, he seeks to recreate the iconographic archetype of the goddess united with Śiva. In imitation of the deities, moreover, he engages his partner in *reversed* sexual intercourse. This, no doubt, is the "special meaning" of Kālī's "standing" on Śiva in the way of the Hero. It is a ritual meaning, a ritual secret.

Often when this ritual secret is discussed in the Tantras and the commentaries, it is surrounded by secrecy and controversy. It occurs, again, for example, in verse 11 of the *Karpūrādistotram* to describe the male aspirant and his subordinate position beneath his female ritual partner. But the commentator again is uncomfortable with such a meaning and so changes the case and gender of the adjective "engaged in reversed sexual intercourse" (*viparītaḥ*) so that it refers not to the male aspirant but to the goddess (*viparītāṁ*) to whom he sings.[7] The commentator will not let the iconography be translated into ritual. He must keep it "out there" in the image. But even images can sometimes be dangerous. There is an oral tradition in Bengal, for example, that states that Kamalakanta Bhattacharya, the famous Śākta poet, used to sing to Kālī on his back, with the image perched on top of him.[8] Nothing is said of the nature of this peculiar position, but its ritual meaning is unmistakably clear. Here Kamalakanta is *viparītaḥ,* engaged in an upside down act of at least symbolic intercourse with the goddess. What the commentators and translators will not allow the devotees of the goddess embody anyway. The ritual precedents are just too strong, too convincing, and too fascinating to ignore.

To conclude, we might say that there are at least three traditional answers to why Kālī is standing on Śiva: to destroy the world, to complete and transform the ontological dialectic of Sāṁkhya, and to engage Śiva (and the Tāntrika) in reversed sexual intercourse. We might call these the mythological, the philosophical, and the ritual dimensions of the iconography. There are, of course, many other interpretations of the goddess on top of the god,[9] but these are the meanings that I want to concentrate on here; all three, at least, are evident and active in the life and teachings of Ramakrishna.

FROM THE PRACTICES ACCORDING TO THE VEDAS TO THE JESUS STATE, 1865–1868

IN CHAPTER 2 I dealt with the biographical details of Ramakrishna's life up to the end of his Tantric practices, completed sometime around the year 1865. Ramakrishna is now thirty. He has watched a father and a brother die. He has tempted death. He has been tempted by life. He has been put through a series of frightening, often bizarre rituals designed to free him from his tendency to retreat from the phenomenal world and its fearfully changing energies. These were the most crucial, most formative years of Ramakrishna's life. Although he would experience a great change in his later years, it would only bring to fruition the seeds planted in the darkness of these secret years. By the time Ramakrishna completed his Tantric practices with the Bhairavī, the basic structure of his religious world had been established. He was now a Child of the goddess. He was now Kālī's Child. This will become especially apparent when we come to these last events of his *sādhana* years, his Vedantic practices with Tota Puri, and see how Ramakrishna's love for the goddess and her dynamic world of duality and devotion cannot be shaken by the monk and his profound but boring *brahman*.

The Secret Years: The Practices according to the Vedas

When a naked monk arrived on the banks of Dakshineshwar and encountered the strange being that was Ramakrishna, he is said to have thought to himself in amazement, "Can there be one so fit to practice Vedānta in Tantric Bengal?" (LP 2.15.9). It was a question that would prove to be prophetic; in the end, it would have to be answered in the negative. Saradananda tells us that this monk's name was Tota Puri, that he was a member of the Naga sect from the Punjab (LP 3.8.23),[10] and that he was skilled in the arts of alchemy (LP 3.8.45). While others often referred to Tota as the Paramahaṁsa (a common title of a monk skilled in Vedānta), Ramakrishna simply called him Nyāṅṭā or "the Naked One," as he and his community wore no clothes as a sign of their complete renunciation of the world and its illusory coverings. Tota was a monk from childhood (LP 3.8.30) and so somewhat harsh and indifferent toward the sufferings of the common lot of men, bound by the ties of their families and worldly lives. Tota had a robust physique (LP 3.8.38). He was said to enjoy the *śānta bhāva* or "state of Peace" (LP 3.8.32). A firm believer in a formless Absolute devoid of duality, the monk often made fun of Ramakrishna's superstitious beliefs in the gods and goddesses of the Hindu pantheon. After watching Ramakrishna dance and sing and clap to the gods each morning, he would sarcastically ask the devout saint if he was kneading doughy chapatis (LP 3.8.33).[11] After he asked Ramakrishna if he would like to practice Vedānta and the saint responded by telling him that he first must go and ask his Mother, the monk assumed that his new pupil was going to ask his flesh-and-blood mother. When he learned that Ramakrishna had gone to ask the goddess's permission—more evidence that Ramakrishna's Vedānta was subordinated to his Tantra—the naked Vedāntin smiled in amused derision. It was a smirk that would soon be wiped off his face by the goddess herself.

After Ramakrishna received permission from the goddess to practice the foreign path, he made Tota promise that he would not tell Chandra (his mother) about the practices, since he feared that she would object to him taking *sannyāsa* or "renunciation" from the monk. The Bhairavī, it seems, also objected to her new competitor and tried to dissuade Ramakrishna from associating with the monk: "*Father! Don't listen to Vedānta!* It will destroy your devotion" (KA 4.240),[12] she warned. It was a warning that he ignored at the time but would later repeat, almost verbatim, to his own disciples.

After having finally satisfied, avoided, or simply ignored the three women of his life—the goddess, Chandra, and the Bhairavī—Ramakrishna finally sat down with the naked man in a small hut tucked away in the trees and began his Vedantic training. The Naked One began by commanding Ramakrishna to give up the unreal world "of name and form" (LP 2.15.16). But the young saint could not. The graceful form of his Mother kept appearing to him, floating in his psychic sky to challenge the command of the monk who had smirked at Ramakrishna's devotion. Finally, Tota took a piece of sharp glass and embedded it in Ramakrishna's forehead: "Concentrate here," he said. Once again the goddess appeared, but this time the saint imagined that his new-found knowledge was a sword and cut the goddess in two. At once his mind ascended past name and form and merged in the formless *brahman*. Within a mere three days,[13] he had attained what it took Tota forty years to accomplish. Not surprisingly, poor Tota was flabbergasted.

Now it was Tota's habit as a wandering renouncer not to stay more than a few days in any one place, but there was something here that attracted the monk. He would stay for eleven months. Unfortunately, like most of the figures of Ramakrishna's story, Tota was eventually downed by dysentery, an illness that Saradananda himself associates with the land of Bengal (LP 3.8.38). Used to dwelling in *samādhi*, now Tota could only wince in pain, all too conscious of his supposedly unreal body. Finally defeated by the condition, Tota attempted suicide one night by walking out into the middle of the bubbling river. But to his amazement, as far as he waded into the dark currents he found himself walking on a sandbar only waist-deep in water. Almost to the other shore, he was wondering how it was that he could not even kill himself when suddenly Tota's mind was dazzled by a great light and he saw: "Ma, Ma, O Ma, the Mother of the universe! Ma, whose form is unfathomable Energy! Ma in the water and Ma in the earth! . . . Everything I see, hear, think or imagine is Ma. . . . As long as one is in the body, if she does not will something, no one is capable of being free from her influence. No one can even die [without her consent]! . . . That One whom Tota has for so long been calling *brahman* and worshiping with heartfelt devotion and love is this very Ma! . . . *Brahman* and the *śakti* of *brahman* are nondifferent!" (LP 3.8.41). Now utterly convinced that the world of the goddess's *śakti* was not a pure illusion to be rejected as unreal, Tota went to Ramakrishna the next day to tell him about what happened the night before. Ramakrishna responded to the monk, who had smirked at his Mother and laughed at his clapping chapatis, with a much-relished "I told you so": "Didn't you not accept Ma before, arguing with me that *śakti* is false, fake? Well now you see that the arguments of your own eyes and ears have turned it all around" (LP 3.8.43). Having realized the (essentially Tantric) identity of *brahman* and *śakti*, Tota bowed his head to Kālī and took his leave (LP 3.3.31). He had found much more than a "fit aspirant for Vedānta" in this land so soaked with Tantra. He had discovered the truths of this Tantric land. He had realized that there is indeed a goddess standing on Śiva, so absorbed in the sleep of *samādhi*. He left a converted man.

But Tota's departure constituted much more than a victory for Ramakrishna. It was also a tragedy of immense proportions, for it was connected to the saint's falling into an unconscious state that would last some six months. Saradananda interprets this almost catatonic state—flies entered freely into his nostrils and ears, his hair grew matted, his bowels functioned uncontrolled, he had to be struck with a stick to rouse him for feedings—as the supreme example of *nirvikalpa samādhi*, that nondual state which is "beyond all states" (LP 2.15.2) and is the goal of all *sādhanas* (LP 2.15.1). Indeed, the saint's faithful biographer goes even further—not only was it *nirvikalpa samādhi*, it proved that Ramakrishna was an incarnation of God, since no mortal can survive such a state for more than twenty-one days and Ramakrishna came back after six full months! Only incarnations return from such an experience. Only they come back to fulfill their world-missions to teach new doctrines to a world hungry for their truths.

Others would differ with Saradananda's account. Jensen, for example, sees Ramakrishna's unconscious state as a reaction to yet another paternal loss.[14] Another male figure had "died," walked away into the sunset. Whatever one thinks of Jensen's theory, it is significant that Ramakrishna's six-month *samādhi* is explicitly connected to Tota's departure, something Saradananda has a hard time explaining. Certainly Jensen is not the only one to read the soul's desire to become absorbed into *brahman* as at least partially generated by an emotional loss. Ramakrishna himself often criticized Vedantic absorption with the very same insight, couched this time, not in the vocabulary of modern psychology, but in the rich and humorous narratives of Hindu mythology: "Before Kṛṣṇa went away to Mathura [to become king], he was about to give the knowledge of *brahman* [to the milkmaids]. He said, 'I am inside and outside of all creatures. Do you all see me in only one form?' The milkmaids responded immediately, 'O Kṛṣṇa, you are abandoning us. Is this why you say, "I am teaching you about the knowledge of *brahman*"'?" (KA 3.80–81). The power and beauty of emotional involvement on the mystical path and the consequent rejection of the loss and separation implied in Vedānta's formless *brahman* are constant themes in the teachings of Ramakrishna. It is possible that such convictions had deep biographical roots in events such as the saint's six-month *samādhi* after the departure of Tota Puri. Tota, after all, much like Kṛṣṇa, would end up ruling his own Mathura-like kingdom. He would become the leader of his monastic community back in northern India (LP 3.8.28). Poor Ramakrishna, the milkmaid, was left far behind with the cold consolations of a *brahman*-knowledge that looks, at least from the outside, as much like a death as it does a realization.

"Remain in Bhāvamukha"

FOR SARADANANDA, it was Ramakrishna's six-month *samādhi* consequent upon his teacher's departure that taught Ramakrishna that all religions lead to the same nondual goal and proved to the world that Ramakrishna was a true incarnation of God. Moreover, it was toward the end of this same six-month state that the saint allegedly heard the Mother's command to "Remain in *bhāvamukha*," a mysterious phrase that deserves careful consideration. Since the category of *bhāvamukha* is absolutely central to Saradananda's theological interpretations—it is perhaps *the* central hermeneutical principle of his biography—and has an interesting prehistory in the texts of Datta and Gupta, it is necessary that I interrupt Ramakrishna's story here and treat the history of this mysterious command.

The command is difficult, if not impossible, to place chronologically in Datta's text, but this, as I have pointed out, is a common feature of the *Jīvanavṛttānta*. Datta treats it in a section entitled "The Reassurance of Ma Kālī." Haladhari (Ramakrishna's cousin), Datta tells us, was especially fit to study the scriptures of Vedānta. Consequently, he was also in the habit of showing his disgust for the worship of forms and ridiculing, much like Tota, Ramakrishna's habit of dancing and singing for the deities. For Haladhari, all such things betrayed an ignorance of the formless nature of the Absolute. Haladhari tried especially hard to teach his cousin these truths and to convince him of his errors. The Paramahaṁsa, it seems, was becoming convinced:

> The Paramahaṁsa, hearing again and again from Haladhari about the wretchedness of his own state, one day entered his room and began to weep, crying "Ma! O Ma!" Just as Ramakrishna called out "Ma! O Ma!" the Primordial Power appeared before him in the form of Kālī. Obtaining a vision of the Mother, he said, "O Ma! Haladhari says that my brain has become bad and that whatever visions I see are the fault of my eyes, that they are only illusions. O Ma! Tell me the truth. What has happened to me?" Taking away his fear then and there, she said, "Remain as you are." With these words, the Mother disappeared. From then on, Ramakrishna listened to no one else or looked to any one else for support. (JV[5], 23–24)

The command to "Remain as you are" is the earliest textual variant of the more classical "Remain in *bhāvamukha.*" It lacks the technical term *bhāvamukha* but occurs in a context that we will see repeated in many of the later passages that do employ the term: it is invoked in response to a Vedantic challenge, and it assures Ramakrishna that his own truths are superior to those of his Vedantic challenger. "Remain as you are," that is, "You are right, he is wrong. Your visions are not simple illusions. I truly exist," the goddess seems to be saying. Ramakrishna's world, defined by the goddess's *śakti,* is thus confirmed.

When we turn to the *Kathāmṛta,* we find that the command appears only once, again without the technical expression *bhāvamukha,* and again as a response to the cruel attacks of Haladhari: "Haladhari used to say that God is beyond existence and non-existence. I went to Ma and said—'Ma, Haladhari is saying these things. So are all forms and things false?' Ma came to me dressed as Rati's mother and said, 'Remain in existence, my child.' I also told Haladhari this. Occasionally I forgot these words and suffered for it. Not remaining in existence, I broke a tooth. And so, when I don't hear divine words or see things, I'll remain in existence—with devotion I'll remain!" (KA 4.2–3). The scene is basically the same as that of the *Jīvanavṛttānta.* Haladhari challenges

Ramakrishna's worship of forms with an abstract philosophical argument. Ramakrishna is bothered by this and goes to the goddess for reassurance, which she promptly gives him with an affectionate command, "Remain in existence, my child." The command is different from that of the *Jīvanavṛttānta* in that it is more abstract, employing the term *bhāva* or "existence." Interestingly enough, it is the same term that occurred in Haladhari's philosophical assertion that the divine is "beyond existence and non-existence" (*bhāva-abhāver atīta*). The command to "Remain in existence," then, answers Haladhari's philosophical challenge in the very terms of that challenge. It does not deny Haladhari's claim that the Absolute is "beyond existence and non-existence," but simply says, "Remain in existence," that is, "Remain as you are, on this side of the dialectic. Go on worshiping forms. You are fine." It answers an abstract philosophical assertion with an affectionate, deeply personal consolation. Ramakrishna, that lover of forms, is reassured and happily goes off to tell Haladhari off. The Paramahaṁsa ends his discussion of the event by discussing what happened to him when he forgot the command: he became lost in ecstasy, fell down, and injured himself. Here he breaks a tooth. Later on in chapter 4, in a crucial passage I will dwell on at length, we will see the saint dislocating his hand in a similar state. In any case, the pattern I have identified above remains constant: the command to "Remain as you are" or "Remain in existence" is uttered to reassure Ramakrishna, caught in the grip of Haladhari's Vedantic criticism, that the goddess's world of *śakti* is not illusory or false.

Although it does not occur in the above passage, the technical expression *bhāvamukha* does occur in another passage in the *Kathāmṛta*. Although here it is used in a strictly philosophical sense, devoid of any biographical context, the expression does intersect with the biographical passages quoted above by its use of the same existence/non-existence dialectic with which Haladhari challenged Ramakrishna. In this passage, Ramakrishna is teaching his disciples that "there is such a thing as consciousness directed away from existence [*abhāvamukha*], and there is such a thing as consciousness directed towards existence [*bhāvamukha*]." Ramakrishna then goes on to associate this *bhāvamukha* or consciousness "directed towards existence" with the path of *bhakti* or devotion. He acknowledges the path of "*brahman*-knowledge," the path concerned with consciousness directed away from existence, but insists that it is too difficult. In this present age, the path of devotion is best since it is the easiest (KA 3.85). Again, as with the scenes involving Haladhari, here Ramakrishna is asserting his own devotional path, intimately bound up with "existence" (*bhāva*) and its forms, as the best path. In other words, in the only passage in which it occurs in the *Kathāmṛta*, the expression *bhāvamukha* is used to answer a Vedantic challenge. Again, the pattern holds.

Prior to Saradananda's *Līlāprasaṅga*, then, the expression *bhāvamukha* was what biblical scholars would call a *hapax legomenon*, a word for whose contextual meaning we seem to have only a "single" (*hapax*) occurrence. When one turns to Saradananda's *Līlāprasaṅga*, however, the term's solitude quickly vanishes into a plethora of uses and meanings, many of which are consistent with the meanings found in the *Jīvanavṛttānta* and *Kathāmṛta* passages analyzed above. But there are also numerous themes and connotations present in Saradananda's use of the term that are not found in the earlier passages, most of them related to Saradananda's theological enterprise and its concern with establishing the incarnational status of its subject. As these latter meanings concern an issue (the process by which Ramakrishna came to be considered an incarnation of God) which, although central to the study of Ramakrishna, nevertheless lies outside the parameters of the present inquiry, I will not treat them in any detail here. They would require another separate study, concerned more with how Ramakrishna's mystico-erotic secret was appropriated and transformed by his followers after the saint's death than with the original biographical content of the secret, the focus of the present study. I will restrict myself, then, to the strictly biographical contexts of the term in Saradananda's account and save a treatment of the term's theological and hermeneutical dimensions for a later study.

Saradananda locates three major occurrences of the command "Remain in *bhāvamukha*" in Ramakrishna's life: two connected with the criticisms of Haladhari and one connected with Ramakrishna's six-month *samādhi* (LP 2.8.17). The first two with Haladhari are in basic agreement with the passages I have analyzed above. The first occurrence, however, does record a number of details never mentioned in the earlier passages. Haladhari has just confused Ramakrishna with his Vedantic scholarship again, leading the saint to believe that his visions are simply delusions of his own brain. Ramakrishna sits down and weeps in Mathur's house: "A little while later I saw a fog-like smoke rising suddenly from the floor and filling the space in front of me. Later I saw in that smoke a beautiful living face of golden complexion, with a beard reaching to the breast! That figure looked at me steadfastly and said with a deep voice, 'My child, remain in *bhāvamukha*. Remain in *bhāvamukha.* Remain in *bhāvamukha!'* This image repeated this only three times and then slowly dissolved back into the fog. The fog then vanished into nothingness. After that vision, I got my peace of mind back" (LP 2.8.18). This time it is an elderly male personage that appears to Ramakrishna, perhaps a sage, perhaps a father. A mysterious fog fills the passage.

When we turn to the second occurrence of the command, "Remain in *bhāvamukha,*" in Saradananda's text (LP 2.8.17), we see that it is virtually identical to the *Kathāmṛta* version, with the goddess appearing as Rati's mother. Indeed, Saradananda seems to be relying on the *Kathāmṛta* version here, for he merely mentions the incident and adds only a single detail, namely, the fact that the goddess appeared near the worship jar in the temple. Once again, the command is in response to Haladhari's Vedantic challenge.

The third occurrence of the command, "Remain in *bhāvamukha,*" in the *Līlāprasaṅga* is placed at the end of Ramakrishna's six-month Vedantic *samādhi.* It is by far the most important of the occurrences for Saradananda. The learned biographer sees profound and intricate theological meanings in Ramakrishna's six-month state and its climactic command to "Remain in *bhāvamukha.*" For Saradananda, the command implies a complicated ontology, strangely Platonic in scope, involving a cosmic mind thinking the thoughts and ideas of the world behind and within every finite mind (a metaphysics quite foreign to Ramakrishna). For Saradananda, it is this cosmic mind that commands Ramakrishna's finite mind to "Remain in *bhāvamukha*" (LP 3.3.12–15). Moreover, the command points to a world mission of teaching that "novel and liberal doctrine" of *yata mata tata patha,* "As many views, so many paths." It was only after the six-month *samādhi,* Saradananda tells us, that Ramakrishna began to awaken fully to the realization that resulted in such a "liberal doctrine," namely, the realization that all religions meet in Vedānta. And it was only after the six-month *samādhi* that he became convinced that it was his destiny to be the divinely ordained teacher of this truth to the world and move away from thinking of himself as "the humblest of the humble."[15] For Saradananda, then, the command to "Remain in *bhāvamukha*" comes at the end of Ramakrishna's six-month Vedantic state to push the saint back into the world so that he can teach the truth that all religions, like his own mystical practices, find their culmination in Vedānta. Ramakrishna turned his "face towards existence" (*bhāvamukha*), in other words, to act as a divine-human channel for an essentially Vedantic revelation.

It is very hard to justify such an interpretation with the textual evidence at hand. The Ramakrishna of Datta's and Gupta's texts *never* connects the command to remain in *bhāvamukha* with the six-month state and seems to be completely innocent of most, if not all, of Saradananda's theological interpretations. Indeed, for the Ramakrishna of all the passages analyzed above, including those recorded by Saradananda, the commands to "Remain as you are" or "Remain in existence" or "Remain in *bhāvamukha*" imply something very different than what Saradananda wants them to mean, for *they are all uttered in response to a Vedantic challenge*. They all say, "Do not be absorbed into the Absolute. It is better that you involve yourself in existence, in the joys of form. Your way is the correct way. Do not listen to the Vedāntins." This is a long way from Saradananda's belief that the six-month *samādhi* and its famous command taught Ramakrishna that the goal of all states is a formless *brahman* and that Vedānta is the highest truth![16]

The whole thrust of Saradananda's narrative, in other words, contradicts the alleged moral of his story, namely, that Vedānta is the highest truth. As with the story of Tota bowing to the goddess, recognizing her dominance in his own life, the narrative forms of the command to "Remain in *bhāvamukha*" all witness to the ultimate truth of the Tantric dialectic and its preference for the dynamic, dualistic, and devotional realities of the goddess over the seemingly dead truths of Śiva's Vedānta. What I will call the "narrative argument" of the story thus weighs against Saradananda's most basic beliefs and assumptions concerning the primacy of Vedānta and the centrality of Tota Puri in the training of Ramakrishna. Perhaps it has taken me too many pages to establish this. After all, we could have come to a similar conclusion with a single passage from the *Kathāmṛta*. "I fell into the clutches of a knower," Ramakrishna tells his listeners. "He made me listen for eleven months to Vedānta, but the seed of devotion did not go away. Turning around, there was that very '*Ma! Ma!*'" (KA 3.173).[17] When the Naked One listened to him sing to the Mother, Ramakrishna reports triumphantly, the Vedantic monk began to cry. That great knower was defeated. So was Vedānta.

Worshiping the Living Liṅgam: Paramahaṁsas, Penises, and Boys

THERE IS A WHOLE COMPLEX of visions and acts that seem to be connected to these eleven months that Ramakrishna spent with Tota Puri, the naked paramahaṁsa. They are all impossible to locate chronologically with any precision. It is possible that some of them may have occurred well before the saint ever met Tota. I treat them here because they seem to be related, at least psychologically, to the naked form of the wandering paramahaṁsa.

As we have seen, Ramakrishna called Tota Puri "the Naked One" because the monk used to remain nude, "like a boy" (LP 3.8.23). This is significant because it reveals in an especially clear fashion what it was about the monk that attracted the saint's attention: his nudity. One can only imagine what it must have been like for Ramakrishna, a homosexually oriented man, to be shut away for days in a small hut with another, stark-naked man. Vedantic instruction or no, it was this man's nudity, and more specifically, his penis, that naturally caught Ramakrishna's attention. How could it *not?* This, after all, was a man who would later get goosebumps and fall into deep ecstatic states at the sight of the male form.

Of course, there are no passages in the texts that state clearly that Ramakrishna was attracted to the paramahaṁsa's penis. There are, however, a number of powerfully suggestive texts that say just about everything else. Consider, for example, a secret talk passage in volume 4. Ramakrishna is describing a vision he used to have of another naked paramahaṁsa: "A naked person used to stay around—I would teasingly fondle his little cock with my hand. Then I would laugh a lot. This naked form used to come out of me. It was in the form of a paramahaṁsa—like a boy" (KA 4.231). The first thing one notices about this striking passage is that it employs the term *nyāṅṭā* or "naked" to describe the visionary form, the very same term that Ramakrishna used to dub his nude Vedantic teacher "the Naked One" (*nyāṅṭā*). The vision, in other words, sets up clear linguistic connections between the nudity of the two paramahaṁsas. The vision, however, does more than hark back to the memories of the hut in the trees: it also *answers* those memories by reversing the relationship that no doubt existed between Tota and the young Ramakrishna, for here the paramahaṁsa, not the saint, appears as the sexual object, as the boy. Not surprisingly, the paramahaṁsa's boyish penis focuses the vision: Ramakrishna arouses this "little cock"[18] with his hand and laughs mischievously. Nikhilananda apparently did not think it was so funny. He castrates the scandalous passage with an innocent, "I used to joke with him" (GSR, 813).

Just a few lines down, Ramakrishna reveals another secret. After telling his audience how he used to perform Tantric rituals with the Bhairavī, who "forced" him to do all of these unspoken acts, Ramakrishna becomes excited and turns to a disciple: "In that state I couldn't help but worship the little cocks of boys with sandal-paste and flowers" (KA 4.232).[19] The vision has entered waking life: the boyish penis he once fondled in a dream-like vision he now rubs with sandal-paste in the light of day; and the laughter of the dream has been replaced by the seriousness and compulsion of the ritual act.[20] Nikhilananda, obviously uncomfortable with the daylight ritual, sends it all back into the darkness (again) with a simple omission. In his "translation," at least, the passage and its ritual no longer exist (GSR, 814). They have been pushed back into the text's unconscious, if you will.

In another passage on the paramahaṁsa's penis, Ramakrishna describes how he used to worship his own penis, teasing a precious "pearl" of seminal fluid out of it, no doubt with the same hand he once fondled the penis of the visionary paramahaṁsa and rubbed sandal-paste on the boys.[21] In volume 4, that book of secrets, the saint speaks of this "worship of the living *liṅgam*": "The paramahaṁsa's state of madness also used to come [upon me]. I would become mad and worship my own penis with the awareness that it was Śiva's penis. This is called the worship of the living *liṅgam* [*jīvantaliṅgapūjā*]. And a little pearl would come out! Now I'm not able to do that" (KA 4.106). Again we see Ramakrishna associate the paramahaṁsa and the penis. Unlike in the earlier vision, however, where the paramahaṁsa functioned as the sexual object, Ramakrishna *as the paramahaṁsa* engages the phallus. Here, moreover, he adds two other dimensions to the symbolic complex: madness and the ritual Śiva-*liṅgam*. Who, we might ask, taught him this unusual practice? Why is it connected to madness? And why is it enacted in "the paramahaṁsa's state"? Given that (1) "the paramahaṁsa" is a Vedantic guru-figure in the texts, (2) Tota was Ramakrishna's Vedantic guru, (3) Ramakrishna explicitly associated Tota with nudity, and (4) Tota's departure was mysteriously connected to a radical six-month alteration of Ramakrishna's consciousness, I think it is reasonable to suggest that it was Tota who taught Ramakrishna to worship (and to fondle) his own *liṅgam* as if it were Śiva's. Through this "paramahaṁsa's state," Ramakrishna seems to be relieving, remembering, and trying somehow to reintegrate something that another paramahaṁsa had done to him; here he fills *both* roles and performs the ritual with himself. Clearly the saint was sexually excited by these memories and this ritual act: his penis responds with a "little pearl" of lubricatory fluid, a physiological response that implies an actual erection. The audacity of such an act, with or without Tota, did not escape the saint. "Now," he confesses, perhaps with a relieved sigh, "I'm not able to do that." Tota, after all, was long gone.

Finally, there is still another secret talk passage, once again in volume 4, that is related to these other passages on numerous symbolic levels. I call it the fog of bliss vision: "The paramahaṁsa boy of fifteen that I saw under the banyan tree, again I saw another just like him! Everywhere there was a fog of bliss!—From within it a boy of thirteen or fourteen arose and showed his face! He had the form of Purna! We were both naked!" (KA 4.259). The "paramahaṁsa boy of fifteen," whose "little cock" Ramakrishna had once fondled with giggles, is here associated with the person of Purna, the flesh-and-blood, fourteen-year-old boy. Ramakrishna notices the similarities between the two visions and immediately makes the connection between the past and the present, between the visionary youth and the historical boy. Nudity again is the key. "We were both naked!" Ramakrishna exclaims excitedly. I have already established that Ramakrishna wanted to sexually engage Purna: "I want to kiss and embrace man . . . as a woman," he frankly admitted, as he talked to M about the boy at the very end of volume 4 (KA 4.271). In another passage, yet again in volume 4, we learn that Ramakrishna's habit of garlanding Purna with flowers and rubbing sandal-paste on his "body" would send the boy into *samādhi* (KA 4.212). Given the explicit connection Ramakrishna himself makes between the visionary paramahaṁsa youth, whose penis he fondled, and the visionary appearance of Purna, whose body he rubbed, it is reasonable to ask if Ramakrishna was worshiping Purna as he once worshiped the boys, "with sandal-paste and flowers." The visionary hints suggest, but by no means establish, a troubling answer. The controversial practices of the village women, who once sent little Gadadhar into very similar states under remarkably similar circumstances, take on new meaning here. No wonder that Purna's parents, like Gadadhar's own mother, worried about such practices and suspected more than religion in this worship (KA 3.149).

What do these scattered references all have in common? They all speak of a fascination on Ramakrishna's part with naked paramahaṁsas, penises, and boys. All three seem to be deeply connected in the associations and meanings that the saint attaches to his visions and ecstatic acts. I would argue that they all stem back to Tota, the naked paramahaṁsa. Ramakrishna most likely experienced Tota's presence as both pleasurable and abusive, hence he "remembers" this paramahaṁsa's naked penis in the visions and acts, and even giggles in delight, but *only* after he has reversed the dynamics of the past relationship to preserve his own integrity and control: the paramahaṁsa (or Śiva), not Ramakrishna, is now the sexual object. Clearly, however, the saint is not in complete control, even within his own acts and visions. There is, after all, a certain compulsion evident in the passages. The "worship of the living *liṅgam*" took place in a state of madness, and Ramakrishna's worship of the boys' penises was something he could not stop: "I couldn't help but . . ." Even the visions that contain no clear reference to compulsion themselves speak of Ramakrishna's lack of control: they appear of themselves and speak their symbolic truths quite apart from the intentions or understanding of Ramakrishna. The passages, in other words, point to an unconscious secret, a dimension of Ramakrishna of which Ramakrishna himself is not yet aware. Granted, he seems to thoroughly enjoy the nature of this secret *within* the secret—"I laughed a lot"—but once outside it, in the light of normal consciousness, he is troubled by its strangely sexual nature. He thus resists its public ritual expression, but in vain.

But most importantly for the purposes of the present chapter, these particular visions and ecstatic acts speak of a tendency on Ramakrishna's part to take a Vedantic figure or category—here the paramahaṁsa or Śiva—and to eroticize it, to awaken it out of its abstract slumber and engage it in erotic acts. In other words, the visions and acts speak once again of Kālī astride Śiva, arousing his penis into an erect acknowledgment of her erotic dominance: Ramakrishna laughs as he fondles a paramahaṁsa boy's penis, worships the penises of young boys in a Tantric state, teases a pearl out of the erect phallus of Śiva, and plays naked with a fourteen-year-old boy, whom he wants to kiss and embrace. He has become the goddess. He is a scandal.

A Painful Reentry, Ramlal, Islam for Three Days, and a Village Squabble

Ramakrishna's six months in *samādhi* was punctured again and again by bouts of severe blood dysentery. Toward the end, these attacks became so severe that they gradually brought him out of his half-year sleep into the light of normal consciousness. Intense suffering thus characterized Ramakrishna's reentry into the world.

And the suffering continued. Saradananda notes that Vedantic paramahaṁsas began coming now, filling Ramakrishna's room with their philosophical debates. Ramakrishna acted as umpire as he took refuge again and again in a chamber pot kept in the corner of the room for him (LP 2.16.1). Shortly after the paramahaṁsas quit coming, babas of the Ramawat community, a religious sect devoted to Rāma, began to arrive at the temple.[22] One of them carried a small metal image of the child Rāma or "Ramlal" (lit. "little Rāma"). In one of the most bizarre episodes of Ramakrishna's life, the image is said to have come alive and insisted on following Ramakrishna everywhere. Ramakrishna fed it, put it down to rest, and bathed it. These chores got more than a little onerous at times for the saint, who had never been a father. The little god's childish stubbornness only made things worse, for no matter what Ramakrishna tried, the god would not listen. Much to the chagrin of the saint, little Ramlal insisted on collecting flowers in thorny bushes, playing in the malaria-infested water, and running in the hot sun. In one scene, when the child would not mind the frustrated saint, an exasperated Ramakrishna began dunking Ramlal into the river until he realized that the god was drowning and quickly pulled him up for air. In the end the child god refused to leave the temple precincts, and his longtime father, the Ramawat baba, had to leave him behind with his new-found friend, Ramakrishna (LP 4.2.16). We are not told what happened to the metal child after this. Whether Ramakrishna's love for him continued through the years or simply faded away shortly after the baba's departure is impossible to say. The fact that we are told nothing else about Ramlal would suggest that the incident was a relatively brief one. At some point the statue was probably set in a corner and forgotten.

Saradananda invokes Vedānta to explain this bizarre episode of the living statue (everything, including the statue, is *brahman,* therefore it too is really alive), but one wonders whether psychological forces consequent upon Ramakrishna's six-month trauma, be it religious or pathological or both, might be better candidates for interpretation. It seems much more likely that the young priest was dealing with the loss of yet another ambiguous father figure (Tota) by symbolically reliving, through the statue and his own actions, memories of his own mischievous youth and the long-lost father who had not died yet. Given the paucity of information, only one thing seems certain: Ramakrishna himself was not ready to be a father. Fathers, after all, do not dunk their children in rivers. The saint, it seems, was still very much a child. Denied his own paternal figures again and again, he himself failed as a father even as he sought to remember and relive the affection of his own.

Sometime after Ramakrishna fully recovered from his dysentery, a Muslim convert named Gobinda Ray arrived at Dakshineshwar.[23] Although one would be hard pressed to find a less Muslim name than *Gobinda* (an appellation of Kṛṣṇa) and Saradananda freely admits that he cannot say whether Gobinda practiced at all the social customs of Islam, the biographer insists that Ramakrishna was "initiated" into Islam by this visitor. Ramakrishna now repeated the *mantra* "Allah," wore Muslim clothes, prayed three times a day, and refused to visit the Hindu deities. He even wanted to eat Muslim food (that is, beef), but a horrified Mathur convinced him otherwise. After three days of this, the saint had a vision of a brilliant human figure with a long beard.[24] Saradananda tells us that after seeing the figure, Ramakrishna first experienced the cosmic, conditioned *brahman* and then merged into "the fourth" state of the unconditioned *brahman* (LP 2.16.12). Seeing God in a human image, merging into an impersonal Absolute—for most Muslims, this would have been a heretical experience through and through. For Ramakrishna's interpreters, however, it signaled that the saint had experienced the very goal of Islam. Saradananda adds irony to irony by claiming that this incident proves that faith in Vedānta alone can bring Muslims and Hindus together, demonstrating once again that his alleged "tolerance" is in fact a form of religious dogmatism, incapable of taking the other tradition on its own terms.

As usual, the vision recorded by Saradananda has variants in the other texts, and, again as usual, these variants do not support Saradananda's Vedantic speculations. This vision of the bearded Muslim, for example, occurs in at least two other places, both in the *Kathāmṛta*.[25] In both passages, one of them listed as secret talk (KA 3.141), the vision clearly carries a Tantric message: the bearded Muslim (a defiled source of food for any good brahmin) distributes grains of rice from a single earthen plate to Ramakrishna and a whole host of unclean creatures (Englishmen and dogs, for example) to demonstrate the ontological truth that Saccidānanda "has become all things, all living beings, the entire world." In one of the visions (KA 3.46), Ramakrishna takes this lesson of the bearded Muslim to his usual Tantric extremes and tastes the disgusting substances of feces and pee with a flaming visionary tongue. Purity is transcended in a typically Tantric fashion. In the end, whether Ramakrishna saw Vedānta or Tantra in the "Muslim" teachings of Gobinda is difficult to say. The textual record is ambiguous at best.

As was his practice, sometime in 1867, Ramakrishna went back to his village for a much-needed rest. Hriday and the Bhairavī accompanied him. Sharada, living just a few miles away, heard of his arrival and showed up to see her mysterious husband. Ramakrishna acknowledged her presence and began to teach her the ways of the Hindu wife. But the Bhairavī, ever jealous of her competitors, was not happy with this new development and began to terrify the young girl. When challenged by the women of the village with the simple fact that Ramakrishna wished to be with his wife, the Bhairavī would snap back with the retort: "What can he say? It was *I* who opened his eyes!" (LP 2.17.10). Finally, when the Bhairavī broke a village custom, a verbal battle ensued that led to her eventual defeat and humiliation. She apologized to Ramakrishna, rubbed his body with sandal-paste, and left for Benares. It was not the last Ramakrishna would see of her.

In Śiva's Holy City and Kṛṣṇa's Vrindavana

MATHUR'S WIFE AND RAMAKRISHNA at some point decided that it would be a good idea to go on pilgrimage to the holy sites of northwestern India. Mathur disagreed: such a journey would cost far too much money and would be filled with physical hardships (JV[5], 64). Mathur was no doubt right—he would spend over one hundred thousand rupees on the venture—but his wife and his saint won out in the end. And so on January 27, 1868, Mathur, his wife, Ramakrishna, Hriday, and some one hundred twenty-five servants set out in one second-class and three third-class rail cars for the holy city of Kashi, today better known as Benares or Varanasi.

On the way, they passed through Deoghar, a destitute village that tugged on Ramakrishna's heart. Unable to bear the sight of so much human misery, Ramakrishna insisted that Mathur give each villager a piece of cloth and feed them all for a day. Mathur, ever the businessman, objected that this might strain the trip's budget, but Ramakrishna threatened to stay until Mathur gave in. Eventually Mathur did just that.[26]

Once the party finally arrived at the holy city, Ramakrishna found that it was not at all what he had expected. Because he did not dress like a holy man and wore no sectarian marks on his body, no one recognized Ramakrishna as the paramahaṁsa he thought he was (JV[5], 66). But how could they? He carried no staff and did not shave his head. Datta complains that the residents of Benares, like beasts, saw only external virtues. They did not recognize his Master. Ramakrishna was equally disillusioned with them: "I thought I would find every one in Kashi meditating all day long on Śiva and merged in *samādhi* . . . but once there, I found everything to be the exact opposite!" (LP 4.3.13). He was particularly disgusted with Mathur and his rich friends, who only seemed interested in talking business in the parlors and drawing rooms. Upset with the whole situation, Ramakrishna cried to his Mother: "Why did you bring me here, Ma? I was happier at Dakshineshwar" (LP 4.3.15).[27] Indeed, the only difference the saint could find between the holy city and his native Bengal was that here they defecated facing west and shit husks and bran, whereas back in Dakshineshwar they faced east and could never digest so powerful a diet (LP 4.3.10).[28] Accurate or not, Ramakrishna loved to tell this tidbit of scatological trivia; it always got him a laugh.

It was in this holy city that Ramakrishna ran into his old Tantric guru, the Bhairavī. She somehow managed to take him to another of her Tantric circles, this one held under the cover of darkness on the bank of the Ganges. The event seems to have made an impression on him, for he would remember it years later talking to some visitors in the *Kathāmṛta*. Ramakrishna describes how the group paired up into sacred couples and began to drink wine, lots of it. "I thought to myself that this time they might meditate or recite their *mantras*, but no, they began to dance! I began to become afraid that they might fall into the Ganges" (KA 2.142).[29] Much to Ramakrishna's disappointment, the Tāntrikas had not changed much since his early adventures with them as the Bhairavī's young initiate. They were still a shady, seedy, drunken lot.

From Śiva's holy city, the pilgrims moved on to Vrindavana, the pastoral scene of Kṛṣṇa's early exploits with Rādhā and the milkmaids. In Vrindavana, Ramakrishna met more disillusionment. The place just did not live up to the Vrindavana of the texts (*śāstrokta vṛndāvana*). Where were the milkmaids, filled with selfless love for Kṛṣṇa? And what were these shopkeepers doing here? (JV[5], 67). And was not Vrindavana *the* place for becoming a woman? Then why was not the Paramahaṁsa happy with all the effeminate men, dressed in women's clothes, whom he found here? "Can one become a woman simply by cutting off the mustache?" Datta asks his readers (JV[5], 67–68).

But unlike in Kashi, here he quickly learned to be happy, for Vrindavana proved to be a place of vision and ecstasy. Watching the young cowherd boys return with their cows in the dust of sunset, for example,

Ramakrishna would fall down unconscious; the boys "reminded" (*uddīpana*) him of Kṛṣṇa (LP 4.3.21).[30] Indeed, Ramakrishna was so happy with this magical place and its pious occupants that he almost stayed, for it was here, in a little hut in the forest, that he at last found someone who had truly mastered the art of loving Kṛṣṇa: a sixty-year-old woman named Gangamata, who was believed to be a reincarnation of one of the girlfriends of Rādhā, Kṛṣṇa's great lover. Upon seeing Ramakrishna, Gangamata immediately recognized him as Rādhā herself. With such a realization, the two of them, now "girlfriends" (*sakhī*), became instant intimates, sharing their love for Kṛṣṇa in gestures and signs that no one seemed to understand but them. At other times, Gangamata would treat Ramakrishna like a child, feeding him with her own hand (JV[5], 68).

So happy were these two girlfriends that, when it came time to leave, Ramakrishna had to be convinced to go. "Who will take care of you when your stomach fails you?" Hriday asked the saint. "I will," answered Gangamata. Hriday then abandoned argument and grabbed the saint's arm. Gangamata grabbed the other and a tug-of-war ensued. In the end, poor Ramakrishna cried out in pain. Gangamata became embarrassed, asked for forgiveness, and reluctantly bid her companion farewell (JV[5], 68–70). In another passage Ramakrishna explains that he finally decided to return home with the party because he remembered his aging mother back at the temple and could not bear the thought of breaking her heart by staying on in Vrindavana (KA 3.29). No mention is ever made of Sharada, his wife. Once again, it is the Mother not the Lover that occupies Ramakrishna's mind and heart.[31]

The Jesus State

RAMAKRISHNA OFTEN VISITED HIS FRIEND, Shambhucharan Mallick, who lived next door to the temple. During these visits, Shambhu would read Ramakrishna passages from the Bible. One day, sometime after the pilgrimage, a strange occurrence took place during one of these friendly visits. On Shambhu's wall hung a picture of the Virgin Mary with the infant Jesus sitting on her lap. On this particular day, this picture came alive for Ramakrishna. A ray of light issued from the image and entered his body. Another transformation had begun, this one centered on what Datta calls the "Jesus state" (*jiśu-bhāva*). Sitting in his own room now back at the temple, Ramakrishna began to see huge Christian churches. He could even hear the teachings of the priests inside (JV[5], 55). Datta ends his account of this Jesus state with the story of "an old man" (probably a reference to Peter) drowning in the sea. "Lord! How do I attain God?" the old man asks. Jesus says nothing but takes his hand and leads him straight into the waves of the sea, where he begins to sink. "Now how do you feel?" Jesus asks the drowning man. "I'm dying!" he screams back as he gasps for air. "When separated from him, if your heart feels like this, *then* you will attain Him" (JV[5], 56). In most Christian interpretations of Peter on the sea, the story is said to be about the necessity of faith. For Datta, it is a lessen in anxious desire. Given the centrality of such a drowning desire in Ramakrishna's life and teachings, Datta's transformation seems an appropriate one, but once again we see how a preeminently Hindu lesson is drawn from an allegedly non-Hindu event.

With much more to prove, Saradananda goes much further than Datta. He too describes Ramakrishna seeing Christian worshipers "offering incense and waving lights" before images of Jesus. But then he continues the story, transforming it into yet another three-day miracle. At the end of the third day, Saradananda tells us, Ramakrishna saw a man of fair complexion coming toward him. He knew that it was a foreigner because "his nose was flat." The foreigner spoke: "Jesus—he who gave his heart's blood in order to save humanity from suffering and pain and who endured death at the hands of men, he is one with the Lord, the greatest *yogī*, the loving Jesus Christ!" (LP 2.21.3). Jesus then embraced Ramakrishna and disappeared into his body. Once again, Ramakrishna entered into an ecstatic state and became one with *brahman* with attributes.

The Hindu contours of Saradananda's version, like those of Datta's, are manifest. Ramakrishna sees images of Jesus being worshiped with incense and lights, a slightly veiled reference to the very Hindu ritual of *arati*, in which incense and lights are waved in front of the deity. It is also significant that the state is inspired, in both accounts, by a picture of the Virgin Mary and the infant Jesus. Such an image would be particularly powerful for someone whose self-understanding was defined by the Mother and the Child. The specifically Christian aspects of this Mother and this Child seem superfluous at best. The ending, like all the endings in Saradananda, are defined by the biographer's Vedantic apologetic: the vision is absorbed back into Ramakrishna, its source, and then Ramakrishna is absorbed into *brahman*. The message is clear, if slightly veiled: all religions are ultimately absorbed by Ramakrishna, the perfect embodiment of the Vedantic sage. Finally, it is probably not insignificant that Saradananda devotes as much space to describing Ramakrishna's fascination with Jesus's Jewish nose as he does to the actual *sādhana* and vision. As we will see below, the marks of the body, be they human or divine, fascinated the saint. Given all of this, it would appear that the doctrinal content of this "Christian" experience seems irrelevant, if it exists at all. A Mother, a Child, and a beautiful male form—these are the central features of Ramakrishna's "Jesus state." We have seen them all before, and we will see them again.

THE MANSION OF FUN AND ITS TANTRIC FORM

I HAVE ALREADY DEMONSTRATED that the narrative argument of the texts point in a direction quite different from that of most traditional Vedantic interpretations. The various commands to "Remain in existence" and the story of Tota's defeat at the hands of the goddess all point to a dialectical world in which the preference is clearly given to the phenomenal energies of the goddess. In the introduction, I have identified this dialectic as one of the general defining features of the Hindu Tantra. Here I want to extend this argument by demonstrating that Ramakrishna's mature teachings, much like the events of his life, are formed around this same dialectic. I want to establish, in other words, that Ramakrishna not only lived in but also taught a Tantric world.

How to Interpret a Chameleon

THIS IS A DIFFICULT TASK, not just because many of the saint's followers have claimed the exact opposite for almost a hundred years now, namely, that Ramakrishna was a Vedāntin, but also because Ramakrishna was not a systematic philosopher. He never wrote a clear consistent treatise on the nature of the world. Indeed, he never wrote a thing. Granted, he *said* a great deal, but these "sayings" (*ukti*), "intimate conversations" (*āḍḍā*), and "talks" (*kathā*) were always uttered to a particular audience at a particular time and then recorded by particular people with specific motives and agendas. The interpreter, then, must always keep in mind, not only to whom Ramakrishna is talking, how he felt at the time, what year it was, and so forth, but also who recorded the teaching and for what purpose.

These problems are particularly acute when we approach a text like the *Kathāmṛta*. I have been arguing that its five volumes portray a Ramakrishna who, however ambivalently, experienced and preached a Tantric world. In other words, I have argued for a particular position by privileging a particular text, M's *Kathāmṛta*. But as I pointed out in the introduction, the early monks of the movement considered M's famous volumes to be only the watered down "Sunday notes" of the Master, delivered to the householders during their weekend breaks. For them, the author of the text (a householder) and the social context of Ramakrishna's teachings recorded in it (a group of weekend householder visitors) renders the *Kathāmṛta* a dubious standard for recording the true message of the Master. Ramakrishna's real message, they claimed, was spoken to them on the weekdays, when the householders were not present. They, not M, are thus the true heirs of the teachings. They alone are fit to interpret it for the rest of the world.

This is a serious charge, rooted in a sophisticated understanding of the nature of texts and their contextual interpretation. But it is also a charge that could just as easily be turned back on the renouncers. After all, the texts that the monks have given us to prove their point (the writings of Vivekananda and Saradananda's *Līlāprasaṅga*) are hardly models of objective reporting. They too were created in a particular social context (a young religious movement) and were intended for a specific audience (middle-class Bengalis deeply influenced by the West). And on both counts, they fail miserably to meet the standards of historical accuracy and scholarly objectivity. Indeed, the manner in which the renouncer texts have cleaned up Ramakrishna for their own audiences and apologetic purposes renders their claims of presenting the "original" Ramakrishna suspicious at best. Like so many of the photographs we have of the saint, Ramakrishna's image has been "touched up" in their writings, even painted over, in order to cover up some of his more troubling wrinkles and undesirable features. The wonderfully human portrait we have of the saint in the *Kathāmṛta* is thus rejected for the fuzzy features of a holy card. Bold detail, complexity, and ambivalence are replaced with monotone colors, simplicity, and dogmatism. I am under no illusion that we have the "historical Ramakrishna" in the *Kathāmṛta*, but I cannot help believing, with a whole host of historians, that here at least we are a bit closer to the full human reality of the Paramahaṁsa from Dakshineshwar. This is one reason that I have privileged M's *Kathāmṛta* over Saradananda's *Līlāprasaṅga*.

But this is simply to admit my own assumptions. It does not answer the renouncers' charge that the *Kathāmṛta* is only a collection of Sunday jottings. Likewise, pointing out that the renouncer accounts are equally influenced by social context and audience only puts into question the monastic reading. It does not establish my own. For this, I want to invoke a more rigorous method. I want to invoke the principle of *total context.* To begin, I want to examine briefly three issues: the problem of genre; the biographical dimension of Ramakrishna's teachings; and the principle of *upāya* or "teaching skill," the Indian notion that the master teacher is able to change his teachings and pedagogy to fit the particular contextual situation of each disciple.

If one examines closely the genres of the writings of the renouncers and of M's *Kathāmṛta,* the monastic claim to the "true" teaching of Ramakrishna loses some of its power. For much of the writings of the renouncers, and especially of Vivekananda, consists of a series of "proof-texting." The writers adduce a saying or a quote from Ramakrishna here and there to prove a point that is often tangential, sometimes even contradictory, to the total movement of Ramakrishna's thought and experience. In this, the monastic writings are exact opposites of M's volumes, for whereas the author's voice is barely present in the *Kathāmṛta,* injecting his hesitant opinions (usually in the form of questions) only in parenthetical remarks, footnotes, and the nuances of his chapter and section headings, the writings of Vivekananda and Saradananda are filled with the loudly proclaimed ideas and confident interpretations (seldom presented as such) of the authors, while Ramakrishna is quoted only to prove a point already made. Saradananda is far more nuanced than Vivekananda, for he often presents a number of interpretations before he tells you his own, and even then, he often leaves the reader with a choice. Saradananda, in other words, seems to realize that he is interpreting. Vivekananda, on the other hand, simply proclaims, and when others beg to differ with his often dubious proclamations, he resorts to hyperbole or simple ad hominem attacks. Sometimes his interpretations had so little to do with Ramakrishna's own self-understanding that he himself was forced to admit it, if only implicitly. Rather than sacrifice his agenda to the fire of historical accuracy, however, the young preacher much preferred to throw his Master into the flames. Consider, for example, his reaction to a fellow monk's charge that, by falsely claiming that social service lies at the core of Ramakrishna's message, he had introduced Western ideas of service and action into a life where they did not belong. Narendra's reply is unambiguous: "What do you know? You are an ignorant man. . . . Your Bhakti is sentimental nonsense, which makes you impotent. . . . Hands off! Who cares for *your* Ramakrishna? Who cares for your Bhakti and Mukti? Who cares what your Scriptures say? . . . I am not a slave of Ramakrishna, but of him only who serves and helps others, without caring for his own Bhakti or Mukti."[32] These are not the words of a man concerned with historical accuracy; rather, they are those of a fiery preacher driven by his own religious vision. They may tell us a great deal about Narendra's concern with spiritual manliness and his disgust with religious forms of escapism, but they tell us almost nothing about Ramakrishna. In Narendra's own words, "I am not a slave of Ramakrishna."

After considering genre and rhetorical style, then, I am led to the following conclusions: whereas M's *Kathāmṛta* seems to be more concerned to present the total context of Ramakrishna's teachings, even if that means recording potentially scandalous revelations and painfully embarrassing remarks (in one passage, Ramakrishna tells M he has bad breath! [KA 4.233]), Saradananda and Vivekananda are more concerned with their own agendas and ideas. Vivekananda is particularly guilty of ignoring the total context of his Master's teachings. The result is two very different appropriations of who Ramakrishna was and what he taught, which in turn seem to issue out of two separate interpretive traditions, what I have called the householder tradition and the renouncer tradition.

The biographical dimension of Ramakrishna's teachings argues against the monastic claim as well. As I have tried to show above, the narrative argument of Ramakrishna's story points in a direction away from the renouncer claim that Ramakrishna's message was a Vedantic one. On the contrary, as I have demonstrated above, his visions and life experiences all moved away from Vedānta toward Tantra. These biographical movements must be taken as part of the total context of Ramakrishna's teachings. His teachings, that is, were expressions of his life experiences.

Finally, there is the issue of Ramakrishna's plasticity and the principle of *upāya* or "teaching skill." Ramakrishna, it is sometimes said, deliberately changed his teachings to fit the particular audience of the day. To householders, it is claimed, he delivered a "watered-down" householder message. To renouncers, on the other hand, he delivered a message of renunciation, his "true" teaching. It is just such a notion that lies behind the renouncers' charge that the *Kathāmṛta* should be subordinated to the monastic writings, since it was delivered to householders. On closer inspection, however, this argument also breaks down.

Ramakrishna himself was aware of the complexities and problems involved in appropriating another human being for one's own purposes, and he warned his listeners against hastily concluding that they knew who he was and what he was about. Everyone, he often noted, is convinced that he belongs to his own sect.[33] Interpretation, after all, goes both ways. It was not, in other words, just a matter of Ramakrishna changing his teachings. It was also a matter of his listeners' perceptions changing as they viewed the world, God, and the saint himself through the different hues and tints of their own "colored glasses" (PDU, 1).[34] But there is more, for at least part of this multiplicity of interpretations was a result of Ramakrishna's own plastic nature. Like the chameleon of his story about the divine shifting colors for different devotees,[35] Ramakrishna did in fact often change his colors to fit the temperament and beliefs of his numerous visitors. One thus must always ask whether one is looking at the "real" Ramakrishna or at some red or green metamorphosis elicited by a passionate discussion or a jaded visitor. *Upāya* did play a role. But this does *not* mean that Ramakrishna's conversations were pure artifice, a "fill in the blanks" exercise for the imaginative. On the contrary, *if taken as a whole,* they reveal consistent patterns of meaning. However elusive he may be in this or that particular tree, the object of our study nevertheless remains a recognizable species, the chameleon, with quite predictable habits. And the instincts of this chameleon can be determined by examining his habits and the contexts of his shifting colors. When this is done, one finds that much of Ramakrishna's teachings on the nature of the world are remarkably, almost monotonously consistent.

All of these considerations of genre, biography, and *upāya* need to be kept in mind as one takes up the monastic challenge and examines very closely the audience and the context of Ramakrishna's teachings. What I hope to show below is that when one combines all of these factors, one comes up with surprising meanings strangely at odds with traditional interpretations. More specifically, I will argue that, when interpreted within their total context, Ramakrishna's teachings on the nature of the world appear as *means to help his listeners, and now readers, to transcend the ways of Vedānta and come to the ultimate knowledge and experience of the goddess and her Tantric world.* Ramakrishna's teachings, in other words, are conveyed to his disciples, just as the command to "Remain in existence" was related to Ramakrishna himself, *in response to a Vedantic challenge.* The Paramahaṁsa's teachings do not prove Vedānta. They subordinate Vedānta to Tantra. They do not preach renunciation, at least in any classical sense; rather they sing of a mansion of fun.

To establish this thesis, I want to begin with a song Ramakrishna liked to sing about this mansion of fun. After locating the image of the mansion in the life of Ramakrishna and briefly analyzing the particular passages in which the song occurs, I will turn to the ontological and experiential dimensions of this mansion. By looking closely at this joke put to music, I will be able to explicate the details of Ramakrishna's world and challenge the renouncers' claim that Ramakrishna's true message centered on Vedānta.

The Mansion in the Life of Ramakrishna

It is often forgotten that Ramakrishna lived in the "mansion" (*kuṭhi*) of the temple complex for sixteen years (1855–1871), and that the Rani as well as Mathur and his family lived in this same mansion whenever they stayed at the temple.[36] As should be obvious by now, these were no ordinary years, nor was this mansion an ordinary place. It was while living here that Ramakrishna practiced his *sādhanas*. It was here that he went "mad" and lost normal consciousness again and again. It was here that the Rani and Mathur orchestrated their temptation scenes. Perhaps it was here also that Ramakrishna kept an eye on Mathur for his wife and reported faithfully any affairs that he had witnessed. Their bedrooms were no doubt very close. Ramakrishna's was connected to the entire second floor by a spiral staircase, the only one in the house.

The tradition explains Ramakrishna's move from this mansion into his new room in the temple grounds in 1871 by connecting it to the death of his nephew, Akshay, who died that same year. Ramakrishna apparently could no longer bear to live in the mansion where his beloved nephew had passed away. It is just as likely, however, that other associations and another death were involved in the move. Mathur also died in 1871. Is it just a coincidence that the saint left the mansion the same year his boss died? Was Mathur "keeping" him there? Certainly, such a practice would fit into the larger patterns of the Handmaid, the Sītā vision, the bedroom scenes, and the Janbajar abduction that I have examined above.

The image of the mansion is thus tied up with the years of Ramakrishna's religious practices (which, as we have seen, were dominated by Tantric themes), with the privilege and prestige of his position at the temple (not everyone got to live in the boss's mansion), and with the rich and sumptuous lifestyle of the wealthy and powerful (Ramakrishna's room was next to the parlor). Above all, it was the place of the householder, Mathur the temple boss. With Mathur's death, Ramakrishna could move out of the mansion and away from all the memories he associated with it. The image of the householder's mansion and the "fun" he no doubt experienced in it all stayed with him, however, and became a focal point for his teachings on the Tantric nature of the world. In a very real sense, Ramakrishna never left Mathur's mansion.

The Mansion of Fun in the Kathāmṛta

THE MANSION THEME enters the *Kathāmṛta* in the form of a humorous song about a certain "mansion of fun" (*majār kuṭi*). We are first introduced to its funny rhythms in volume 1. Ramprasad, Ramakrishna tells his disciples, thought that the world is a mat of deception, a dark illusion to be rejected. But this is only a half-truth, for if one obtains devotion, the world appears in its true colors, as a mansion of fun:

> This world is a mansion of fun,[37] I eat, drink and roll around
>   having fun.
> Was there any lack in King Janaka's might?
> Holding to both directions, he downed the bowl of milk.
> (KA 1.46)

King Janaka was a saintly ruler who, after spending many years performing ascetical practices standing on his head,[38] returned to his kingdom and became known for his ability to attend to both the divine and human worlds. He was thus an ideal sage, a perfect ruler, and a model for all householders (KA 1.105). He could "down the bowl of milk" as he held "to both directions," that is, he could attend both to his worldly duties and to the demands of God. He lived in a dialectical world, in what the poet called a "mansion of fun." Such is the world of the goddess's devoted householder, who, unlike the "dry" renouncer, enjoys both social duties (*dharma*) and release (*mokṣa*), both mystical union (*yoga*) and pleasure (*bhoga*) (KA 4.49). Everyone who listens to this song thinks Janaka's mansion of fun is a very funny world.

In volume 2, the song appears again, this time immediately after a householder disciple sings a Sanskrit song in praise of Śaṅkara, the famous Vedantic philosopher. In the Sanskrit song, the world is described as a deep well and a terrible wilderness, something to get out of. Ramakrishna responds to such Vedantic Sanskrit with his own challenge: "Why do you say the world is a well and a forest?" he complains. "That is what people say in the beginning. But when one attains him, then is there such fear?" With that, he breaks into the song of the mansion of fun, making fun of all that Sanskrit and its noble talk of renouncing something that is in fact divine (KA 2.204). Here we see a familiar pattern: Ramakrishna is challenged by Vedānta and responds with his

Śākta faith in the divinity of the mundane world. Perhaps, as the renouncers charge, such a response can be explained by taking into account the audience, here a householder foolishly flirting with the ascetic profundities of Vedānta. It is just as likely, however, that Ramakrishna's response was rooted in his own biography and all those commands to "Remain in existence" and "Remain as you are." They too, after all, answered a Vedantic challenge with an essentially Śākta faith.

In a similar passage in volume 3, Ramakrishna is talking to a scholar. When the scholar gets to speak (which is seldom), it is only to ask a question or to admit his ignorance: "I don't understand," he confesses, as Ramakrishna explains his dialectical world. "This is very difficult to understand!" the scholar exclaims again, after another series of attempts on Ramakrishna's part. Unable to enlighten his dull pupil, Ramakrishna finally changes tactics and breaks into a series of metaphors, all leading up to the mansion of fun and Ramakrishna's glosses on it:

> When there is buttermilk, there is butter. When you think of buttermilk, you have to think of butter—because without butter, there could be no buttermilk. And so if you honor the eternal, you have to honor the play as well. With the grain, and then against it. After the direct experience of form and the formless, this state occurs! Form is made of consciousness, and the formless is the unbroken Saccidānanda.
>
> She herself has become everything—thus the mystic's "This world is a mansion of fun." For the knower, "This world is a mat of deception." Ramprasad called the world a mat of deception. Then someone else responded:
>
> > This world is a mansion of fun; I eat drink and
> > roll around in fun.
> > O Mr. Sen, you're not very bright; you
> > understand only a little.
> > King Janaka of great energy, how happy he was.
> > Keeping to two directions, he drank his milk
> > from a cup.
> >
> > (Everyone laughs)
>
> The mystic enjoys the bliss of God in a special way. Some people hear about milk, some people see it, and some people drink it. The mystic drinks milk, obtains bliss, and is nourished. (KA 3.77)

"When there is buttermilk, there is butter," that is, the sweet world and its rich *brahman*-essence cannot be separated. Likewise, one must accept both sides of the dialectic, the eternal (*nitya*) and the phenomenal world of the divine play (*līlā*). One must go "with the grain" and then against it, that is, one must first reject the world (the usual religious pattern), and then, after realizing that it is in fact divine, again accept it, even though this goes "against the grain" of one's learned assumptions.[39] Switching metaphors, Ramakrishna asserts that form and the formless are both true. The dialectic is omnipresent. It is rooted in the goddess's immanence, in her incarnation not "in" but *as* the world. She has literally become everything, making this world a mansion of fun for the mystic, a place to eat, drink, and make merry. Only the true mystic (*vijñānī*) knows this and so can drink the milk of the world and be nourished. Others only hear about and see such delight. Once again, the song is sung to answer a Vedantic challenge.

In volume 4, the mansion still stands in defiance of Vedānta and its doctrine of illusion, but here the saint is much more specific. Here he explicitly equates Vedantic renunciation—*neti neti,* "Not this, not this"—with Ramprasad's mistaken "mat of deception" and teaches that after one has seen him the world is no illusion but a mansion of fun (KA 4.244). In another, more philosophical passage in the same volume, Ramakrishna explains that his mansion of fun stands beyond the polarities of human thought: "The knower says that 'This world is a mat of deception.' But he who has gone beyond both knowledge and ignorance says that this world is a 'mansion of fun.' He sees that the Lord has become everything, the soul, the world, the twenty-four cosmic principles" (KA 4.146). For Ramakrishna, the knower (*jñānī*), the Vedāntin, still deluded by his "Not this, not this" renunciation, cannot see. Only the mystic, who has transcended the duality of the world in the Tantric dialectic, can see that the world is in fact a mansion of fun and enjoy it as such.

In volume 5, Ramakrishna is still singing the song (KA 5.134). And again, as in volume 4, he equates the "mat of deception" with what he calls "the Vedānta view." This view, Ramakrishna goes on, states that the world is completely false, like a dream. But in "the Purāṇa view" (*purāṇa mata*) of the devotional scriptures one says that the Lord has become the twenty-four cosmic principles, and so one worships him both inside and outside. Again, Ramakrishna relates how Ramprasad described the world as a "mat of deception" only to be answered by another man's "This world is a mansion of fun" (KA 5.51). For his part,

Ramakrishna identifies with this mansion of fun. "My state is always to eat and drink and have fun!" he tells his listeners (KA 1.49).

Finally, in that secret volume, volume 4, a passage occurs that, although never mentioning the song explicitly, clearly owes much to it. M calls this section "Ramakrishna's Visions and a Secret Interpretation of Vedānta—Nondualism and Qualified Nondualism—Is the World False?" M begins by noting that the "German pundits," Kant and Hegel, saw a little of the truth. They were "faint echoes" of Vedānta. But it was Ramakrishna whom the goddess caused to actually *see* the truth of Vedānta in his visions. But what did he see? And what does M mean by "a secret interpretation of Vedānta"? A little further down the page, M is talking to his Master on the western verandah outside the saint's room:

> M: "Is the world false?"
>
> Sri Ramakrishna: "Why false? This is all the talk of reason.
>
> "First one rejects the world by saying, 'Not this, not this.' God is not the soul, not the world, not the twenty-four cosmic principles—all this is like a dream. After going with the grain, then one goes against the grain. Then one feels that she herself has become everything." (KA 4.34)

On the very next page, Ramakrishna relates the famous Kālī Temple vision that I have discussed above under "The Goddess in a Cat." In this vision, as we remember, everything in the temple, from the marble floor to a stray cat, is revealed to Ramakrishna's eyes as "made of consciousness." Everything is revealed to be the goddess: she has indeed "become everything." It is this divine world of the goddess that M seems to have in mind when he refers to a "secret interpretation of Vedānta." Although Ramakrishna certainly would never have described such a world as "Vedantic" (he knew better), M's secret interpretation contains a provocative truth, for it suggests that Ramakrishna's ontological teachings move through and past traditional Vedānta ("Not this, not this") to the dialectical experience of Tantra ("She has become everything"). In other words, what M calls "a secret interpretation of Vedānta" is Tantra.[40]

Brahman and Śakti

NOT SURPRISINGLY, Ramakrishna commonly talks about this mansion with the categories and symbols of his dialectical Tantric world. To demonstrate this, I will take the mansion of fun passage from volume 3 analyzed above (KA 3.77) and exegete a few of its themes, namely: the unity of butter and buttermilk; the eternal and play; and the all-important phrase, "She herself has become everything." Such an ordering is admittedly an arbitrary one, but, as I have been trying to show all along, it really does not matter where one starts since all the paths of Ramakrishna's soul lead to the same truth, to the dialectic of Tantra. Virtually every metaphor and theme, almost every image and abstraction eventually stems back, through a forest of intertwined associations, to this shimmering truth.

Let us begin, then, with a series of images: "When there is buttermilk, there is butter. When you think of buttermilk, you have to think of butter—because without butter, there could be no buttermilk. And so if you honor the eternal, you have to honor the play as well. With the grain, and then against it. After the direct experience of form and the formless, this state occurs!" Each of these themes speak of the same truth: the dynamic union of the Absolute and the world of everyday experience. One may not see the butter in the buttermilk, but it is there. And one may want to deny that the butter has anything to do with the buttermilk, but it does. In truth the two cannot be separated. In other passages Ramakrishna speaks of the inseparability of milk and its whiteness (KA 5.66), of the jewel and its radiance,[41] of fire and its power to burn (KA 3.14), of the snake and its coiled nature (KA 2.73), of water and its power to wet (KA 5.66), and of water and its power to move (KA 1.100).[42] Each of these images is part of a larger, more abstract whole, Ramakrishna's all-important belief that *brahman* and *śakti* are "nondifferent" (*abheda*). This unspeakable something and this always speaking energy are not equal, for that would collapse the eternal delight of their union. They are "nondifferent," paradoxically One yet Two. This doctrine of the nondifference of *brahman* and *śakti* is so central to Ramakrishna's world that Datta devotes an entire chapter to it in his metaphysical treatise on Ramakrishna's teachings, his *Tattvasāra* or "The Essence of Reality" (TS, chap. 3). It is just as central to the *Kathāmṛta,* where it forms the structure upon which the Paramahaṁsa hangs most of his metaphors and sayings. This is the doctrine that supports the mansion of fun. This is the frame that holds the marble and stone in place and gives the whole creation a recognizable, and classically mystical, form. This is the doctrine that makes the fun possible.

But most important for our purposes, Ramakrishna's belief in the nondifference of *brahman* and *śakti* was a conviction that took its form and power from the saint's Tantric experiences. This becomes especially apparent in passages such as this one found in volume 4. Ramakrishna turns toward the Panchavati or "Place of Five Trees" and says to M: "I used to sit in this Panchavati. In time I became mad! O what happened! *Kālī is brahman.* She who has sex with Śiva is Kālī, the Primordial Power! She arouses the Unmoving. . . . There is the Self of Consciousness and the Power of Consciousness. The Self of Consciousness is a man, the Power of Consciousness is a woman. The Self of Consciousness is Kṛṣṇa, the Power of Consciousness is Rādhā. The devotee is a particular form of this Power of Consciousness" (KA 4.60). Ramakrishna begins with his early period of madness, a madness that led him to the conviction that Kālī is indeed "she who has sex with Kāla [Śiva]." Kālī, in other words, is called "Kālī" because she has sex with Kāla. Even her name is erotic. She alone can arouse the Absolute, "the Unmoving," Ramakrishna tells M. A few lines down, he takes this erotic dialectic and applies it, first to an interpretation of the Vaiṣṇava deities, and then to the human plane of devotion and religious practice: the devotee, an embodiment of feminine energies, erotically relates to the divine as male, as consciousness. For Ramakrishna, this Śākta world, with Kālī on top of Śiva arousing him out of his immobility, structures all the worlds, be they human or divine. Vaiṣṇava figures, like Vedantic figures, are transformed into Śākta symbols. The world is read through Tantric eyes.

But Ramakrishna is not specific about what happened under those five trees that brought him to the conviction that the goddess indeed is on top of the god. In a secret talk passage, again in volume 4, however, we learn a bit more. Here Ramakrishna relates a similar vision, perhaps the same one, and explicates the specifically Tantric nature of the secret: "One day *Śiva and Śakti* were shown to me everywhere. I saw the love-making of Śiva and Śakti. People, animals, trees, within them all I saw the love-making of this Śiva and Śakti—the cosmic man and woman! . . . All this is very secret talk" (KA 4.56).[43] "*Brahman* is nondifferent from *śakti.*" This is the language of philosophy and the intellect. "I saw the love-making of Śiva and Śakti." This is the language of myth and the imagination. It is also the language of the Tantras. "All this," Ramakrishna concludes, "is very secret talk."

But this identity between *brahman* and the goddess as *śakti* was a deceptive sort of equation, for the goddess was not really the same as *brahman*. Rather, she was its form, its energy, its creative, nurturing, and destructive power: "That which is *brahman* is that which is *śakti*. When we think of it as being inactive, then we call it '*brahman*.' When we think of it as creating, maintaining, and destroying the universe, then we call it the Primordial Power, we call it Kālī. *Brahman* and *śakti* are nondifferent" (KA 3.14).[44] So they are the same, and they are not the same. They are "nondifferent" (*abheda*). They exist in relation, in a dialectic that is very common in the history of mysticism and mythology. Both the myth and the mystic strive to resolve the contradiction, to transcend it in a dialectical coincidence of opposites. The mythologist might say that they must always fail: a contradiction is a contradiction, a pair of opposites that cannot be united. The mystic might disagree: a contradiction may be just a pair of opposites whose categories have not yet been transcended.

Ramakrishna's ontology, then, was neither strictly monistic nor dualistic. The truth lies between light and darkness, in the twilight of the middle (KA 5.86–87). To get there, one must look at both the Many and the One as two thorns. One must dig one out with the other, and then throw *both* away.[45] Such an understanding leads to a certain attitude toward the eternal (*nitya*) and the play (*līlā*) of the world: *both* must be accepted as real (KA 4.286). Such was his "mature opinion" (KA 5.58) and his "ripe" devotion (KA 4.147); both had moved through the polarities of existence to the dialectic of the truth. Unlike Vedānta, which asserts that only the eternal is really real, Ramakrishna emphatically insisted that "*the play is also real,*" and so, "when one arrives at the eternal, it is good to remain in the play" (KA 2.58). Here we hear echoes of a more famous command, the command to "Remain in existence" that Ramakrishna heard so often in his earlier years. This teaching on the reality and divinity of the world, then, is not just the result of Ramakrishna's merciful *upāya*. It is rooted in Ramakrishna's own life. It goes back to the beginning.

"She Herself Has Become Everything"

Perhaps the radical nature of Ramakrishna's Tantric world is best expressed in the saint's oft-repeated claim that "She herself has become everything." Certainly, it is this omnipresent goddess that makes possible the mystic's mansion of fun: "She herself has become everything—thus the mystic's 'This world is a mansion of fun'" (KA 1.94).

There are three types of aspirants, Ramakrishna taught. The lowest sort believes that God and the world are separate, that God is "up there" somewhere. The middle aspirant believes that God dwells *in* all creatures as the "inner controller" but is still somehow separate from them. The highest aspirant, on the other hand, sees clearly that "She herself has become everything," that the divine exists in and *as* the twenty-four cosmic principles that constitute all that is. In such a world, everything and everyone is truly divine: father, mother, son, neighbor, every living creature. The good and the bad, the pure and the impure, all are God (KA 1.116). Narendra would joke about this world in which even the cup on the shelf was God, and all would laugh (KA 3.68), but this divine utensil was much more than a joke. For Ramakrishna, the cup truly vibrated with divine energies and the laughter was part of the mansion of fun. He who sees the world's divinity, he taught, has only spittle for that Vedantic "analysis" that falsely splits the world asunder: "Pthu! Pthu!" (KA 1.94).

Ramakrishna's disgust for Vedānta is fairly clear: spit and saliva do not lend themselves easily to misunderstanding or subtleties. But the assertion that "She herself has become everything" is not so precise, for it raises a number of important issues that are not apparent in my (or any) translation. I will address only two of them here: the problem of determining the gender of the divine in this phrase and in Ramakrishna's discourse in general; and the manner in which Ramakrishna's belief in the goddess's material immanence stemmed from his own experiences.

As with many religious texts, there is a real problem in determining the gender of the divine in Ramakrishna's language. It is a problem internal to the texts. Indeed, a character in one of the saint's stories asks simply, "Is Kālī a man or a woman?" (KA 5.68). Given the constant gender transformations that take place in the mythology of the goddess, it is not an unreasonable question. At least part of the difficulty stems from a simple linguistic fact: Bengali pronouns do not distinguish gender. One result of this linguistic indifference to gender is an unusually fluid religious world in which a masculine "Lord" (*iśvāra*), a feminine "goddess" (*devī*), and a neuter Absolute (*brahman*) all are referred to by a single pronoun, *tini*, "he," "she," *or* "it." Because of this ambiguity, the translator must rely primarily on context to determine the gender of the pronoun. Unfortunately, only rarely does the immediate context help with the maddeningly ambiguous phrase, "She/He/It herself/himself/itself has become everything." I usually translate it as "she" because of the more general religious context in which the phrase is uttered, namely, Ramakrishna's Śākta world.[46] As I have already pointed out, such a world is defined by a dialectic between transcendent consciousness, conceptualized as the masculine Śiva, and an immanent dynamic energy, conceptualized as the goddess Śakti. In Ramakrishna's

Tantric world, then, the world of form, energy, matter, and phenomenal experience was the world of *śakti*, the feminine force of the goddess, hence my translation, "She herself has become everything." But such a choice of translations should not blind us to the fact that Ramakrishna himself was quite open to changing the gender and terms of this divine omnipresence. "The universe is completely filled, above and below, with the Lord," the saint taught (KA 2.219).[47] Given such theological and linguistic nuances and the profound effect they seemed to have had on Ramakrishna's own self-understanding, I can only insist that my choice not be taken as an exclusive preference for a single gender. For a being such as Ramakrishna, a biological male who liked to wear women's clothes and is said to have menstruated, such an either-or approach to gender can only lead to serious misunderstanding and distortion. Indeed, when asked by a disciple whether he was a man or a woman, the saint confessed with a smile, "I don't know" (LP 3.1.35).[48] Neither do I. I would only insist that when approaching such questions of gender in Ramakrishna's language and behavior, we keep that smile.

It seems obvious that Ramakrishna's belief that "She herself has become everything" was rooted in his own mystical experiences. The experience that he quotes most often to prove his point is the famous Kālī Temple vision in which he saw everything as "made of consciousness" (*cinmaya*). This notion that "everything is made of consciousness" occurs again and again in Ramakrishna's teachings and visions. It happens "in a flash," lighting up the saint's consciousness as if it were a match being struck. Suddenly, without warning, there is light (KA 5.87).[49] In such a flaming state, human beings appear as pillows bobbing up and down on the ocean of consciousness (KA 3.68), or as leather bags with someone else wagging their hands and feet and heads (KA 3.249).[50] Souls are like countless bubbles in the water, or like globules (KA 4.42). Nature too is transformed. Trees appear as cosmic bouquets, perched on the head of the cosmic man (KA 2.192).[51] The field, moving with ants, takes on a new life: "Everything in this place is filled with consciousness!" the saint would shout. The flowers appear with layers and layers of brilliant petals bubbling with life: "Little bubbles! Big bubbles!" (KA 4.42). The streams too are dazzling and alive with their swarming minnows, their shiny scales shimmering with this same brilliant consciousness. The whole world sizzles with this consciousness, like the hot earth soaked with a summer rain (KA 3.33–34).[52]

Such visions led Ramakrishna to another conviction, namely, that it is false to think that one can see God only "within" in meditation: "I used to meditate with my eyes shut, but is the Lord not there if I open my eyes? When I open my eyes, I see that the Lord dwells in all creatures, in man, animals, trees, the sun and the moon, the water and the ground" (KA 2.128). People who think God is only inside are living in dark mud houses, he explained. But after the realization that God is within *and* without, the world itself becomes a glass house. The sun of gnosis can now enter in and shine its discerning light on the secrets of the soul (KA 3.193). In *samādhi,* the "face" of his consciousness is "turned inwards" (*antarmukha*), but when he turns this "face outwards" (*bahirmukha*), he still sees that "She herself has become everything." "I see both sides of the mirror as he!" Ramakrishna exclaims (KA 4.176). Again, the dialectic structures both the visions and Ramakrishna's discourse about them. We are back to *bhāvamukha* and a "face" turned simultaneously "in" toward the divine and "out" toward the world of existence.

Finally, one quality of these "Visions of Everything Filled with Consciousness" (KA 4.35)[53] or "Visions of Brahman" (KA 2.237)[54] should not go unnoticed, namely, their shining, shimmering, mercurial natures. It is significant that Ramakrishna's visions speak of a consciousness vibrating with energy and power and not of a "pure consciousness" devoid of every relation and quality. In Ramakrishna's world, such purity is reserved for the sleeping Śiva, blissfully aloof from the phenomenal world of bag-like people, bubbly animals, tree-bouquets, and shimmering schools of divine minnows.

THE LOVE-BODY OF THE GODDESS

"SHE HERSELF HAS BECOME everything." Yes, but this vision and the mansion of fun that it reveals are reserved for a certain stage on the religious path. Not everyone sees the omnipresent goddess. Not everyone can live in the magical mansion. There is a general method or path upon which the aspirant must embark to become a true "mystic" (*vijñānī*). Before I can explicate the contours of the final goal, then, I must first treat very briefly that which must be left behind. As with the rest of this chapter, the pattern will remain the same: Vedānta must be transcended for Tantra. The knower may be a Vedāntin, but he must eventually abandon his boring *Not this*'s and reach the radical affirmation of the Tantric mystic. He must renounce his renunciation and see that the world is no mat of deception but a mansion of fun.

Boring Vedānta

WHAT DID RAMAKRISHNA UNDERSTAND by the expressions the "knower" and the "mat of deception"? As we have seen above, each was an expression of what Ramakrishna called the "Vedānta view." But what was this "Vedānta view"? I have no intention here of wading into the literature on the broad and often contradictory system of Indian thought known as Vedānta. Such an enterprise would take us far from our present path and, in the end, would be quite superfluous, since Ramakrishna himself pursued no such understanding. In the end the essential prerequisite for this study is that we understand what *Ramakrishna* understood by Vedānta. Unfortunately, many (too many) of the books written about the saint completely ignore this one prerequisite and approach Ramakrishna through the "Vedantic" categories of others, particularly Vivekananda. But although what Vivekananda thought about Vedānta is of great historical interest, it is virtually useless and often quite distorting when we come to the simple preacher of Dakshineshwar, who had a penchant for summing up thousand year traditions in simplistic, almost jingle-like phrases. The "essence" of the *Gītā,* he taught, consists in repeating the title (you don't have to read the text!) over and over until it reverses itself: Gītā, Gī-tā, Gī-tā Gī tā gī Tā-gī, Tāgī." The essence of the *Gītā,* in other words, is *tāgī* or *tyāgī,* "renunciation."[55] Likewise, Ramakrishna loved to tell the story of a wandering holy man who carried a fat book with him wherever he went. When Ramakrishna opened it, he found only a single word, "Rāma." This, for the unlearned preacher, was an example of the highest devotion, the very essence of the *Rāmāyāṇa.*

And Vedānta? Its essence is only a little more complex. The essence of Vedānta, Ramakrishna taught, is the belief that *brahman* is real and the world is false, "like a dream." Because the world is illusory, not really real, it must be rejected with the famous chant of *neti neti,* "Not this! Not this!" until the coverings of society, the body, the mind, and finally the human subject are all annihilated in the pure existence that is *brahman* (KA 5.66). Such a state is beyond words. It is what is, pure and simple. This, "in essence," as Ramakrishna would say, is Vedānta.

But the knowers are boring, Ramakrishna complained, and their doctrine of *māyā* or "cosmic illusion" is too "dry" (KA 4.286). Their monotonous "Not this! Not this!" was something that the saint rejected as inadequate, a half-truth that encompassed only the first stage of the mystical quest. "But beyond the knowledge of *brahman,* there is something else," Ramakrishna taught. Beyond the Vedantic "analytical knowledge" (*jñāna*) is the "dialectical knowledge" (*vijñāna*) of the mystic (KA 3.55). Unlike Vedantic knowlege, which is exclusive, rejecting everything for the Absolute, the knowledge of the mystic is inclusive, including both the Absolute and the phenomenal world in its dialectical embrace. Such a mystic is like the cow that eats everything and so gives her milk in torrents, instead of in driblets as she did when she rejected everything like the knower (KA 1.180). Life flows now, like rich white milk.

This mystical life, far from being a lifelong struggle to renounce the world, is deeply sensual and profoundly emotional. The spiritual senses are employed in acts of talking, tasting, seeing, and laughing. Reality is no longer an impersonal Absolute. Now it is both other and self: "He is I, he is everything. The name of this is mystical knowledge [*vijñāna*]" (KA 3.9). There must always be this he, this other, for without "him" as other, the dialectic collapses back into the boring Absolute. The mystic falls back and becomes a dry knower again.

The Three Marks of the Mystical

BOTH THE STATES of the knower and the mystic can be approached through a study of a single preposition, *vi-*. Some years ago Betty Heimann alerted Indologists to the philosophical implications of seemingly innocent prepositions.[56] The study of mysticism has followed similar leads, concentrating largely on the linguistic nature of mystical experience and the structuring power of language and grammar. With these currents of thought and scholarship in mind, I want to look very briefly at what we might call the grammars of the knower and the mystic. By examining their respective uses of the preposition *vi-*, I will be able to isolate three characteristics or marks of the mystical as it is traced in the grammar and vocabulary of the *Kathāmṛta*.

First, let us look for a moment at the grammatical nature of the knower, the Vedantic sage who has renounced the world for the never-changing stability of *brahman*. The knower's primary method on the path to *brahman* is *vi-cāra* or "discriminating analysis," that mental discipline with which the knower cuts through every form to lay open its aggregate, and therefore illusory, nature. *Vi-* here implies division, discrimination, a cutting in two. It is the same *vi-* of *vi-veka* or "discrimination," and of Vi-veka-ananda ("the bliss of discrimination"), the religious name of Ramakrishna's most famous disciple. The grammatical lines of the knower here point to division and dualism. The *vi-* of the knower's *vicāra* and *viveka* functions as a grammatical analogue to Ramakrishna's mythical sword, that mental weapon that he used to cut the goddess in two and separate *brahman* from the world of forms.

But in Ramakrishna's teachings on the mystic, this *vi-* and its discriminating sword are eventually set down for another very different sort of *vi-*, that of *vi-jñāna* or "mystical knowledge." Nikhilananda translates the term as "super-knowledge." It could be translated more accurately as "dialectical knowledge," for here *vi-* implies, not a transcendence, a *super-*, but a dialectic of transcendence *and* immanence, a going back-and-forth. Such a truly mystical knowledge implies not division but synthesis, not a cutting in two but a holding together, not a renunciation or "cutting off" but a dynamic and often erotic union. The mystic's *vi-*, then, is a prepositional analogue of all of those commands to "Remain in *bhāvamukha*." Its grammatical bidirection mirrors the biographical directions of Ramakrishna's life and its attempt to hold in tension the demands of the phenomenal world and the attraction of the transcendent divinity. This dialectical character of *vi-* is the first mark or characteristic of the "mystic" (*vijñānī*), that possessor of the knowledge that reality is both One and Two.

This mystical *vi-*, then, is not that of the Vedantic sword that cuts the world into a real *brahman* and an unreal illusion, as in *vi-cāra* ("analysis") or *vi-veka* ("discrimination"). This *vi-* is the mystic's preposition. It is also the grammatical form of Kālī and Śiva's mystico-erotic union, that oneness that is both dialectical (as in *vi-jñāna*) and yet somehow upside down (as in *vi-parīta-rati*). Such a unique experience, then, not only unites ontological opposites but also transcends or transgresses the norms of society. And these two functions are themselves related, for every moral norm or social rule is inevitably built around a dualism between the world and the divine, the good and the bad, the pure and the impure, the proper and the improper. Consequently, an experience that has transcended every opposite by uniting them in a dialectical state is, *by definition*, beyond the purview of social or moral dualisms. This asocial or even amoral character of the unitive state is the second mark of the mystical in Ramakrishna's life and teachings.

But the mystic is more than someone who is convinced of the ontological dialectic of the real beyond and behind the deceptive mats of society. He is also someone who has experienced this reality *intensely*. The *vi-* of *vijñānī*, then, also implies intensity, depth, and emotional power. Hence Ramakrishna often glosses the experience with yet another *vi-* word, *vi-śeṣa* or "special." "The mystic enjoys the bliss of God in a special way," the saint taught. "Some people hear about milk, some people see it, and some people drink it. The mystic drinks milk, obtains bliss, and is nourished" (KA 3.77). This intense experiential nature of the mystical event is the third mark of the mystical in Ramakrishna's discourse.

The *vijñānī* or mystic in Ramakrishna's discourse, then, is *someone who has experienced intensely the dialectical nature of the real beyond the dualistic dichotomies of society.* An ontological *coincidentia,* a transcendence of social mores, and an experiential intensity—these are the three marks that characterize the mystic's experience in Ramakrishna's discourse. All three marks, moreover, are carried in the *Kathāmṛta* by a single preposition, *vi-*. Such a mystic embodies in his life and teachings the union of Kālī and Śiva, whose intensely erotic, socially improper, upside-down union constitutes everything that is.

Ramakrishna's Bhakti: When Lust Is Not Lustful

WHAT IS THE PRECISE NATURE of this "special way," this intensity that characterizes the mystical experience for Ramakrishna? For Ramakrishna, the nature of the mystical experience varies according to psychological temperament and the consequent *bhāva* or "identity" that the aspirant takes on to approach the divine.[57] For Ramakrishna, mystical knowledge is intimately bound up with these *bhāvas* and the *bhakti* or "devotional love" that they attempt to awaken: "To feel for sure that the Lord exists, this is called knowledge [*jñāna*]. To talk with him, to take him and enjoy bliss—as a Mother, a Friend, a Servant, or a Lover—this is called mystical knowledge [*vijñāna*]" (KA 3.56). The *vi-* of *vijñāna,* then, signals a deeply relational, dialectical sort of experience that is awakened within human-divine encounters modeled after human social and family relationships. It manifests itself in the mystery of emotion, in that dynamic in-between of human experience.

This in-between nature of the *bhāvas* (TS, 43) renders them particularly suitable to carry the experiential truths of true mystical knowledge, for their natures, like the reality to which they relate, are essentially dialectical. Accordingly, Ramakrishna can often be heard talking about these states and their *bhakti* in the same ontological categories I have examined above. In a whole series of sayings that Datta records for us, for example, the saint can be heard teaching in his usual Tantric style. In the first state of one type of practice, he tells his listeners, there is form, in the second there is formlessness, and in the third and final there is the state "beyond form and formlessness" (TP, no. 23). Knowledge (*jñāna*) is associated with the formless eternal, devotion (*bhakti*) is associated with the forms of the play (TP, no. 76), but this simple knowledge and this simple devotion (and the orders of reality they pertain to) become one with the appearance of the special "mystical knowledge" (*vijñāna*) that the direct experience of God produces in the Tāntrika's mind (TP, no. 73).[58] For Ramakrishna, in other words, both Vedantic knowledge and devotional love are subsumed (again) under the dialectics of his Tantric world.[59]

Ramakrishna has two basic typologies for these dialectical relations "beyond form and formlessness," one based on Vaiṣṇava states, the other working out of a Śākta model. In volume 3 of the *Kathāmṛta,* he sets out the classical Vaiṣṇava typology of the five states: the Peaceful, associated with the ancient sages, who "had no desire to enjoy anything else"; the Servant, practiced by Hanuman, who "worked for Rāma like a lion," and by the wife, who "serves her husband with all her heart"; the Friend, associated, among other things, with climbing on another's shoulders, as Kṛṣṇa's friends used to do to him; the Mother, whose model is Yaśoda, Kṛṣṇa's mother; and finally, the Lover, practiced by Rādhā, Kṛṣṇa's sweetheart. In this last state "are all the others" (KA 3.21–22).[60] In the same volume, Ramakrishna outlines a slightly different typology, this one influenced by Śākta states and their emphasis on the Tantric identities of the Hero and the Child: "In order to attain him, one must rely on a single state: the Hero, the Friend, the Servant, or the Child" (KA 3.83). At other times, the saint spoke of the Vaiṣṇava state of the Handmaid of Rādhā and the Śākta state of the Female Servant of the goddess. Basically what we have then is a religious world with nine major options: the six Vaiṣṇava states of the Peaceful, the Servant, the Friend, the Mother, the Handmaid, and the Lover; and the three Śākta states of the Hero, the Child, and the Female Servant of the goddess. Ramakrishna is said to have employed them all at some point or another. "What's my state?" Ramakrishna asks. Narendra replies: "The Hero, the Handmaid—all the states" (KA 3.253). Even for Narendra, a true master of hyperbole, such a statement was not much of an exaggeration.

Why does the mystic, so attuned to the basic unity of existence, take on such states and seek the experience of devotional love? Because, as hard as he may try, the "I" will not go away, and "*as long as he keeps the 'I' in the devotee, the path of devotional love is the straight one*" (KA 3.110).

But if this stubbornly persistent "I" needs love to attain God, this love also needs an "I" and a "mine." It must be possessive, and passionately so. Accordingly, the milkmaids were known for their passionate desire to possess Kṛṣṇa for themselves (KA 4.47). They did not want to be absorbed into the formless. They had already experienced that and had found it lacking: "There is a view that in their former lives Yaśoda and the milkmaids believed in the formless. They found no satisfaction in this, so taking Kṛṣṇa they enjoyed bliss in the play of Vrindavana. Kṛṣṇa one day said to them, 'You all should see the eternal realm. Come and let us bathe in the Yamuna.' As soon as they sunk under the waters, they immediately saw Golaka [the eternal realm]. After that, they saw the unbroken light. Then Yaśoda said, 'O Kṛṣṇa, I don't want to see all this—now may I see you in the form of man. May I take you in my lap and feed you'" (KA 5.99). This passage easily could be read as autobiographical, for, as we have seen in chapter 1, Ramakrishna had sunk into the formless waters in his First Vision and found it frightening. Perhaps this is why he described it as a drowning. Consequently, he would spend the rest of his life seeking meaning in relations that were at once human and divine. He would become a Mother to his disciples, and sometimes a Lover. Like Yaśoda, he would feed them, bathe them, and hold them in his lap. Sometimes he would even try to nurse them. And like Rādhā, he would yearn, "wrung like a wet towel," for their erotic presence. When they finally did arrive, he would joke with them as a Friend. Like Yaśoda and the milkmaids, he found Vedānta's formless Absolute less than satisfying. Rising back out of the waters, still gasping for air, he opted for the joys of a dialectical world and its mansion of fun. It was a world, after all, in which he could love.

Ramakrishna insists that this love for God contains no specifically sexual dimensions. The milkmaids' love was free from lust, he says repeatedly, as if to reassure himself.[61] So too, there was not even a "smell of lust" in the love the poet Chandidas felt for the washer-woman, Rukmini (KA 5.105). Likewise, only the forms of the passions remain in the mystic, the saint taught (KA 3.76). His lust has been "flattened," like the screws in the temple door that Ramakrishna saw pounded by lightning (KA 3.95). Or again, the mystic's desire is not like the frayed thread, split by lustful thoughts and desires and so unable to be threaded.[62] True devotional love, on the other hand, is like the trunk of the tree, thrust straight up out of the ground. It does not branch out (KA 5.39). Reversing the metaphor (and its meaning) in order to explain the relationship of "lust" (*kāma*) and "desire" (*kāmana*),

Ramakrishna taught that lust is the root of the tree and desires are its branches (KA 5.116).

It would not be too much to say that Ramakrishna's metaphors are somewhat confused, alternating back and forth between a denial and then an affirmation of sexual desire. Somehow devotional love is lustful, and somehow it is not. Or in Ramakrishna's words, "the lust of devotional love is not within lust" (KA 3.246). In the categories of this present study, one might say that this love is "erotic," at once mystical and sexual, "mystico-erotic." The Bengali resorts to the same hyphen in order to express this relationship between the mystical and the sexual. Ramakrishna, for example, often spoke of what he called his *bhakti-kāmana,* literally his "devotion-lust" or "lust of devotional love."[63] The hyphen is not terribly convincing, for it never quite defines the precise nature of this relationship between the mystical and the sexual, but it at least acknowledges, even if Ramakrishna wants to deny, that such a connection, perhaps even identity, in fact exists.

The Love-Body and Sex with the Self

THIS LUSTFUL AND YET lustless love, at once mystical and sexual, informs all of the senses. Ramakrishna thus insists that the mystic not only knows about the milk of mystical experience, he actually *tastes* it. He so completely absorbs its essence that he is "nourished" by it. He has eaten the mystical, so to speak. Similarly, Ramakrishna rejects the notion that religious experience is restricted to the sense of sight, to "visions" (TP, no. 27). The mystic, he insists, also "talks" to God and enjoys his intimate company: "In play we cracked knuckles. Then we talked. We talked! One talks to God! It's not just a matter of visions. One actually talks. Under the bel tree I saw God arise from the Ganges and come to me. Then how we laughed!" (KA 4.238). Such experiences are not "auditions" but "talks" (*kathā*) (KA 5.113 et al.) and "chats" (*alapa*).[64] Moreover, they are part of the experience itself, not just something that comes after it when one returns to normal consciousness. The mystical, if you will, is talkative to its dialectical core.

But this deeply personal love of the mystic goes much further than the mouth of taste and speech, for it creates an entire second body, what Ramakrishna calls the "love-body" (*premer śarīra*). With this new love-body and its "spiritual senses,"[65] the mystic communes with God in deeply sensual ways. Consider, for example, the following secret talk passage:

M: "Can the Lord be seen with these eyes?"

Sri Ramakrishna: "He can't be seen with these eyes of flesh. As one practices *sādhana* a love-body forms—with eyes of love and ears of love. With these eyes one sees him—with these ears his voice can be heard. Again, genitals of love form."

Hearing this, M broke out laughing, "Ho! Ho!" The Master became annoyed and spoke again.

Sri Ramakrishna: "With this love-body one has sex with the Self."

M again became serious. (KA 3.22)

As he had done with the paramahaṁsa boy, here again the saint takes a Vedantic category—"the Self" (*ātman*)—and eroticizes it. He arouses it out of its sleeping abstraction and engages it in deeply sensuous, explicitly erotic ways: quite bluntly, he "has sex" with it.

Now what it might mean "to have sex with the Self" is an open question. And unfortunately, this secret passage leaves the reader with more questions than answers. The phrase "genitals of love form" (*premer liṅga yoni hae*) is particularly ambiguous, since it could mean either "genitals of love form" or "a love phallus and a love vagina form." Although linguistically "genitals" is perhaps the preferable translation, the logistical quandaries involved in something like "sex with the/(one)Self" might also lead to a reading of the passage as an expression of Ramakrishna's androgynous, or even hermaphroditic, nature.

Fortunately, other passages in the *Kathāmṛta* can help us with Ramakrishna's love-body and its ability "to have sex with the Self." There are numerous passages, for example, that refer to Ramakrishna "erotically delighted in the Self" (*ātmārāma*).[66] Although most of these passages cannot be construed as explicitly erotic, when the same phrase is used to describe Kālī, its erotic meanings become more obvious. In a song Ramakrishna liked to sing, for example, Kālī is described as *ātmārāmā* when she engages Śiva in intercourse (KA 2.173–174). It is also relevant here that Ramakrishna often talked about "having sex" with the Self or with Saccidānanda. When one turns lust "around the corner," Ramakrishna teaches, one can "have sex with the Self" (KA 4.17).[67] It is interesting to note that there is only one figure in the *Kathāmṛta*, other than Ramakrishna, who is consistently described as having sex with *brahman*—Kālī, "who has sex with *brahman*" (KA 1.162).

Ramakrishna's tendency to give the neuter *brahman* a distinct gender is also important here, since it fits well into that general pattern of eroticizing Vedānta that I have examined above. In one passage, for example, Ramakrishna explains that the experience of *brahman* is ineffable. Just as the embarrassed wife gazes at her husband through a slat and becomes silent when her giggling girlfriends finally figure out which one he is, so too the experience of *brahman* can only be expressed in silence (KA 3.44). In this humorous passage, the male gender of *brahman* is only implied. In other passages, however, it is made more explicit. In one such passage, Ramakrishna explains how he used to take on "the state of Rādhā and Kṛṣṇa" and "the state of Caitanya." These, he explains, are the states of "the union of the male and female states" in which he would see Caitanya continuously. When such conditions eventually left him, his state began to change again as it alternated back to the other, formless side of the dialectic. Now he took down all of his pictures and began to think only of the unbroken Saccidānanda. But even here, in the formless, the erotic and its "union of the male and female states" appeared, for the saint now meditated on the unbroken formlessness as "the primordial man." He remained, he tells us, in the state of the Female Servant, "the Handmaid of the man" (KA 3.137–138).[68] He then goes on to describe another vision of having sex with the Self, a vision which, on closer inspection, turns out to be a variant of the cunnilingus vision that I have analyzed above. None of this should strike the reader as new. Saccidānanda (yet another Vedantic category) is imagined as male, Ramakrishna becomes female, and his numerous states form themselves around erotic "unions" and "sex with the Self." Boring Vedānta has become sexy.

The Goddess-Body and Sex with Brahman

RAMAKRISHNA'S SECRET LOVE-BODY, then, is part of that larger pattern that I analyzed in chapter 2 in which Ramakrishna, like Kālī, has sex with Vedantic states and figures. When we turn to another complex of passages, this love-body becomes identified with the goddess's own divine body, transforming the experience of "sex with the Self" into a more explicit Tantric state.

Consider, for example, a passage in volume 4. Ramakrishna is talking again about his "love" (*prema*) for Saccidānanda. This love, he teaches, is the same love that drove Sītā and Parvatī to practice asceticism in order to acquire female bodies with which they could "know" God as man. Ramakrishna then describes his Sītā vision in which he saw her "filled with *rāma*" (*rāmamaya*) (KA 4.36). As I pointed out in chapter 2, this vision draws on a wordplay: *rāma* can refer to the god "Rāma," the object of Sītā's passion, or to the erotic passion itself. "Being filled with *rāma*," in other words, describes a state in which one's desired object (*rāma*) and one's desire (*rāma*) are linguistically identical. We are back to "having sex with the Self," a nondual sort of eroticism.[69]

This passage on love's ability to turn one into a divinely passionate woman is related to two others. In the first, Ramakrishna refers to four types of bodies, the third of which he calls "the goddess-body" (*bhagavatīr tanu*). Ramakrishna describes it thus: "This is the body with which one enjoys the bliss of the Lord and takes pleasure" (KA 1.250). He then goes on to associate this goddess-body with the Tantras. In the second passage, Ramakrishna contrasts the ancient Vedic seers, who saw the divine as supersensual consciousness, with the devotee, who takes on a love-body to actually "see" this consciousness. Here he explicitly equates this love-body with the goddess-body (KA 5.36).

If we take all of these passages together, we can safely conclude that the love-body of the secret talk passage quoted at the beginning of this subsection is Ramakrishna's version of the Tantric goddess-body, that female spiritual form which the devotee, in imitation of Sītā and Parvatī, acquires through asceticism and *sādhana* in order to engage the divine male in mystical intercourse. The mystic, in effect, takes on the body of the goddess and becomes Kālī to "have sex with *brahman*."

The Pansomatic Orgasm

The love-body, then, is a Tantric entity rooted in mythology and Ramakrishna's experience of a male *brahman*. But what about the curious phrase, "having sex with the Self"? What does it refer to? We know that Ramakrishna used it to describe at least two moments: his secret vision of himself licking vagina-shaped lotuses; and the end result of turning one's lust "around the corner." But what does such an experience *feel* like? Ramakrishna tries to tell us in that most secret of volumes, volume 4: "Sex with a woman—what pleasure is there in that! When one has a vision of the Lord, one experiences a bliss ten million times greater than the pleasure of sex. Gauri used to say that when the great love [*mahābhāva*] occurs, all the holes of the body—down to the hairpores—become great vaginas. In each and every hole, one experiences the pleasure of sex with the Self" (KA 4.36).[70] It would be difficult to imagine a more thoroughly orgasmic state than this, with every hairpore and hole now a vagina being penetrated by the phallic

Self. It is important to point out, however, that the experience described in the passage is *not* Ramakrishna's. It is Gauri's. Gauri was one of Ramakrishna's numerous Tantric friends. Perhaps Ramakrishna approved of Gauri's description of the mystical state because it described so well what he himself had been experiencing all along, or perhaps he simply found the description compelling.

In any case, these hairs and holes appear elsewhere in the texts. Examining the context of their textual appearances is, as always, instructive. Throughout the *Kathāmṛta,* for example, Ramakrishna keeps shouting about the hairs of his body standing on end, "erect" in their vaginal holes, Gauri might say. "Look! Look! My body is all a tingle. Look with your hand! I have goosebumps all over my body!" (KA 5.60). It is a common scene. In one such scene, Ramakrishna looks at the boy Rakhal and gets these same erotic goosebumps (KA 4.4). Again, talking about Naren's lack of lust, Ramakrishna's body catches fire: "Look with your hand! My body is tingling." M ponders this scene and thinks to himself: "Wherever there is no lust the Lord is present. . . . Is this why Ramakrishna gets so excited?" (KA 3.263). Ramakrishna's "lust" (*kāma*), that trunk of the psychic tree, has disappeared only to be transformed into a mystico-erotic "love" (*prema*). Indeed, he is now equipped with an entire body of this mystical love, complete with genitals. Every hair stands erect, every hole shakes with pleasure. He has taken on a love-body, a goddess-body filled with divine passion for the male god.

"Ramakrishna Paramahaṁsa"

RAMAKRISHNA LIVED IN AND PREACHED a Tantric world. Voices commanded him to "Remain in *bhāvamukha,*" to remain poised within that dialectical union of the Absolute and the phenomenal world that defines Tantra. He struggled to unite the goddess and the god, the world of *śakti* and the world of *brahman.* And he saw. He saw his world literally shaking with the bliss of Śiva and Śakti engaged in sexual intercourse. Appropriately, he sang of the goddess on top of the god and preached a mansion of fun that left the renouncing ways of Vedānta far behind. When he did encounter Vedantic figures and personalities in his life and visions, he engaged them in erotic encounters in an attempt to awaken them out of their abstract slumber. Often, these arousals took a phallic form. He worshiped his own penis as Śiva's living-*liṅgam.* He fondled the penises of young paramahaṁsas, both human and divine. He had sex with neuter Vedantic abstractions turned male—the Self, *brahman,* and Saccidānanda. Finally, he quoted approvingly a Tāntrika's description of the mystical state: the body aroused with thousands of vagina-like holes and tiny phallic hairs, all engaged in orgasmic intercourse in every nook and cranny of the body. This was the love-body, the body of the goddess that has sex with *brahman*, with Śiva, with the Self. In all of this, almost uncanningly, Ramakrishna embodied the goddess's *śakti*. Taken as a whole, his numerous visions and ecstatic states amount to a nuanced and sensuous description of Kālī's body, "delighting in reverse sexual intercourse with Śiva."

When we encounter the traditional interpretations of Ramakrishna as a Vedāntin, then, we should be very careful. It seems clear that by opting to call Ramakrishna a "paramahaṁsa," Ramakrishna's followers have sought to emphasize the traditional and the philosophical, the Vedantic nobility, if you will, of their Master. But by doing so, they have nevertheless omitted another side of the saint, perhaps the most important side. For, as I have shown in this chapter, Ramakrishna's experiences of the Vedantic paramahaṁsa diverge radically from the perceptions of his followers. In the secret visions and revelations of Ramakrishna, the paramahaṁsa is almost always naked, he is often a boy, and he is usually an erotic object. He appears in secret visions and is worshiped in secret ritual acts over which Ramakrishna himself has little if any control. Above all, the paramahaṁsa's phallus fascinates Ramakrishna: the saint fondles it, worships it, teases shining pearls out of it. This is what seems to have attracted Ramakrishna to the paramahaṁsa figure. Certainly it was not Vedānta. That was all too dry and boring.

When we come across the name, "Ramakrishna Paramahaṁsa," then, we should look twice. Certainly such a name points to the tradition's attempt to present a Sanskritic figure poised in the truths of Vedānta. But it also carries other secret meanings connected to the saint's homoerotic desires and Tantric categories. "Ramakrishna Paramahaṁsa," in other words, is an ironic title. On the surface it may be superficially Vedantic, but in its secret depths it is profoundly, provocatively Tantric. As with his life and teachings, even the saint's name points to the iconography of Kālī, the Tantric goddess who stands on top of the Vedantic god and "has sex with *brahman*."

CHAPTER FOUR

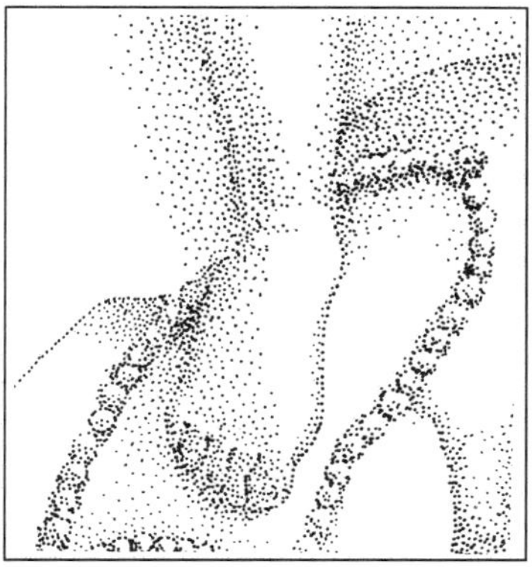

Kālī's Feet: Ramakrishna's Descent into the Forms of Man

> Who has seen such a crazy woman,
> Standing on the heart-lotus of her husband!
>
> Ramprasad

IN HIS GODDESS-BODY of mystical love, Ramakrishna sought out the divine man. As Kālī engages Śiva in sexual intercourse, Ramakrishna had sex with the Self, with Saccidānanda, with *brahman*. His mystico-erotic energies had been transformed, turned away from the social world and "around the corner" to the Absolute. The energies were ascending. But there was another, equally meaningful movement in his life. Voices commanded him to descend, to come back, or at least to keep looking back. He was to keep his ontological "face turned towards the world of form" (*bhāvamukha*). Somehow he was to balance the ascending and descending energies in a dialectical rhythm. But at first he did not listen. He could not look back. He could not turn his face around and descend back into the very world he had tried so hard to escape. Eventually, as we have seen, he did look back and return to this world. Through the eyes of a face looking out from the Absolute into the phenomenal world, the world no longer appeared as something to reject as unreal or renounce as impure. It shimmered now with the goddess's own energies. It had revealed itself as a mansion of fun, a place of song, dance and laughter.

I have examined the doctrinal results of this return in chapter 3, but I have said nothing of its biographical dimensions. Consequently, many important questions remained unanswered: When did Ramakrishna finally begin to listen to the voices and return to the human world? What happened in his life that brought him back to the mansion of fun? And finally, when he did return to the world, in what ways were his now simultaneously ascending and descending energies integrated into the social world? It is to these questions that I now want to turn.

I will argue in the course of this chapter that Ramakrishna's descent back into the world was related, both psychologically and chronologically, to the coming of his disciples. I will demonstrate this by focusing on one of Ramakrishna's most important secret visions, the vision of Jagannath. This particular experience occurred sometime in 1884, when most of the disciples had arrived and a community had begun to form around the saint. I will argue that the community provided the context for the vision and acted as its catalyst. The explicitly erotic context of this vision, its command to Ramakrishna, and its painful consequences (the Paramahaṁsa dislocated his hand within the vision) lie at the center of the present chapter. As a result of the experience, Ramakrishna finally began to descend back into the human world and, in the words of the secret vision, "delight in God in the forms of man." I will advance the thesis that it was this turning around and descent that eventually led, through a complex social process of debate and belief, to the declaration that Ramakrishna was an incarnation or "descent" (*avatāra*) of God. Psychologically speaking, as a result of the vision and its command to "delight in God in the forms of man," Ramakrishna's energies *had* descended into the world in order to incarnate themselves in social forms and human relationships. The mythology of the incarnation gave both Ramakrishna and the disciples a language with which they could express the power and depth of their experiences of these descending energies. The change instituted by the vision and the dislocated hand thus took on its final and most developed form. The mystical and the erotic were transformed into the mythological and the theological.

To establish such a reading, I begin once again with a particular iconographic feature of Kālī—her feet. As we shall see shortly, these crimson feet function in primarily two ways: they charge the corpse-like Śiva with the goddess's divine *śakti;* and they enable the goddess's human devotees to have some access to her seemingly distant and fearful divinity. Kālī's feet thus act as erotic channels (with Śiva) and as mediators between the divine and human worlds (with her devotees). They can thus function as proper symbolic foci for the present chapter, so concerned with the erotic dimensions of Ramakrishna's descent back into the human world of his devoted followers and the theological debate that such an erotic descent generated.

KĀLĪ'S FEET

WHAT DO KĀLĪ'S FEET MEAN? First of all, Kālī's feet are Indian feet, and feet in India mean certain things. Perhaps most significantly for our purposes, feet are the sacred meeting point of the human and the divine in Indian culture. They are the "bridge" that unites the world of the gods and the world of human beings. Accordingly, that which is lowest on the body of God or the guru (who embodies God for the devotee) is the very highest that humanity, caught in its sufferings and delusions, can ever hope to reach: at the sacred feet, the highest of the low may touch the lowest of the high. Consequently, common forms of homage to one's guru include drinking the water with which his feet have been washed, placing one's head (the highest part of one's body) on his feet (the lowest part of his), and massaging his feet. Related to this symbolism of the low and the high on the human body is the fact that feet also represent that which is most humble, even that which is despised. As early as the *Ṛg Veda* in the famous "hymn of man" (10.90), for example, the four castes of Indian society are created when *puruṣa*, the cosmic man, is sacrificed and dismembered: his mouth becomes the sacred priest, his arms the mighty warrior, his thighs the people, and his feet the lowly servant.[1] The body of society, modeled on the body of the cosmic man, is thus structured hierarchically. That which is high is pure. That which is low is less pure or impure.

These ancient meanings are reworked and expanded upon in the Tantric literature, where Kālī's feet often dominate the imagery as the primary focus of devotion and meditation. Indeed, Kālī's feet seem to be everywhere in the Śākta songs. In an attempt to order their numerous connotations, I will adopt the traditional division of Tantric culture into its conservative or "right-handed" tradition and its radical or "left-handed" tradition and, somewhat playfully I admit, divide Kālī's crimson feet into what I will call their "right-footed" and "left-footed" meanings.

Right-Footed Tantra

IN GENERAL, the right-footed meanings of Kālī's feet correspond to her right hands, those that offer boons and dispel fear. This right-handed, right-footed Kālī is a nurturing, motherly goddess, who cares for her children involved in the world. Accordingly, right-footed Tantra concentrates on Kālī's feet as objects of refuge, mediation, and union.

Above all, the poets pray again and again to Kālī's feet as a place of *refuge.* For the sake of analysis, we might divide this refuge into three general types: refuge within the world of *saṁsāra,* refuge or freedom from fear, and refuge or protection from death. Because the way of the Śākta, like most Tantric paths, is the way of the householder, the Śākta poets often pray for refuge, not from the world but *within* the world: "The householder's life is the supreme religion," Ramprasad sings. But precisely because he is a householder, Ramprasad confesses that he cannot renounce the world. He must remain in it, and so he sings, "Let me have my abode at your feet."[2] Kālī's feet, then, offer the householder some haven in which to rest for a moment from his busy schedule and numerous concerns.

In this troubling world of the householder, Kālī's feet, much like her top right hand, also grant "fearlessness" (*abhaya*). "O mind! Be absorbed in the feet of Mother who destroys all fears," Ramprasad sings.[3] The poets also sing of Kālī's feet as a refuge, not from the world, but from Kālī herself: "I'm lying here holding your feet and you don't even look at me once, Ma! . . . All shut their eyes in fear, hold your feet, and cry out, 'Ma! Ma!'" (SP, no. 189). Her waist is covered with bloody hands, her breasts are adorned with lopped-off heads, and half her arms threaten immediate death. Where else could the Child go?

Kālī's feet thus protect the poet from the Mother who inspires terror. But they also protect the poet from the Father who lies prostrate below her. For he is death, and since even this death is subdued by Kālī's feet, the poet prays to her feet to be spared from that ultimate of fears: "How can he fear death who remembers Ma's feet and their gift of fearlessness?" (RJS, no. 291). Like her right hands, then, these feet are truly right feet, protecting the poet both from the terror of the goddess's left side and from the pale corpse beneath her feet.

Kālī's feet, in other words, lie in between the comfortable human world and the awful divine world. As such, they are particularly suited to offer *mediation.* They are thus likened to places of pilgrimage (SP, no. 332), those sacred and yet earthly places where the divine is especially manifest. Because they offer this mediation, Kālī's feet are also the objects of meditation: "For the sake of liberation, the yogī ponders in his heart the lotus feet of Kālī" (RJS, no. 67). Such meditation leads eventually to immersion and absorption, to *union* in these feet. "O Tārā, I long to merge in those rosy feet" (RJS, no. 47). Soon the poet's music merges with the tinkling bells of the goddess's feet. They become one in a new state of being, a new land: "Merging my life in your feet and blending my tune with your anklets' sound, I have learnt a song of that land."[4] This is the state of *mokṣa* or "liberation" (SP, no. 182).

Left-Footed Tantra

THE RIGHT-FOOTED FEET of Kālī, then, carry connotations of refuge, mediation, and union. These are all respectable, public meanings. The left-footed meanings of Kālī's feet, on the other hand, are more secret. They tend to focus on Kālī's feet as instruments of sexual contact and oedipal struggle. Unlike the right-footed passages, which are usually uttered as heart-felt prayers and devout assertions, these left-footed passages are often characterized by their troubled questions and amazed exclamations. They are marked by ambivalence, wonder, and complaint. "O mind, tell me how this can be! She kicks the Lord in the chest!" (RJS, no. 315). And again: "Who has seen such a crazy woman, standing on the heart-lotus [of her husband]!" (RJS, no. 57). In such left-footed passages, Kālī's feet are not a place of refuge, mediation, or union. *They are a problem.*

And like her left-handed rituals, these left feet are strangely, troublingly sexual: "The naked woman, the naked man. Father plays with her feet," Ramprasad sings (SP, no. 262). In other songs, the poet is more explicit about the sexual dimensions of his Mother's feet: "She is immersed in sexual delight on top of her husband. He trembles as he tries to hold the weight of her feet" (KA 1.196). In this passage, there is a clear association between Kālī's feet "standing" on Śiva and the upside-down posture of *viparītarati* or "reversed sexual intercourse." The goddess is standing on top of her husband for sexual reasons, and the poets know this. Because of this, their songs about Kālī's feet perched on the chest of Śiva are often filled with expressions of shock, amazement, and, as we shall see in chapter 5, shame. In many paintings and icons, moreover, as Kālī "stands" on Śiva, Śiva's penis stands erect. Something other than refuge and mediation is transmitted by her beautiful feet.

Occasionally, another left-footed dimension peeps through the songs. There is something oedipal about this dimension, for it is revealed in contexts defined by the poet's complaint and challenge directed at his divine Father, Śiva: "After stealing Ma's feet, whom does Śiva vainly threaten with death? Ma's treasure goes to the son. What right does he have to this treasure?" (SP, no. 312). Banking on his Mother's grace, the poet challenges his own Father, if in vain: "O Ma!

When I ask for my riches [her rosy feet], all I get is trouble and lots of tricks" (SP, no. 314). In other songs, the Child seems to acknowledge this unjust favoritism and resorts to disgruntled complaints: "O Ma Tārā! You've tricked me and given your feet . . . to Śiva" (RJS, no. 48). In still other songs, the singing Child speculates that Śiva pretends to be a corpse beneath Kālī's feet in order to deprive him of her feet: "He fakes death, O Ma, in order to get your feet . . ." (RJS, no. 72).[5] The Child suspects a trick.

Finally, it is important to point out that Kālī's feet often are compared to red lotuses,[6] those blossoming petals whose crimson color is associated with fertility and active sexuality in the culture and whose shape, as we have already seen, suggests far more than the simple nature of a floating flower.

To sum up, one might say that the many meanings of Kālī's feet can be divided into two general patterns: those meanings readily apparent to the public culture and accepted as traditional (refuge, mediation, and union); and those meanings implicit in the symbolism but not widely accepted by the public culture (sexual contact and oedipal focus). As I hope to demonstrate below, similar patterns of mediation and sexual contact were embodied again in the life of Ramakrishna. Certainly Ramakrishna's feet became an object of devotion and faith. But, very much like Kālī's feet, they also constituted *a problem*. How that problem was solved, or at least muted, is the topic of the present chapter.

THE COMING OF THE DISCIPLES, 1868–1885

I ENDED THE LAST CHAPTER'S biographical section with a discussion of Ramakrishna's pilgrimage to Benares and Vrindavana and a short analysis of his "Jesus state." For both Datta and Saradananda, this Jesus state concluded Ramakrishna's *sādhana* period (JV[5], 57). For the swami, the pilgrimage too was filled with meaning, for it was on this pilgrimage that Ramakrishna came to see clearly that only he had fully realized that all religions lead to the same goal. According to Saradananda, he now desired to know who would grasp and accept this "modern noble state."[7] He now anxiously longed for the coming of his disciples. His universalist realization was thus followed by a long period of anxiety and longing. For Saradananda, the doctrine seems to be the most important thing. For Ramakrishna, it was most certainly the desire.

The pilgrimage took place in 1868. Mathur died in 1871. Sharada showed up at the temple in 1872 and at some point (depending on which biography one believes) was worshiped as "the sixteen-year-old girl." But still there were no disciples. Often, it seems, the saint grew impatient, even depressed. Was his prediction that the disciples would come soon a mere delusion? Before he died, Mathur tried his best to console his young priest, pointing out that he was a host of disciples in one person, but that did not seem to help much (LP 2.19.17). At some point, we are told, the Mother assured Ramakrishna that his beloved disciples would begin coming if only he could become known in a certain place, the garden of Belgharia, where the famous religious leader, Keshab Chandra Sen, met with his disciples (LP 4.4.56). Accordingly, Ramakrishna sought out the garden and its inhabitants in the year 1875. With that visit, Ramakrishna entered written history.

Keshab's Newspapers

RAMAKRISHNA'S VISIT TO BELGHARIA deeply impressed Keshab. Keshab responded by writing about the saint in the numerous Brahmo newspapers of the day. All the Brahmo journals were full of talk about Ramakrishna, Saradananda notes. The biographer is quite clear that it was Keshab's writings that brought the disciples to Ramakrishna: "the general Calcutta public was able to know about Ramakrishna only after his meetings with Keshab Chandra [Sen]," he writes (LP 5.1.1.1).[8] Keshab seems to agree. He told Ramakrishna that he published articles about him in order that people might come to him (KA 4.89). "Now you shall remain for sometime a secret. But gradually this place will become a forest of people," Keshab told his saintly friend (KA 5.210). Ramakrishna responded to Keshab's faith in the printed word by telling him that such newspaper articles were unnecessary. If the Lord wants to make a man famous, he told Keshab, nothing will prevent the man from becoming famous, not even living in a lonely forest. "What can man do?" (KA 5.224).

But Ramakrishna did not live in a forest and, despite his skepticism regarding human agency, Keshab's newspaper articles greatly influenced the coming of his disciples, almost all of whom showed up only *after* Keshab took up his cause in print. Indeed, until the famous religious leader began writing articles about "the Hindu saint" from Dakshineshwar, Ramakrishna remained little more than an unknown priest, tucked away in a comfortable temple somewhere north of Calcutta. It was Keshab's newspapers that changed all that. They put Dakshineshwar "on the map." Indeed, one of the many ironies of Ramakrishna's life is the fact that although he despised newspapers as Western intrusions into India's spiritual landscape and avoided them with religious fervor, they nevertheless proved to be one of the single most important instruments in bringing his beloved disciples to him. Again and again in the *Kathāmṛta,* Ramakrishna criticizes his followers for not believing in anything unless it appears in "the newspaper." Accordingly, he liked to tell the story of two friends, one of whom had just seen a house collapse. As the event had not yet made it into the local headlines, the other friend refused to believe him. Such a lack of faith leads to the present predicament, he continued, in which people now have a difficult time believing in the existence of incarnations. Since "such a thing is not in their English writings," it must not, it cannot exist (KA 3.187–188).[9] Such comments constituted a trenchant criticism of Western forms of thought and writing uttered by an indignant saint operating with completely different notions of reality, authority, and social legitimacy. It was a criticism that bordered on disgust and manifested itself in physical behavior. Ramakrishna could not even touch a newspaper, lest its worldly ways rub off on him (KA 1.199). Indeed, so much did he mistrust the printed word that he would not even handle a hand-written letter, unless of course it dealt with religious topics (KA 4.248).

But the printed word ignored the saint's reproaches and continued on its way. In the process, it was instrumental in making famous the very saint who could not touch it. The first recorded mention of Ramakrishna in a published document appears in 1875, in a short article by Keshab entitled "A Hindu Saint." It appeared in the Brahmo Samaj paper, the *Indian Mirror,* and spoke of Ramakrishna's "depth, penetration and simplicity" and of the "never-ceasing metaphors and analogies in which he indulged."[10] Two very short articles followed, both in the *Indian Mirror,* in February of 1876 and 1877. The 1877 article focused on Ramakrishna's physical appearance and ecstatic states: "His physical condition being very debilitated and his heart susceptible of strong religious impulses he cannot bear the pressure of feelings and often becomes unconscious and is subject to cataleptic fits."[11] In 1879, Pratap Chandra Mozoomdar, a disciple of Keshab, published another piece, an article in *The Theistic Quarterly Review* entitled "Sri Ramakrishna Paramahamsa." Mozoomdar opened the short piece with a strikingly honest question: "What is there in common between him and me? I, a Europeanized, civilized, self-centered, semi-sceptical, so-called educated reasoner, and he, a poor, illiterate, shrunken, unpolished, diseased, half-dressed, half-idolatrous, friendless Hindu devoteee?"[12] Mozoomdar then went on to describe Ramakrishna's austerities as having "permanently disordered his system, inflicted a debility, paleness, and shrunkenness upon his form and features that excite the deepest compassion." "He has nothing extraordinary about him," Mozoomdar informed his readers, except his "absolute conquest of lust" and "his avoidance of woman and wealth." This, for Mozoomdar, is "the whole secret of his matchless moral character."[13]

Anxious Longing from the Music Tower

IT WAS SUCH "GOOD PRESS" that issued in one of the most important periods in the life of Ramakrishna, the coming of the disciples. In most of the major biographies, this coming of the disciples is portrayed as a major event in Ramakrishna's life, and indeed it was. Ramakrishna had visited a number of famous scholars, religious leaders, and saints, all of whom had followings. He seems to have been impressed by this and wondered whether he would have similar disciples. This desire soon translated itself into vision. Ramakrishna thus began "seeing" his future disciples in visions. These "marked" disciples would come to be known as "the disciples who had been seen."[14] He thought he could make out their faces, but, as we will see, he was often mistaken.

At first Ramakrishna thought that Keshab's Brahmo disciples would follow him, but he was quickly disappointed: "It did not take him long," Saradananda writes in his typical polemical style, "to understand that, influenced by Western learning and ways, they were quickly falling far from the national religious ideal, and many at times were considering social work to be the highest form of religious practice" (LP 5.1.1.4).[15] Disappointed by the Westernized Brahmos, who were so deluded by their social projects, Ramakrishna turned again to his desire. Soon it developed into a form of that anxious desire that I studied in chapter 1. Ramakrishna, "wrung like a wet towel," would climb the music tower of the temple precincts and literally cry for his disciples. Some passages claim that the saint's longing was so great that it actually caused the disciples to come, as if the energies of the desire somehow cast out a series of magnetic attractions over the streets of Calcutta from the music tower. Like so much else about Ramakrishna's life, his anxious desire for the disciples was believed to be "synchronous," in tune with the actual sequence of events. Desire and history worked together.

Whether it was a cosmic desire or the printed word or both that brought them, eventually the disciples did in fact begin to come. It is to the events of these arrivals that I now want to turn. But before I do, I need to say something about the textual record of these years, for like other aspects of Ramakrishna's life, the textual record, if taken as a whole, is interesting and provocative as it sometimes offers us a very different picture of things than has usually been presented in the official literature of the Ramakrishna Order. If one should read only these renouncer texts, one would get the overwhelming impression that Narendra's appearance totally eclipsed all others in importance. Almost one hundred pages, for example, are given to Narendra's first few visits in Saradananda's *Līlāprasaṅga*. I do not want to belittle the importance of Narendra's visits. On the contrary, I will spend the rest of this section treating those crucial visits. But I also think that it is important to point out that not every text considers Narendra's arrival to be so central.

As I have already pointed out, Narendra's cousin, Ram Chandra Datta, does not even mention Narendra, much less his first visits, in his *Jīvanavṛttānta*. In this account, it is *Ram's* first visits that merit the pages. When we turn to another householder text, M's *Kathāmṛta*, we find a similar pattern: whereas M's first visits are given nearly twenty full pages at the very beginning of the volumes, Narendra's are only mentioned in passing. We, I think, can conclude from such a pattern that these three texts are formed around three very different impressions of what constituted "the coming of the disciples." The one renouncer text, Saradananda's *Līlāprasaṅga*, predictably argues for the centrality of Narendra. The two householder texts, on the other hand, argue for the importance of the householders, and more specifically, of the authors themselves. Again, we are back to conflicting visions that seem to polarize themselves around the renouncer/householder conflict. Although the early visits of Datta and M are important, and in some places quite revealing in their honest descriptions of the financial and emotional costs supporting such a new religious movement entailed, the specific meanings of these visits are not as central to the themes of the present study and its attempt to uncover the erotic dimensions of Ramakrishna's life and teachings. Ramakrishna may have accepted Ram and M as his disciples, but he truly loved Narendra. For the sake of brevity and focus, then, I will only discuss here the first meetings, or what the texts more accurately, I think, call "visions" (*darśana*), of this "beloved disciple."

The Problem of Narendra's First Three Visits

UNLIKE DATTA'S FIRST ENCOUNTERS with the Master, which are virtually unknown, there is perhaps no series of events in the life of Ramakrishna recounted more often and with more fascination than Narendra's first three visits to the Dakshineshwar temple. In the fifth and final volume of his famous *Līlāprasaṅga*, Saradananda writes of them in an engaging account that has become permanently etched into the Bengali religious consciousness. With its appearance, all others seemed to have fallen into line. In the preface to the second edition of *The Life of Swami Vivekananda*, for example, the editors note that they have "re-written" their account of these first meetings to bring them into line with that of Saradananda.[16] In fact, their new account amounts to little more than a collection of huge verbatim quotes drawn directly from Saradananda's text. Datta's text suffers a similar fate. Despite the troubling fact that Narendra never appears in its pages, the editor of its sixth edition took the liberty of "correcting" and rearranging its contents until the text agreed with the canonical volumes of M and Saradananda (JV[7], "editor's note to sixth edition").

Given the importance and centrality of these first three visits, especially as they are recorded by Saradananda, it is essential that I spend some time with them. As I will approach them, the events of these first visits will reveal a number of patterns that I have already identified as lying at the center of Ramakrishna's secret: the erotic nature of Ramakrishna's "anxious desire"; the troubling, perhaps even scandalous, nature of Ramakrishna's relationships with his boy disciples; and the accusations of madness. I want to add another pattern here, one most appropriate for this present chapter so concerned with Kālī's feet: the strange power of Ramakrishna's touch, especially as it manifested itself in the Paramahaṁsa's feet. All of these elements are present in Narendra's first three visits. I will argue that they constituted *a problem* for Narendra, for Ramakrishna, and for Saradananda. Here I want to define the specific nature of this problem and show how these three interpreters—the visitor, the visited, and the biographer—tried to solve it. But first, I need to recount the visits themselves.

Sometime in 1881, perhaps in November, Ramakrishna was enjoying a gathering at the home of Surendra Mitra, one of his householder disciples. Ram Chandra Datta was there with his eighteen-year-old cousin, Narendra, then a college student and a frequent participant in the Brahmo Samaj. Surendra had invited Narendra to sing at the gathering. Ramakrishna was immediately taken with the teenager. He asked Surendra and Ram to bring the boy to Dakshineshwar, but then, perhaps not willing to wait, examined Narendra's body and invited the student himself. The Paramahaṁsa was quite open about the effects this initial meeting had on him. So anxiously did he desire the boy's presence, he told his disciples, that he felt as if he were a wet towel being wrung. So distraught was he over the teenager that he would go to an abandoned part of the temple precincts and weep loudly for Narendra. Only after such crying could he control himself. This, we are told, went on for some six months (LP 5.3.6).

Sometime during these six months, or perhaps shortly after, Narendra finally showed up at Dakshineshwar. Saradananda tells his readers that he learned "from a reliable source" that Ramakrishna would cover up many of the strong feelings he had felt for Narendra during that first meeting when he later spoke about the event to the disciples (LP 5.3.7). There was something secret about the event. Because of Ramakrishna's reticence to talk about the experience (a rare form of silence for the saint), Saradananda has to rely on Narendra's account of the meeting. According to Narendra, Ramakrishna led him to the northern porch and closed the door behind them. Since it was winter, screens covered the porch from the outside, so the spot of their encounter was concealed from all eyes. As soon as Ramakrishna got the college student inside, he grabbed his hand and began to "rave and weep," complaining all the while that Narendra had waited too long to come. At this point, Ramakrishna's mood changed. He stood before an already confused Narendra, folded his hands in homage, and said: "I know, Lord, that you are that ancient sage Nārāyāṇa . . . who has taken a body again in order to take away the sufferings of souls."[17]

That was about all poor Narendra could take. "This one is completely insane," Narendra thought to himself. "If he is not, then why does he say all these things about me, the son of Bishwanath Datta?" While Narendra puzzled over the scene, Ramakrishna left the porch and came back with some sweets and candy. He insisted that Narendra eat them and then asked him to return again, this time alone. Narendra, for some reason, promised that he would.

When the scene finally ended and Narendra reentered the room, he found to his amazement that Ramakrishna was acting quite normal with everyone else. The Paramahaṁsa, it seemed, was only "mad" in relation to Narendra. Narendra watched him closely. He was deeply impressed with Ramakrishna's teachings and the purity of his soul, but he finally concluded, with the help of some Western psychology, that Ramakrishna was a "monomaniac" (LP 5.3.9).[18] The problem was solved, at least for now, through psychology. Narendra was pathologizing Ramakrishna.

Saradananda believes that Narendra waited so long to return a second time because he believed that Ramakrishna was a "monomaniac."

Mad men, after all, make people nervous. They are not normally sought out as conversation partners. Thus when Narendra finally did return, he was on his guard. Narendra entered the room and saw that Ramakrishna was in a "strange state," muttering something to himself as he approached him. A nervous Narendra was certain that this "crazy man" was about to create another embarrassing scene. What happened next deserves a full account:

> As I was thinking this, he quickly approached me and placed his own right foot on my body,[19] and immediately I had an unprecedented experience at his touch. As I looked, I began to see that all the things in the room, with the walls themselves, were spinning wildly and dissolving into somewhere. It was as if my sense of self was rushing all at once into an all-consuming Great Nothing. Then I was overcome with a terrible fear as it occurred to me that with the destruction of one's sense of self comes death, and that this itself was at the threshold of death—so close! Not able to restrain myself, I cried out, "Hey! What are you doing to me? I have a father and a mother!" When he heard me say such things, the strange crazy man laughed out loud, touched my chest with his hand, and said, "Then enough now, the work doesn't have to be done all at once. It will come about in good time." (LP 5.4.2)

Narendra was amazed that the experience ended as fast as it began. Who was this madman who could shatter his mind with a touch and then put it back together? (LP 5.4.4). Was this an incident of mesmerism or hypnotism? And his behavior—the madman treated Narendra like a dear relative or friend (LP 5.5.5)—it all made Narendra very nervous. But although Narendra, by his own confession, was a skeptical, if not hostile, subject, there was no doubt in his mind that a "revolution" had taken place in his soul (LP 5.4.3), even if it was affected at the hands (or feet) of a lunatic. Narendra left, confused, troubled, and upset. The problem remained unsolved.

Soon Narendra returned for a third visit. He would be strong this time, he thought to himself, as he entered the temple precincts. Soon the skeptical yet fascinated teenager found himself taking a walk with Ramakrishna along the river. When the two of them got to Jadu Mallik's garden, they sat down in the parlor. Jadu's home was always open to Ramakrishna. As Narendra sat there looking at his problem, it suddenly got up and walked toward him. Narendra was on guard, but again to no avail. Ramakrishna extended his foot and touched him "as before." When Narendra came to, Ramakrishna was passing his hand over Narendra's chest and smiling. Something had happened again, but Narendra did not know what.

Saradananda points out that Narendra never told the other disciples about his experience under Ramakrishna's foot during this third visit. They all assumed that he said nothing because these things concerned "special secret talk" (*viśeṣa rahasyer kathā*). But later they learned from the Master himself that Narendra did not tell them about the incident because *he did not know himself what had happened.* This secret, in other words, was secret even to Narendra:

> When Narendra lost consciousness, I asked him various questions that day: who he was, where he came from, why he came (i.e., why he was born), how many days he would remain here (on earth), etc. . . . All his answers at that time were in conformity with everything that I had seen and felt about him. It is forbidden to say all these things. . . . The day he (Narendra) realizes who he is, he will no longer remain in this world. Due to his firm resolve on the path of yoga, he will abandon the body that very moment! (LP 5.4.8)

So we have another secret: Narendra's status as a divine visitor on earth. He has descended from the gods. Ramakrishna, however, cannot reveal this to Narendra, because as soon as Narendra learns of his own secret, he will disappear, he will die. The secret that is revealed must then be concealed. We will see this same pattern again in Ramakrishna: as soon as the world realizes who he is (an incarnation of God), he too will disappear, he too will die. When the secret is revealed, it immediately conceals itself again. Narendra and Ramakrishna, then, both have secret selves that must remain concealed, at least for a time. Moreover, for Narendra at least, this secret self is an unconscious self. Narendra himself is not even aware of it. Interestingly enough, Saradananda refers to these revelations as "secret talk" (*rahasyakathā*) (LP 5.5.6).

This third visit did little to solve Narendra's problems. If it did anything, it only complicated things further. Who was this strange man? And what was he doing with that foot? And that hand: how did he calm the psychic storm so easily by passing his hand over the chest? And why did he treat Narendra so lovingly, so intimately? What was it about this man and his actions that made Narendra so nervous? Different people answered these questions differently. I want to look at three such answers here: those of Narendra, Ramakrishna, and Saradananda.

Narendra's Pathology: The Master as a "Monomaniac." According to Saradananda, after this second experience under Ramakrishna's foot, Narendra abandoned his opinion that Ramakrishna was a "monomaniac." Perhaps he did not know who this strange man was, but somehow his earlier pathologizing interpretation did not do justice to the facts of his experience. He had not solved the problem. He had merely abandoned, for the time being at least, one of his answers. He would nevertheless continue to pathologize his Master. Saradananda, for example, tells us that Narendra often would try to explain to Ramakrishna how "the investigations and researches of Western physical science" had disproven the allegedly divine status of the saints and mystics (LP 5.6.1.17). Narendra was also fond of explaining to Ramakrishna that his visions were nothing but the delusions of his brain; he was "a brain-sick baby, always seeing visions and the rest."[20] To make matters worse, Narendra accused Ramakrishna of considering him to be great simply because he wanted to (LP 5.6.1.16). In effect Narendra was saying that Ramakrishna's love blinded him. The young disciple even went so far as to scold Ramakrishna for thinking too much of him. Was not king Bharata, thinking too much of a deer at his death, reborn as a deer? Ramakrishna was troubled by such questioning, but the visions and locutions he received from his Mother always confirmed his own previous beliefs. Narendra was a "son-of-a-bitch" to think otherwise (LP 5.6.1.22). Moreover, Ramakrishna claimed, the goddess herself had told him that the moment he did not see the god Nārāyāṇa in Narendra, he would have nothing to do with Narendra (LP 5.6.1.22). Narendra's criticisms were thus answered with a vision, a theology of divine immanence, and with anger.

Ramakrishna's Mythology: The Sage and the Child. But Ramakrishna's relationship to Narendra was not simply a problem for Narendra. It was also a problem *for Ramakrishna.* There was something shameful or embarrassing about it for the saint. Was not he an old man and Narendra a mere boy? What would people think? "But I just can't restrain myself," he confessed (LP 5.5.14). Ramakrishna usually solved the problem through two different but related strategies, one that might be called mystical and one that might be called mythological. In one passage, for example, Ramakrishna justifies his extraordinary love for Narendra by pointing out the boy's unusual meditative abilities: "He sees a light when he sits to meditate. Do I love Narendra so on my own?" (LP 5.6.1.7). Ramakrishna seems to be arguing that he loves Narendra because of Narendra's mystical capabilities and uncommon closeness to the divine.

In another, much more complex move, Ramakrishna legitimates his anxious desire for Narendra by placing it within a mythological context and by literally "seeing" it in a vision. There are two major textual accounts of this vision, one in the *Kathāmṛta* and one in the *Līlāprasaṅga*. Although they are clearly variants of the same vision, they nevertheless are also very different. In a footnote, Saradananda acknowledges that he has embellished Ramakrishna's own much simpler account of the vision. He also assumes—with little evidence, it seems—that the vision took place before Narendra arrived. In the *Kathāmṛta* version, however, Ramakrishna makes no such claim. There is absolutely nothing in the accounts themselves to suggest that the vision occurred before the two met. Taken together, then, these two accounts of the same vision present us with a powerful example of how a vision, simple and relatively uninterpreted in the mind of the visionary, becomes embellished and reworked in the minds of the disciples. We have here, in other words, a lesson in the history of visions.

The *Kathāmṛta* version is much simpler, certainly closer to Ramakrishna's language, and probably more authentic. I will begin with it. It occurs, like most important visions, in volume 4. Ramakrishna is talking about how "in this [pointing to himself] there is something special." To prove his point, he recounts how a boy named Gopal Sen once came to him. "He who is within this put his foot on the chest of Gopal." In such a state, that someone complained, "You've delayed for so long. I can't bear to be with worldly people" (KA 4.239). After this strange conversation between a mysterious someone and the boy, Gopal went home. A few days later he was dead. Ramakrishna believed that the touch of his foot awakened the boy to his true divine nature. Gopal thus realized that he was Nityagopal, a reincarnation of Kṛṣṇa himself. Having realized his divine nature, it was impossible to remain in the world and so he abandoned his body. That someone inside Ramakrishna was talking to that someone inside Gopal. Having recognized one another through the magic touch of a foot, one left and the other stayed behind.

Having told the story of Gopal, Ramakrishna then immediately begins to describe another vision, a "vision of the indivisible Saccidānanda":

> I saw a fence splitting that [indivisible Saccidānanda] into two levels. On one side, there was Kedar Cuni and many other devotees of form. On the other side of the fence, there was a light that looked like a sparkling heap of red brick dust. Within it sat Narendra! He was absorbed in *samādhi!* As I looked at him absorbed in meditation, I said, "O Narendra!" He opened his eyes a little. I understood that he was taking the form of a Kayastha boy in the neighborhood of Simla. Then I said, "O Ma, bind him in illusion. If you don't, then he'll become absorbed in *samādhi* and will abandon his body." Kedar and the other devotees of form peaked into this region, trembled in fear, and fled. (KA 4.239–240)

Ramakrishna has a vision of *brahman* in its *svarūpa* ("with form") and *nirūpa* ("without form") aspects. A fence divides these two regions or worlds. The devotees of form dwell on one side. Narendra sits alone on the other, in a brilliant and yet fuzzy red light, perhaps a veiled reference to Narendra's fiery *rajas* nature. Ramakrishna understood, within the vision apparently, that as Narendra opened his eyes his meditation was broken and he assumed a body of a Kayastha (a caste) boy somewhere in the Simla neighborhood, where in fact Narendra's ancestral home was. Ramakrishna prays to his Mother that she keep him bound and his secret nature concealed from him, lest he become absorbed in *samādhi* again and descend back into the formless red light. Ramakrishna ends his description of the vision with a comment that makes his own preferences quite clear. Whereas Narendra dwells in such formless and yet fiery heights, the other devotees of form can only peak into such a realm. Their hair stands on end in fear, and they run away. Narendra is far superior to the rest, Ramakrishna seems to conclude.

The vision in Saradananda's *Līlāprasaṅga* is much more complicated. The basic plot remains unchanged, but the emotions and images of the vision have been molded into more mythological forms. Upanishadic motifs and references to gods and goddesses are also added, giving the vision a more traditional, more mythological ring:

> One day I saw that the mind on the path of *samādhi* was rising up on a path made of light. . . . Gradually it came to the furthest border of that realm. There I saw a fence made of light spread out, splitting the realm into the divisible and the indivisible. Jumping over the fence, the mind gradually entered the realm of the indivisible. I saw that there there were

> no personal forms or anything else; even all the gods and the goddesses with their divine bodies hesitated to enter here, for the scope of their respective powers remained far below. But the very next moment I was able to see seven persons, ancient sages with bodies made of divine light, seated there established in *samādhi*. . . . Then I saw a part of the homogenous circle of light of the room of the indivisible, devoid of any difference, appear before me, congeal, and develop into a divine infant in space. This divine infant, descending to one of the sages, hugged him lovingly around the neck with his own most tender arms . . . and began to make great efforts to wake him from *samādhi*. At the tender and loving touch [of the infant] the sage rose from *samādhi* and gazed at this amazing boy with half-shut, unblinking eyes. . . . The strange divine infant then expressed endless bliss and said to him, "I am going. You have to come with me." Although the sage made no reply, his love-filled eyes expressed his inner assent. . . . Amazed, I then saw a part of his body and mind develop in the space of burning light and descend to earth along the reversed path. As soon as I saw Narendra, I understood that he was this person! (LP 5.4.9)

Ramakrishna is now a divine infant and Narendra one of the seven sages of Hindu mythology. Moreover, it is now the gods and goddesses, not the devotees of form, who fear the realm of the formless. The formless light takes a form, becomes a child, and descends to embrace one of the sages. The sage assents to descend with the infant. The description of the vision ends with the assertion, never made in the *Kathāmṛta* version, that Ramakrishna immediately recognized Narendra at his first visit as the sage of the vision.

We probably will never know whether the vision occurred before or after Narendra's first visit. In a sense, it does not matter. After all, it is quite possible that Ramakrishna did indeed have such a vision before the disciples began to arrive, but that the face of the vision, like in many a dream, was unclear in the red brilliance of the dusty light. Perhaps Narendra was not the first person to arrive at the steps of Dakshineshwar to be identified by Ramakrishna as his long-awaited companion. Indeed, the Gopal scene quoted above would seem to suggest that Ramakrishna thought that it was *this* boy for whom he had been anxiously longing: "You've waited too long," Ramakrishna tells the boy, *exactly* as he would say to Narendra years later. Perhaps, then, the countenance of the vision was unclear and Ramakrishna kept attaching his visitors' identities to it until he got it right, or until one of his visitors finally believed him. This at least would explain Ramakrishna's strange behavior at Narendra's first visit to Dakshineshwar, when the Paramahaṁsa complained that Narendra had waited too long to come (exactly as he had with Gopal). Clearly this was not the first time Ramakrishna had used such language with a total stranger.

In any case, it is clear that Ramakrishna understood his anxious desire for Narendra in mythological terms. He saw it in visions. And the visions, no doubt, in turn strengthened and refashioned his desire. When Ramakrishna was criticized for his excessive love for Narendra, he would answer, at least in the *Līlāprasaṅga:* "Look, Narendra is a man of absolute purity. I have seen that he is one of the four persons from the realm of the indivisible and one of the seven sages."[21] There was something special, something divine, something of mythological proportions about Narendra that justified and legitimated this old man's raving and weeping for the boy. Others would be puzzled. Even Ramakrishna would experience shame at the thought. But in the end, it was a vision and its myth that bonded the Paramahaṁsa to his chosen disciple, the college boy named Narendra, who had waited too long, much too long, to come.

Saradananda's Theology: The Hidden Meanings of the Incarnation. So whereas Narendra initially answers the problem of Ramakrishna's strange love for him by pathologizing the saint, Ramakrishna solves the problem by mythologizing it. Saradananda too finds it necessary to address "the cause of their strange attraction for one another" (LP 5.6.1.6), explaining such an attraction as stemming partly from Ramakrishna's visions (the saint's mythological hermeneutics) and partly from Ramakrishna's fear that Narendra would be lost in the desire for a wife, wealth, and fame "under the influence of the modern way."[22] In short, Saradananda seems to be saying, Ramakrishna was so anxious over Narendra because he did not want to lose him. But Saradananda does not stop there. He goes on to develop a more sophisticated, primarily theological approach to the problem of Ramakrishna's strange love for Narendra.

The biographer begins by admitting Narendra's own initial pathologizing hermeneutic. During those first days, he tells us, Narendra considered the Master to be "half-mad" on account of all those strange things that he said. Such a move, however, is then replaced by a theological approach to the problem of Ramakrishna's strangeness: "If only he would have accepted him as an incarnation, all those words would have made sense" (LP 5.4.14). Narendra would have then realized that he and Ramakrishna shared a common mission and that all the saint's strange words and actions were designed to realize that common vocation.

"If only he would have accepted him as an incarnation"—this, in a nutshell, is Saradananda's hermeneutic as he struggles with all the strange events of Ramakrishna's life. This is the key, the incarnational key, that opens the door to the meanings of both Ramakrishna's life and Saradananda's biography. With this key, with the knowledge that Ramakrishna was God incarnate, that which is strange or puzzling in Ramakrishna's life becomes understandable and that which is seemingly mundane or trivial takes on great significance. Biography becomes hagiography, a revelation of the sacred meanings secretly enfolded into Ramakrishna's life. "Even though it seems amazing," Saradananda writes, "this attraction of the Master for Narendra can be understood as natural and inevitable through a little thought and a careful eye."[23] The incarnational key has rendered Ramakrishna's unusual relationship to Narendra understandable and reasonable.

With Saradananda's theological approach to the problem of Ramakrishna's strange desire, we have moved from the pathological through the mythological to the theological. What was, at least on some level, a powerfully sexual experience of an illicit and shameful "anxious desire" for a boy became, through vision and mystical states, a mythological reality of profound depth and power. This mythical vision, itself formed through a theological focus, was then embellished and expanded upon—I would not say distorted—with Saradananda's hagiobiographical method until it was capable of carrying what Saradananda calls the "hidden meanings" (*gūḍha artha*) of the incarnation. Through a complex process of interpretation and reinterpretation, we have passed from the "secret talk" (*guhya kathā*) of the *Kathāmṛta* to the "hidden meanings" (*gūḍha artha*) of the *Līlāprasaṅga*, from the erotic to the theological.

Narendra pathologized, Ramakrishna mythologized, and Saradananda theologized. Most likely, all three perspectives bear truths that deserve our attention. But whichever approach we take, one thing seems clear: for the tradition at least, in the end, a madman had become a god.

THE CHANGE AND THE SECRET OF THE DISLOCATED HAND

IT WOULD BE DIFFICULT to overestimate the importance of the coming of the disciples. The roles the disciples played, both in the creation of Ramakrishna's own self-understanding and in the appropriation of that understanding for the larger culture, lie at the very center of the history of the Ramakrishna phenomenon. Perhaps it is not too much of an exaggeration to say that "Ramakrishna Paramahaṁsa" would not exist without the disciples. Certainly Gadadhar, the simple temple priest, would have lived his life out at Dakshineshwar. But it is doubtful that we would know anything about him today if it were not for the early efforts of Mathur and the Bhairavī, of the ever-publishing Keshab and his Brahmos, of the first householder disciples and their writings, and finally, of the boy disciples who would become the first monks of the Ramakrishna Order. These last two groups of disciples, the householders and the renouncers, are especially important, not simply because they recorded for posterity the personality and deeds of Ramakrishna, but, much more significantly, because they more than anyone else actually formed and helped determine Ramakrishna's own self-understanding and actions. That is to say, from a historical perspective at least, *Ramakrishna the incarnation was socially created through human interaction and the processes of interpretation and debate.* When Ramakrishna asked a disciple, "Who do you say I am?" he did not ask the question because he was already absolutely certain of the answer. Rather, he asked the question to be reassured that the answer that he had already been given many times before was in fact the correct one. He was named by others. Mathur, the Bhairavī, and their Tantric friends had identified him as an incarnation of God. The householders and the renouncers would reinforce and expand on this early declaration. Eventually, as the believers began to outnumber the revilers—and there were many skeptics—Ramakrishna began to believe them. As a result of all this, before he died the Paramahaṁsa was confidently declaring his divinity in cryptic statements and seeing it in secret visions. The social process of interpretation and debate had entered deeply into his soul: "He who was Rāma and he who was Kṛṣṇa is now Rāmakṛṣṇa," he declared.[24]

It was only within this social process of naming, interpretation, and debate that Ramakrishna saw his visions confirming the truth that he was in fact an incarnation of God. The social process, in other words, helped to create the visions. But the visions also helped to create the social process. In a very real sense, there was no "inside" or "outside" to the process. As with his Tantric dialectic, the inside of Ramakrishna's psychic visions and the outside of his social community formed a single dynamic whole. Psyche and culture formed one another.

This dialectic process of vision and social interpretation had been going on for some years when Ramakrishna experienced a secret command that would effectively complete his transformation from a troubled mystic into a confident god. I have called this final transformation "the Change." The Change was part of Ramakrishna's gradual movement away from Vedānta and its renunciation of the world to Tantra and its radical delight in that same, but now transformed world.[25] It also seems to be related to all of those commands to "Remain in existence" and to "Remain in *bhāvamukha*." But what the commands only hinted at the Change seems to have finally accomplished. At first, Ramakrishna did not listen. He kept turning away. At some point, however, he finally gave in. He finally obeyed and experienced the Change.

The Vision of Jagannath

THE CHANGE CANNOT be placed chronologically with any accuracy, for it occurred gradually over time. But its definitive climax seems to have occurred in 1884 with a secret vision and a painful dislocation. At this point, despite the presence of numerous disciples, Ramakrishna is still trying to direct his energies "up" toward the Absolute. He is still trying to "have sex with the Self." But something occurs in one of these attempts that leads him to believe that he must now turn around and redirect his love to the divine incarnate in the social world. He finally realizes that his numerous ascents must now be balanced by an equally passionate descent.

This descent and this Change are signaled by a dislocation, not just of a psychological state, but also of a hand. It took pain to bring him back. The secret talk passage relating this spiritual and physical dislocation occurs, like most important passages, in volume 4: "Now I'm telling you something very secret—why I love Purna, Narendra, and all the others so much. I broke my arm while embracing Lord Jagannath in the erotic state. Then it was made known to me: 'You have taken a body. Now remain in the different states—the Friend, the Mother, and the rest—in relation to other forms of man'" (4.227–228).[26] There is something secret, even scandalous, about this incident. Rakhal seems particularly embarrassed by the event. He insists on covering the arm lest others see it and begin to slander the saint: "What precisely *was* Ramakrishna doing in the vision when he dislocated his hand?" we can almost hear them asking. Rakhal also refuses to talk to the doctor about the event unless they both go behind a screen (KA 4.72). Ramakrishna responds with a complaint: "Rakhal doesn't understand my state." Ramakrishna was hurt enough to consider leaving the temple altogether, but where would he go? (KA 4.73) There is something about the vision and the hand, then, that is troubling, something others should not hear about.

In other passages, we learn a few details but not much more. Ramakrishna, we discover, was on his way to the pine grove, probably to defecate, when he found himself stumbling along "filled with ecstasy" (KA 5.107). In such a drunken state, he tripped over an iron rail and dislocated his left hand.[27] Ramakrishna does not understand: "Can you give me a lecture why I broke my arm?" he asks Ram (KA 2.103). Eventually an answer comes, not from Ram, but from the Mother. The Mother, Ramakrishna relates, showed him that he was controlled by her: "I'm an instrument and you are the controller," he confidently declared (KA 4.63).[28] The event was thus given a religious meaning. It pointed to Ramakrishna's radical dependence on the Mother (KA 4.100) and suggested that Ramakrishna was really two: "There is she and the devotee," he said. "The devotee broke his arm and is sick now—'There are two in here'" (KA 3.251). Even a dislocated hand leads to the incarnation at this point in the story.

But despite such analyses of the meaning of the event, we are never told when the vision occurred in relation to the fall, how it was connected to the act of defecation, or in what sense it was erotic. Rakhal's attempt to keep things covered up behind a screen seems to have worked. If, however, we place the vision in the larger context of Ramakrishna's religious world, we can bring it out from behind the screen and place it within the space of some degree of understanding. Consider, for example, Ramakrishna's statement that the fall was associated with "the erotic state" (*madhura bhāva*). As we have seen, the erotic state is commonly accepted as the highest of the Vaiṣṇava states, for it alone subsumes all the others.[29] Ramakrishna's secret vision bears this out, for what we see taking place in it is the transformation of the erotic state into the other states. What is particularly significant here is the fact that in the erotic state Ramakrishna's energies were directed toward the divine, to "Lord Jagannath," whereas the other states are to be taken on "in relation to other forms of man." From "embracing Lord Jagannath in the erotic state," Ramakrishna will turn to his disciples as a Mother, as a Friend, and as a Lover. Accordingly, in volume 5, the saint explains how he is no longer capable of experiencing God as pure consciousness, for now he wants to see, touch, and literally embrace God in form. Once again, he recounts the command of the secret vision: "You have taken a body. So delight in God in the forms of man." So important is this Change to Ramakrishna that he leaves the steps he is sitting on and scoots closer to his disciples to reveal this secret talk (KA 5.122).

So the vision of Jagannath and the Change that it led to are related, somehow, to Ramakrishna's secret. Little wonder, then, that the distribution of the passages on Ramakrishna's dislocated hand approximate the distribution of Ramakrishna's secret talk. As with the secret talk passages, there are no passages on the dislocated hand in volume 1 and only a few in volumes 2 and 3. The vast majority of passages occur in volume 4, with a few extras saved over for volume 5.[30] Moreover, the single passage that relates what Ramakrishna was seeing and hearing in his inebriated state occurs, not surprisingly, in volume 4. The dislocated hand, then, shares the same textual pattern as Ramakrishna's secret talk: it is held back in volume 1, mentioned in volumes 2 and 3, and fully revealed in volume 4. M, in his typical fashion, has taken down the screen that Rakhal tried so hard to keep up.

Vaishnavacharan's Truth

CERTAINLY THE MOST IMPORTANT ELEMENT of the vision of Jagannath was its concluding command: "You have taken a body. Now remain in the different states—the Friend, the Mother, and the rest—in relation to other forms of man." It was this aspect of the vision no doubt that acted as a powerful catalyst for Ramakrishna's Change. From here on, he would turn his energies around and redirect them into the human world and experience them "in relation to other forms of man." In another variant of the same vision, this one in volume 5, Ramakrishna gives a slightly different account of the experience. Here, however, Ramakrishna relates the final command as his own interpretation of what the vision meant to him rather than as a divine voice spoken from above. "It is *as if* it were saying . . . ," he tells his disciples. I quote the passage in full and include Ramakrishna's comments on how he is translating the vision's meanings into his social experience:

> (To the devotees): "Look, on account of hurting this arm, my state is turning around. Now I'm seeing the special mani-

> festation of God in human beings. It's as if it were saying, 'I dwell within man, so take delight with man.'
>
> "He is especially manifest in pure devotees—this is why I'm so anxious for Narendra, Rakhal, and the rest." (KA 5.114)

The "it" of which Ramakrishna is speaking is most likely his arm, or perhaps the incident of dislocating it. As with the passage of volume 4 quoted earlier, here again this incident is associated with a radical change in the Paramahaṁsa's orientation to the divine and human worlds. He is now "turning around." Having once taken his lust and "turned it around the corner" in order to engage Lord Jagannath in an erotic encounter, Ramakrishna feels himself turning around once again. In the terms of the present study, one could say that he is at last beginning to complete the circle of his dialectical world. Finally, having described the meaning of his experience of the dislocated hand, Ramakrishna can then take his new discovery and use it to legitimate his "anxious desire" for the boy disciples. The erotic vision of Jagannath is thus brought down to the human world and translated into social and psychological forms. Ramakrishna's passion has descended.

Whether it was a command that Ramakrishna heard within the vision or a meaning that seemed to him to be implied by the vision's content, either within or after the vision, Ramakrishna's realization that the bliss of God can be experienced in the social world of human forms did not come to him as a new revelation. Like most other aspects of the saint's mystical life, the realization and its command spoke of truths that ultimately stem back to Ramakrishna's Tantric days. This particular truth—that God can and should be loved "in man"—Ramakrishna first learned from his old friend, Vaishnavacharan. Vaishnavacharan, we might recall, was a major player in the early years of Ramakrishna's Tantric training. He was a Vaiṣṇava scholar well-versed both in the devotional scriptures of the Vaiṣṇava faith and in the secret practices of Tantra (LP 4.1.29). Like so many other figures of the texts, he seems to have lived two lives. Such a dual personality, incorporating both the "right-handed" and "left-handed" traditions of the culture, made him an especially capable leader of a local Tantric sect, the Kartābhajās of Kacchibagan.

According to Saradananda, Vaishnavacharan was first invited to Dakshineshwar in order to advise Mathur on the nature of one of Ramakrishna's many illnesses. He would later be summoned again to help determine whether Ramakrishna's strange bodily signs were symptomatic of pathology or were marks of divinity. He would confirm the

Bhairavī's opinion that the signs spoke of divinity rather than madness. Ramakrishna, he proclaimed to the assembly, was indeed an incarnation of God (LP 4.1.35). Mathur apparently learned of Vaishnavacharan from the Bhairavī (LP 4.1.18). This is no accident. The texts, after all, state clearly that Vaishnavacharan, like the Bhairavī, practiced a *sādhana* "of a secret type" (LP 4.1.21).[31] It is quite likely that Vaishnavacharan and the Bhairavī frequented the same communities and knew the same texts. Their names come up again and again in the texts, often together.

Vaishnavacharan's teachings can be reconstructed by piecing together a number of passages in the texts, especially in the *Kathāmṛta*. From such passages we learn that he preached a doctrine of divine immanence. In this, he was probably merely developing the Kartābhajā belief that the guru is God into a much more encompassing faith in the divinity of humanity itself. "If one can worship God in an image," the Tantric scholar taught, "why not in a living man?" (KA 2.192). According to Vaishnavacharan, such worship leads to an ultimate truth: "When you see God in man, your knowledge is complete" (KA 2.98).[32] The proper object of such a complete knowledge Vaishnavacharan called "[God's] play as man" (*naralīlā*).[33]

For Vaishnavacharan, such a faith certainly carried homoerotic dimensions. Ramakrishna, for example, points out that Vaishnavacharan liked to look at pictures of men, for they aroused in him feelings of "tenderness" (*komala*) and "love" (*prema*) (KA 4.75). Ramakrishna, we might recall, sexually aroused himself with a very similar practice (KA 5.108). Perhaps he learned it from his Kartābhajā friend. More to the point, Datta records a rhyme of Ramakrishna's that explicitly connects Vaishnavacharan's "depraved" Kartābhajās with the Hijras, a religious community of castrated men known for their homosexual practices: "When the woman is a Hijra and the man is a *khojā* (eunuch), then you will be a Kartābhajā" (TS, 99).[34] This unusual saying, recorded by Datta in his *Tattvasāra*, might help us explain the same author's stubborn refusal to describe the lifestyle of the two "women" who, under Vaishnavacharan's instruction, no doubt, sucked a big toe and performed "a very obscene gesture." They were not prostitutes, Datta goes out of his way to tell us, "but their way of life is of a kind so repugnant that I am unable to reveal it to the public" (JV[5], 37). Such an obvious, self-confessed omission cries out for explanation, especially when it occurs in an author who remained silent about very few "secret things." Given the equation the rhyming saying sets up between "the woman" and "a Hijra" and Datta's adamant refusal to describe the women's repulsive lifestyle, worse than even that of a prostitute, I think it is likely, indeed probable, that these two "women" were not women at all, but Hijras who were trying to engage the saint in some sort of homosexual act: "When the woman is a Hijra . . ."

There were, of course, other types of disciples, and so other types of sexual practices, in Vaishnavacharan's community. There were women, for example, for whom Vaishnavacharan's teaching of God's play as man awakened heteroerotic desires. Did he not teach them to look on a man, any man, as God? "Whom do you love?" he would ask them. "So-and-so," they would answer. This chosen man would then become their chosen or "desired" (*iṣṭa*) deity (KA 4.80).[35] Through loving him they could attain the divine. It is a seldom discussed, virtually unknown fact that Ramakrishna's own wife had once been initiated into a Kartābhajā community. Sharada would later recall how she feared Ramakrishna's reaction but was relieved to discover that he did not become angry upon learning of her hidden Tantric past (LP 5.11.9). Given what we now know about Vaishnavacharan's community, we can well understand her fear but only wonder about what she was doing with such a group and why Ramakrishna did *not* become angry. He, after all, was often quite upset with these communities and their practices. Indeed, he blasts the Kartābhajā women, who take "so-and-so" as their chosen deity only to end up scandalously pregnant (KA 3.52). Ramakrishna's visits to Vaishnavacharan's Kartābhajā community probably did little to change his opinion: "These people talk big," Ramakrishna complained, "but they misbehave" (KA 4.80). The saint's final conclusion was ambivalent at best: "You're not to act like them or mix with them, but you also must not hate them" (LP 4.1.21). For Ramakrishna, then, Vaishnavacharan's truth that God could be realized in one's love for a human being was more of a Tantric perversity than a powerful theology of divine immanence. It should be tolerated but not emulated.

But the dislocated hand and the vision of Jagannath changed all that, for after he dislocated his hand and found himself "turning around," Ramakrishna began to realize that Vaishnavacharan was right after all (KA 4.75). In the saint's mind, the dislocated hand and Vaishnavacharan's truth are intimately related. They are often mentioned together in the *Kathāmṛta*. Consider, for example, the following passage in volume 4. Ramakrishna is talking about his dislocated hand and the Change that it effected in him: "Vaishnavacharan used to say that when one has faith in God's play as man one's knowledge will be full, but I didn't listen to him. Now I see that he was right" (KA 4.75).[36] Ramakrishna, it seems, knew when to acknowledge his masters, even if it took him years to do so. In the end, just as Vaishnavacharan had predicted, the saint was won over: "Now I only like God's play as man," the Paramahaṁsa noted calmly, as if it were now a self-evident truth instead of a detested Tantric practice (KA 4.75).[37]

What took the saint so long to realize Vaishnavacharan's truth? Perhaps Ramakrishna did not listen to the Tantric scholar because he did not trust him. After all, it was this same Vaishnavacharan who had taken the young Paramahaṁsa to his Tantric community and "tested" the young priest. Ramakrishna, we might recall, left outraged after two women forced him to experience their symbolic and not so symbolic obscenities. The saint definitely did not want his "toe" sucked by such a woman. Such incidents, no doubt, contributed to Ramakrishna's resistance to Vaishnavacharan's truth, but this was probably not the primary reason for the saint's rejection. It seems just as likely that Ramakrishna resisted Vaishnavacharan's method of loving God "in the forms of man" simply because he lacked a man in which to love God. We must never forget that it was only at the end of his life that Ramakrishna had any real disciples, and only toward the very end that he had any disciples who were his juniors. The coming of the disciples in the early 1880s provided the social context in which Vaishnavacharan's truth could be advanced again. This time, however, Ramakrishna had a community to descend back into. He finally had a man, indeed, young attractive boys, to desire. Accordingly, he could now accept Vaishnavacharan's Tantric approach to God and experience its depths in his own human relationships. He could "delight in God in the forms of man."

The disciples also found Vaishnavacharan's concept of God's play as man very useful, for they saw in it yet another way to talk about the mystery of God's incarnation in Ramakrishna. Vaishnavacharan did not develop this aspect of the doctrine—at least we have little evidence to suggest that he did—but Ramakrishna and the disciples certainly made the most of it. M, for example, refers to the *avatāra* as God's play as man (KA 3.48) and declares that, of all the doctrines, he likes this one the best. This, then, gets him speculating on the incarnational status of Ramakrishna (KA 3.212). Ramakrishna is also quick to see the *avatāra* in Vaishnavacharan's truth. In God's play as man, the Paramahaṁsa taught, God is "covered up" in the human. It is thus very difficult to recognize an incarnation. He is a secret being. Only twelve people, for example, recognized Rāma as one (KA 4.44). Kṛṣṇa and Caitanya were also such *avatāras*. They descended into the human in order to enact God's play as man (KA 5.114). Ramakrishna also relates God's play as man to his general Tantric ontology of the eternal and the play (KA 4.75). In the divine-human nature of the *avatāra*, the dialectic is fully embodied. In the language of the present study, one might say that in such a god-man the Absolute and the phenomenal world, the transcendent consciousness of Śiva and the dynamic energies of Śakti, are united. He is a Tantric being.

Vaishnavacharan's truth that God should be worshiped and loved in man (or a man) was thus picked up by Ramakrishna and the disciples and transformed into something new. Ramakrishna, no doubt, attacked the doctrine's obvious abuses and for many years rejected even its less scandalous practices, but in the end, with a community of men to descend back into, he was finally converted. The disciples, perhaps ignorant of the doctrine's Tantric origins in Vaishnavacharan's Kartābhajā community, listened enthusiastically as Ramakrishna told them about God's play as man. It seemed to them that Ramakrishna was speaking about himself. Perhaps he was. In any case, it was through such a social process of debate, interpretation, and belief that Ramakrishna the Tāntrika became Ramakrishna the incarnation of God. *What began as a Tantric truth, rooted in the mystico-erotic practices of Vaishnavacharan's Kartābhajā sect, was transformed into a theology of incarnation and community.* In the process, Ramakrishna's secret too was transformed. Once seen in the twilight of private visions and subjectively experienced as intense desire, it now was debated in the light of day. With Ramakrishna's descent from the erotic heights of mystical union into the forms of man, his secret too descended and became public. As a socially debated and defined reality, this secret was quickly transformed into a theological truth that the wider culture could appropriate. Ramakrishna's experiences were no longer simply his own.

Nārāyāṇa: The Divine Human

VERY MUCH RELATED to Vaishnavacharan's doctrine that God is best loved and worshiped in a man is Ramakrishna's doctrine that every human being is in fact a form of the god Nārāyāṇa. According to this teaching, humanity is essentially divine. Indeed, its very terms are structured around a theological wordplay that equates the human and the divine: "man" (*nara*) is in his essence "God" (*Nārāyāṇa*). But God in a special way, for Ramakrishna's teaching on the divine nature of every human being is unconcerned with the moral worth of the person in question. God plays *every* role in the play of the world. Thus after having watched a play about the life of Kṛṣṇa, for example, Ramakrishna declares: "I saw clearly that she herself had become everything. I saw that whoever was dressed up [in a female role] was the Blissful Mother herself! Those who were dressed up as cowherds in Golaka I saw were Nārāyāṇa himself. He himself has become everything" (KA 3.107).[38] The world is a play in which the god and the goddess play all the parts. In a similar but more striking vein, the Paramahaṁsa taught that it does not matter at all whether the person in question is a violent thug or a holy man; he is still divine, a manifestation of the god Nārāyāṇa. Ramakrishna can thus speak of Nārāyāṇa the thug and even of Nārāyāṇa the tiger (KA 3.55).[39] God can be violent. This is why one must worship the divine even in people who are evil and bad. This is why, Ramakrishna calmly notes, he can worship the goddess in a "shitting, pissing, runny-nosed girl" (KA 4.199).[40] God is God. The goddess is the goddess. Morality and purity are irrelevant.

Almost. The Nārāyāṇa doctrine is not simply about worshiping God in the impure dregs of humanity. On the contrary, for Ramakrishna at least, it is more about loving God in pure male disciples. "I love them," Ramakrishna admits, "I see Nārāyāṇa in them" (KA 4.143). The doctrine somehow justifies and legitimates the desire. Certainly the doctrine helped the disciples, and especially M, to explain to themselves and to others Ramakrishna's strange dealings with his boy disciples. M, for example, notes in one of many passages that Ramakrishna's relationship to Rakhal strikes him as "strange" (*adbhūta*). "Perhaps," M speculates, "he sees that Nārāyāṇa himself has taken the body of the boy Rakhal" (KA 1.83).[41] In other passages, M is less sure of himself. Question marks begin to appear in the Bengali text. In one such passage, Ramakrishna is caressing the body and mouth of Narendra. "Why?" M asks himself and his readers. "Is it because he sees Nārāyāṇa himself in Narendra? Is he having a vision of God in a man?" M's question is not answered as Ramakrishna rubs and presses Narendra's body and feet in an ecstatic state. M asks again, not at all sure of himself: "Is he transmitting his *śakti?*" (KA 1.204).[42] M still receives no answer.

So close is Ramakrishna's Nārāyāṇa teachings to Vaishnavacharan's truth that it seems reasonable to ask whether the saint also got this teaching from the Tantric scholar and his Kartābhajā community. Nārāyāṇa, after all, is considered to be a form of Viṣṇu. As such, the deity would fit well into Vaishnavacharan's general Vaiṣṇava world. But we have much more than this bit of mythological coincidence to suggest that Ramakrishna got the doctrine from his Tantric friend. We have texts in which Ramakrishna clearly associates the Nārāyāṇa doctrine with both the Change and Vaishnavacharan's truth. "If one can worship him [Nārāyāṇa] in an image," the saint points out, no doubt mimicking his former teacher, "why not in a human?" (KA 5.114). Once again Vaishnavacharan's truth peeps through. In another passage, Ramakrishna explicitly connects the Change, Vaishnavacharan's truth, and the Nārāyāṇa doctrine: "Now I'm seeing that this state is changing again. Long ago *Vaishnavacharan* said that when one has the vision of God in a human one's knowledge is complete. Now I'm seeing that he wanders about in each [human] form" (KA 2.98–99). "Long ago Vaishnavacharan said . . . Now I am seeing that . . ." Once again, Ramakrishna is converted, changed. Having recorded the nature of his changing state, Ramakrishna then goes on to use the Nārāyāṇa doctrine to explain why he loves to feed the disciples (KA 2.99). As he did with the vision of Jagannath and the doctrine of God's play as man, Ramakrishna feels a need to translate the Nārāyāṇa doctrine into a concrete social expression. He must turn around and descend into the forms of man. He must feed God in a disciple. But not just any disciple. He prefers boys, and only morally and sexually pure boys at that. Nārāyāṇa may be a cheat and a holy man, a snotty-nosed girl and a sexually pure boy, but Ramakrishna much prefers the holy men and the boys to the cheats and the virgins. When it comes to his social relations, he is quite willing to discriminate, despite the radical unity of his ontological world.[43]

The Nārāyāṇa doctrine, then, alternates between a radical affirmation of the divinity of every human being and Ramakrishna's use of the doctrine to justify his obviously preferential treatment of a few boy disciples. Moreover, in its insistence that one can love God in a man, the Nārāyāṇa doctrine seems to be connected both to Vaishnavacharan's truth and to the doctrine of God's play as man. Clearly all three doctrines carry both erotic and theological dimensions for Ramakrishna. The disciples, no doubt uncomfortable with the erotic aspects of the teachings (M's continuous use of the word *strange* is a case in point), tended to downplay the erotic and emphasize the theological. They thus helped translate Ramakrishna's secret into the public realm. In their company and through their interpretations, Ramakrishna and his secret descended. But in the midst of this descent, both were changed, for, as we shall see now, when they entered the social arena of "God in the forms of man," both the saint and his secret were immediately subject to debate, interpretation, and sometimes rejection.

Phallic Love and the Incarnation's Erotic Community

So far I have only hinted at this process of interpretation and debate in my discussion of Vaishnavacharan's truth, the doctrine of God's play as man, and Ramakrishna's teachings on Nārāyāṇa. It is now time to examine this descent more closely and try to begin to answer a few questions. Once Ramakrishna finally turned his ontological face around to the human world (*bhāvamukha*) and descended to delight in the forms of man, how did he experience that world and those forms? In what ways were his now descending energies experienced, both by him and the disciples? What was the precise nature of God's play as man?

Ramakrishna's Phallic Love

As should be apparent by now, *this* God's play as man expressed itself in symbolic forms and acts that can be described as broadly Tantric, for they shimmered with energies that were at once mystical and sexual. Like so much else about the saint, Ramakrishna's descending energies were profoundly erotic, even phallic. But how? The renouncers, after all, like to quote a passage in which Ramakrishna refers to his penis as "all dead and gone." Like Śiva himself, it was a living corpse, pulled back into its tortoise-like shell in an unusual act of renunciation. But Ramakrishna's penis was not dead, nor was it gone. For, much like Śiva's, at the touch of Kālī's feet, Ramakrishna's phallus showed itself in other more symbolic but still profoundly erotic ways. Ramakrishna, for example, described his love for God as *rāgabhakti*, a "passionate love" that, unlike conventional love driven by prescription and duty (*vaidhibhakti*), is spontaneous and deep-rooted, "like Śiva's *liṅgam* that stretches down even to Benares." In a strikingly translucent passage, Ramakrishna explains that it is this love, likened to a mystical phallus, that the incarnation shares with his disciples (KA 4.193). In other passages, Śiva's phallus and the incarnation are equated. In one such passage, M, awed by the person of Ramakrishna, asks himself, "Is Sri Ramakrishna an incarnation, a Śiva-*liṅgam* thrust straight up from the underworld?" (KA 5.62).[44] In another place, Ramakrishna spits on rituals and rosaries, comparing himself to a self-born *liṅgam* "thrust straight up from the underworld," in no need of forced acts and constructed intentions

(KA 2.147).[45] He is no ordinary mortal. He needs no rituals or prayers. His mystical, essentially divine nature is as obvious as Śiva's erect *liṅgam*.

But what is obvious about this self-born *liṅgam?* That it is divine? Or that it is a phallus? Its mystical or its sexual nature? We are back to the basic problem of the erotic in Ramakrishna's language and experience. It has been argued, of course, that Śiva's *liṅgam* is not really a phallus at all but an abstract symbol of the Godhead, despite the fact that Śiva does all sorts of phallic things with it. In the Purāṇas, for example, he seduces the forest sages' wives with it and then, when angered by their husbands' protests, cuts it off and sends it crashing to the earth where it burns out of control until the sages promise to worship it. Completely ignoring such texts—and there are hundreds of them—the argument against a phallic interpretation usually proceeds by pointing out the fact that many modern Hindus are completely unaware of its history and sexual connotations. For them, it is argued, the *liṅgam* is nothing more than an abstract symbol of divinity.[46]

Perhaps, but such was certainly not the case for Ramakrishna, who, we must remember, worshiped his own penis "with a pearl" as the living *liṅgam* (KA 4.106), prayed to the "place of the father" (*liṅgam*) and the "place of the mother" (*yoni*) not to be born again (KA 2.155), and matter of factly described sexual intercourse as the joining of the "penis" (*liṅgam*) and "vagina" (*yoni*) (TP, no. 201). Nor would such an argument likely convince the Tāntrika who one day paid Ramakrishna a visit. The "stem" and "lotus flowers" of *kuṇḍalinī* yoga, the Tāntrika pointed out, symbolize Śiva's phallus (*liṅgam*) and the goddess "in the form of a vagina" (*yonirūpa*) (KA 5.103).[47] Ramakrishna, then, whether he was conscious of it or not, knew quite well what a *liṅgam* was and what it symbolized: the essential unity of the mystical and the sexual. Consequently, it is little wonder that he used it to describe the manner in which he wanted to relate to his male disciples. For Ramakrishna, at least, his was a homoerotic community, united through an erect passion that was at once profoundly religious and provocatively sexual.

Techniques of Arousal

RAMAKRISHNA USED various techniques to arouse this "passionate love," likened to a symbolic phallus, among his disciples. Among them, singing and dancing, nudity, the examination of bodies, and the pairing up of his disciples into spiritual couples were particularly important.

Singing and dancing were especially popular in the incarnation's erotic community. Often, Ramakrishna would dance naked, surrounded by his male disciples, or pace, or sit naked among them.[48] Sometimes the boys would dance naked (KA 3.99). Such practices did not always sit well with the locals. One scholar, after visiting the saint and witnessing such a show of dancing and singing, was supposed to have commented curtly: "Yes, a paramahaṁsa indeed."[50]

Naked bodies were also common. For Ramakrishna, nudity was a natural expression of the mystical state: when the *kuṇḍalinī* rises "from the feet to the head," he taught, one's garments automatically fall off (KA 1.237). Nakedness was also seen as an instrument to loosen the bond of shame (LP 3.8.29). It was particularly as "the Paramahaṁsa" that Ramakrishna practiced his mystical nudity. M described Ramakrishna in "the state of the paramahaṁsa" thus: "He moves like a child! He grins again and again! He is wearing nothing around his waist. He is naked. His eyes float in bliss!" (KA 2.67). It should also be noted that many of the personages that appeared in Ramakrishna's secret visions were naked. Most of them were boys.

Just as nudity is a naked sign of the mystical state, it is also necessary in order to reveal a man's mystical potential, recorded for the trained eye in the curves, colors, and shapes of the male body. Accordingly, Ramakrishna would ask to examine the bare chests of men and boys in order to determine their spiritual fitness (KA 3.119). Sometimes, he would go further: one day, for example, he asked the boy Prasanna to strip for him, whereupon Ramakrishna exclaimed, "What a boy!" (KA 3.124). Another day, he was explaining to a boy how he could not keep his loin-cloth on: "I, a man so advanced in age, have to go about naked, but I don't feel my nakedness." But, Ramakrishna adds, he has abandoned that practice for all those who feel shame in his naked presence. Having identified himself as a man who has gone beyond the bond of shame, Ramakrishna then tests the boy with the same standard by asking him to take off his clothes, wrap them around his head like a turban, and walk around the temple courtyard. The boy does so and then notes that he could only do such a thing before Ramakrishna. Apparently, many others had stripped for Ramakrishna before this boy, for the Master acknowledges the boy's lack of shame as the usual response: "Many others say that. They say, 'Before you we don't feel shame when we take off our clothes, but we do before others'" (LP 5.7.15).[51]

On Becoming a Woman

Finally, Ramakrishna paired his disciples up into "masculine" and "feminine" disciples in order to awaken their devotion and love. This is a particularly interesting technique, since its logic demonstrates, once again, the secret that lay at the heart of Ramakrishna's life and teachings. It has often been pointed out that Ramakrishna took on the mannerisms and moods of women in order, in his own words, "to conquer the enemy of lust" (KA 4.4).[52] If a man can act exactly like a woman—dressing like one, brushing his teeth like one, talking like one—then he can conquer lust (KA 4.4). According to Ramakrishna, the effeminate actors of Bengal, who had mastered such techniques for their trade, were models for the male devotee and should be imitated (KA 4.4). Ramakrishna was a master of such imitations. In numerous scenes, Ramakrishna acts like a woman, making fun of her gestures and foibles, to the roar of his all-male audience (KA 2.50). In one scene, for example, he rolls on the ground, imitating a woman wailing for her dead husband while she carefully holds her nose-ring lest it break (KA 4.272). A dead husband is a tragedy, but so is a lost or broken nose-ring. Becoming a woman, then, was not just a sacred duty for Ramakrishna. It was also a lot of fun, an opportunity to laugh at the other, slightly despised gender.

Such a discipline may seem unnatural, a dangerous translation of the stage into real life, but in the symbolic world of Ramakrishna it is not, for in such a world every human being is already a woman in relation to the divine. There is a view, Ramakrishna pointed out, that says "whoever has nipples is a woman." And only two beings born in this world did not have nipples: the heroic Arjuna and his divine charioteer, Kṛṣṇa. Everyone else by definition is a woman (KA 2.155). Becoming a woman on the stage of life, then, even if one thinks he is a man, is not only spiritually helpful, it is theologically natural.

But whether natural or not, this ascetic technique of becoming a woman in order to conquer lust is a tricky thing, since, at least in Ramakrishna's case, it is built on a mistake that in the end rights itself *within* the technique. The mistake is this: same-sex love is impossible. Such is the logic of Ramakrishna's teachings. If a man can become a woman, his desire for a woman will die, since sexual desire exists, by definition it seems, only between a man and a woman. But clearly, given all that we know now about Ramakrishna's secret, such an assumption is patently wrong, *especially* in Ramakrishna's world. For homosexual love not only exists in Ramakrishna's world, it is absolutely central to that world. So what are we to make of Ramakrishna's teaching on becoming a woman?

If we look carefully at the contexts in which Ramakrishna becomes a woman, it becomes apparent that he did not "become a woman" simply to conquer desire. True, he became a woman when he lived with his wife, Sharada, in order to conquer his desire for her. And he succeeded: "I'm not able to call you a he," she confessed (KA 2.154–155). But he also took on the nature of a woman to live with and lie down with Mathur, to sing to his beloved Narendra, and to mother little Rakhal. *As a woman, Ramakrishna was ascetic to women and erotic to men.* It is also important to point out that this sexual nature of the woman, which he rejected when he found it in actual women, he affirmed and nourished in his own actions, metaphors, and teachings. Devotional love is a woman, he taught, for it has access into the inner harem of the house, whereas male knowledge only makes it into the outer courtyard: the feminine, in other words, is not only better, it is more erotic.[53] Likewise, the lover of God dwells in the world like an unfaithful wife, a naughty woman who does her chores but constantly thinks of her lover, her God (KA 1.251). Once again, to be female is to be erotic. To be female is also to be Tantric, or at least to complete the Tantric polarity. Again and again, Ramakrishna relates how the devotee takes on a female identity to approach a masculine God: "This," Ramakrishna proclaims, "is the last word" (KA 4.60).

Ramakrishna, then, became a woman not just to conquer his desire but also to *increase* it. Whereas his love for women died, his love for men and male deities was nourished, set afire. I would argue, moreover, that within this dual movement of asceticism and eroticism, the erotic was more primary, more basic. Becoming a woman—that dweller of the harem and naughty wife of the world—enflamed Ramakrishna's desires more than it extinguished them. Given his teachings on women, it is likely, indeed probable, that he was not particularly attracted to women in the first place. Assuming the nature of women allowed him, then, to kill what desire he had for women and to nourish his more natural desire for men. He could thus preach that a woman cannot love a woman, that this same-sex love was impossible, while he, a man, sang to his beloved disciples, nursed them at his breasts, and fondled them in his lap. The teaching, though appearing to deny the reality of same-sex love, actually ended up affirming it. On the outside, it was ascetic. On the inside, it was erotic. This outside-inside nature of the teaching should not surprise us, for we now know that Ramakrishna's teachings and experience were built on a paradox that he did not see, on a secret of which he was not aware. His teaching on becoming a woman in order to conquer "lust" is just one more example of this secret and the power of its unconscious truths.

It was in this sexually charged context, moreover, that the saint encouraged his male disciples to pair up into couples, to become spiritual men and women. Narendra, little Naran, and Purna (who, it might be added, figure most prominently as the objects of Ramakrishna's "feminine" love) all have a "masculine essence" (*puruṣasattā*) (KA 4.212).[54] Narendra in particular has a man's nature and so naturally tends to a "very high state," to a formless state (KA 4.228). Since Narendra's nature is masculine, he sits on the right side of the carriage, whereas Ramakrishna, having a woman's nature, sits on the left (KA 4.228). The saint also explains that since Narendra has a man's nature and he a woman's nature, "I am submissive to him" (KA 5.131). They are a couple. Other disciples had "feminine" natures. For example, Bhaburam, whom Ramakrishna "sees" dressed up like the goddess, along with Manindra, Bhabanath, Nityagopal, and Harish all have a "woman's nature" (*prakṛtibhāva*).[55] Harish even sleeps in women's clothes (KA 4.99).

According to Ramakrishna, these spiritual genders result in different types of religious experiences. Whereas the feminine disciples are more likely to undergo the "states" (*bhāva*) and experience their bodies as flushed, masculine disciples tend to become dissolved in the Absolute. Hence Ramakrishna notes that as his own states "go in," his feminine nature leaves him and he becomes a boy (KA 4.214). We might say, then, that feminine souls are religiously "extroverted" while masculine souls are religiously "introverted." It is interesting to note that, although many men are said to have feminine souls, the saint never speaks of women as having masculine souls. Indeed, when women show masculine marks, at least in their bodies, the saint rejects them as malformed.

Ramakrishna was interested in such genderizing for a specific reason. It was not simply a matter of curiosity. Rather, it was intended as a means to arouse desire and devotional love. To encourage this love, for example, Ramakrishna asked Bhabanath to rent a house near Narendra's, for the two in Ramakrishna's eyes were like "man and woman" (KA 4.164).[56] Likewise, he described the disciples' love for Dr. Sarkar with a fairly obvious sexual metaphor: "Because you are coming," he told the good doctor, "the lovers stay awake, dress up, and tidy up the bedchamber" (KA 1.253).[57] So important is this male-female polarity that even the doctor's little round pills take on Tantric natures. Two of them are called *puruṣa* and *prakṛti*, "man" and "woman" (KA 3.256). In Ramakrishna's erotic community, then, even a doctor's visit is experienced in sexually charged metaphors.

The Communal Incarnation and the Subtle Body of the Inner Circle

RAMAKRISHNA USED TWO fascinating theological models to express the mystico-erotic nature of his community—the notion that he and his disciples constituted what I will call a "communal incarnation"; and the identification of his disciples with the different lotuses of the subtle body.

Ramakrishna tells us that when an incarnation descends to earth, his retinue of disciples descends with him. These disciples are of three types: the "inner circle," the "outer circle," and the "providers" (KA 4.283). Ramakrishna spoke of particular disciples in the inner circle as "parts" (*kala*) or "pieces" (*aṁsa*) of him: Purna, for example, was considered such a "part" of Ramakrishna (4.213). It was these "parts," as inseparable elements of the communal incarnation, who have incarnated along with Ramakrishna as his "friends and followers" (*sāṅgopāṅga*). Accordingly, Ramakrishna once saw "with open eyes" Caitanya and his disciples dancing in the temple precincts. Later, when certain disciples finally showed up at the temple, Ramakrishna would "stand up with a start," recognizing them as members of the retinue he had seen in his vision.[58] Caitanya and his disciples had reincarnated *en masse* as Ramakrishna and his disciples.

This communal incarnation was held together through relationships charged with erotic energies. Ramakrishna's secret Change becomes important here. We might recall that in his experience of making love to Jagannath he was told to turn his energies back to the social world and "take delight in God in the forms of man." He was no longer to "have sex with the Self." Now he was to become a Mother, a Friend, and a Lover of the disciples. All of these relationships, to the extent that they were all transformations of "the erotic state" of his secret experience, were erotic: they were transformed, redirected from his erotic experience with the divine. Ramakrishna "came down to earth" to make love to his community, to "take delight in God in the forms of man." Just as the Godhead became two and incarnated as Rādhā and Kṛṣṇa "in order to taste his own sweetness" (KA 5.83),[59] so now Ramakrishna and his disciples constitute "the forms of man" in which God can incarnate again and experience his own mystico-erotic "bliss" (*ānanda*). Accordingly, Ramakrishna often addressed a boy disciple with the expression "I've come for you" or "You've come into a human form and taken a body for me" (KA 4.227). Incarnating, for Ramakrishna, was as much a sexual experience as it was a theological truth. It was "aimed" at specific male presences.

God's play as man, then, is an erotic reality for the saint. The descent of God is an erotic descent. Thus Ramakrishna explains that God's play as man in the incarnation comes about so that God can "taste the juice" of experience. A little of this "juice" (*rasa*), sought by the incarnation, manifests itself in every devotee. It can be extracted only by a continuous "sucking," as one sucks the honey out of a flower (KA 3.179). This, according to M, is the "secret meaning" (*guhya artha*) of the incarnation and his play as man. The communal incarnation, then, is the place of God's bliss. Social relations provide the duality necessary for the mystico-erotic joys of Rādhā and Kṛṣṇa. The incarnation and his disciples descend for one another. The sweetness that was once experienced in the erotic state of Ramakrishna's mystical experiences of the divine is now sought in the living juices of male disciples. We are back to a secret language charged with homoerotic meanings only slightly concealed from the unbelieving. We are back to the erotic dialectic of Ramakrishna's Tantric world.

But Ramakrishna's disciples were flowers in more than one way. Not only did he suck out their sweetness. He also united with them in the subtle body of the inner circle. He did this by identifying different disciples with particular lotuses in the subtle body in a manner similar to that in which presiding deities are placed on them in the yoga manuals and Tantras: "I saw that some were of the ten-petaled lotus, and some were of the sixteen-petaled lotus, and some were of the hundred-petaled lotus." But Narendra, Ramakrishna reports with an excited exclamation point, was in the middle of the thousand-petaled lotus in the head, where Śiva sits waiting for his lover, the goddess Śakti (KA 4.228). The vagina-shaped lotuses that he had once licked in his vision and the sweet lotuses that he "sucks" in his disciples are now peopled with male disciples. This might help explain Ramakrishna's belief that whenever he looked at Narendra his mind "dissolved in the Undivided." This, after all, is exactly what is supposed to happen when the goddess Śakti finally reaches the thousand-petaled lotus and unites with her lover, Śiva, in its midst. Narendra was Śiva himself in the thousand-petaled lotus *of*

Ramakrishna's own subtle body. Narendra and the disciples were indeed "parts" of Ramakrishna, intimate parts with whom he, as the feminine Śakti, could unite in the subtle body of the communal incarnation. Like Ramakrishna's love-body, which he fashioned in his mystical practices, the subtle body of the inner circle, which he gradually molded out of his social relations, was a reality at once mystical and sexual.

RAMAKRISHNA'S FOOT: THE SINFUL TOUCH OF GOD

I BEGAN THIS STUDY with Ramakrishna's foot placed provocatively in the lap of a young male disciple. I took this act as a symbol for the entire study, advancing the thesis that Ramakrishna's foot points to a secret of which he himself was not aware, namely, that his mystical experiences and visions were constituted by erotic energies that he neither fully accepted nor understood. We saw this foot again in the present chapter, when Ramakrishna extended it in his first meetings with Narendra. I noted that for Narendra, as for many others, Ramakrishna's foot constituted a problem, a problem for which, in the beginning at least, Narendra could only invoke pathology as an answer. For his part, Ramakrishna never denied that he stuck his foot in strange places. But neither was he willing to take any blame. He made no attempts, at least recorded ones, to interpret the foot's meaning. That he left to others. In the course of the last four chapters, I have attempted my own interpretation. Having discussed in some detail the symbolic and social contexts of Ramakrishna's ecstatic act, it is time now to return to that foot and its secret.

Ramakrishna's extended foot, like his other techniques of arousal, served as a means to generate and awaken his and the disciples' energies. By all accounts, it was a very effective one. Walls spun for Narendra at the foot's touch. Other disciples fell into trances and saw visions. But unlike Ramakrishna's practices of reading bodies and pairing his disciples up into spiritual genders, it was the action of his foot that attracted the most attention, both negative and positive. There was something about Ramakrishna's foot that bothered people, that made them nervous and sometimes angry. But there was also something about Ramakrishna's foot that evoked great devotion and faith. Like Kālī's feet, Ramakrishna's foot seemed to invoke feelings of both devotion and shock.

This dual nature of the foot becomes especially explicit in a passage in the *Kathāmṛta* in which Dr. Sarkar, who was at the time treating Ramakrishna for throat cancer, argues with Girish Ghosh, the famous playwright and devout disciple of the saint, about the meaning of this foot:

> Doctor Sarkar: "Well, when you go into ecstasy, you place your foot on people's bodies. This isn't good."
>
> Sri Ramakrishna: "I can't tell whether or not I place my foot on anyone's body!"
>
> Doctor Sarkar: "That's not good. Don't you feel this, just a little?"
>
> Sri Ramakrishna: "What happens to me in that state of ecstasy, can I explain this to you? After such a state I have thought that perhaps this is why I am ill now. In order to experience God I've become mad. When I enter such a maddened state, what can I do?"
>
> Doctor Sarkar: "He admits it. He expresses regret for what he does. He is aware that this act is 'sinful.'"[60]
>
> Sri Ramakrishna (to Narendra): "You're very bright. Why don't you say something? Why don't you explain it to him?"
>
> Girish (to Dr. Sarkar): "My good sir! You're mistaken. He hasn't become ill on account of this. His body is pure, without sin. He touches people for their own good. Taking their sin upon himself, he has become ill, such is his thought from time to time. . . ."
>
> Doctor Sarkar (becoming embarrassed, to Girish): "I've been defeated by you. Give me the dust of your feet." (He takes the dust of Girish's feet.) (KA 1.254)

Dr. Sarkar suggests that Ramakrishna believes he is ill because of his "sinful" acts. The "shame" that led to Ramakrishna's initial suicide attempt with Kālī's sword becomes the "sin" of his last years: Christianity has begun its attack on Hinduism. Ramakrishna, not at all sure why he does such things and quite unable to defend himself, turns to his beloved Narendra for help. But the ever-fiery Girish steps in and insists that Ramakrishna is sick because he has vicariously absorbed *other* people's sins. Dr. Sarkar admits defeat and takes the dust, interestingly enough, of a foot.

But the argument is not over. Dr. Sarkar will insist again and again that the devotees are spoiling Ramakrishna by taking the dust of his feet and filling his head with the idea that he is an incarnation. Such actions can only produce "egotism" in an otherwise positively delightful soul (KA 2.218). For Sarkar, a foot is a foot and a man is a man. But it was Ramakrishna who had the last word in the matter, or perhaps better, the last act: Ramakrishna fell into ecstasy and placed his foot in Dr. Sarkar's lap, explaining to the doctor upon his return, "You're very pure! Otherwise I wouldn't be able to place my foot there!" (KA 4.278). The reader can only smile.

So we see a whole range of opinions focused on Ramakrishna's foot "there." Dr. Sarkar considers Ramakrishna's habit of touching people with his foot while in ecstasy to be "sinful." Girish, employing a strangely Christian model of transference and vicarious suffering,[61] believes that Ramakrishna touches people in order to take their sins upon himself. Ramakrishna's foot: Sinful? Or the foot of God? The debate, in which we have been involved all along, was, and perhaps still is, a very real one.

RAMAKRISHNA VIPARĪTARATĀ

IN THE CONTEXT of the present study, I would argue that Ramakrishna's foot is best understood as an embodied symbol of the mystico-erotic base of his Tantric experiences, what I have called Ramakrishna's secret. I would also argue that it functioned as a powerful symbol for Ramakrishna's descent back into the social world. With the arrival of his young disciples in the early 1880s, Ramakrishna finally could listen to Vaishnavacharan's Tantric truth and all those mysterious voices that all along had been commanding him to "Remain in existence." Now, with a community of men in which to love God, the aging saint could finally turn around his ontological face (*bhāvamukha*) and descend back into the social world. Now he could "take delight in God in the forms of man." His foot became a symbol of this descent, for, like the incarnation himself, it mediated between the divine and the human worlds. Through it, Ramakrishna could transmit his mystico-erotic energies into the bodies and hearts of his disciples. He could come down.

But such a descent was troubling for the disciples, for the secret that lay behind it constituted a problem. Like Kālī's feet, Ramakrishna's foot invoked both devotion and scandal. It seemed to carry both "right-footed" and "left-footed" meanings. Many believed that it was an instrument of grace and purification, and indeed it was. But others complained of its strange actions and "sinful" behavior. In their voices, the complaint of the poet could be heard again: "Who has seen such a crazy woman, standing on the heart-lotus of her husband!" "Who has seen such a strange man?" M often asked himself. "You place your foot on people's bodies. This isn't good," Sarkar complains. Kālī, still *viparītar-*

atā, "delighting in reversed sexual intercourse," had descended into their midst.

Ramakrishna's descent into the forms of man was deeply influenced by this upside-down, contrary act of the goddess. Like the goddess herself, arousing Śiva from his deathlike slumber with her beautiful feet, Ramakrishna awakened his disciples into radically new forms of consciousness with his foot. He frankly described the love that he shared with his all-male community as Śiva's *liṅgam,* the same phallus that he had once worshiped in madness and fondled in visions. By pairing his disciples up into mystical couples, through the dance and song of devotion and the nudity of innocence, renunciation, and shock, he sought to awaken their phallic love, "thrust straight up from the underworld" of their unconscious depths. He was the goddess standing on top of the ithyphallic god.

The disciples apparently did not see this unusual coincidence of iconography and bodily form. Perhaps they did not want to. Instead, they offered their own interpretations of Ramakrishna's foot. Narendra at first advanced a pathological explanation. Many others claimed that the actions of the foot proved that Ramakrishna was in fact a god. Some even claimed that the foot absorbed the sins of others. This is why, they said, Ramakrishna was sick. At least one man, however, thought that it was the foot itself that was sinful. Pathology, mythology, theology, and moral deviancy, then, were all advanced as possible answers to the problem of Ramakrishna's foot. It would take years, many years, before the problem would be resolved. And in this process of interpretation, debate, and belief, the secret of Ramakrishna, embodied in his foot, would be transformed. Like Ramakrishna himself, the secret too had descended. It too would be changed.

CHAPTER FIVE

Kālī's Tongue: Shame, Disgust, and Fear in a Tantric World

> O Ma! Is this your family's way, to stand on your husband?
> You're naked. Your husband is naked. And you both roam about
> from cremation ground to cremation ground!
> O Ma! We could all just die! Now woman put on your clothes!
>
> Ramprasad

AS WE HAVE SEEN in chapter 3, Kālī is on top of Śiva in the Tantras and in the *Kathāmṛta*, both in an erotic and in a philosophical sense. In chapter 4, we saw Ramakrishna embodying this iconographic form as he descended into the forms of man and extended his ecstatic foot into the bodies of his disciples in order to awaken their phallic love. Not surprisingly, such an act elicited outrage as well as devotion. Ramakrishna's foot and its strange habits thus became a focal point around which his disciples and friends argued about the meaning of the Paramahaṁsa's life and teachings. Much was symbolized by that foot and the goddess who seems to have been the source of both its form and power.

But there is still more, for there is something essentially shameful about a woman—even if she happens to be a goddess—standing on top of a man. Bengali wives, after all, do not normally stand on top of their husbands. Only whores and illicit lovers dare to stand on top of their men.[1] Mothers especially should remain mothers, at least in the eyes of their children. Certainly they are not supposed to be naked Lovers: "You're a Mother, so why are you naked before your boy?" the poet asks (SP, no. 143). Nor do Bengali women normally deck themselves out in morbid garlands and gory skirts and choose the rotting smoke of a cremation ground as their place of intercourse. The cremation ground, after all, is a place of fear, of disgusting sights and smells. It is a place of horror.

But this shame, this disgust, this fear bordering on horror is what Tantra is all about, or perhaps better, this shame, disgust, and fear is what Tantra is *not* about: "Shame, disgust, and fear" (*lajjā, ghṛṇā, bhaya*), Ramakrishna taught, are the three major bonds that must be severed if one is to realize the goal.[2] But to sever these bonds, to conquer like a true Hero these awful emotions, the aspirant must first engage the shameful, the disgusting, and the horrible directly in ritual, in myth and in iconography. Fear must be dissolved with a steady stare. But Ramakrishna could not look. He turned away from the naked woman's lap, that place of disgust, or simply fell into an unconscious state. The Bhairavī, in his own words, "forced" him to perform the repulsive rituals. He had to be pushed, screaming all the way as it were, into this Tantric realm. And in the end, Ramakrishna would fail to become a Hero. He would remain a Child.

From the householder's perspective, Ramakrishna failed. But this failure was tied up with a rejection, not just of the householding Hero, but of Tantra itself with all its macabre rituals and images. This failure to become a heroic householder and this rejection of Tantra must be kept distinct, for whereas Ramakrishna's failure to be a phallic male was often judged negatively by the culture, his rejection of Tantra met little opposition or challenge. Many people severely criticized the saint for his seeming impotence and mistreatment of women, that is, for his failure to become a householder. Almost no one, however, criticized him for his rejection of Tantra. Ramakrishna's rejection of Tantra, in other words, must be seen as only a moment in a broader cultural rejection of Tantra. And this cultural rejection of Tantra must be seen in its own context, as the flip side of Tantra itself. After all, by adopting for its rituals the very things that the culture deems grossly unacceptable (the Five M's), Tantra defines itself as anticulture. It *must* be rejected. It expects, it *wants* to be rejected, for the moment it is accepted it loses its salvific power to free the aspirant from his or her social conditionings and becomes itself a conditioning. Ramakrishna's rejection of Tantra, in other words, is a rejection of something that is already rejected.

Ramakrishna's rejection of Tantra, then, was part of a larger Bengali rejection of Tantra. At some point in time—we will never know when—this cultural shame or embarrassment over Tantra was projected onto the goddess herself and became focused on, of all places, her tongue. Kālī's tongue, much like Ramakrishna's foot, thus became a focal point of a cultural debate that in the end changed, indeed *reversed*, the meanings of that tongue. Now it is said Kālī is sticking out her tongue, that incredibly long tongue, not to lick up the blood of slain demons, as she did in the Pūraṇas, nor to eat the ritual offerings of goat and human meat, as she did in the Tantras. Now, her devotees say, she is sticking out her tongue *in shame*. She is embarrassed, they say, because she is standing on her husband and she knows that this is wrong. In the context of this present study, one could say that her tongue is expressing the shame of her feet.

What does a protruding tongue have to do with shame? When Bengalis are embarrassed, they stick out their tongues ever so slightly. It is actually more of a biting the tongue, a slight extension as the teeth bite or "cut" (*kāṭā*) it, but few seem to notice the conflation here. Never mind Kālī's cannibalistic history in Hindu mythology or her unabashed eroticism in the Tantras and their rituals. Never mind that her tongue often hangs down well past her chin, *way* past any cultural cue of embarrassed shame: one text has it extending nine miles![3] All that history and all those texts are forgotten now. Now she is supposed to be ashamed, embarrassed by her improper acts, by her upside-down eroticism. *Viparīta-rati*, after all, implies a reversal, a contrariness, an upside-down act that goes against the norm. It is not supposed to happen that way.

I find this shamed tongue fascinating, not so much because it is such a prominent theme in contemporary Bengali interpretations of Kālī, but more especially because it is virtually absent in the Purāṇas and Tantras that form the textual and ritual base of the tradition.[4] This, I would argue, signals something important in the culture. Contradictions after all often point to hidden truths. They suggest that there may be more to a particular cultural form than the culture itself is often willing to acknowledge openly. The present study is a case in point, for the Ramakrishna that I have uncovered in the historical record is in many ways not the Ramakrishna that contemporary Bengali culture acknowledges as its own. Ramakrishna, in other words, very much like Kālī's tongue, is a problem for Bengali culture. The problem of Kālī's extended tongue can thus function as an especially effective iconographic focus to get at and see clearly the problem of Ramakrishna. The saint aids us immeasurably here by sticking out his own ecstatic tongue again and again, not to express a sense of shame, but to commune with the disgusting and the impure. Ramakrishna's tongue, in other words, is a Tantric tongue, and precisely because it is neither ashamed nor embarrassed, it is, much like Kālī's tongue, a contradiction or "problem" for the culture.

This final chapter is based on the assumption that the problem of Kālī's tongue and the problem of Ramakrishna are both emblematic of the more general problem of Tantra in Bengali culture. In other words, the shame the culture sees in Kālī's extended tongue, and by extension in Ramakrishna's ecstatic tongue, is in fact a projection of the shame Bengalis feel about the Tantric tradition in general. It is Bengalis, not the ecstatic Ramakrishna and *certainly* not the goddess of the texts, who are "ashamed." Of course, I have been treating this theme of shame, disgust, and fear throughout the study. Indeed, without shame the present study would not exist, for it was shame that created Ramakrishna's secret talk, that twisted M's five volumes into a complex cycle of concealing turns, and that drove Nikhilananda to bowdlerize or omit entire passages in his translations (introduction). Shame again was central to Ramakrishna's initial crisis. Without it, it is doubtful that the young saint would have brought Kālī's sword to his throat and been drowned in the ocean of light (chapter 1). Likewise, shame, disgust, and fear were all central to Ramakrishna's rejection of the Lover for the pure sexless Mother. Such reactions forced Ramakrishna's numerous Tantric experiments underground until they only appeared in unconscious visions and ecstatic states over which the saint had little control (chapter 2). Finally, shame was central to the debate that Ramakrishna's foot and its descent into the forms of man generated (chapter 4). "He admits it," Dr. Sarkar claimed, "He expresses regret for what he does." But did he? It seems unlikely. Ramakrishna was no more ashamed of the actions of his foot than Kālī is ashamed of hers in so many of the Tantras. Hence the problem of Kālī's tongue.

KĀLĪ'S TONGUE

THE HISTORY OF KĀLĪ'S TONGUE, like the history of the goddess herself, is a story rich in detail but poor in plot. We know a great deal about what the tongue symbolized in specific texts at different periods, but we know very little about how, why, or when the different meanings of the tongue developed. Nevertheless, the work of different scholars has resulted in something of a consensus in a very general history of Kālī and, by extension, of her lolling tongue.[5] Such a history can be divided into four broad stages: the tongue as consumer of blood sacrifices in tribal culture; the tongue as consumer of demons in classical Hinduism; the

Tantric tongue in medieval Hinduism; and finally, the tongue as an emblem of embarrassment or shame in modern India. These stages are at best preliminary hermeneutical devices designed to place the discussion that follows in a broad historical context. They argue, not so much for some sort of historical precision, which they do not claim, but for the importance of historical development and change in analyzing the complexity and internal conflict inherent in so many religious forms. Moreover, these stages should not be understood as mutually exclusive. Like most religious forms built up over time, Kālī's tongue never truly sheds any of its earlier meanings. Preserved in myth, ritual, and iconography, these different layered meanings are always potential realities for those capable of tapping into their latent power. As we shall see shortly, it is precisely this historical process of layering and this ever-present latency that produce what I have called the problem of Kālī's tongue.

Tribal Origins: "That Sonthal Bitch"

Most scholars now agree that Kālī originated in the mountain tribal societies of South Asia, where she, or some variant of her form, seems to have been worshiped with blood sacrifice and fertility rituals. In these contexts, Kālī's tongue seems to have functioned primarily as a consumer of blood and, if we are to believe the reports (which were often explicitly polemical or embedded in literary works), human sacrifice. Kālī here is a goddess of outsiders, of the peripheries of Hindu culture. She dwells in the mountains and on the geographic extremities of Hindu India. She is black-skinned, like the tribal aboriginal peoples of the mountains who worshiped her. Perhaps one of Ramakrishna's disciples summed up this troubling history best when he capitalized on Kālī's popularity among the Sonthal tribes and jokingly referred to her as "that Sonthal bitch."[6]

The Early Sanskrit Literature: Long-Tongue, Fire, and Fury

The Kālī of the early Sanskrit literature is no less fantastic than the Kālī of the tribal peoples and does little to ennoble her image. Consider, for example, the demoness Long-Tongue (*Dīrghajihvī*) of the *Jaiminīya Brāhmaṇa,* a figure whom O'Flaherty has identified as a precursor of the later, equally long-tongued Kālī.[7] Long-Tongue licks up the juice of the Vedic ritual and has "mice" (vaginas) all over her body. She is slain through a trick whereby the god Indra grants a certain Sumitra penises on every limb. Sumitra lays down with the demoness and locks into her so that Indra can cut her down. Long-Tongue, she who licked up the ritual juice and had vaginas "on every limb," was thus slain. In this story, the demoness's tongue illicitly licks up the sacrificial offerings that belong rightly to the gods and seems to be connected, however symbolically, to an overly aggressive female sexuality: the unusual length of her tongue seems to mirror the exaggerated number of her "mice." The sacrificial theme, if not the sexual one, appears again in the *Muṇḍaka Upaniṣad* (ca. sixth-century B.C.E.) but this time rights itself back to a more proper meaning. Here for the first time we come across the name "Kālī." It refers, however, not to a goddess, but to one of the seven tongue-like flames of the sacrificial fire.[8] Long-Tongue's tongue, once the aggressor, has become part of the sacred fire. The *Muṇḍaka* passage, however, still contains no clear reference to a goddess. For that we have to turn to the *Mahābharata* where a dark goddess named Kālī appears in the dreams of the Paṇḍava warriors to warn them of their own imminent deaths.[9] The sleeping heroes see her black bloody form leading them away with a noose.

In these passages, a Kālī-like goddess (Long-Tongue) or a goddess named Kālī is still a figure on the very periphery of Indian society and consciousness. She threatens to destroy the sacrifice. She challenges the Vedic gods with the dangers of multiple sexual organs. She appears in dreams to lead the Paṇḍava warriors away to their death. Kālī and her blood-hungry tongue are brought a bit closer into Hindu society with the appearance of the sixth-century C.E. Sanskrit text, the *Devīmāhātmya,* an approximately seven-hundred line battle hymn reciting the glorious battles of the goddess Durgā against the forces of evil. In the course of the hymn, Kālī assists Durgā twice, once to slay the demons Canda and Muṇḍa and once to kill Raktabīja. In the first scene, Durgā's forehead darkens into an inky black anger out of which a horribly emaciated Kālī appears, armed with a sword and a noose, "with gaping mouth and fearful with her lolling tongue."[10] Kālī devours the elephants of the demon army and lops off the heads of Canda and Muṇḍa to present to Durgā. The demon leader now decides to march with all of his army on the stubborn goddess and her inky companion. Amidst the battle, the demon Raktabīja proves to be particularly powerful, for every time he is cut down in battle each of his semen-like drops of blood (*rakta-bīja*) spring into an equally powerful Raktabīja. Soon there are thousands of him. But Durgā simply commands Kālī to open her mouth wide and gulp down the drops as Durgā herself slays the demon: "Stricken with many weapons, the great demon Raktabīja fell to the ground bloodless."[11] The male demon's vital forces were thus consumed by a devouring female.

In both of these scenes, we see Kālī's tongue and huge gaping mouth employed to consume not a human sacrifice but a demonic army. Her terrible violence has been harnessed for the good of the world. She still retains her dark, bloodthirsty nature, but her darkness is now an angry aspect of the great goddess. Kālī and her tongue have entered the Hindu fold, if only as an incarnation of fury and as a consumer of demonic blood and semen.

The Tantric Tongue: Blood and Passion

THE TANTRIC TEXTS preserve these earlier meanings of wild bloodthirst, sacrifice, and battle, although the descriptions now become somewhat stylized. Kālī's face is thus commonly described as "smiling with two streams of blood oozing from the corners of her mouth" (KT 1.32). Her mouth is still said to be gaping, its huge teeth protruding, smeared with blood. Her lolling tongue is yet a marker of horror and fear. Violence, even if it has been purified with devotion, is still very much a part of her worship. Thus the goddess is said to be greatly satisfied with the flesh of both animals and men: "cats, camels, sheep, buffaloes, goats, and men" (KS, v. 19), as one list goes. Kālī's origins in the sacrifices of the tribal peoples are still very apparent.

But there are developments as well in the Tantras, for the texts describe aspects of Kālī and her tongue that were not so apparent in the earlier traditions. In the Tantras, for example, Kālī is a great goddess in her own right and not simply an emotional appendage of Durgā. Moreover, she is now joined to Śiva, one of the major deities of the Hindu pantheon, erotically engaging the god in reversed sexual intercourse. This upside-down erotic act takes on cosmic proportions when the philosophical tradition of Sāṁkhya is employed to interpret the union of the goddess and the god as the creative union of primordial nature (*prakṛti*) and the eternal spirit (*puruṣa*).

What does Kālī's tongue mean in the Tantras? Many things, no doubt. It is a consumer of blood sacrifice and a provoker of horror. Perhaps it also signified the goddess's sexual arousal. The tongue, after all, is commonly associated with the category of passion (*rajas*) and is extended while Kālī engages Śiva in aggressive intercourse. In Hindu mythology, moreover, the female sexual organ can become "teethed." And there are later texts in the culture in which both the mouth and the tongue become sexual organs. As we have already seen, a woman once used her mouth to sexually suck her own big toe as a symbolic substitute for Ramakrishna's penis. Finally, I might add here that in a secret talk passage in volume 4 of the *Kathāmṛta*, Ramakrishna sees the goddess's "cosmic vagina" (*brahmayoni*) "lolling" (KA 4.232), the same expression that is often used to describe Kālī's tongue. Clearly, then, there are numerous symbolic cues that could give a sexual meaning to Kālī's gaping mouth and its blood-red tongue.

The Tongue of Shame

BUT MORE IMPORTANT than such acts, visions, and myths in uncovering the sexual dimensions of Kālī's tongue is the profound reversal or denial that takes place in respect to the tongue and its meaning in contemporary Bengali culture. Kālī's tongue, we must remember, is said now to represent the goddess's sense of shame for "standing" on her husband. The Tantras are clear enough about why Kālī is "standing" on Śiva: she is engaging him in reversed sexual intercourse, delighting in the waves of passion and arousal that flow from such an act.[12] There is certainly no shame here. If Kālī, then, is said now to be ashamed for standing on Śiva, and the Tantras state that Kālī is standing on Śiva to engage him in an upside-down erotic act, then it is clear, *at least from a Tantric perspective,* that the shame the culture sees in Kālī's extended tongue is, quite simply, misplaced. It is not there.

Misplaced or not, however, it is precisely this shamed tongue that becomes Kālī's tongue in the modern period. If one asks people on the street why Kālī is sticking out her tongue, this "shamed tongue" answer is precisely the explanation that will most often be given. In a fascinating piece of research, Usha Menon and Richard Shweder have recently established this "culturally correct" interpretation of Kālī's tongue in contemporary Orissa.[13] But there are important dissenters in Menon and Shweder's study, foremost among them two Tāntrikas. In a second article, Shweder and Menon quote a third source, the story of P. C. Mishra, an Oriya narrator Frédérique Marglin interviewed in Puri, to further amplify this Tantric reading of Kālī's tongue. According to Mishra, Durgā became furious when she learned that, due to a boon the gods had granted the buffalo demon, she could kill him only by showing him her genitals. After exposing herself and slaying the buffalo demon, the goddess goes on a wild rampage, so upset is she about being humiliated by the male gods:

> Her anger grew so terrible that she transformed herself, grew smaller and black and left her lion mount and started walking on foot. Her name then became Kali. With tongue lolling out and dripping with blood, she then went on a blind destructive rampage. . . . The gods and the people became extremely worried and appealed to Siva for help. Mahadev agreed and lay himself down, sleeping on the path on which the furious, black and naked Kali was coming. In her blinded anger she did not see him and stepped on his chest. At that moment Siva's penis became erect and entered Kali. At that instant Kali recognized her husband and pulled out her tongue in ecstasy and her anger disappeared.[14]

Here Kālī's tongue retains its Tantric nature. It is a marker of sexual ecstasy, not of shame. It extends itself as Śiva's penis becomes erect, as if to signal that it too is a sexual organ, capable of arousal. The story thus reverses the "culturally correct" version of the myth and returns the icon of Kālī "standing" on Śiva back to its earlier Tantric meanings.

But P. C. Mishra's story is the exception. Indeed, so rare is his account of Kālī's tongue that an interpretation such as his would turn up on Menon and Shweder's statistical scale as a "cultural dud."[15] Although Mishra most likely speaks of the earlier Tantric intent of the icon, he nevertheless appears as wildly heterodox, as "wrong." Kālī's tongue, then, has reversed itself from a sexually aggressive organ of wild proportions to a marker of feminine modesty. Sumitra's ancient act of slaying the sexually aggressive Long-Tongue has been reenacted in the culture. In the words of Vivekananda, Śiva has finally reclaimed his rightful dominance over the goddess and made her a "servant" (*dāsī*) (KA 4.296).

But has he? As Menon and Shweder point out, narrators commenting on the manner in which the goddess returns to her wifely senses usually insist that she does so entirely of her own accord. She could stamp Śiva into the ground if she wished, but instead she chooses to reign her power in and control her justified anger in an act of public "shame." Menon and Shweder articulate some of the implications of this self-imposed shame: "The ultimate message of the icon, therefore, is to display the cultural 'truth' that it is women who uphold the social order. . . . Curiously enough, this view of women coincides with the Tantric one that also sees women as the power that upholds the universe. The difference is that while the Tantric view sees women achieving this position through the unchecked exercise of power, the narrators in the sample see it as being attained through the moral self-control of such power."[16] Paradoxically, then, even in the culture's denial of the explicitly Tantric meanings of Kālī's tongue (the tongue as a marker of sexual aggression and arousal) the culture ultimately returns to Tantra and its divinization of feminine power. The shy housewife, biting her tongue in a public act of restraint, controls by that act an immense reservoir of power capable, at any moment, of dissolving what Ramakrishna called the "bonds of shame, disgust, and fear" and returning the culture to that Tantric midnight "where all jackals howl in the same way" (LP 4.4.30).

Kālī's tongue, then, has reversed itself from a fiery consumer of bloody flesh and demons to a marker of feminine modesty. The violent aspects of the goddess are no doubt still present in the myths, images, and rituals, but they are now eclipsed by a domestication process focused on the tongue. The sexual dimensions of the tongue, moreover, perhaps once obvious in the Tantric images and rites, are now only hinted at in the symbols and myths and suggested by a series of nervous denials. One of the purposes of this final chapter is to expose the source of that nervousness by uncovering the Tantric dimensions of Kālī's tongue as they are revealed in the secret visions and ecstatic experiences of Ramakrishna.

THE LAST DAYS, 1885–1886: THE SECRET REVEALED AND CONCEALED

ALL BUT ONE of the "marked" disciples (those whom Ramakrishna had seen in previsions) had arrived before the close of 1884. The boy Purna, the "Full One," arrived in the early months of 1885, completing or "fulfilling" the coming of the disciples. As one of Ramakrishna's most beloved disciples and the object of numerous secret rendezvous, hidden carriage rides, and special gifts, Purna the Fulfiller occupied a place in the spiritual hierarchy of the community just below Narendra. With his arrival, the community of the incarnation was complete. "From now on, no one else of this class will come here," Ramakrishna is said to have declared (LP 5.9.1).[17]

Thanks to Keshab's efforts, Ramakrishna had become quite well-known. Crowds gathered to look at him and to listen to his stories, teachings, and famous metaphors. All this fame, however, eventually began to annoy the Paramahaṁsa. Too many "wretched people" took too much of his time, he complained. Accordingly, he asked the Mother to give some of his householder disciples a little *śakti*, so that they could teach the crowds and he could concentrate on more important things (LP 5.11.4). And concentrate he had to, for his days were numbered. Within a little over a year, he would be dead, his cancer-racked bony body consigned to the flames of the funeral pyre.

One of the most striking aspects of these final days was Ramakrishna's belief that he would disappear in death as soon as it became known that he was an incarnation of God. As soon as the secret of who he really was got out, the secret would have to be concealed again. Accordingly, many times he was heard to say, "When many people regard this as a god and show faith and devotion, it will immediately disappear" (LP 5.11.5). Like the textual aspect of the secret, then, defined as it is by patterns of revealing and concealing, the theological aspect of the secret was patterned after a similar movement of revelation and occultation. That which was revealed must be concealed again. The last days of Ramakrishna, like the texts that record his teachings, bear this truth out.

Throat Cancer and the Good Doctor

IT WAS NOT LONG after the last marked disciple came that the Paramahaṁsa began to feel pain in his throat. Perhaps it was in the month of April 1885 (LP 5.10.3). At first the doctors thought that it was just a common cold, the result of Ramakrishna's body and feet being overexposed to the cold and rain at a recent religious festival. Like a pouting child, Ramakrishna blamed it all on poor Ram. Had he not made him go to the festival? (LP 5.11.1). But the doctors soon changed their mind and diagnosed the saint's condition as nothing more than a case of "clergyman's sore-throat" (LP 5.11.2). In other words, Ramakrishna was talking too much. The condition, however, was aggravated by more than just talking. Ecstatic states also seemed to inflame it: "It got worse when he talked a lot and after he went into *samādhi*" (LP 5.10.4). The two activities that more than anything else defined who Ramakrishna was—*kathā* and *samādhi*, "talking" and "ecstasy"—were thus diagnosed as leading causes of the pain. In a sense, Ramakrishna was his own problem now. He was told to stop talking so much and to avoid, as best he could, his ecstatic states. But he could not. How could he? Talking and ecstasy *were* Ramakrishna.

As the days wore on, Ramakrishna's body weakened and streams of blood began to flow from the boils that had developed in his throat. He could no longer eat solid foods. Doctors were summoned, but to no avail. Ramakrishna seemed dejected. The disciples were positively depressed. Datta describes the mood of the hour: "We arrived at Dakshineshwar in the morning and saw that the Paramahaṁsa was sitting alone in a very depressed mood. No one had ever seen such a heart-wrenching scene. Seeing his face, devoid of any joy, it seemed to us that everything was empty" (JV[4], 137). Such scenes of empty despair provoked the disciples to move Ramakrishna into Calcutta for treatment. At first, Ramakrishna was excited about the adventure of living in a rented house, but only until he actually saw the place and decided that he did not want to live there at all. He turned around, walked out the door, and proceeded immediately to Balaram's home, which happened to be in the area. There he stayed for two weeks as an uninvited guest while the disciples anxiously looked for another place. They soon found a house, this one fortunately to Ramakrishna's liking, on Shyampukur Street. Here he would stay for three months. It was at this time that the doctors rediagnosed Ramakrishna's disease as a form of cancer. Deciding that drugs would have a deleterious effect on the Master's tender constitution, the disciples decided to avoid English doctors and hire a series of homeopathic doctors, among them, a certain Dr. Mahendralal Sarkar. Sarkar would be with Ramakrishna until the very end.

This ambivalence toward "English doctors" would continue throughout the illness. Datta struggles in his writings with the question of whether to summon an English doctor, noting at one point that Ramakrishna forbade them to. When the situation became desperate and it was clear that homeopathy was getting them nowhere, an English doctor was finally called in, a certain Dr. Coates from Calcutta Medical College. But his Western medicine was equally impotent before the disease. All he could do was pronounce that Ramakrishna's cancer was in fact incurable (JV[4], 144). From his perspective, there was no hope. But the disciples continued to hope anyway, some of them going so far as to believe that the Master was actually feigning his illness for some hidden purpose. He would surely recover, they claimed, when that purpose was fulfilled. A suffering god was more than they could take. Denial seemed the best way out.

The English doctor only reinforced such feelings. He could bring nothing but despair in the form of an unwelcome diagnosis. The homeopath Dr. Sarkar, on the other hand, played a very different sort of role in these final days, acting as much as a friend and companion as a professional doctor. He would come to treat Ramakrishna, ask a few questions, and then stay for hours to talk to the saint and argue with the devotees about their beliefs, about the merits of Western science and physiology, and about the meaning of Ramakrishna's *samādhi*. Datta tells us that his was a modern, reformed sort of religion, that is, he worked for the social welfare of others (JV[4], 139). He believed in God but did not honor the scriptures, the gods and goddesses, or the strange powers that the sages were said to possess. He had taken the attacks of the Christian missionaries very seriously.

The *Kathāmṛta*, the *Līlāprasaṅga*, and the *Jīvanavṛttānta* all dwell, almost lovingly, on the numerous scenes involving the good doctor. In a sense, Dr. Sarkar is the model of what the texts would like all Western-educated Indians to be: skeptical but sincere, and ultimately convertible, pliable, ready to believe. Many of the doctor's arguments must have rung true for M, for Saradananda, and for Datta, all of whom were trained in Western forms of thought and criticism. All three authors, at least, give Sarkar pride of place in these last days, presenting his arguments in considerable detail. True, in the end, the doctor is always defeated in argument by the faithful Girish, by the fiery Narendra, or by Ramakrishna himself (although, as if the argument was cleaned up in the texts to end in the right way, it is often not at all clear why Sarkar was defeated). But at least he gets to argue. Unlike poor M, who gave up the practice after his first few visits, Dr. Sarkar challenges the disciples and the saint until the very end, and he does it with words and a spirit that were filled with conviction, honor, understanding, and compassion.

Dr. Sarkar had treated Ramakrishna years before. When he was brought this time, by M, he was amazed to find Ramakrishna surrounded by devotees. "Whose devotees are these?" he asked. When M began to introduce him to Ramakrishna's community, Sarkar expressed his surprise. Certainly this was not the Ramakrishna he knew back at Dakshineshwar so many years ago. Then he knew Ramakrishna simply as "Mathur Babu's paramahaṁsa," as if the wealthy Mathur somehow owned Ramakrishna for himself (perhaps not far from the truth) or made him into who he was (again, not entirely false). Now, however, Mathur was dead and Ramakrishna was in the newspapers. The tables had been turned. Sarkar seemed impressed, but he was not yet convinced of the transformation that seemed to have taken place.

Accordingly, the texts are filled with scenes in which Sarkar criticizes the disciples for ruining Ramakrishna, the simple preacher, by treating him as if he were a god. As we saw in the last chapter, the practice of taking the dust of Ramakrishna's feet was particularly upsetting to the doctor. His own modern democratic notions conflicted sharply with the special treatment, indeed, the adoration, Ramakrishna received from his disciples (JV[4], 140–141). On more than one occasion, it seems, he stated his belief that *bhāva* and *samādhi* were manifestations of mental perversions (JV[4], 140). In one humorous scene, Sarkar says as much only to discover that the disciples are dropping like flies all around him as they fall into the very "mental perversions" that he had been attacking. Sarkar shakes them, but to no avail. "Perhaps Doctor Sarkar," Datta speculates, "could not understand such events" (JV[4], 141). The scene thus ends with the doctor defeated, not by a rational argument but by a group of seemingly unconscious disciples.

Saradananda plays such conflicts and arguments down, claiming that in the end Sarkar was convinced that the disciples were not turning Ramakrishna into some "sensationalistic fashion" (LP 5.12.2.19), but the biographer's case is not convincing. M presents a very different picture of things in the *Kathāmṛta,* and Saradananda gives himself away when he points out that Sarkar could not understand how one could revere someone as an incarnation, "because he was so influenced by Western education" (LP 5.12.2.19). Even in Saradananda's text, then, Sarkar is and is not brought around to the disciples' interpretation of things. He remains, to the end, a friend, but certainly not a disciple.

Ramakrishna as the Image: Kālī-pūjā, 1885

WHILE RAMAKRISHNA was staying at Shyampukur and was being treated by Dr. Sarkar, many strange events were taking place (JV[4], 142). According to Saradananda, the disciples were experiencing Ramakrishna's "divine power" and "god-nature" day and night. The biographer is careful to point out, though, that such revelations "did not take place before all or all the time" (LP 5.12.2.27). Ramakrishna, it seems, preferred to reveal his secret self only to a few. One such secret revelation took place on the night of Kālī-pūjā in 1885, the last such pūjā the saint would ever see. Ramakrishna had instructed a few disciples the day before to prepare for a brief worship of Kālī. Accordingly, flowers, incense, sandal-paste, fruits, roots, and sweets were all collected and made ready for the annual worship to take place the following night. No arrangements, however, were made for an actual image of the goddess. When the night finally arrived, nothing seemed to be happening. The flowers and the sweets just sat there, and much to the surprise and confusion of everyone present, Ramakrishna made no move to perform the worship himself. He just sat there as well. This unusual and perhaps uncomfortable silence prompted the disciples to begin speculating. At some point they concluded that the Master was intending to worship the Mother in himself, as he had done on so many earlier occasions. Perhaps this was why he had given no instructions to arrange for an image. But Ramakrishna made no moves that would substantiate their theory. He still just sat there.

Finally it occurred to the ever-faithful Girish that it was the disciples who should perform "the worship of the Mother of the Universe in the living image of his bodily form" (LP 5.12.2.25). Inspired with such a faith, Girish took the flowers and the other offerings and began to offer them to the feet of Ramakrishna. Something was triggered in the saint. His body hairs stood on end as his limbs spontaneously assumed the iconographic form of the goddess. His two hands became Kālī's right hands, offering boons and granting freedom from fear. He now was the goddess. Cries of "Victory to Ramakrishna!" filled the room as the disciples offered fruit and sweets to Ramakrishna's feet and recited their chants. The roof shook with their excitement (JV[4], 143).

Eventually, Ramakrishna came to, ate a little of the offerings, and blessed the disciples. The pūjā had come to an end. Ramakrishna had manifested his secret divine nature to a select group of disciples. He had done it, moreover, in a way that dramatically demonstrates two of the basic theses of the present study, namely: that Ramakrishna embodied in his visions, his teachings, and his life the iconographic form of Kālī; and that his divinization was effected through a social process of interpretation and belief over which he often had little, if any, control. If Ramakrishna had become the image of his own accord, he was transformed into a god by the desires and interpretations of others. For his part, he just sat there in silence. It was Girish and the faithful brothers who theologized upon that silence and filled it with meaning. Ramakrishna responded with more silence and an iconographic pose.

The Cosmic Ramakrishna: The Secret Fully Revealed

RAMAKRISHNA AND THE DISCIPLES stayed three months at Shyampukur Street, until the landlord wanted them all out and they had to move yet again. They landed this time in a beautiful complex, complete with a garden. It would become known simply as Kashipur. The almanac was consulted, and the move was made on December 11, 1885. It would be the group's last move.

According to Saradananda, it was at Shyampukur and Kashipur that the inner and outer circles fully defined themselves, for it was at this time that Ramakrishna's many moves and intense suffering served as a test, separating the devout from the lukewarm. The community of devoted disciples now became closer than a family. According to Saradananda, only twelve stayed until the very end and completed their "vow of service" (GM 5.13.2.6).[18] They would become the pillars of the early monastic community after Ramakrishna was gone. Saradananda seems to identify these twelve with the inner circle, but falsely I believe. As I pointed out in the introduction, Ramakrishna never equated the inner circle with his renouncing boy disciples. For Ramakrishna, the inner circle always contained both householders and renouncers.

For many of these last disciples, be they householders or renouncers, serving Ramakrishna carried serious costs. M, Ram, Surendra, and Girish, for example, had to meet each month to try to figure out who would foot the bills. Surendra seems to have picked up the expenses of renting the different buildings (JV[4], 144), while the other householders provided for the needs of the boy disciples. The boy disciples also suffered. Narendra had to give up his law studies, a particularly difficult choice given the fact that his family, having lost Narendra's father a few years earlier to death, was in serious financial trouble. Other boys found great opposition when they returned home. The parents were not at all happy with things. Ramakrishna, they believed, was ruining their children (GM 5.13.2.10). It is little wonder that some of the disciples never showed up during these last days or left Kashipur never to return. Purna, for example, one of the most beloved of all the boy disciples, is not listed among the final twelve. He had married (LP 5.7.34). And poor Harish: Saradananda tells us in a footnote that, "a few days after he returned home, Harish became mentally ill" (GM 5.13.2.7, n. 1). It was not an easy time for any one.

The community moved into the Kashipur house the second week of December. Within a few short weeks, an event of unusual consequence and meaning would take place at Kashipur. It is still celebrated every year on the very date it occurred in 1886: January 1. The day began with Ramakrishna feeling especially well and deciding to take a stroll in the garden. Datta, for some reason, tells us that he was wearing a silky green hat that covered his ears (JV[4], 146). At some point during the stroll, Ramakrishna asked Girish[19] a question that he often asked his disciples: "Who do you say that I am?" Girish immediately answered that he was convinced that Ramakrishna was God incarnate, come down to earth out of mercy for humankind. Ramakrishna responded to Girish's faith with a single sentence and a simple gesture. He raised his right hand and said, "What more shall I say. May you be awakened."

Saying this, Ramakrishna entered into an ecstatic state and began touching his disciples.

As he touched them, with both his hand and his foot, the disciples saw visions and experienced new states of consciousness. As Ramakrishna's hand touched Akshay's chest, for example, Akshay felt a "lightning bolt of *śakti*" (JV[4], 146). With a similar touch, Ramlal, long discouraged by his partial visions of his chosen deity, now saw the full iconographic form of his god (GM 5.13.3.3). Ramakrishna had become the image during Kālī-pūjā. Now he completed the image for a disciple.

Everyone present in the garden at Kashipur received a special awakening on that day, everyone except poor Haramohan. Peeved, no doubt, that the boy had married a woman (KA 4.109), Ramakrishna would not touch him. "May you remain as you are today," he said simply, and then walked away (JV[4], 147–148). Ramakrishna had done something similar on another occasion, again to Haramohan (JV[4], 146). One can imagine the disappointment the left-out disciple must have felt as he watched all of his friends enter ecstatic states. Marrying a woman apparently had made him an unfit object for the saint's homoerotic energies. Haramohan, after all, was now engaged in explicit heterosexual activity. He had dared to defile himself with lover-and-gold.

Vaikuntha's experience at Ramakrishna's touch on that day is especially interesting. He had what might be called a cosmic vision of Ramakrishna: "Wherever I looked, I saw the form of the gently smiling Master within the sky, the houses, the trees, and the people" (LP 5.13.3.6). Ramakrishna was everywhere. The universe seemed to smile. This cosmic vision continued for days, too many days it seems: "Because I could not concentrate on the work at hand, it suffered. . . . Even though I tried to control the vision for sometime, I could not do it. I then understood a little why Arjuna, after seeing the universal form of the Lord and becoming afraid, prayed to him to take it back. . . . At times I thought to myself, 'Am I going mad?' I then prayed again to the Master in fear, 'Lord, I am not able to contain this state, make it stop.' . . . after I prayed in this way, the vision and the state went away in a day" (LP 5.13.3.7). Ramakrishna had experienced again and again that "She herself has become everything." Here this vision of "She herself has become everything" is replaced by another. Now "Ramakrishna himself has become everything." Something has happened. What began as a subjective experience of Ramakrishna has become an objective, cosmic truth for a disciple. Vaikuntha sees Ramakrishna "out there," in the houses, trees, and people of the external world. Everything is suddenly ensouled with the smiling presence of the Paramahaṁsa from Dakshineshwar. The cosmic body of the goddess has been transformed into the cosmic body of Ramakrishna himself. Ramakrishna, in effect, has become God. Vaikuntha is quick to grasp the religious meaning of the vision. He thus recalls for us the famous vision of Arjuna the archer in the *Bhagavad-Gītā,* in which Kṛṣṇa, Arjuna's charioteer, appears to Arjuna in his terrible cosmic form and frightens the archer into asking him to hide his divine form again. Vaikuntha follows Arjuna's example and prays to Ramakrishna, the "Lord," to cover his divinity again, to take the vision away. Ramakrishna's secret was too much for Vaikuntha and his comfortable sanity: "Am I going mad?" he asked himself again and again. The life of the office and the everyday world could not carry on with such a cosmic secret fully revealed. It *had* to be concealed again.

Saradananda marvels that there was not a single renouncer present for this event (LP 5.13.3.4). Narendra and the other students were all back in the house, cleaning things up or sleeping after staying up all night with their dying Master. Saradananda seems puzzled by this troubling absence of the renouncers at such a profoundly significant event, but Saradananda's problem is just that, Saradananda's problem. Once one acknowledges that the boy disciples held no monopoly on Ramakrishna's revelations, something the biographer seems incapable of, such anomalies cease to be anomalous. As I have shown, Ramakrishna's secret was as much for the householders as it was for the renouncers. The events of January 1, 1886, are just one more example of this seemingly obvious truth.

Datta refers to the events of this day as the "Kalpataru Day," the day on which Ramakrishna became a "wish-fulfilling tree" and granted to each of the disciples present a uniquely personal experience. For Datta, the events of that day constituted the "last act" of the "secret of the play" of Ramakrishna. The "stage curtain" came down on that day: "After that, we did not see him again like this," Datta writes (JV[4], 147). Whereas Datta adopts the vocabulary of myth and dramatic theory to capture the excitement of that day, Saradananda opts for an explicitly theological approach, preferring to call it "The Bestowal of Freedom of Fear within the Manifestation of the Self." It was on this day, the biographer writes, that Ramakrishna revealed that he was a god-man and removed the fears of the disciples. Both Datta's wish-fulfilling tree and Saradananda's manifestation capture something of that day for us. But whatever one chooses to call it, it seems clear that the events of that day carried meanings and memories of cosmic import for the disciples.

January 1, 1886, left a deep impression on the disciples, convinced them that Ramakrishna was no ordinary mortal, and, perhaps most importantly, prepared them for Ramakrishna's death. They very much needed their fears allayed at this point, for the next few months would bring much horror.

Narendra and the Peahen

THE MONTHS ROLLED ON and things only got worse. Datta's memories of those last few days are telling: "When I remember all the blood, I shiver in terror," he writes (JV[4], 147). Creepy it was. Ramakrishna's body was terribly emaciated. His flesh seemed to barely hang on a rack of bones. Boils in his throat would swell until he could barely breathe and the doctors had to lance them. A stream of thick mucous would hang dangling from his mouth. Pus oozed out of the boils in his throat. Blood flowed freely. When he tried to drink, milk dribbled pathetically from his mouth (JV[4], 145). Ramakrishna was suffering terribly. In his own metaphor, he had been reduced to a mere paper frame with a hole punched in the throat (JV[4], 149).

Toward the very end, only weeks before he died, Ramakrishna called Narendra to his side and in an ecstatic state transmitted his mystical energies into him. Afterward, Narendra claims, his body was so charged that, when he asked another disciple to touch it, the disciple received a palpable shock (KA 3.274).[20] Ramakrishna's mystical energies thus chose erotic channels to the very end. They flowed in the same directions as Ramakrishna's loves. Now finally embodied in the saint's beloved object, Ramakrishna could die.

Related to this transmission of energies is Ramakrishna's famous commission to Narendra to teach, symbolically preserved in a fascinating drawing that has not received enough attention or comment.[21] His throat swollen with cancer, Ramakrishna drew Narendra's bust facing left with a peahen behind it, facing the back of Narendra's head. Written (in poor Bengali) above the drawing is: "Victory to Rādhā, the embodiment of love! Naren will teach. When he goes outside, he will give a shout. Victory to Rādhā!"

The peacock is an erotic symbol in Vaiṣṇava poetry, for its dance ushers in the rainy season, the season for making love. Accordingly, Ramakrishna tells us that when Rādhā sees a dark cloud or the blue neck of a peacock, she is "ecstatically reminded" (*uddīpana*) of her dark blue Kṛṣṇa, and falls down unconscious.[22] But peacocks are also proud teachers for Ramakrishna. The saint, for example, once described how he saw in a vision the form of his friend, Keshab Sen, before he ever actually met him in person: Keshab appeared in the vision as a proud peacock showing off his colors in order to attract a great following as a teacher of men (KA 4.239). With his images and words, then, Ramakrishna seems to be identifying himself both with Rādhā, the lover of Kṛṣṇa, and with the peahen, who arouses the peacock to display for all men its gorgeous feathers. If we continue to unpack the symbolism, we might speculate that Ramakrishna's commission to Narendra to teach was an essentially erotic act, for the peacock's display is intended primarily for its mate (in this case, the feminine Ramakrishna); that it also gives delight to any onlookers seems almost beside the point. But beside the point or not, Narendra's presence and words, like the peacock's display, would indeed be very colorful, a delight for many, just as they had once "lighted the fire" of his peahen, Ramakrishna (KA 5.133).

The Great Union: The Secret Concealed

THE SUFFERING CONTINUED until the morning of August 15. It was almost one o'clock in the morning. Ramakrishna lay down and fell asleep, but shortly before one he awoke and ate a little wheat flour. At 1:05 A.M. he slipped into an ecstatic state. He never came back. Many of the disciples believed that he was only in *samādhi.* Had not they all seen this a hundred, a thousand times before? The same still body, the same frozen eyes, the same stiffness—it was all there. But this time, Ramakrishna would not come back. He would not reemerge from the beyond. He was dead, or in the language of the texts, he had entered the "great union" (*mahāsamādhi*) (JV[4], 152). Dr. Sarkar was called in to confirm the disciples' fears. He noticed that the backbone was still hot (JV[4], 152), perhaps still warm from the coiled departure of the mystical energies that were Ramakrishna.

Datta describes how everyone felt in the darkness of that night: "Our hearts began to thump and the house felt empty" (JV[4], 150). Ramakrishna was gone. The secret, suggested to the disciples at Shyampukur during Kālī-pūjā and fully revealed to the householders in the garden of Kashipur, was now concealed again. Despair set in.

A Pot of Bones in a Householder's Garden

THE NEWS SPREAD QUICKLY, and with it the pain. Pain and sorrow had replaced the bliss and joy of Ramakrishna's company. But there was work to be done. The body was cleaned, dressed in ochre robes (the color worn by renouncers), rubbed with sandal-paste, and laid in a bed of flowers. A photograph was taken, and the body was burned. Rain began to fall. Within a single hour, what Datta calls the "form of Ramakrishna" had been returned to the five elements from which it came. The relics were collected and put into a pot. On the way back from the pyre, a disciple was mysteriously bitten by a black snake. The wound, Datta notes, was bruised for a full five months. The poison reminds Datta of Śiva's throat that turned blue when he mercifully drank the deadly poison from the cosmic ocean. Ramakrishna, like Śiva, suffered in his throat, Datta points out. Like Śiva, he too took our sins upon himself. Again and again he had told the disciples that this is why he became sick (JV[4], 155). And now he was dead, dead for the disciples' sins. Perhaps the mysterious snake bite pointed to this truth. It was not much of a consolation. Like the disciple's swollen ankle, the group would be bruised for some time.

Ramakrishna had possessed a secret. But where was it now? Perhaps, we might answer, it was in the pot of bones. Datta tells us that he took the pot home and buried it in his garden. Nothing was left of Ramakrishna's physical form now except a pot of bones in a householder's garden. But love and faith burned in the hearts of the disciples. They would write many books. They would found an order. They would declare their Master to be an incarnation of God. Datta had declared the "secret of Ramakrishna's play" to be over with the events of January 1, 1886. On that day the "pot of love" had been broken, its contents freely dispensed to all present (JV[4], 147). Perhaps, in some sense, Datta was right. The pot *had* been broken. Ramakrishna's mystico-erotic energies had been dispersed into his disciples. But in another sense, the play had just begun. That secret, once revealed in Ramakrishna's life and now concealed in his death—perhaps it could be revealed again. Perhaps the "secret of Ramakrishna's play" was not yet over.

With Ramakrishna's death his legacy in fact did not come to an end. Indeed, from a history of religions perspective, it had only begun. After all, there was another pot now, a pot of bones. A shrine would be built over this pot. It would be worshiped. One pot had been broken, but only to be replaced by another. And which pot would prove to be more important? The body of Ramakrishna that only a handful actually saw? Or the pot of memories that would become the texts, the rituals, and the beliefs of a religious movement? In many ways, the pot of whitened memories would prove to be the more important. Certainly it would have a longer history.

GAURI'S QUESTION

THE LAST DAYS of Ramakrishna were marked by more than doctors, cancer, and self-revelations. They were also marked by intimate revelations of the saint's deep ambivalence regarding his own Tantric world. Ramakrishna's throat may have turned blue from drinking the poison of his disciples' sins, but it also seemed to possess its own poison, an impurity that it could never quite get rid of. In the remainder of this chapter, I want to turn to this ambivalence, to this poison, and demonstrate just how troubled Ramakrishna's relationship was to Tantra and its powerful images. I want to examine for a moment the blueness of Ramakrishna's swollen throat.

I begin with a Tantric scholar named Gauri. He was known to be a Śākta Tāntrika. It was from Gauri, we might recall, that Ramakrishna got his description of the mystical experience, with every hole of the body, down to the smallest hair pore, likened to a great vagina shaking with pleasure as it is penetrated by the phallic Self. Long before Ramakrishna decided (or was commanded to) worship Sharada as the sixteen-year-old girl, Gauri was worshiping his own wife as the goddess incarnate. He was a man steeped in the Tantric culture of his day. Because of this unique training, he had a particularly insightful perspective on the Paramahaṁsa from Dakshineshwar. In a fascinating passage in volume 5, we catch a glimpse of the depth of this insight in the form of a startling question. Ramakrishna is speaking, reminiscing about Gauri. Ramakrishna tells his listeners that, after watching him eat, Gauri used to ask him: "Did you take the Bhairavī in your *sādhana?*" (KA 5.73–74). Ramakrishna says nothing more. As suddenly and unexpectedly as the question and its implications are raised, it is again dropped.

Gauri's question, however, seems too important to drop. Why did he ask it? Gauri's question no doubt implies that the Tantric scholar, having been initiated into the secrets of Tantric culture, saw some connection between Ramakrishna's Tantric practices with the Bhairavī and his eating habits. Unfortunately, Gauri's insights were not particularly welcome. M and Nikhilananda both tried their best to keep Gauri's question unanswered or even unasked. M, at least, was willing to ask it, but only in his very last volume, and then only after he himself was dead (the volume was published posthumously). Nikhilananda, on the other hand, was not even willing to have it asked, much less answered. He completely omits it from his allegedly faithful translation (GSR, 294).

But Gauri's question is still there in the text, asking, not only for an answer to the immediate question—"Well, *did* you?"—but also for a closer examination of the relationship between Tantric eroticism and Ramakrishna's eating habits. What was it about Ramakrishna's manner of eating that could elicit such an unusual question from the Tantric scholar? And what was it about Tantric culture that made it so easy, almost natural, for Gauri to associate sexual intercourse and food? It is to these questions that I now want to turn.

If one looks carefully at the texts, Ramakrishna's relationship to food can only be described as tortured. By the Paramahaṁsa's own confession, his life was torn between an early period in which he would eat just about anything from anyone at anytime and a later period in which he could eat only certain foods cooked by certain people and offered by certain hands. That is to say, his life moved from a Tantric world structured around a transgression and transcendence of the category of purity back to the Brahmanical world of the socially acceptable and the proper. "Before I was in such a state that the smell of corpses used to come across the river to Dakshineshwar, and these smells struck my nose as sweet," he related. But now, the saint confesses, he can eat food only if it has been prepared by a brahmin cook (KA 2.131). In another passage, Ramakrishna explains with wonder how, after seven years of madness, he returned to his village and was able to accept food even from a prostitute. "But now I can't do this" (KA 2.151).

Through both of these periods of the impure and the pure, Ramakrishna suffered from severe bouts of dysentery, especially during his *sādhana* years, when he lived with Mathur, the Bhairavī, and Tota. The texts are filled with constant references to the problem. As we will see later in this chapter, the problem was so central that it often appeared in Ramakrishna's visions and metaphors. The Master's body, like his mind, was continuously expelling the world out through his bowels. His cousin suspected that there was more to these loose bowels than simple physiology. The always stinging Hriday was all too clear about his own theories on the psychological origins of Ramakrishna's intestinal sufferings. When the poor Ramakrishna had been reduced to skin and bones by dysentery, the proud Hriday would taunt him: "Look here how I eat," he bragged to the Paramahaṁsa. "You can't eat because of your mind." This, we must remember, was the same man who once told

Ramakrishna that he was an idiot and that "if I weren't here, you wouldn't be famous." Such taunts were so pointed (and convincing) that Ramakrishna walked to the bank of the river and almost jumped in at high tide to escape their truths (KA 1.168–169).

So Ramakrishna's relationship to food was a tortured one. Contemporaries saw both sexual and neurotic dimensions in it. Moreover, his relationship to food had a well-defined history, one that moved from a Tantric transgression of purity to a Brahmanical acceptance of purity. By now, this pattern should be a familiar one, for it replicates on the plane of food and the digestive process the same general pattern that we have looked at above: Ramakrishna's struggle to realize, sometimes successfully, sometimes not, the Tantric dialectic of the "pure" Absolute and the messiness of the phenomenal world.

Ramakrishna, we might recall, was trained to accept the phenomenal world through Trantric practices and was commanded to "Remain in existence" by mysterious voices. But he could neither integrate the Tantric world nor obey the commands. Instead, he rejected the Lover for the Mother and continued to seek erotic satisfaction with the Absolute, with the Self. As we saw in the last chapter, only when his disciples arrived did the Paramahaṁsa finally begin to turn his energies back to the phenomenal world, for only then did his mystico-erotic energies find objects suitable to their own natures. I have called this turning back, this descent back into the world, the Change. It was very much related to the beginnings of Ramakrishna's speculations on his status as an incarnation: he had taken a body for the boys in order to delight in the bliss of human relationships. The consumption of food was part of this delightful descent. At times, Ramakrishna would even use food, or the joyous sharing of food, to explain why the incarnation cannot "stay home," that is, why he desires to be born in the world: "May I not have to come again. But there is a saying that when one feasts at invited meals and then goes home, the sauce and rice are no longer so good" (KA 3.251). The world is not such a bad place, the saint seems to be saying, especially when one is constantly being invited to lavish feasts and colorful celebrations. Such things keep one embodied, and happily so. Along similar lines, I might point out that food was often used to bring Ramakrishna "down" from his ecstatic states. Offering him a bit of food, a sweet, or some water was usually all it took (KA 2.140). Food and embodiment, then, whether in an incarnational or in a psychological sense, were very much related. The consumption of food at feasts brought Ramakrishna and his disciples together as a community, the

Paramahaṁsa used food to explain why he descended into this world, and his disciples used it to bring him back down to the world. Food, moreover, acted as an especially powerful focus for Ramakrishna's acceptance and rejection of Tantra and its integration of the world, the body, and sexuality. In a very real sense, food for Ramakrishna became a metaphor for existence itself.

To demonstrate all of these symbolic connections, I want to turn to the texts and first identify what might be called the Tantric and the Brahmanical stages in Ramakrishna's relationship to food. Having identified these two stages and the structural polarity that they reproduced on the biographical plane, I then will show how food became a place of "intercourse" with the coming of the disciples. Finally, I will tie these different symbolic strands together by hooking them all up to the Tantric ritual of the Five M's and show how, like so many other dimensions of the saint's life, Ramakrishna's ambivalent relationship to food can only be properly understood if one approaches it through Tantra and its use of food and sex as symbols for a willing and involved existence in the world.

Tongues of Flame

EARLIER IN THIS CHAPTER, we saw that the textual history of Kālī's tongue began with its association with the sacrificial fire and the metaphor of the tongue of flame. As the flame "licks" about as it eats the sacrificial offering, so does the goddess's fiery red tongue consume whatever is offered to it. These same associations appear in our texts. Saradananda, for example, uses the metaphor to poetically describe the sacred fire burning before the Master and Tota Puri (LP 3.8.34), and a disciple tells his companions about some mysterious phosphorous wells, complete with tongue-like flames, that he had seen on a trip (KA 4.125). But these passages are for the most part restricted to the world of poetic description and literary metaphor. There are other passages, however, that, if taken together, link up Kālī's tongue and the flame in an explicit and more specifically Tantric fashion.

To begin to unravel these connections, I begin with a secret talk passage in volume 3. "This is very secret talk," the Master proclaims. He then hesitates as if prevented from speaking—"How many more things I could say but cannot. . . . It is as if someone were holding my mouth shut"—and then goes on to reveal yet another series of secrets: "I used to see no difference between the sacred tulsi tree and horse-radish. She pushed the distinguishing mind far away. I was meditating under the banyan-tree when a bearded Muslim (Muhammad) was shown to me. He came before me with some rice in an earthen plate. From the plate he fed some foreigners and gave me a little bit. Ma showed me that without One there is not Two. Saccidānanda takes on various forms. It itself has become all things, all living beings, the entire world. It itself has become food" (KA 3.141). A bearded Muslim (an unclean source of food for a brahmin) approaches the saint in a vision and offers him and some foreigners the same rice. All share the same food, an act which for Ramakrishna points to an ontological truth: "without One there is not Two." Reality, he seems to say, does not share society's dualistic categories of caste and purity. Finally, the famous expression that "She herself has become everything" is here replaced with "It itself has become food." Saccidānanda, as food, is being eaten, uniting everything to itself in the mystical meal shared amongst the saint, the Muslim, and the foreigners.

This same scene is told again in an earlier passage in the same volume, but this time the account is glossed with another vision, this one of a lolling tongue of flame:

> One day I saw that *consciousness is one—nondifferent.* At first it was shown to me that there were many people and animals—within that there were babus, Englishmen, Muslims, myself, a cremator, and dogs. Moreover, a bearded Muslim man was standing there with a plate of rice in his hand. He gave the mouths of everyone a little of this rice from the plate. I also tasted a little.
>
> And another day it was shown to me—feces, pee, food, and cooked dishes—all sorts of food. All were lying there. Suddenly from within [me] the personal soul came out and tasted all of these things as if it were a tongue of flame. It was as if a lolling tongue were tasting everything! Feces, pee—it tasted everything! It was shown to me *that all things are one—nondifferent!* (KA 3.46)

Rich babus, the hated English, unclean Muslims, a cremator, and some dogs—the visionary crowd is constructed out of the cultural elite, foreign imperialists, a non-Hindu, impurity, and defilement, all radical "others" for Ramakrishna. The Muslim man distributes the same unifying rice, again pointing to an emboldened philosophical revelation: "*Consciousness is one—nondifferent.*" Ramakrishna then immediately relates another vision, apparently because he feels it pointed to the same truths. The "personal soul" (*jīvātmā*), he tells us, appeared as a lolling tongue of flame and tasted the disgusting substances of feces and urine. By so doing, it transcended the laws of purity and perceived that reality lies beyond such distinctions.

There is a passage in Datta's *Jīvanavṛttānta* that throws an even more revealing light on these secret visions and their meanings, for it hooks them up explicitly with Kālī. In its details, it is very close to the scene discussed above involving the lolling tongue touching feces and urine. Indeed, it is so close that we are probably dealing here with the earliest version of the same event (Datta's text, we might recall, was published in 1890, eighteen years before Gupta's volume 3). Datta entitles the section dealing with this scene "Discriminating with Sandal-paste and Feces."

While worshiping the goddess, Datta tells us, Ramakrishna decided to test the powers of his mind. Accordingly, he held his own feces in one hand and sandal-paste (a perfumed cosmetic) in the other. As he held them in his two hands and pondered their natures, he realized that "all things on earth" become feces and that the two substances were really the same. All things he saw in the light of this ontological "sameness" (*samatā*). Here we are reminded immediately of the two realizations that formed the heart of the visions discussed above: "*Consciousness is one—nondifferent*" and "*All things are one—nondifferent.*" All three visions speak of a reality behind the social world, accessible only through a transgression of that society's laws and norms.

Ramakrishna was convinced that he had seen into the nature of things. Just about everyone else, however, thought he had gone stark raving mad. Datta explains why: no one, except for the Tantric Aghorīs, was known to have used feces in their *sādhana*. This lack of respectable precedence (apparently, the Aghorīs were considered to be a shady lot) rendered Ramakrishna's analysis of feces and sandal-paste particularly controversial. Accordingly, Haladhari tried to take the young saint aside and persuade him from his fecal ways, but nothing came of his pleadings. Finally, someone—we are not told who—stepped in and addressed Ramakrishna with these words: "I have heard that you took your own shit in *sādhana*. Everyone can be called this kind of knower of *brahman*. Who does not touch his own shit? Unless you are able to touch another person's feces, you cannot be called a true knower of *brahman*" (JV[5], 19). If such words were meant to dissuade the young saint from his troubling practices, they failed miserably, for Ramakrishna took them, not as a scolding, but as a challenge. As was his practice in handling criticisms and challenges, he then relayed the words to Kālī. Apparently, the goddess also took them as a challenge, for she responded by entering Ramakrishna's body. At that moment, possessed by the goddess and her lolling tongue, the saint went down to the river where people defecate and urinate. There he took some clay smeared with feces and touched it to his tongue, "and he felt no disgust." Datta glosses the scene with his own authentification: "I have heard from his mouth that when he touched the tongue to the feces, it didn't smell bad" (JV[5], 19).[23]

In another similar scene, this one in the *Līlāprasaṅga,* Saradananda explains how Ramakrishna at first felt great disgust when the Bhairavī asked him to touch his tongue to a piece of rotting human flesh. At that point, he had a vision of the terrible form of the Mother (that is, of Kālī) and entered into an ecstatic state. He could then touch his tongue to this human "meat" and feel no disgust (LP 2.11.9). The scene is basically the same as the sandal-paste and feces scene told by Datta. Only the impure substance has been changed.

Both of these passages, in turn, are related to a number of passages involving Ramakrishna's ambivalent relationship to wine. Despite the fact that wine is central to Kālī's cult, Ramakrishna could not bring himself to drink it. But he knew that he at least had to touch the substance, lest he anger the goddess. He would thus touch a drop or two with his tongue, extending it to commune, however briefly, with the Tantric liquid. Here one can detect what might be called a scared tongue. It is repulsed by the illicit substance of wine, but it extends itself anyway in order to touch it for Kālī.

Finally, along these same lines, we might recall two passages discussed above in chapter 2. The first one occurs in volume 4. Ramakrishna is talking about his Tantric practices under the bel tree that the goddess enacted through him. All things were one. The sacred tulsi tree and the horse-radish looked no different to the young saint at this point. Such a state had profound consequences for his eating habits. He would eat the leftovers of jackals, follow dogs around to share his bread with them, and wash his mouth out with muddy water (KA 4.175). It was as if he sought out the impure and the disgusting to commune with it through his mouth.

If we take all of these passages together, we might speculate that, at least from Ramakrishna's perspective, it was not *his* tongue that ate the Muslim's defiled rice, that licked the feces and urine, that tasted the flesh of a corpse, and shared its food with jackals and dogs. Psychologically speaking, it was Kālī's. Ramakrishna, after all, could not perform such acts by himself. The texts state clearly that such events were only enacted in visions and maddened states of possession, that is, at times when Ramakrishna was under the control of the goddess.

Under her control, then, the tongue ecstatically extends itself to commune with wine, human meat, fish, polluted rice, even feces and urine. Again and again, it reaches out to commune with that which society deems disgusting and shameful. There is something Tantric about this tongue. All that wine and meat, all that emphasis on impurity—it all seems strangely coherent and meaningful. But what of the specifically sexual dimensions of the tongue? Sexual intercourse, after all, is an integral part of Tantric ritual. If Ramakrishna's secret tongue is indeed a Tantric tongue, we would expect to see it reach out, not only for meat and wine but also for sexual union. Here we are reminded of the secret cunnilingus vision in which Ramakrishna sees himself arousing vagina-shaped lotuses with his tongue. As with the visions and states discussed here, the tongue in this secret vision functions as an instrument of union. It extends itself into the heart of reality by communing with that which society considers impure, that "place of disgust" called the vagina. It breaks the bond of disgust and initiates its possessor into an experience of ontological Sameness, Unity, or Nondifference. The tongue, be it Ramakrishna's or the goddess's, thus fulfills a basically mystical function.

But Kālī's tongue, we recall, is supposed to represent shame. In Ramakrishna's secret visions and maddened states, however, this same tongue expresses, not a bond, but a *breaking* of a bond. Ramakrishna's tongue licks vagina-shaped lotuses, touches feces and urine, and eats the leftovers of jackals and dogs. The tongue unites with the impure, and through it, with reality. It fulfills an eminently Tantric function. Kālī's tongue, then, secretly functions in vision, possession, and ritual in a way radically different from that in which it is supposed to function in society. Kālī does not stick out her tongue in shame for her improper position here. She sticks it out to unite with the disgusting and to prove that such feelings are illusory bonds to be destroyed on the path.

The Brahmanical Tongue

THIS KĀLĪ-LIKE TONGUE and these Tantric states of indiscrimination contrast radically with the social world in which Ramakrishna lived. It should not surprise us, then, that Ramakrishna soon returned to his Brahmanical ways and the proper behavior of the Vedas and the

Purāṇas. If once he could eat the food cooked by a low-caste boatman—as Mathur screamed in horror, "Father, get away! Get away!"—now Mathur too could rest at ease, for, in Ramakrishna's own words, "this state is no more" (KA 2.113). Ramakrishna can still eat a little of the goddess's fish soup offering, but her goat meat is another matter. He must force himself to taste a little of it on his finger, lest she get angry (KA 3.30). Again, the contrast is remarkable. Once he had tasted rotting human flesh. Now he can barely sip some fish soup. He has come back to the world of discrimination, difference, and defilement.

Food as a Place of "Intercourse"

ONE OF THE MOST interesting aspects about these differences in purity and caste is how Ramakrishna employed them to posture himself into and out of various human relationships. If one examines the texts carefully, it becomes apparent that Ramakrishna uses food to reject figures and personalities that he finds undesirable and, likewise, to get closer to people whom he loves. Food thus acts as a place of "intercourse" for the Paramahaṁsa, not in the literal sense of sexual intercourse, but in the broader sense in which Ramakrishna defined the "eight kinds of sexual intercourse" with a woman: listening to talk about women, talking about women, whispering in private to women, keeping anything of a woman with one, touching a woman, and so forth (KA 5.141). Here I want to extend the metaphor a bit, adding what we might call a ninth type, and look at Ramakrishna's sharing of food as a similar place of "intercourse."

There are two basic ways Ramakrishna uses food in relation to other people: to push them away and to draw them near. Both strategies are extremely common in the texts. In one scene, for example, the saint is not getting along with a group of holy men and so sits alone at the meal. When he gets to eat first, the holy men complain, "Hey, who's this?" (KA 2.56). The saint thus distanced himself and established his superiority with a single plate of food. In another passage, Ramakrishna describes frankly the four types of people whose food he will not eat: lawyers, thieves, doctors, and rich kids (KA 5.135). Sometimes these scenes of rejection were quite dramatic. In volume 1, for example, Ramakrishna boldly states that "one shouldn't feed bad people. When such people, who sin greatly and are very attached to objects, sit down to eat, that place is impure for ten feet down." Having said that, Ramakrishna then immediately relates how Hriday once fed some people in his village. Among them were many of these "bad people." Ramakrishna objected: "I said, 'Look Hriday, if you feed them, then I'll leave your house'" (KA 1.124).

The patterns were complicated further by Ramakrishna's willingness to abandon the categories of caste and purity at a moment's notice when they interfered with his loves. For example, he quickly abandoned his practice of eating only food cooked by brahmins when he was in the company of Narendra. Narendra may not have been a brahmin, but, according to Ramakrishna, he possessed enough pure *sattva* to render his food pure (LP 5.8.2.5). In one particularly intimate scene, Ramakrishna makes Narendra puff on a smoke through his own hands and then, much to Narendra's dismay, proceeds to puff himself on the same, now unclean, smoke. The saint had only vulgarity for the boy's objections to all of this: "Geez, you son-of-a-bitch, you're sure focused on differences" (LP 5.8.2.24). The saint, it seemed, used the categories of caste and purity deftly for his own purposes. Social distinctions were stressed and even exaggerated when Ramakrishna wanted to get rid of someone but conveniently forgotten when a beloved disciple or friend was involved. Food was thus a locus or a sign of both the saint's grace and rejection.

Usually these food scenes involved men, especially boys, but sometimes women were also involved, or more accurately, not involved. It is noteworthy, for example, that Ramakrishna refused to send the sweets he was given by visitors to his wife, working in the kitchen; he much preferred to keep them for his boys. Such a scene is symbolic of the saint's dealings with women in general: he kept himself for his young male disciples and distanced himself from women. Sometimes, however, he was forced to bridge the chasms he and his culture had built between the genders and classes. In a scene in the *Jīvanavṛttānta*, for example, a poor woman complains that Ramakrishna's disciples are rich and their celebrations very expensive. "You're not the Master of the poor," she complains. Ramakrishna responds to this (very common) criticism by eating one of her sweet *rasagollas*. She seems appeased (JV[4], 133). The act fulfilled two functions: by eating her sweets, Ramakrishna could please her and yet keep his distance. Here food mediated though it did not unite.

Ramakrishna was quite open about what determined whether he would eat someone else's food: "If they show devotion to God, then there's no fault. But if they have desires, then this stuff is no good" (KA 2.195). The nature of these desires seems to have been sexual, for often it was a person's sexual practices that defiled his or her food. This would explain why it was a sign of great wonder when Ramakrishna accepted food from a prostitute in his early maddened state (KA 2.151). This criterion of sexual continence becomes especially important when the person in question is a male. Generally speaking, if a boy or man is sexually active with a woman, Ramakrishna wants nothing to do with him. Thus Ramakrishna explains how he rejected a boyhood playmate who married and would not touch the young Haramohan, who brought his new wife to the temple (KA 4.109). In both instances, the boys were considered to be defiled by their active heterosexuality. But those who remained celibate won both Ramakrishna's favor and his food. Hence an ecstatic Ramakrishna feeds the little Nityagopal by grabbing both of his hands and intimately putting them to his mouth (KA 5.129). But the Chatterjee boy was another story. Ramakrishna touches some sweets brought by the boy and angrily asks Latu, "What son-of-a-bitch brought these sweets?" After throwing the cup down, he exclaims, "I know everything." The English reader is left hanging, for Nikhilananda omits what follows (GSR, 522), but M tells his Bengali readers that this boy was going to a "Ghoshpara bitch," that is, to a Kartābhajā woman (KA 4.145). Again, Narendra relates how Ramakrishna refused to touch the glass of some people. This then inspires Hazra to tell how the saint turned his back on a Vaiṣṇava, who we learn (in still another passage omitted by Nikhilananda [GSR, 511]) was sleeping with his aunt (KA 4.130). In yet another half-translated scene (GSR, 717), Ramakrishna explains how he used to feed the boys back in his village. But only some of them. Those who slept with their sisters-in-law he refused to feed. "Who could feed such people!" he exclaimed (KA 3.117). To receive food from Ramakrishna, then, a male must be sexually continent. He must be both ready and worthy of Ramakrishna's love expressed in the food.

As he did with his relationships to his boy disciples, Ramakrishna gradually developed a sophisticated theology to explain his intimate practice of feeding boys and young men. Sometimes he would use the ancient Indian metaphor of the sacrificial fire: "He is in all souls like fire. Feeding people is like sacrificing to him" (KA 1.124). But more often, he would employ Vaishnavacharan's Tantric theology of divine immanence. As we saw in chapter 4, Vaishnavacharan had taught the Paramahaṁsa how to see and love God in man. "Nārāyāṇa is especially manifest in pure souls," Ramakrishna taught. This is why he loved to feed the boys (KA 3.117). Such a theology, despite its rather common appearance, was in fact profoundly Tantric, for it was used by Vaishnavacharan to support the erotic practices of his own Kartābhajā sect. Ramakrishna's practice of feeding the boys was explained within this general Tantric worldview. In such a world at least he could worship God in man and offer his love as food in a tangible and socially acceptable way. Food thus offered Ramakrishna a means to commune with man, and through him, with God. In the manner in which Ramakrishna manipulated it to define his social relationships, in its numerous sexual overtones, and its often intimate expression, food for Ramakrishna was indeed a "place of intercourse."

On the Origin of the Tantras

SO RAMAKRISHNA'S RELATIONSHIP TO FOOD was erotic in some sense. Gauri saw this. Taking his lead, I have tried to identify some of the patterns of this erotic eating. But there is still something more to the Tantric scholar's question. After all, Gauri's question did not just associate food and intercourse. It associated food and *ritual* intercourse: "Did you take the Bhairavī in your *sādhana?*" What was it about Ramakrishna's Tantric rituals that formed such a stable bond between eating and the erotic?

The question should really be reworded: What was it about Ramakrishna's Tantric rituals that did *not* lead to such a bond? Very little if anything, we might answer. Consider for a moment the Five M's: are not they all about eating and sex? Meat (*maṁsa*), fish (*matsya*), wine (*madya*), fermented grain (*mudrā*), and sexual intercourse (*maithuna*): everything is either consumed or sexually enjoyed. The Five M's, in other words, are constructed around the same pattern that we have seen forming Ramakrishna's eating habits: the sharing of food as a symbol for (or prelude to) intercourse. This pattern is extended and focused further in Ramakrishna's secret Tantric life to the point where eating *is* sex, thus the Ramakrishna-*homunculus* licks the lotuses shaped like vaginas in order to arouse them into new states of consciousness. The female sexual organ, in some sense, is eaten. Although certainly the graphic details of this vision are unusual in the history of mysticism—cunnilingus is not a common symbol for mystical union—they are almost predictable in a tradition that employs food and sex together in its central ritual. Indeed, so central is this erotic eating to Tantric culture that Ramakrishna himself used it to explain how the Tantras themselves were formed: "There is a tradition that says that this *goddess of great illusion* herself swallowed Śiva with one gulp. When the six *cakras* became conscious inside Ma, Śiva came out Ma's thigh. Then Śiva created the Tantras" (KA 5.68).[24] The goddess eats Śiva with a single gulp. Inside, Śiva awakens her energies and emerges from her thigh to create the Tantras. The allusions to the vaginal consumption of the penis, to the awakening or arousal of the goddess's energies, and to Śiva "coming out" (we might say "pulling out") onto the goddess's thigh are all fairly transparent sexual metaphors.

If these images are placed within their mythological, ritual, and textual contexts, their sexual connotations become even clearer. There are, after all, myths in which a demonic female figure bears an actual *vagina dentata* and tries literally to eat a phallus[25] and Tantras in which the vagina is described as the *yoginīvaktra,* the "mouth of the yoginī."[26] As for the references to awakening the goddess's *cakra*s, it should be noted that sexual intercourse, be it imaginal or actual, is commonly used in Tantric ritual to awaken or arouse the drooping *cakra*s. Finally, the reference to Śiva creating the Tantras immediately after his unusual trip from the goddess's mouth to her thigh is particularly revealing, for in the Tantras themselves it is often said that the Tantras were created either during or immediately after intercourse. Thus the Tantras are often written in the form of an intimate colloquy that takes place between the divine pair either during or after their erotic union. Given all of these diverse mythological, ritual, and textual meanings, then, it is symbolically reasonable to see the goddess's "eating" of Śiva as an allusion to sexual intercourse.

Ramakrishna's version of the origin of the Tantras retains this basic structure: the god and the goddess unite and then the god creates the Tantras. The union of eating and being eaten has simply replaced the union of penetrating and being penetrated. Given the fusion of eating and intercourse in Tantric ritual, it seems an easy, almost natural, substitution. But it is a substitution that is also a transformation and a reversal. In "normal" sexual intercourse, that is, in that form sanctioned by the culture as appropriate, the man is active and the woman passive. He penetrates her. He is on top of her. The substitution of eating for intercourse in the myth allows for this active/passive structure to be reversed. The goddess cannot penetrate the god, but she can eat him, and she does. She thus puts herself back "on top" and reverses the normal pattern of male/female relations. The god, of course, awakens the goddess's different *cakra*s, most likely by penetrating their lotus forms, but we are not told this in the myth. The emphasis remains on the goddess eating the god.

Given all of these numerous mythological and ritual connections between the act of eating and the act of sexual intercourse, it seems rather obvious that it was Tantric culture, and especially Tantric ritual, that formed the bond in Ramakrishna's life between eating and intercourse and allowed Gauri to ask his question. I would argue, moreover, that it was this same secret culture that defined both the history of the saint's eating habits and the general structure around which he struggled. In a certain sense, Ramakrishna ate his way into the opposition between Tantric and Brahmanical culture. His tongue moved from Tantric states in which it united with jackal food, feces, and symbolic vaginas to states in which it could only touch the food of brahmins and pure celibate boys. As Kālī's tongue, it delighted indiscriminately in the impure. As the brahmin's tongue, it split the world asunder into the impure and the pure. Through all of this, Ramakrishna was struggling, among other things, with Tantra and its use of food and sex as embodied symbols for life in an already divine world. Just as "She herself has become everything," so too "It itself has become food," *all* food, *all* things. Ramakrishna was very much attracted to these truths. Indeed, he saw them in his visions and enacted them in his secret, unconscious states. But in the end, he could never truly make them his own.

Lover-and-Gold

Ramakrishna, then, never quite assimilated Tantra's radical acceptance of the phenomenal world. Like the Tantric rituals themselves, Ramakrishna's contact with this world and its impurities was restricted to unconscious psychological states and the secret times and spaces of ritual. The Paramahaṁsa's Tantric experience, in other words, was bounded on every side, kept in check by the larger Brahmanical world. Through food he accepted and then rejected the Tantric world.

Very much related to Ramakrishna's rejection of Tantra through his rejection of certain types of food was his rejection of Tantra through a rejection of certain types of women. The two, again, seem to be related on some deep symbolic level. Just as the saint's rejection of Tantra through food was structured around the opposition between purity and impurity, so too was his rejection of Tantra through women expressed through a similar opposition, that between the pure, sexless Mother and the impure, disgusting Lover. It was an opposition that the saint would never transcend. It was a problem he could never solve.

Given the saint's insistence that the Mother must always be separated from the Lover, the presence of numerous women who embodied both roles in their persons constituted for Ramakrishna what only can be called a profound crisis. Their very existence elicited from the saint an emotional contradiction that he simply could not resolve. Accordingly, there is probably no topic that receives more attention in the *Kathāmṛta* than the renunciation of what Ramakrishna called *kāminī-kāñcana* or "lover-and-gold." Saradananda calls it Ramakrishna's "first teaching" (LP 5.7.42), and M describes it as Ramakrishna's *mūlamantra* or "primary chant" (KA 2.245). And a "chant" it was, appearing more than 250 times in the *Kathāmṛta*. Understanding what Ramakrishna meant by "lover-and-gold," then, is absolutely central to understanding Ramakrishna. Like the saint's Tantric practices, the renunciation of "lover-and-gold" lies at the heart of who he was. It is an integral part of his secret.

And like most other aspects of his secret, this is a topic surrounded by a long history of controversy and concealment. The story of this particular controversy begins its published history in 1879 with Pratap Chandra Mozoomdar's article, "Sri Ramakrishna Paramahamsa."[27] The piece was on the whole appreciative of the saint, but Mozoomdar, by his own confession, was telling half-truths. In a letter to Max Müller, Mozoomdar referred to the article and admitted that he had written about only one side of Ramakrishna. There was "another side" of Ramakrishna's character, he told Müller, but one he could not take up in the article, "because it was not edifying."[28] In his own article, "A Real Mahātman," Müller refers to Mozoomdar's letter and its charge of Ramakrishna's "almost barbarous treatment of his wife."[29] Müller defends Ramakrishna against the charge, partly out of sincere conviction, partly out of ignorance of the materials. Ever since then, the debate has raged on, resulting in a series of articles, books, and false translations. Nikhilananda, for example, no doubt aware of the controversy, concealed many of Ramakrishna's outrageously misogynous statements beneath polite English phrases. Even M participated in the cover-up. His English King James paraphrase of the *Kathāmṛta*, published as early as 1907, is conspicuously silent on the topic.

There are two general camps in this debate: one sees Ramakrishna as a misogynist who hated and feared women; the other sees Ramakrishna as an infallible saint who loved all human beings and who worshiped women as embodiments of the divine. Whereas scholars, both Western and Indian, usually have sided with some version of the misogynist reading,[30] the devotional camp has been populated almost solely by devotees and swamis, some of whom have gone so far as to claim that the saint was a modern prophet of women's rights, a sort of proto-feminist. For the purposes of this study, it is significant that this second, devotional camp often shows signs of a certain nervousness. For example, just as the English preface to *The Great Master* "craved" the thoughtfulness of its readers and tried to suggest the "right attitude" for approaching the chapters on Ramakrishna's mystico-erotic practices (GM, v–vi), the Bengali preface to the 1986 Udbodhan edition of the *Kathāmṛta* addresses only one issue concerning the content of the text: Ramakrishna's teachings on "lover-and-gold." The phrase *kāminī-kāñcana,* the editors insist, really means *kāma-kāñcana,* "lust-and-gold,"[31] since it was an abstract vice, "lust," that Ramakrishna preached against, not a flesh-and-blood human being: "He never hated (*ghṛṇā*) or looked at anyone with contempt—rather, by merely looking at a woman's form his most pure mind saw the great goddess and became sunk in *samādhi.*"[32]

It is very curious that the only issues that the editors feel a need to address revolve around Ramakrishna's secret *sādhanas* and the topic of "lover-and-gold," both central to this study and its basic thesis that Ramakrishna's mystical experiences were constituted by erotic energies that he neither fully accepted nor understood. In volume 5 of the *Kathāmṛta,* M sums up Ramakrishna's teaching with these same two topics: "There were various secret things [*guhya kathā*] said about *sādhana* and talk about renouncing lover-and-gold" (KA 5.96). The modern editors, in other words, are nervous about the very topics that M recorded as lying at the very core of Ramakrishna's teachings. Like Ramakrishna's stutter, this editorial nervousness supports my general thesis. It witnesses to a half-conscious, half-known secret against which the editors feel a need to defend themselves.

But, as always, things are more complicated than first meet the eye. As Ramakrishna himself noted in another context, the floor always hides complex structures beneath its smooth surface (KA 4.120). Granted, there is *no* basis for a feminist Ramakrishna: when asked about the (Western-influenced) Brahmo Samaj and its concern with the "freedom of women" (*strī-svādhīnatā*) and the abolition of the caste system, the saint replied that such things are the impermanent concerns of beginners temporarily lost in the "dust storm" of their early and misguided enthusiasm. When the dust clears, Ramakrishna insisted, they will see clearly that such concerns are impermanent and unimportant. Only God is truly real and worth one's energies (KA 5.20).[33] But even given this, one still must acknowledge that there is truth in the devotional camp: after all, there *are* numerous passages on worshiping the goddess in women.

How, then, are we to reconcile these two views? I would suggest that the debate between these two views is a false one, as it rests on the illusory foundation of a misguided translation—*kāminī* as "woman"—and the false category that it generates. When the phrase *kāminī-kāñcana* is translated at all, it is almost always translated as "woman-and-gold." Nikhilananda's *The Gospel of Sri Ramakrishna* has made the English phrase virtually canonical. But "woman" barely exists in Ramakrishna's world. In Ramakrishna's symbolic universe, a woman is almost always defined *in relation.* She is a mother to a child, a wife to a husband, a sister to a brother, a lover to a lover, a prostitute to a client, and so forth. There are a few general terms for "woman"—for example, *strī* (interestingly enough, the term chosen for such Western notions as the "freedom of women")—but Ramakrishna seldom uses it. When Ramakrishna refers to women in his discourse, he usually has something much more specific in mind.

As I have demonstrated in chapter 2, it was woman as Mother and Lover that structured Ramakrishna's Tantric practices. These same two identities structured the saint's discourse on *kāminī-kāñcana.* If approached with these two categories in mind, Ramakrishna's comments about women are consistent and meaningful: he hated and feared women as Lovers and worshiped them as Mothers. If, on the other hand, one approaches Ramakrishna's teachings on *kāminī-kāñcana* with the false category of "woman," they immediately become confusing and contradictory: he both hated and worshiped woman. The confusion surrounding Ramakrishna's attitudes toward women, in other words, is a function, not of Ramakrishna's understanding, but of ours. Or to put it another way, whereas Ramakrishna's behavior toward "women" is confusing and inconsistent, his behavior toward women as Lovers and Mothers is very consistent, indeed predictable. Once again, the chameleon, of whatever color, remains a chameleon. We just have to figure out which tree he is on.

"Woman-and-gold," then, is a false translation, yet another strategy in the concealing of Ramakrishna's secret. The word *kāminī* does not mean "woman." Literally, it could be translated as "lusty woman" or "sexy woman." It certainly is not an abstract term for woman, much less for an even more abstract vice. Specifically, it refers to woman as a sexual being, to a potential lover capable of arousing one's own sexual desires (*kāma*). It thus must be translated more *literally*, more *physically*. After all, it was flesh-and-blood women whom Ramakrishna *literally* could not touch: a simple brush sent excruciating pains through the saint's flesh, as if he had been stung by a horned fish, and took away his breath.[34] It was the gory contents of their *physical* bodies—blood, intestinal worms, fat, phlegm, piss, guts, and bad smells—that disgusted him (KA 3.19).[35] And it was their culturally specific habits that he loved to ridicule: they blow their noses as they cry (KA 2.233), and they weep and roll on the ground but hold their precious nose-rings all the while, he observed and then did the same as his disciples rolled on the floor in fits of laughter.[36] As Sumit Sarkar has pointed out, Ramakrishna's *kāminī* is historically specific to nineteenth-century Bengal.[37] It is an embodied, historical concept, specific to Ramakrishna's world. It must be interpreted as such.

Given all of this, I would suggest that Ramakrishna's understanding of *kāminī* is an analogue of what I have called the Lover, that feminine role in Tantric culture defined by its sexual relation to the male aspirant. I translate the expression *kāminī-kāñcana*, then, as "lover-and-gold." Here I want to analyze the teaching in three parts: the numerous metaphors that Ramakrishna used to explain it, the quandaries that resulted from it for his householder disciples, and the cultural and historical contours of Ramakrishna's misogyny. I begin with a flurry of metaphors and images.

The Worldly Family: "The Bitch and Kids"

THE MOST COMMON GLOSS Ramakrishna attached to the expression *kāminī-kāñcana* was *saṁsāra*, "world" *or* "family."[38] The worldly man, the man attached to lover-and-gold, is the family man, the husband caught in the net of sexual desire, familial responsibilities, and financial needs. Ramakrishna was horrified by this state and of what he called, rather tactlessly, "the bitch and kids" (*māga-chele*).[39] A quick trip through some passages dealing with this troubling woman and her equally troubling kids reveals a great deal about how Ramakrishna felt about being a husband and a father. The Paramahaṁsa, for example, associated his own "bitch," Sharada, with the pots and pans of her tiny room in the music tower that doubled as a kitchen (KA 3.155) and described worldly happiness as "the happiness of the bitch." This bitch and these kids spell endless trouble for the unsuspecting man. Once married, man is trapped in a long series of expensive weddings, toilsome jobs, and lawsuits.[40] The roof leaks, and there is no money to fix it. His kids will become addicted to prostitutes, marijuana, and alcohol (KA 1.136). His wife no doubt will give his money and possessions to her lover. And forget about pilgrimages: the householder will be stuck carrying all the bags and will have to fight with the kids in the temple. There is no time to think of God. There is only lying, cheating, flattery, and deceit (KA 1.57–58). The rich are especially hounded, for they lose their money from four sides: lawyers, thieves, doctors, and bad boys (KA 5.135). In such a state, devotion can be little more than a drop on a frying pan. It sizzles for a second and is gone.[41] The cute cooing and babbling of little children is like the deadly murmur of the water running through a fish-trap. Once the unsuspecting fish-father follows the seductively innocent sound in, he is trapped (KA 5.16). Lost in this awful world, he is now like a dog who cannot get rid of his fleas, a pitcher with a hole in it that cannot hold water, or a blind man in a marvelous library (PDU, 14–15). He is pathetic.

But there is more to this worldly family than the bitch and kids. There are *in-laws,* those dreaded "black snakes" filled with venom.[42] Such a family, Ramakrishna taught, is like the sweetened puffed rice that farmers lay out in front of their storehouses for the rats: the rats eat it and are satisfied, never knowing how much lies untouched in the storehouse (KA 2.167). Again, a man living in the world is like a snake trying to swallow a mole: it is an excruciatingly painful experience and never quite finished (KA 1.70).

And all this ultimately stems back to woman as Lover. It is all her fault. Lover-and-gold, to be truly accurate, should be LOVER-and-gold. Everything bad for Ramakrishna pales before the problem that is the Lover. Marrying a woman leads to the necessity of "gold," which in turn necessitates taking a job.[43] All this spells the end of the man's freedom (KA 1.72), for now he is a slave to woman, money, and land, to his boss, and to his stomach.[44] Ramakrishna noted with disgust how a man could bring home a fat salary and yet still cower before his wife: "If she says 'Stand up!' he stands up. If she says 'Sit down!' he sits down. And still everyone praises his wife!"[45] The Captain, a disciple of Ramakrishna, praises his wife, that nasty hag, as if he were possessed by some ghost and did not know it.[46] Another disciple, this time unnamed, is described as a "slave of a black hag" (KA 3.30). The saint, it seems, thought very little of his disciples' wives.

As long as a man is attached to this world of lover-and-gold, "nothing will happen."[47] Yoga, mystical absorption, devotional states, and meditation will be impossible. What is worse, the longer a man is attached to this lover-and-gold, the less he realizes just how shitty a state he is in. Accordingly, the saint likened the worldly man to the low-caste worker who carries baskets of gooey "poop" (*gu*) all day long: eventually the smell of the stuff no longer bothers him (KA 3.31). Or he is like the lowly feces-worm pining for its pile of excrement (KA 1.70). Or again, he is like the fly, who will land on a piece of sweet candy one minute and on feces the next. Unlike the bee, who will only land on sweet things, he cannot distinguish between the sweetness of God and the stench of the world and of woman.[48] Again, the renouncer still attached to lover-and-gold is like someone who swallows his own spit,[49] or a beautiful woman with body odor, attractive and yet defiled (KA 4.96). The scholar attached to lover-and-gold is no better. He is like the vulture who, although soaring high in the sky, sets his sights on the rotting flesh of the carrion pit or the cremation ground below.[50] In a similar vein, Ramakrishna spoke of women as corpse-ash when compared to God (KA 4.28) and counseled his listeners to abandon lover-and-gold as quickly and as anxiously as they let loose their own shit and piss (PDU, 4). In an even more graphic image, Ramakrishna talked about the householder "pacifying" his wife and family so that he could practice his *sādhana* in peace: just as the *sādhaka* "cools" or pacifies the ritual corpse with a mouthful of rice when it warms and comes alive in Tantric *sādhana,* so too should the householder pacify his wife with this or that trifling.[51] Above all, keep them quiet, keep them dead. For Ramakrishna, then, the worldly family is a pile of shit, the abode of worms and flies, or a corpse, a terrifying body one sits on while practicing *sādhana*.

"But You Do Bite!"

RAMAKRISHNA KNEW that his householder disciples could not renounce lover-and-gold. He knew that, like the camel who continues to bloody his mouth while eating thorns, or like the woman who soon forgets her labor pains and becomes pregnant again, men attached to their families would remain in the world.[52] He thus counseled them to practice their religious exercises in private, away from their families. They then could reenter their households and live in the world like the mudfish, unaffected by the sliminess that surrounds them, or like the waterfowl, whose feathers repel the water.[53] He also encouraged his disciples to look upon their wives and children with a distant compassion. When a man loves everyone equally, he practices "compassion" (*dayā*). When, on the other hand, he loves a particular person to the exclusion of others, he is caught in the bonds of "illusion" (*māyā*).[54] His true desire should be reserved for the divine. If a man can practice in this way, he can live in the world. Such a man is like the circus rider that Ramakrishna once saw, riding on the back of a horse on a single foot.[55] As impossible as it may seem, with much practice, it can be done.

This theme of difficulty and precarious balance is itself balanced by another theme in Ramakrishna's discourse on woman and the family: the theme of "fighting from the fort." The home is like a "fort" (*kellā*), Ramakrishna taught, and a strong one at that.[56] After all, in this darkest of ages, food is necessary, and a wife will cook for you (KA 1.73). Things are very "convenient" at home (KA 3.97). Why sleep in seven beds when you can sleep in one? (KA 1.73).[57] The life of the renouncer, Ramakrishna seems to be saying, is not all that it is cracked up to be. The householders have their own advantages, their own strengths, which they should draw on. In a few scenes, Ramakrishna goes so far as to throw his previous cautions to the wind and encourages particular disciples to "have a little fun" with their wives. In one such scene, for example, he sends young Rakhal home to fulfill his "remainder of pleasure" (KA 4.163). In another, he complains that "Bhabanath talks all night with his wife!" "I said to him, 'Have a little fun with your wife!'" Bhabanath did not take such advice well. He was angered by Ramakrishna's comments (KA 3.115). In another similar scene, M can be seen grinning (KA 4.206).

This double message—the family is at once a pile of shit and a convenient fort—produced great ambivalence and doubt in Ramakrishna's disciples. Ramakrishna, after all, often told the story of Vaśiṣṭha's instruction of Rāma on the ontological silliness of renunciation—"Rāma," the sage asked his confused disciple, "why should you renounce the world? . . . Is the world other than the Lord?" (KA 5.90)[58]—but also insisted that the two great evils of the aspirant are lover-and-gold and that renunciation is essential to realize *brahman* (KA 4.31). Such glaring inconsistencies did not go unnoticed. One disciple accused Ramakrishna of "biting," of saying one thing and then the exact opposite. Another disciple decided to press the issue: "Hearing about the renunciation of lover-and-gold, he said to me one day: 'Why have you renounced all those things? "This is money and this is clay"[59]—is not this distinguishing mind a product of ignorance?' What could I say? I said: 'Who knows, my boy, why I don't like money and all that stuff'" (KA 1.88). Ramakrishna does not deny the seeming contradiction. Was not this the man who had his "distinguishing mind" pushed far away by the goddess and saw (indeed, *tasted*) that sandal-paste and feces were "nondifferent"? What *could* he say?

For his part, M believed that Ramakrishna often "gave in to the weak" when he preached on the fort and the necessity to have fun with one's wife (KA 2.97). It is not difficult to see why. In their first meetings, Ramakrishna scolded M for having children and showed his "disgust" with all that blood.[60] M left a shamed man, his self-esteem "pulverized" by Ramakrishna's shattering remarks. Passages in which M struggles over his married status and the possibility of renunciation in the world are strewn throughout the *Kathāmṛta*.[61] It must have been very painful for him. To make things worse, his wife was going mad. When M first met Ramakrishna, he was contemplating suicide. Clearly these family troubles contributed to M's decision to seek out Ramakrishna. Ramakrishna seems to have sensed this. In one scene, the saint speculates that M is not coming as often because he is on better terms with his wife. Everyone laughs (1.136). But it was not always so funny. In another scene, Ramakrishna suggests to M that he "Let her kill herself" if she is an obstacle on his path to God (KA 2.11),[62] a troubling comment indeed from a person often billed as a feminist.

Defining Ramakrishna's Misogyny

I WOULD ARGUE that the disciples were ambivalent about their family lives with "the bitch and kids" because Ramakrishna himself was profoundly ambivalent about his own relationship to women and the world. Ramakrishna's answer to this ambivalence was clear enough, at least in his own mind. As he had done with the goddess, he split the women he encountered into two distinct natures, those that possessed the "power of delusion" (*mohaśakti*) and those that possessed the "power of gnosis" (*jñānaśakti*). Those women who embodied the powers that led a man further into the trap of *māyā* and the entanglements of the world manifested the power of delusion (KA 3.23). It is fair to say that Ramakrishna hated such women. Certainly he feared them. Their intimate connection to the bodily processes of birth and menstruation disgusted the saint. Those women, however, who embodied the powers that led a man to God manifested the power of gnosis (KA 5.34).[63] Ramakrishna did not hate such women, nor did he fear them, although he often preferred to keep his distance.

Unfortunately, although such a distinction was clear enough in the saint's mind—he seldom, if ever, failed to determine the nature of a woman standing before him—Ramakrishna's disciples often lacked the saint's ability to distinguish between the powers of delusion and gnosis. Accordingly, to them it often seemed that the saint was preaching a simple misogyny: "Well then should we hate women?" they asked more than once. It is not difficult to see why the disciples would ask such a question. Ramakrishna's teachings on women *are* profoundly misogynist, but in a very specific way. To understand the specific contours of this misogyny, it is crucial that the interpreter distinguish with Ramakrishna the powers of delusion and gnosis. If the hermeneut fails to make the distinction between these two sorts of women in Ramakrishna's own understanding, the texts are hopelessly confusing. If, however, the distinction is kept in mind, the texts fall neatly into line. In scenes in which the saint is convinced that a particular woman poses no threat to his spiritual powers, that she is a pure Mother, a possessor of the power of gnosis, he is quite comfortable in her presence. Numerous passages thus relate how groups of women felt "no shame" in his presence. The sexual charge, as it were, had been effectively removed by Ramakrishna's assumption of the child state and by the women's (perceived, at least) assumption of the mother state. The relationship was rendered pure, sexless, devout. In scenes, however, in which a woman is perceived by Ramakrishna to possess the power of delusion, the saint inevitably reacts with scorn, hatred, fear, and, at times, unconsciousness. The Lover is resolutely rejected. Thus there are no "women" in the texts. Rather, there are Mothers and Lovers, possessors of the power of gnosis and possessors of the power of delusion. If we keep such distinctions in mind, Ramakrishna's reactions are not only consistent, they are predictable.

Ramakrishna's misogyny, then, needs to be qualified. He did not hate or fear all women. Certainly he feared women as sexual beings, as Lovers. But he also worshiped women as pure sexless beings, as Mothers, even if this "worship" was as much a defensive tactic born out of fear as it was a religious act arising from genuine devotion. His attitudes, in other words, were dual. They were split like Ramakrishna himself. I should also add that his misogyny was not so much a misogyny, a "hatred of women," as it was a "disgust" (*ghṛṇā*) of female bodies. True, the saint was very upset about men losing their social prestige and privileges to their female counterparts. A grocery shopping man or a husband groveling before a whining wife was just more than Ramakrishna could stomach. As Sumit Sarkar has astutely pointed out, there was an issue of power in Ramakrishna's misogyny.[64] But the primary elements seemed to revolve more around the issues of ritual purity and the rejection of an active heterosexuality. Ramakrishna may have been afraid of women dominating men, but he was absolutely terrified of the polluting substances of the female body and the contact with them that sexual intercourse inevitably brings. To sum up, then, I would say that Ramakrishna's debated misogyny was neither a simple "hatred" (*miso-*) nor a hatred of "woman" (*gyny*). Rather it was a "disgust" (*ghṛṇā*) of woman as "lover" (*kāminī*). To be precise, we must abandon our Greek and adopt his Sanskrit and say that it was a *kāminī-ghṛṇā* or "lover-disgust," an emotional reaction culturally defined and historically specific to nineteenth-century Bengal.

THE SECRET DOOR

SHAME, DISGUST, AND FEAR. As markers of Ramakrishna's rejection of Tantra, we have seen one, two, or all three of these bonds focused first on food and then on women. But perhaps nowhere are these three emotional reactions and the rejection that they record expressed so boldly as in Ramakrishna's metaphor for Tantra as the latrine of the house. Following Tantra, the Paramahaṁsa taught, is like entering the house of mystical experience through its most disgusting opening, the latrine. In another metaphor, Tantra is described as a "dirty path." Ramakrishna, in other words, accepts Tantra as a path to God, but only reluctantly so. It will get you there, he seems to say, but only if you want to wiggle through a very tiny gutter running with the most disgusting of substances.

There is a great irony in the textual history of Ramakrishna's metaphor of the latrine. Nikhilananda refuses to translate the image, but in his attempt to clean up his Master's latrine he leads us into an unsuspected and probably unintended revelation. In the swami's translation, Ramakrishna compares the Tantric path to entering a house through the "back door" (GSR, 513). Of course, there are no respectable back doors in the Bengali text, only disgusting latrines. Unlike the other bowdlerized passages, however, this bit of mistranslation, if handled properly, can lead us into yet another dimension of Ramakrishna's secret. For if we look for other "back doors" in the *Kathāmṛta*, we find them. As we shall soon see, in one secret talk passage there is a door to a hidden room, a "thief's chamber," that Ramakrishna sees in a vision on his way to defecate in the pine grove. In other passages, both the anus and the opening to the *suṣumnā* or central channel of the subtle body are called the "secret door" (*guhya dvāra*)[65] Finally, in another secret talk passage, the *cakra* connected to the powers of evacuation whose opening signaled the early awakening of Ramakrishna's *kuṇḍalinī* energies is called simply "the secret" (*guhya*), a word that can also refer, again, to the anus (KA 4.238).

Nikhilananda's "back door," then, leads us into a whole series of linguistic and symbolic associations hooking up Tantra (the back door), the act of defecation (the hidden door of the thief's chamber), the anus (the secret door), the hidden opening of the central subtle channel located near the anus (the secret door), and the energy center that controls the process of evacuation and initiates early mystical experiences (the secret). In his attempt to conceal Ramakrishna's latrine behind a "back door," Nikhilananda has thus unknowingly led us into yet another dimension of Ramakrishna's secret, its anal or fecal character. His prudish piece of censorship has become a moment of ironic revelation.

I will take this hidden or secret door as my final organizing metaphor. After briefly studying the latrine that lies behind it, I will explore the contexts—temporal, spatial, relational, and textual—in which it appears and suggest a possible interpretation of its seemingly random openings and closings. My reflections on this secret door will serve as the final and perhaps most dramatic instance of this study's basic thesis, namely, that, Ramakrishna's religious experiences were unconsciously structured around Tantra's dialectic of the mystical and the sexual. As we will see here, sometimes this connection could be as tragic as it was profound.

The Tantric Latrine and the Mystical Use of Bodily Fluids

THERE IS A DEVELOPMENT in Ramakrishna's use of the dirty path and latrine metaphors through the volumes of M's *Kathāmṛta* that I hope by now will strike the reader as a familiar one. The dirty path image is introduced in volume 2, although no details are given. We are told that there are dirty paths, but we are not told why they are dirty. They are associated with Tantra but only obliquely. Moreover, no mention is made of the latrine. In volumes 4 and 5, however, the graphic details of this dirtiness are revealed and explicitly hooked up to both Tantra and the latrine image. This dirtiness, moreover, is associated with a particular text, the *Rādhā Tantra*. The latrine image, in other words, follows the basic textual development of Ramakrishna's secret talk that I have analyzed in the introduction: it goes unmentioned in volume 1, is introduced in the middle volumes, and is fully revealed in the later volumes, especially volumes 4 and 5. Even in its textual history, then, Ramakrishna's metaphor of the latrine is linked to his secret.

The first passage occurs in volume 2. Ramakrishna has just explained that his state, the state of the Child, is very pure and that there is no danger in it. The states of the Lover (for a woman) and the Hero (for a man), on the other hand, are very difficult and dangerous. "Some paths are pure, and other paths are dirty," Ramakrishna notes. "Taking a pure path is good" (KA 2.143). That path that is associated with the innocence of childhood and the purity of the Mother is considered to be good, safe, and above all, pure. That path, however, which is associated with a woman or a man as a sexual being is considered to be dirty and dangerous. In the terminology of this study, the paths are split into those associated with the dangers of the Hero and the Lover and those which reject those dangers for the purity and innocence of the Child and the Mother. We are given a basic dichotomy, then, but not many details.

In volume 4, however, Ramakrishna fills in the bare lines of volume 2 with some very graphic colors. The Paramahaṁsa is talking about the Bauls and how they "refine" (the English word is used) their experience into ever sweeter forms. The Bauls were known for their erotic forms of *sādhana*. In a line further down, for example, Ramakrishna relates how they despise pious devotion—"the smell of Kṛṣṇa," as they call it—and seek rather to "sit on the lotus without sipping the honey" (KA 4.134). Taking this Tantric approach to conquering the senses, Ramakrishna explains how a man can know that he is truly perfected. A man is truly perfected, the saint relates in a play on words, when *"he remains with a sexy woman [ramaṇī] and does not have sex [ramaṇa]."* Having got that out, Ramakrishna then proceeds to tell his listeners about the practices of a certain "they": "Many of them follow the view of the *Rādhā Tantra*. They perform *sādhana* with the Five Essences. Earth, water, fire, wind, and space [become in their *sādhana*] shit, piss, menstrual blood, and semen. All these are the essences! All these *sādhana*s are very dirty *sādhana*s, like entering a house through the latrine" (KA 4.134). Since the passage is surrounded with comments about the Bauls and the Kartābhajās, it is likely that the "they" refers to these Tantric sects. And indeed, in volume 5, the entire passage is repeated almost *verbatim*, but this time Ramakrishna explicitly links it up with a specific community, Vaishnavacharan's Kartābhajā sect. Ramakrishna relates the information as if he were a firsthand witness to its truths: "Vaishnavacharan followed the views of the Kartābhajās. . . . They don't like to worship images. They want the living man. Many of them follow the view of the *Rādhā Tantra.* The essences of earth, fire, water, wind, and space [become] shit, piss, menstrual blood, and semen" (KA 5.180–181).

Here we might recall that it was Vaishnavacharan's Kartābhajā sect that put Ramakrishna to the "test" in his Tantric days by subjecting him to sexual temptations. It was Vaishnavacharan, again, who taught Ramakrishna to worship God in man and so helped catalyze the Change. With such passages as these, it is perhaps not unreasonable to suggest that this same sect may have taught the young Ramakrishna to discriminate "with sandal-paste and feces," to lick vagina-shaped lotuses, and to see his "toe" in the mouth of the naked "woman." After all, the substances of shit, piss, menstrual blood, and semen must be consumed somehow. We are back to the tongue. Given the close link that exists in the texts between the metaphor of the latrine and Vaishnavacharan's community, I think it is also reasonable to suggest that Ramakrishna got the image from Vaishnavacharan himself. This is not insignificant, since Vaishnavacharan's homosexual tendencies may have played into the original creation of the latrine image, which, as we shall soon see, itself carries definite homoerotic dimensions. Certainly this community's ritual use of the bodily fluids played an important role in forming Ramakrishna's mystical experiences. For even if the saint never actually participated in the ritual of the Five Essences, or Four Moons as they are called elsewhere,[66] it will become increasingly clear that the basic Tantric intuition lying behind that ritual—that pollution and impurity can be used to induce mystical states—deeply informed the manner in which Ramakrishna experienced the world, his body, and the divine.

The Open Door: The Dislocated Hand, Captain's Latrine, and Ecstatic Diarrhea

THERE ARE AN UNUSUAL NUMBER of instances in which Ramakrishna associates, whether implicitly or explicitly, the act of defecation and the moment of religious experience. Some of them are rather commonplace, for example, his story about the man who realized the unity of God in all religions when, on his way to defecate, he saw a chameleon change its colors.[67] Others are more graphic, for example, when, after asking Kālī for supernatural powers (*siddhi*), he sees in a vision an old "fat-ass" (lit. "basket-ass") whore squatting with her back to him as her shit "plops" to the ground. Super-powers, he concludes, are no better than the noisy shit of a fat-ass whore (KA 3.140). But such teachings and visions are primarily didactic; they carry a moral lesson or an easily translated religious truth. Other passages in the texts are far more obscure in their fecal languages. They can be divided into those that deal with the *open* secret door and those that deal with the *closed* secret door. I will treat three "open" passages first: the dislocated hand, Captain's latrine, and the ecstatic diarrhea scenes.

The dislocated hand scene I have already treated at some length in chapter 4. I will only mention it here to point out that Ramakrishna dislocated his hand as he tried to embrace a male god in an erotic state on his way to the pine grove, that is, on his way to defecate (KA 4.63). Defecation, God, and homoeroticism were all integral to the experience. Moreover, the event was filled with profound meanings for Ramakrishna, for it initiated the Change that eventually redirected Ramakrishna's mystico-erotic energies back into the social world, or what the saint called "God in the forms of man." It would be hard to overestimate the event's importance. That it occurred in the pine grove only adds to its mystery. Certainly the spatial context of the vision, and perhaps its content, also added to the event's illicit nature. Hriday, we recall, would not talk to the doctor about the incident until they were both safely ensconced behind the privacy of a curtain. There was something about the event that needed to be kept secret.

In another unusual passage, this time in volume 1, Ramakrishna relates the day he went to visit one of his disciples he called "the Captain" and fell into an unconscious state in, among all places, his host's latrine: "One day I became unconscious in the latrine of his house. He's so concerned about purity, and yet he sat down with his foot in the hole [of the latrine] and pulled me out" (KA 1.178). When the secret door opens, Ramakrishna falls into ecstasy, and this in a room defined by its disgusting impurity. The fact that the Captain had to put his foot in the hole of the latrine to lift the saint out suggests that Ramakrishna was frozen in a defecating posture, squatting over the hole. He "became unconscious," in other words, in the very act of defecation.

Perhaps it was just a coincidence that Ramakrishna was embracing a male god on his way to defecate and became unconscious in the Captain's latrine. After all, the saint often fell into such states. Perhaps there is nothing intrinsic about the admittedly fecal context of these particular incidences. Such objections, however, lose much of their power when we come across this striking passage in volume 4: "It can't be said how many divine forms used to be seen in visions. At that time I had stomach problems. In all of these states the stomach problems got worse and worse. That's why when I saw a form, finally I would spit at it, but it would hold me again like a ghost that runs one down from behind! I would become filled with ecstasy and lose track of time! The next day the ecstasy would flush through my bowels and come out! (laughter)" (KA 4.232). It might be possible to explain some elements of this passage by simply noting what at least one text goes out of its way to point out, namely, that the climate of Bengal often has extremely adverse effects on the stomach and bowels (LP 3.8.38). Any traveler knows that. But this is hardly a simple case of "drinking the water" and its consequent diarrhea, for here Ramakrishna not only experiences ecstasy while he defecates, *he defecates ecstasy.* The symbolic association between the act of defecation and ecstasy has become literalized in the bowels. Here, moreover, the fecal ecstasies are likened to ghosts and a haunting. For some reason, the past and its fearful memories "that run one down from behind" can only be exorcised through Ramakrishna's anus.

There seems to be some connection, then, between the open secret door and Ramakrishna's ecstatic states and visions. He makes love to God on his way to defecate. He falls into unconscious states while he is defecating. He even defecates ecstasy. The door is wide open, too open, it seems.

The Closed Door: The Thief's Chamber and the Hero's Pose

But there were other times when this secret door was shut tight. Here I want to look at two examples of this closed door.[68] The first passage occurs in volume 3 in a vision Ramakrishna describes in one of his secret talk passages. It reads as follows: "Listen up! I'm telling you *something very secret!* As I was shitting, I saw in front of me in the direction of the pine grove something that looked like the door to a thief's chamber. I couldn't see what was inside the chamber. With a finger-nail file I began to dig a hole, but I couldn't, for as soon as I would dig a hole, it would fill up again! Then all at once there was such a hole!" (KA 3.33). A "thief's chamber" (*cora kuṭhari*)[69] is a secret room or compartment used by members of a household to hide their valuables, a type of safe if you will. Whereas wealthier families often cement the door to an entire room shut to create such a hidden chamber, poorer villagers are more likely to bury their much simpler safes in the ground. Here Ramakrishna sees such a village "thief's chamber" before him. But he cannot tell what valuables the buried door hides, so he tries to dig it out with a small fingernail file, no doubt as he squats to defecate. But like the images of the dirty path and the latrine, this particular door is a "dirty" one; it keeps filling in with symbolic dirt as the saint tries to see what is inside. Suddenly, however, the "hole" caves in, most likely at the very moment Ramakrishna's own secret door opens. Does the door to the thief's chamber open? Is it already open? We are not told. The passage is silent; indeed, it goes completely uninterpreted in the *Kathāmṛta*. Perhaps this is why it made it into the relatively early volume 3. Although revealed in Ramakrishna's secret talk, it is still a secret kept secret. It is still highly symbolic. Nikhilananda further obfuscates things by removing the context of the vision, the phrase "as I was shitting" (GSR, 260). The English reader is thus deprived of the one piece of information that might make the vision intelligible.

The thief's chamber, hidden in the dirt, is most likely a symbol for the anus, that dirty "secret door" or "latrine" of the body. Such a symbolic connection would be quite natural in a culture that refers to the anus as both the "secret door" and as a "hole" (*chidra*) (JV[5], 16). But this thief's chamber is more than an anus. It is also an intentionally hidden household safe, a container of family secrets. It is likely that this safe's contents relate to the saint's past. We are dealing here, in other words, with "buried memories" connected somehow to Ramakrishna's family history. In the end, of course, the chamber's valuables are kept hidden, certainly from us, and perhaps from Ramakrishna himself. We are thus left asking questions. What was inside the chamber? And why did its apparent "opening" coincide with the physiological act of defecation? More specifically, why do Ramakrishna's memories seem to be buried in his anus? And why are they released, like the ghosts of the previous passage, or revealed, like the chamber of this vision, through a literal opening of Ramakrishna's bowels?

The second closed door passage occurs very late in volume 4. It is eleven in the morning. The Master is sitting in his room with some devotees talking to a Christian devotee named Mishra, literally "the Mixed One." Mishra was born into a Christian family. Although he wears the clothes of an Englishman, he proudly dons an ochre loincloth beneath them. Both in his name and his manner of dress, Mishra embodies his name, for he struggles to reconcile or "mix" two different worlds. On the surface, he seems to have opted for the West and its religion, but underneath he is still very much a Hindu, an orange-clad renouncer. In the course of the conversation, Mishra advances a number of interesting theological claims:

> Mishra—"The son of Mary is not Jesus. Jesus is the Lord himself."
>
> (To the devotees)—"He (Sri Ramakrishna) is now this one—again at another time he is the Lord himself.
>
> "All you (devotees) are not able to recognize him. I saw him earlier—now I see clearly. . . .
>
> "In this country there are four gatekeepers. In the area of Bombay there is Tukaram and in Kashmir Robert Michael—here there is he—and in the east there is another man."
>
> Sri Ramakrishna—"You're able to see such things?"
>
> Mishra—"Yes, when I was at home a vision of light always used to occur. After that I had a vision of Jesus. How will I describe this form! Compared to this beauty what is the beauty of a woman!" (KA 4.276–277)

Mishra begins by advancing a Christology that in effect functions as an analogue for his own understanding of who Ramakrishna is: "The son of Mary is not Jesus. Jesus is the Lord himself." That is, Jesus was not a human being born of a woman. He is God himself. In the same way, although Ramakrishna now appears to be a human, he is in fact God. Ramakrishna, in other words, is like Jesus: appearing to be human but in reality remaining God. Mishra then goes on to criticize the disciples for not recognizing this incarnation in their midst. He even claims a prevision in which he saw Ramakrishna among the four "gatekeepers" guarding the holy land of India. This naturally whets Ramakrishna's curiosity. Mishra quickly satisfies it by describing his vision of Jesus, more beautiful than any woman. The homoerotic nature of this vision and its beautiful male form is implied but not clearly stated. We are reminded immediately of Ramakrishna's own vision and the "Jesus state" that induced it.

Such divine male beauty fascinated Mishra. It would prove to be too much for Ramakrishna as well. The text continues:

> After a little while, as he was talking with the devotees, Mishra took his pants and shirt off and showed them an orange loincloth inside.
>
> The Master, coming from the verandah, said: "I couldn't shit. I saw him (Mishra), standing there poised like a Hero." Saying this, the Master entered into *samādhi.* (KA 4.277)

Mishra opens his pants to reveal an ochre garment wound around his loins. Certainly this act had theological implications, for the English garment was pulled down to reveal Mishra's deeper ochre nature. On the outside, Mishra was a Christian. On the inside, he was a Hindu. This, no doubt, delighted Ramakrishna. But surely there was more. Pulling down one's pants, after all, carries meanings other than the purely theological. Certainly the act struck Ramakrishna as erotic, for he describes the half-naked Mishra as a Hero, that phallic male of Tantric culture that he himself had so often rejected as dangerous and dirty. Perhaps Ramakrishna found this particular Hero attractive rather than dirty because of Mishra's own brand of mystical homoeroticism. Surely it was no accident that Mishra the Hero was fascinated, not with the *śakti* of women, but with the beauty of a divine male form that he eventually identified with Ramakrishna himself. As a Christian dressed in English clothes, he saw Jesus, "more beautiful than any woman." Now, as a Hindu dressed in an ochre loincloth, Mishra sees Ramakrishna as "the Lord himself." Although Nikhilananda completely omits the all-important phrase, Ramakrishna himself was very clear about how Mishra's half-naked form affected him: "I couldn't shit." Coming back from the porch, where he perhaps kept a chamber pot, the excited Paramahaṁsa entered into *samādhi*.

What did Ramakrishna see while he was gone? M has his own theories: "Perhaps the Master was in the Jesus state! Are he and Jesus one?" (KA 4.277). M's is an interpretation charged with theological meaning and a long sexual history. What was it about this "Jesus state" that resulted in visions, both imaginal and actual, of beautiful male forms? Ramakrishna had seen them in his earlier days. Mishra too had seen them amidst visions of light. Here, Mishra equates Ramakrishna with the beautiful Jesus while Ramakrishna, in M's "Jesus state," sees erotic beauty in Mishra and enters an ecstatic state. The sexual and the mystical can hardly be distinguished.

This passage on the Hero's pose is connected to the thief's chamber passage in a number of ways. Textually speaking, both passages are tied together by the simple fact that Nikhilananda omitted the very same piece of information from both of them, namely, the fact that Ramakrishna was defecating (or trying to defecate) when the visions occurred. But they are also related on a symbolic level. I have already interpreted the thief's chamber to be a symbol for the anus, that "secret door" of Tantric culture. We see similar anal dimensions in the Hero's pose passage. But whereas in the thief's chamber passage, the secret door is closed and then, perhaps, opened, in the Hero's pose passage, the door remains shut tight. Unlike in the thief's chamber passage, moreover, where we are left with uninterpreted symbols, here we are told very clearly *why* the door is closed: "I couldn't shit [because] I saw him (Mishra), standing there poised like a Hero." The Hero's pose passage, in other words, suggests that the closing of the door, at least at *this* time, had something to do with Ramakrishna's homoerotic desires. Somehow homoerotic feelings both excited the saint (he entered *samādhi*) *and* blocked the secret door of the anus (he could not defecate). If we add to this simultaneous arousal and closing the saint's other experiences of a simultaneous arousal and *opening* (e.g., the dislocated hand, the Captain's latrine, and the ecstatic diarrhea scenes), we are left with the striking image of an uncontrollable secret door that swings open and shuts tight in contexts defined by three consistent markers: the physical act of defecation, ecstatic states, and homoerotic desire. What does all this mean?

The Thief's Chamber in the Texts: Digging up Buried Memories with Ramakrishna

I HAVE LOCATED A PATTERN, but only a pattern. There is no linear argument here, no clear-cut revelation. There are only symbolic acts that connect up to symbolic visions, which in turn can be associated with symbolic acts, and so on. This elaborate weave of the texts creates a situation in which the individual scenes in themselves seem to lack meaning, for, when they are taken out of their proper context, that is, out of their pattern, they cease to make sense and become simply bizarre. The thief's chamber or the Hero's pose, for example, prove nothing in themselves. Taken alone, they appear as merely two more strange scenes in the life of a mysterious, inexplicable saint. But they are not bizarre, and Ramakrishna is not inexplicable. Insofar as this chamber in the dirt and this reaction to Mishra's pose are human expressions, they possess definite meanings that can be deciphered.

To get at these meanings, however, I must begin by momentarily stepping out of the symbolic web of the texts to advance a clear thesis, a "linear argument." I will then return to the textual weave and its patterns in order to support my original thesis. For the sake of this particular argument, I will view the texts as hiding a kind of cultural thief's chamber and see my speculations as a type of "digging." As usual, I see this practice as a digging *with* and *for* the saint; he, after all, wanted very badly to know what was inside. Even when I am finished, however, and we can finally peek inside the chamber with Ramakrishna, my original thesis will not be proven. Indeed, for many, as in the saint's vision of the thief's chamber, the dirt of doubt and disbelief will seem to collapse the hole back into a pile of meaningless mud. For others, however, this "digging with Ramakrishna" will succeed, and they will be able to exclaim with the saint, "Then all at once there was such a hole!"

Let me begin, then, with a thesis regarding the seeming confusion of Ramakrishna's opening and closing secret door. Put simply, I would argue that such a pattern points to the conflicted nature of Ramakrishna's memories of being "entered" by others through the secret door and his equally conflicted desire to enter the same secret door of others. On some level, Ramakrishna seems to have enjoyed the energies these memories invoked: he thus falls into pleasurable ecstasies that are initiated by the opening of the secret door (no doubt, the physiological event that "clicks" the memory of an earlier, equally physical opening), associates its closing with the beauty of Mishra, and actively initiates new homoerotic, if still highly symbolic, encounters in his adult years. On another level, however, he clearly feared such memories, hence he experiences strange fecal ecstasies that "possess" him like ghosts until he expels them out violently through the very door they entered: the anus. It is as if this uncontrollable secret door swung wide open and shut back tight to answer Ramakrishna's conflicted fears and desires. Its seemingly random swingings were symbolic embodiments of the saint's own confusion, pain, shame, and desire.

Of course, it would be easy to dismiss such speculation—and it is that—as the product of Western forms of thought that have little relevance to a South Asian culture such as nineteenth-century Bengal. But then what *are* we to make of the mysterious coincidence of ecstatic states and fecal contexts in Ramakrishna's life? What is God, sex, and feces doing together here, and so often? Why did the physical, literal opening of Ramakrishna's secret door consistently initiate ecstatic states? And why was its closing associated with homoerotic desire? And what about Hriday, that cousin-critic of the saint, who argued pointedly that Ramakrishna's bowel troubles were psychologically induced (KA 1.168)? Until someone offers a better explanation, I cannot help but believe that Ramakrishna's rejection of Tantra as the latrine of the house and his inability to open the secret door before Mishra are more than a rejection of Tantra and a simple case of constipation. Given the text's play on the "secret" nature of the anus, the consistently contorted nature of Nikhilananda's handling of the passages, and the hinted realities of Ramakrishna's troubled past, I cannot help but believe that this latrine and this wildly swinging "back door" are part of what I have called Ramakrishna's secret.

Given all of this, I do not think we can avoid here the problem of sexual abuse and its relationship to Ramakrishna's mystical states.[70] I realize, of course, that the issue is a difficult one, weighed down as it is with a particularly sticky history in Indological discourse,[71] the problems of cultural relativism,[72] and the complexities of human memory,[73] *especially* when those memories are recorded, as they are here, by others in texts that in turn have been edited and often altered by succeeding generations. But however sticky, problematic, or complex, the question remains: what *are* we to make of the suggestive link between traumatic sexual experiences and Ramakrishna's mystical states?

Sil, drawing on a number of scattered textual references and symbolic cues, was the first to speculate that Ramakrishna was sexually abused by a whole series of women and men throughout his childhood and early adult life.[74] Although I differ with him on a number of theoretical and historical points,[75] Sil is right about very many things, and this no doubt is one of them. Granted, even given the fears of Gadadhar's mother concerning the holy men and their stripping of young Gadadahar (to make a loincloth and cover his body with ashes) and the suspicious religious practices of the young village women (who worshiped him as their divine lover, Kṛṣṇa), we must admit that there are no clear indications of early sexual abuse in the biographies. But why should there be? These are, after all, hagiographies, and hagiographies rarely dwell on such forbidden subjects as the sexual complexities of childhood.

Despite this surface silence in the texts, however, the symbolic connections and religious teachings of the saint do point in just such a direction, as does the general textual pattern of revealing and concealing that I have analyzed throughout this study. Is it just a coincidence that repeated traumatic events, much like Ramakrishna's Tantric experiences, often result in symptomatic signs that, in the words of one psychiatrist, "simultaneously conceal and reveal their origins . . . [and] speak in [the] disguised language of secrets too terrible for words"?[76] It is indeed remarkable that the vast, if young and still debated, literature on sexual trauma suggests that individuals who have experienced abuse often become adept at altering their state of consciousness, "split" their identities to separate themselves from the traumatic event, lose control of their bodily, and especially gastrointestinal, functions, experience visions and states of possession, become hypersensitive to idiosyncratic stimuli (like latrines), symbolically reenact the traumatic events, live in a state of hyperarousal, regress to earlier stages of pyschosocial development, develop various types of somatic symptoms (including eating disorders and chronic insomnia), become hypersexual in their language or behavior, develop hostile feelings toward mother figures, fear adult sexuality, and often attempt suicide.[77] The list reads like a summary of Ramakrishna's religious life. Certainly it is not simply a matter of the saint manifesting one or two such symptoms, as is often the case with traumatized children and adults. Perhaps we could overlook that. But Ramakrishna manifests virtually all of them and displays them with an intensity that even the experienced psychiatrist might find alarming.

I have analyzed the symbolic equations of the Vedantic paramahaṁsa, nudity, boys, and penises in the saint's visions and language, suggesting that something more than "Vedantic instruction" went on between Ramakrishna and the naked Tota Puri in the small hut tucked away in the trees. Ramakrishna's six-month long "*nirvikalpa samādhi,*" traditionally connected with the departure of Tota, looks *very* different from such a perspective. Saradananda places the state shortly after Tota's departure in order to demonstrate the magnitude and depth of Ramakrishna's Vedantic realization. But again, we must ask ourselves whether Saradananda's Vedantic hermeneutic is believable here. I have already demonstrated that Saradananda's attempt to connect the six-month state with the famous command to "Remain in *bhāvamukha*" finds no support in the texts of Datta and Gupta and quickly falls apart in the face of internal evidence alone. Given, then, the paucity of reliable information we have concerning the exact timing and motives of Tota's departure and the wealth of symbolic material we do possess that links up nudity, paramahaṁsas, and the fondling of penises, I think it is just as possible to read the six-month state as a reaction to Tota's abusive presence and to see the condition not as the crown of but as *the reason for* Tota's otherwise unexplained departure. Of course, Tota simply may have been leaving a friend after too long a stay, but then what are we to do with six months of unconsciousness, force-feeding, and bloody bowels that would not be controlled? It seems much more likely that Tota was in fact escaping.

I have also demonstrated the sexual context of Ramakrishna's handmaid state, its connection to Mathur's demonic "abduction" of the saint, and the state's association with a form of unconsciousness that, at least from the outside, strongly resembles a traumatic reaction: one does not remain unconscious for days on end at the home of one's boss without a very good reason. It is also more than a little curious that Ramakrishna often slept in Mathur's bedroom, lived in his mansion for sixteen years, and knew so much about his sexual exploits. In this same context, we must also ask why the young Gadadhar lost both his consciousness and the control of his bowels shortly after his brother died and left him alone at the temple, at the mercy of Mathur; is it just another coincidence that the first textual appearance of the saint's uncontrollable secret door coincides *exactly* with the advent of Mathur's unchallenged authority over the boy? These unconscious "slimy mud" (JV[5], 22) scenes and the states of madness that brought them on would continue for years and would let up only when Ramakrishna was taken back home to his village, far away from Mathur. Jensen has noted the curious connection that seemed to exist between Ramakrishna's states of madness and the temple precincts.[78] It was almost as if the temple made Ramakrishna mad. In the light of these diggings, we might speculate that it was not so much the temple as the *temple boss* that gave these states their energy and purpose. Here we might also guess at the import of those "scandalous" interpretations that were advanced by the saint's contemporaries to explain Mathur's practice of dressing Ramakrishna in expensive women's clothes. Certainly not everyone was naive.

The connections, however, by no means end there. The manner in which the saint anxiously tried again and again to turn the sexually aggressive Lover, in the form of a woman or the goddess, into a sexless, pure Mother by falling into unconscious states and desperately calling "Ma! Ma!" is highly suggestive of early traumatic experiences at the hands of sexually aggressive "mothers."[79] Moreover, the saint's vehement rejection of the Gopāla state, in which a man or a boy becomes Gopāla (the child Kṛṣṇa) in relation to a woman as Yaśoda (Kṛṣṇa's mother), also fits in well here: "Many women look at handsome boys, see that they look good, and set new traps of illusion. *This* is the Gopāla state!" The tone and detail of Ramakrishna's language would suggest that he was speaking from bitter experience. Such negative reactions were probably not restricted to Ramakrishna. Indeed, the fear of such sexually aggressive mothers seems to have been so strong and pervasive in the culture that it took the form of a stylized rhyme: "From such maternal affection (*vātsalya*) comes deception (*tācchalya*)," the saint angrily quipped. Certainly such childhood experiences would go a long way in explaining Ramakrishna's extreme fear and hatred of women as sexual beings.

Finally, I might point out that mothers are sexualized to an unusual and unnecessary degree in Ramakrishna's discourse. Consider, for example, his teaching that "every vagina is Mother's vagina," a teaching, we might recall, that Ramakrishna advanced to explain to himself and to others why he could not engage any woman as a sexual being. Why, we might ask, did the saint so easily associate women, mothers, and vaginas and then use this equation as a reason to avoid women in general? Certainly many of his contemporaries found his understanding of sex with *any* woman as an act of incest to be bizarre to the extreme. What was he afraid of? What happened in his hidden past that finally resulted in such extreme if still symbolic reactions? Clearly, *something* did.

But if Ramakrishna feared such advances in others, he also relived these childhood and adolescent experiences of sexually aggressive adults by reenacting the forgotten events in symbolic and ritual contexts that simultaneously revealed and concealed their secret meanings.[80] If once Ramakrishna was seduced by sexually aggressive "mothers," he would later become himself an erotic Mother and engage his boy disciples in maternal relationships that even in M's eyes seemed "strange": a thirteen-year-old boy sitting in the lap (that is, on the genitals) and nursing at the breasts of a forty-eight-year-old man is simply more than M, or most anyone else, could understand. Again, if he once was sexually manipulated by Tota, the naked paramahaṁsa, he would later relive the experiences by uncontrollably rubbing sandal-paste on the penises of boys, by fondling the penis of a visionary paramahaṁsa youth, and by worshiping his own erect penis "in the state of the paramahaṁsa." The pattern, although admittedly speculative in its attempt to move backward from known biographical events to the *if* of alleged childhood and early adult scenes, is too consistent and too suggestive to be ignored. The pattern, moreover, is only strengthened and confirmed when we can remove the *if* and discuss with confidence both the childhood scene and the later adult acts. Take, for example, Ramakrishna's strange behavior with the Ramlal statue. We know that Ramakrishna lost his father when he was only seven. Taking up our pattern, then, we could easily, and I think reasonably, read the saint's pathetic attempts to engage the statue, as a father would engage his little boy, as symbolic acts by which he desperately tried to relive and somehow reintegrate a fatherly affection that he had lost, or never had, as a boy.

If this reenactment pattern seems too speculative and appears to be only loosely connected to the secret door passages discussed above, consider the following scene. Narendra and Ramakrishna are taking a nap at the home of a disciple. Narendra has his back to Ramakrishna. At some point, the saint gets up, crawls toward Narendra and "touches" him softly. Narendra wakes up and shouts in English. "Lo! the man is entering into me!" Ramakrishna laughs and replies, "You son-of-a-bitch! Do you think I don't follow your jabbering in English? You're saying that I'm entering into you!"[81] Ramakrishna thus attempted to do to Narendra what Mathur and Tota had done to him: enter him "through the latrine." Narendra's secret door, however, was shut tight.

The House and the Latrine: Relating the Mystical and the Socially Reprehensible

I BEGAN WITH A SERIES of doors in the text whose symbolic associations with the anus enabled me to locate a number of "openings" and "closings." I advanced the thesis that these contrary movements pointed to the conflicted natures of Ramakrishna's sexual past and present desires. To support my argument, I turned to the thief's chamber vision as a symbol of buried memories and family secrets, realities of Ramakrishna's past for which we admittedly (still) have very few hard facts. Once, however, I located the thief's chamber in its proper fecal context, I was able to dig through the texts and uncover a good deal of related material that calls us back to this sealed safe through symbolic webs that never proceed in straight lines but rather wrap around and around a central spider-like truth. With the right texts and the proper methods, in other words, I was able to dig up the thief's chamber with Ramakrishna and peek inside, if only for a moment.

What have we seen? We have seen that, despite Ramakrishna's rejection of Tantra as the latrine of the house, it was *precisely* through this secret door that he entered many of his ecstatic states. We have seen, moreover, that the latrine image is a metaphor that speaks to us of the ambiguities that marked Ramakrishna's homoerotic mysticism: of his fears of being entered by others, of his disgust with the dirtiness of sex, of his own profound ambivalence toward Tantra and its use of the bodily substances on the mystical path, and finally, of his own hidden desires to enter the secret door of others. It is to Ramakrishna's credit that he did not categorically reject Tantra. Perhaps he sensed, or even knew, that its truths had been embodied in his own life, that somehow his ecstatic states were connected to his earlier erotic, and sometimes abusive, encounters, and that he himself desired to enter the secret door. Perhaps this is why the saint insisted that one *can* get into the house of mystical experience through the latrine. Had he not done it? His rejection of Tantra, then, was not a categorical rejection. It was a rejection that was also a disgruntled, and perhaps embarrassed, acceptance of a truth displayed in his own life.

Perhaps many of us wish we had never peeked, never looked inside. Some, no doubt, still do not see, and do not *want* to see, the gaping hole which so amazed Ramakrishna. I, at least, have seen things that I did not want to see, that I had no idea were there when I began my research. But there it was, the thief's chamber, seen and opened in the very act of defecation. And there was the dislocated hand, Captain's latrine, and the Hero's pose, again all explicitly associated with the act of defecation. There, moreover, were texts that talked about ghosts connected to the saint's bowels, sexually aggressive "mothers," holy men stripping a little trusting boy desperate for a father figure, village women worshiping this same little boy as their mythical lover, a worried mother, suspicious neighbors, a boss whose "demonic" presence could send a young priest into prolonged states of unconsciousness, and a phallic guru whose unexplained departure was connected with *half a year* of more unconsciousness and some very bloody bowels. I have refused to be naive about such things, despite a long and noble tradition to the contrary. Perhaps others wish to be, lest their thoughts become too "imperialistic"[82] or "Western" or, God forbid, "psychoanalytic." Such reactions, no doubt, can be expected. After all, anyone who dares dig up another culture's hidden safe and talk openly about its contents is likely to be labeled not a digger but a thief.

But I am not a thief. I am a digger, and I admit that some of what I have dug up is neither obvious nor easy to accept. Let me be very clear, then, about exactly what I think these last "diggings" mean and do not mean. Clearly, I would not deny that Ramakrishna suffered what Masson calls "massive traumas" in his childhood and early adult life. Indeed, of the three types of trauma Masson lists as essential components of the ascetic's past—sexual seduction, overt or covert aggression, and the loss of a loved one[83]—Ramakrishna clearly suffered the last (twice) and most likely endured the first as well, and many times at that.[84] Nor would I question the importance of such events in setting up the *psychological conditions* for Ramakrishna's mystical experiences; indeed, I have spent the last five chapters establishing and analyzing those conditions. I *would*, however, question the assumption that such conditions are sufficient to explain the *meaning and content* of the experiences themselves. It is one thing to suggest that Ramakrishna was abused as a child and again as a young adult, and that this set up certain psychological conditions that made the saint particularly prone to unusual states of consciousness. It is quite another to claim that this somehow explains away the religious meaning and genuine depth of all such states.[85] It does not. No matter how many dark secrets we uncover about the saint's hidden past, the fact remains that Ramakrishna experienced many of his later ecstasies as profoundly pleasurable and that healing and revelatory energies were often transmitted from these states into his disciples. Yes, Ramakrishna was clearly angered and disgusted with many of the personalities that haunted his past, but he just as clearly and just as passionately expressed joy and wonder when confronted with the realities of his mystical experiences. If we are to understand the whole Ramakrishna, we must acknowledge both these emotional poles.

Ramakrishna's life, then, *was* tragic, but it was also ecstatic. The abuse he seems to have received as a child and young adult *was* reprehensible, both to him and to us, but it was also connected, in ways we do not yet understand, to his later mystical realizations. Once again, it is absolutely crucial to recall Ramakrishna's dogged insistence that the house of mystical experience can be entered through something as horrible as a latrine. The house *can* be entered through the latrine, but this does *not* mean that the house, once entered, is nothing but a latrine. Whatever we think of such an entrance, the possibility remains that, under the proper conditions, even the latrine might very well open up into a very large and very wonderful house. The ethical and religious implications of such entrances, both for the researcher who digs them up and for the culture that symbolically supports and yet publically denies them, remain to be addressed. I would hope in the meantime that researchers could be sophisticated enough to keep the admittedly troubling conditions of entrance and that which is entered distinct in their discussions. Only then will we be able to share both Ramakrishna's deep disgust with certain aspects of his own latrine-like entrance and his obvious joy at truly being in the house.

"Bite Your Tongue!"

I BEGAN THIS CHAPTER by noting that when Bengalis are embarrassed or ashamed they stick their tongues out slightly. We would say that they "bite" them, as in our own English expression, "Bite your tongue!" With this in mind, it is interesting to note that in some of Ramakrishna's secret talk passages, the saint complains that as he struggles to speak someone is "holding" his mouth shut.[86] Someone will not let him speak the secret. Ramakrishna senses this act of internal censorship and responds to it with feelings of shame and guilt: "Well, have I done something wrong?" he asks, "Should all this (secret) talk have been spoken?" (KA 3.141). The extended, bitten, or held back tongue, then, represents in the public culture and in Ramakrishna's own socialized conscience a state of shame or reticence.

In stark contrast to this public meaning, Tantra takes the same tongue and extends it to accomplish something radically different. If it once extended itself to express shame in the social conscience, Tantra uses it to transgress and transcend the emotion of disgust in its secret rituals. In this last chapter, we have seen this reversal of meanings worked out in the texts. Although Kālī is *supposed* to be ashamed for standing on her husband, in these texts, at least, she most definitely is not. Thus Ramakrishna, possessed by Kālī, extends an ecstatic tongue to commune with rotting human flesh, polluted rice, river-bank feces, and symbolic vaginas, that preeminent "place of disgust." Kālī's tongue here is not about shame but about the destruction of disgust. Moreover, it is stuck out in ritual and ecstatic contexts that, taken together, impressively reproduce the Five M's of Tantra: wine, fish, meat, and intercourse, at least. For Ramakrishna, the tongue is *the* Tantric organ. Indeed, so central is the tongue to Ramakrishna's Tantra that, when the saint must fulfill the only M that does not necessarily involve it, *maithuna* or "sexual intercourse," he uses it anyway.

Most dramatically, the tongue functions in the Kartābhajā practice of the Five Essences as a means to ingest the bodily substances of "shit, piss, menstrual blood, and semen." It is here, within this ritual context, that Ramakrishna commonly spoke of Tantra as the latrine of the house. This latrine image and its consequent bowdlerization as the "back door" hook up to an interrelated complex of sexual abuse, physiological reaction, and repressed memory, all expressed through hidden doors, which in turn help generate a whole discourse of secrets that both reveal and conceal their terrible truths in symbol, ritual, and vision. The tongue that touched the feces and urine and menstrual blood to conquer disgust now reaches out again, this time to speak the unspeakable. Halfway through its own revelations, however, it "bites itself" and reverts to symbols and secrets. The tongue that conquered disgust is conquered again by shame.

Kālī's tongue, then, is split, like Ramakrishna himself, into two separate worlds of meaning. It fulfills a public function (it expresses shame) and a secret function (it destroys disgust). Just as Tantra defines itself in opposition to Brahmanical culture, so too does Kālī's secret tongue define itself over and against her public tongue. What is shameful, even reprehensible, to society is salvific for Tantra, that "dirty path" that winds its way through the texts as a tradition at once cruelly abusive and religiously profound. Society may insist, in the form of Ramakrishna's conscience (and Nikhilananda's omissions), that he not speak of this path and its secrets, that he remain silent. But driven by the secret goddess, Ramakrishna speaks anyway and tells his secrets with a tongue that is as much Kālī's as it is his own. In many ways, the *Kathāmṛta* is a result of that extended tongue. Its patterns of revealing and concealing merely replicate on a textual dimension the ambivalence and reluctance embodied in Kālī's tongue, extended to both express and destroy the bonds of "shame, disgust, and fear."

EPILOGUE: THE FOG OF BLISS

THERE IS A SECRET TALK PASSAGE in volume 4 of the *Kathāmṛta* that sums up many of the themes I have been analyzing during the course of the last five chapters. Ramakrishna has just emerged from an ecstatic state and is speaking "very secret things" to M in private:

> Do you know what I saw all this time in the ecstatic state?—*A field with a road to Sihore extending for some six to eight miles.* I was alone in this field!—The paramahaṁsa boy of fifteen that I saw under the banyan tree, again I saw another just like him!
>
> *Everywhere there was a fog of bliss!*—From within it a boy of thirteen or fourteen arose and showed his face! He had the form of Purna! We were both naked!—Then the two of us ran around in the field and played joyfully!
>
> Running around so much, Purna became thirsty. He took a drink with a leaf and then came to give me some water. I said: "Brother, I can't eat your leftovers." Then he laughed, cleaned the glass, and brought me another glass of water. (KA 4.259)[1]

This is a complicated vision in need of a good deal of interpretation. Even Ramakrishna finds the vision hazy as he watches it take form in a psychic fog of memory, emotion, and desire.

Although the ecstatic state takes place in the present, the vision that accompanies it is structured around archaic material, that is, around images from Ramakrishna's childhood, adolescence, and early Tantric practices. Sihore, for example, was a village not far from Kamarpukur, where Ramakrishna grew up. The open field stretching between the two towns would have been a natural playground for Gadadhar and his friends,[2] who most likely romped naked through such fields as village boys are wont to do: "We were both naked! . . . Then the two of us ran around in the field and played joyfully!" The vision as a whole, then, like a dream, harks back to Ramakrishna's childhood, both in its geographical setting and in its boyish content. Though seen in the present, it speaks of the past.

But some of the vision's material is of later origin. For example, the paramahaṁsa boy of fifteen whom Ramakrishna saw under the banyan tree most likely refers to the "naked form" (*nyāṅgta mūrti*) that used to materialize out of his body during his early years of *sādhana*. Immediately after this paramahaṁsa boy appears, another boyish figure takes shape in the fog, this time with the face of Purna, Ramakrishna's fourteen-year-old disciple, whom we saw play such an important role in Ramakrishna's anxious desires (chapter 1). By associating the boy of his present vision with this most recent boy disciple, with the "naked form" of his *sādhana* years, and with his naked playmates of his childhood, Ramakrishna is setting up homoerotic associations stretching some forty years between his early childhood and final secret visions. The vision thus encodes a personal history, a psychic transformation. Gadadhar's naked boyhood playmates (chapter 1) became the stuff of his mystico-erotic visions and Tantric practices (chapter 2), which in turn were transformed into the visages of his present beloved boy disciples (chapters 1 and 4). Childhood pals, a naked visionary form, and a boy disciple are all condensed into a single form within the psychic fog of bliss. Thus, in this secret vision of Ramakrishna, the inner circle of his final days finds its psychic roots in his earlier Tantric encounters, and even farther back, in the childhood exploits of his village life. The disciples are indeed intimate "parts" of Ramakrishna. They have become focal points for the saint's lifelong associations.

But there are gaps in the vision, periods in Ramakrishna's life that cannot be reconciled. Whereas in Ramakrishna's Tantric years Ramakrishna laughed after he fondled the paramahaṁsa's penis, here the naked Purna laughs *at* Ramakrishna for his unenlightened attitude to purity—"In a Tantric world," Purna seems to say with his laugh, "everything is pure. So why do you refuse my glass?" The vision thus reveals to us something of Ramakrishna's present ambivalence toward Tantra and its transcendence of the Brahmanical laws of purity (chapter 5). Ramakrishna's Tantric days are definitely over, something he was often quick to admit. Now much older, he is no longer comfortable with such methods. He is a good brahmin now. But his Tantric days still tempt him with their secrets, and they laugh at him with a form that Ramakrishna finds beautiful, the form of the boy Purna.

CONCLUSION: ANALYZING THE SECRET

All this is very secret talk. What will you understand by analyzing it?

Ramakrishna in the *Kathāmṛta* 4.56

I DOUBT whether Ramakrishna himself grasped the meaning of his fog of bliss vision. It was too close to him, too immediate. He himself was lost in the fog. But the historian of religions is outside it. He can enter the fog of bliss at will through his imagination and then reemerge to ponder its meanings and their relationships to other texts and visions. Such visions, moreover, are not subjective dream-like experiences for the historian. The historian does not witness their drama in unconscious states; rather, he encounters them in the light of his waking reason and its interpretive powers. Nor do the visions disappear for him. They have been recorded, etched in ink, if you will. Such a process, no doubt, has changed the secrets—any translation from one human being to another is bound to effect some transformation, however slight—but the secrets nevertheless remain relatively stable. They are there for anyone who can read the texts. They do not appear and disappear at will in some psychic space.

They are there, but they still do not speak to us in any intelligible fashion, for they appear in the texts, as they most likely appeared to Ramakrishna, as a series of seemingly unrelated parts. As a confused mélange of strange images and mysterious voices, the secrets often seem to lack meaning. Perhaps this is one reason Ramakrishna referred to them as "secrets." They did not make sense to the saint. Their meanings, their message, remained hidden, even from him. Beginning with this assumption, I introduced this study by ordering these secrets into a textual pattern, identifying their cyclical distribution throughout M's *Kathāmṛta* as itself meaningful. The text, I argued, is ambivalent in its simultaneous efforts both to conceal and reveal a secret. I then proceeded in the body of the study to interpret the various "secret talk" passages by placing them within their proper iconographic and biographical contexts and by glossing them with other associated passages in the texts. In short, I tried to understand Ramakrishna's secret by contextualizing it within a series of wider symbolic, historical, and textual worlds. What have I uncovered through such a method? Or to be more precise, what *is* Ramakrishna's secret? And in what sense were its mystical dimensions related to Ramakrishna's homosexual desires? It is with these two questions that I want to conclude.

EMERGING FROM THE FOG OF BLISS: DEFINING THE SECRET

WITH FIVE CHAPTERS of material behind me, I can now return to my initial assertion that Ramakrishna possessed a secret and spell out in a more systematic way its different dimensions. As a way of concluding, then, I want to define very briefly the following eight dimensions of Ramakrishna's secret: (1) the textual; (2) the political; (3) the psychological; (4) the social; (5) the ontological; (6) the ritual; (7) the anal; and (8) the theological. I have summed up each dimension with a single phrase, each of which, except for the first, is taken directly from the texts themselves.

The Textual Dimension: Patterns of Concealment, Omission, and Absence

I BEGAN by demonstrating how the texts themselves are informed by a secret. In the case of M's *Kathāmṛta*, this secret drove M to order his volumes in a cyclical pattern and to tuck the more explicit "secret talk" passages away in the later volumes. Nikhilananda, M's translator, carried this process further by mistranslating or simply omitting those passages that he found personally troubling or that he considered unfit for a Western audience. M's pattern of cyclical concealment was thus replaced by a strategy of censorship and omission. Absence is yet another strategy in this textual element of the secret. To this day, the secret is made present by the absence of certain key texts in the bookstores and markets of Calcutta, most prominent among them, Ram Chandra Datta's *Jīvanavṛttānta.* While M's *Kathāmṛta* and Saradananda's *Līlāprasaṅga* are everywhere, Datta's biography, except for one or two editions in a library here and there, is nowhere to be found. For all practical purposes, it does not exist. It does not count. The secret, then, manifests itself on a textual level by structuring, distorting, and even eliminating the texts that record its varied contents.

The Political Dimension: "I Won't Give Them to Anyone."

RELATED TO THIS TEXTUAL DIMENSION of the secret is another, equally pervasive dimension, the political element. Anyone who has tried to locate M's diaries knows what I mean. The researcher soon discovers that the powers that control the archives and historical documents do not want these texts to be studied too closely. Certainly this reluctance on the part of M's descendants and the Ramakrishna Order explains why no Western researcher has ever seen, and may never see, the original manuscripts of M's diaries. They do exist. Thanks to the foresight of Swami Prabhananda and the Ramakrishna Order, they have been carefully photographed. Unfortunately, however, they are kept under lock and key. Like the contents of Ramakrishna's thief's chamber, they contain a secret that is kept hidden from the public's eye. And this hiding, this refusal to submit to public scrutiny, itself has a very long history. Indeed, it goes back to M himself. In one passage in the *Kathāmṛta,* for example, Girish Ghosh asks M if he could see his diaries, about which he had heard. M replies honestly, "No . . . I won't give them to anyone. I wrote them for me. They are not for others!" (KA 2.242).[1] It also goes back to Vivekananda, who threatened to sue his own cousin if he included his name in that "bosh and rot" of a book, the *Jīvanavṛttānta.* To this day, M's refusal, backed up by the political forces of Vivekananda's community of renouncers, stands unshaken.

The Psychological Dimension: "I Have No Control"

THESE TEXTUAL AND POLITICAL DIMENSIONS of Ramakrishna's secret are extraneous to Ramakrishna himself. They are part of what might be called the appropriation of Ramakrishna in Bengali culture. Other dimensions of the secret, however, can be seen to be functioning in Ramakrishna's own life. The psychological aspects of the secret, for example, are particularly evident. The Paramahaṁsa sees visions filled with symbols that, if interpreted within the total context of his discourse, can be arranged into recognizable (Tantric) patterns of meaning and show clear connections to his own half-forgotten past. He falls into ecstatic states that on closer examination are found to occur consistently under certain circumstances and in certain contexts. He admits frankly that he does not know what his visions mean, that he does not know why he cannot touch metal or women, that he has no control when he is in "that state." In other words, Ramakrishna is *unconscious* of his own secret. It is a secret kept secret from the saint himself.

I have uncovered the secret unconscious side of Ramakrishna by approaching the texts through Kālī's iconography, which, as I have argued in the introduction, manifests in an unusually graphic way the latent meanings of the Tantric psyche. With such a method, I have identified two Ramakrishnas: Ramakrishna the Child and Ramakrishna the Tantric Hero. The Hero, who appears in the saint's unconscious visions, obviously knows the secret, but the Child of his consciousness does not. The Hero, the worshiper of Kālī as Lover, licks vagina-shaped lotuses, sees God in the heat of a bitch, and ecstatically worships his own and other people's *liṅgam*s. Granted, he is an ambivalent Hero, for the heterosexual structure of his Tantric world often grates against his own homosexual desires, but he is a Hero nonetheless. The Child, on the other hand, rejects Kālī as Lover and insists on approaching her only as a pure, sexless Mother. He is a boy of five, innocent, pure, likened to the Vedantic paramahaṁsa sage. The agonistic relationship that existed between this Child of consciousness and this conflicted homosexual Hero of the unconscious both created the secret and foreshadowed the patterns of concealing and revealing so evident in the texts.

The Social Dimension: "No One Else Is Here Now"

BUT THE SECRET structured more than Ramakrishna's psyche. It also ordered Ramakrishna's social relationships and the manner in which he defined his community of disciples. The saint will only speak his secret talk to certain disciples, those whom he includes in his inner circle. "No one else is here now," he whispers excitedly to a few of his close disciples before he breaks into another revelation. His secret talk thus functions as a means to separate the inner circle from the rest of the crowd and draw his most intimate disciples into a closer communion with him. By sharing secrets, Ramakrishna wins their hearts and binds them to himself. Likewise, by refusing to reveal these same secrets, he pushes others away. They are not "his own." The secret thus divides Ramakrishna's listeners into the inner and the outer circles, and by implication, locates the saint in the center of these concentric circles of discourse, revelation, and power.

The Ontological Dimension: "A Secret Interpretation of Vedānta"

THROUGHOUT THIS STUDY I have argued that Ramakrishna's mystical and sexual energies were inseparably united. This too is an integral part of the secret but one ultimately subsumed under its ontological dimensions and what they imply about the hidden structure of the cosmos and the human being. "She herself has become everything," Ramakrishna taught. The very walls vibrate with her energies. Goosebumps speak of her arousal. Everything *is* the goddess. This radical vision of things is the secret that M clumsily calls "a secret interpretation of Vedānta" (KA 4.34). Of course, it is not Vedānta at all. It is Tantra. As I have demonstrated in chapter 3, the world is formed around the dialectic of the goddess standing on top of the god. She is the mistress of Tantra and its energies, he the master of Vedānta and its pristine consciousness. Together, this energy and this consciousness, this energy that is conscious, constitutes everything that is. Ramakrishna's world was thus a Tantric world, secretly structured around the upside-down, mystico-erotic union of Śiva and Śakti. Despite a host of prudishly pedantic "interpreters" of Tantra, the implications of such statements are clear enough: everything is divine, including and, from a Tantric perspective, *especially* the sexual powers. This is one of the "secrets" of the world, a hidden truth revealed in Tantric experience. From the perspectives of psychoanalysis and textual analysis, my original statement that Ramakrishna's religious experiences were constituted by mystico-erotic energies is both reasonable and defensible. From the perspective of this ontological vision, it is utterly redundant.

The Ritual Dimension: "Everything about a Tāntrika Is Secret"

RELATED TO THIS ONTOLOGICAL ELEMENT of the secret was its experiential base in Tantric ritual and symbolism. As I have demonstrated in chapter 2, the ontological structure of Ramakrishna's Tantric world was first revealed to the saint in his Tantric practices with the Bhairavī. Those rituals and those years would define everything that came after them. Ramakrishna's secret, then, was rooted in Tantric ritual, rituals that were by definition kept secret from the public. Indeed, the very nature of Ramakrishna's secrecy is itself a Tantric characteristic. All those secret talk passages, all those concealing cycles, all that bowdlerizing on Nikhilananda's part—all this can be explained by seeing Ramakrishna as a Tāntrika and his secret as a Tantric ritual secret. For the Tāntrika is the secret man *par excellence.* As the saint put it, "Everything about a Tāntrika is secret" (KA 4.166). Ramakrishna himself was no exception.

The Anal Dimension: "The Secret Door"

BUT THE TANTRIC DIMENSIONS of the secret bothered Ramakrishna. He found Tantra's use of the bodily fluids and its stress on human sexuality as a source of ritual potency particularly appalling. Tantra was the "latrine of the house" for Ramakrishna. The Tantric aspects of the secret thus took on fecal or anal dimensions, both in the original Bengali and, ironically, in Nikhilananda's English translation ("the back door"). I have suggested that this association between the secret and the act of defecation is rooted in Ramakrishna's experiences of being "entered" through the secret door of the anus and his consequent desire to enter the same secret door of others. Such a theory, at least, would help explain Ramakrishna's unsuccessful attempts to control the opening and closing of his own secret door and the numerous instances in which he fell into unconscious states while he defecated. Mythologically speaking, he was reliving (and resisting) buried memories of Sītā's abduction.

The Theological Dimension: "The King Who Comes in Secret"

FINALLY, THERE IS a theological dimension to the secret. Relatively uninterpreted by Ramakrishna himself, the saint's secret visions became impressively plastic elements with which the disciples could and did mold different theologies of incarnation and community. We saw this process begin with the three Tantric figures, the Bhairavī, Gauri, and Vaishnavacharan, who declared as early as the late 1850s that the saint's bodily signs were symptomatic of divinity. It seems to have abated somewhat in the 1860s and early 1870s but picked up considerable momentum with the coming of the disciples in the late 1870s and 1880s. Toward the end of his life, when Ramakrishna finally turned around from the Absolute to the phenomenal world and descended into the forms of man, this process of interpretation and debate became more central as it focused on the strange actions of Ramakrishna's foot and what Ramakrishna meant to the community that was forming around him. The secret was being transformed.

Although I cannot go into the details of such a transformation here (such a project belongs properly to a future study on the appropriation of Ramakrishna), I can explain the process briefly by positing a secret with two primary levels: Ramakrishna the Tāntrika and Ramakrishna the incarnation. Seven of the eight dimensions outlined above are related somehow to Tantra. The textual and political dimensions can be seen as an attempt to cover up the Tantric elements in the texts. The psychological dimension took its form around classical Tantric identities, the Child and the Hero. The social dimension, moreover, was a function of the revelation of secrets that were themselves primarily Tantric in orientation. Finally, the ontological dialectic, the notion of Tantric ritual secrecy, and the anal nature of the latrine of the house were all explicitly connected to Tantric texts and their worldview. Ramakrishna's secret was clearly a Tantric secret.

But not entirely. There was one other major level to it, the incarnational, that is, the belief that the secret pointed to Ramakrishna's status as a new incarnation of God. We have seen this aspect of the secret developed in Saradananda's "hidden meanings" hermeneutic, in the debates that surrounded Ramakrishna's foot, and in Datta's description of the Kalpataru Day, when Ramakrishna, like the mythical wish-fulfilling tree, magically distributed his god-like *śakti* to his disciples according to their own "imagined desires" (*kalpa*). There are also a number of visions in the *Kathāmṛta*, some of them related in secret talk passages, that contain clear references to the belief that Ramakrishna was God.[2] Although it lies outside the parameters of the present study, this is important to keep in mind. Certainly it was what the later tradition picked up and developed.

There are two primary levels to the secret, then: the Tantric and the incarnational. Both the secret's content and its interpretation seem to have changed over time, swinging back and forth between these Tantric and incarnational meanings. The secret's earliest strata seem to be primarily Tantric, but even here already show incarnational patterns. As we have seen in chapter 2, Ramakrishna's Tantric practices occurred very early in his life and constituted the foundation—structurally, doctrinally, and mystically—of the rest of his career. Accordingly, many of Ramakrishna's reminiscences concerning this early period of his religious practices are preceded by the heading *pūrvakathā*, "talk about the past." They are thus prior, certainly in a chronological sense and, I would argue, most likely in a developmental one as well. At some point, however, as Ramakrishna's ecstasies and visions were witnessed and interpreted by a community of disciples, Ramakrishna's Tantric secret undergoes a transformation: a series of mystico-erotic experiences become the grounds for Ramakrishna's incarnational status. Ramakrishna, through a complex social process of interpretation and appropriation, is declared to be an incarnation of God.

By the time we get to Saradananda's *Līlāprasaṅga* in 1911, the "secret talk" (*guhya kathā*) recorded so faithfully, if reluctantly, in Gupta's *Kathāmṛta* had become the "hidden meanings" (*gūḍha artha*) of the *Līlāprasaṅga*, Saradananda's term for those deepest levels of interpretation that are capable of uncovering Ramakrishna's status as an incarnation of God. Ramakrishna is now identified with the divine king "who comes in secret" and is recognized by only a select few. By now, the specifically Tantric dimensions of Ramakrishna's secret have been omitted or covered up and the incarnational aspects have been emphasized. The two primary meanings of the secret—Ramakrishna the Tāntrika and Ramakrishna the incarnation—have flip-flopped. Ramakrishna the incarnation is now primary and Ramakrishna the Tāntrika is secondary, if he is admitted at all.

The structures and styles of the *Kathāmṛta* and *Līlāprasaṅga* reflect this social process of interpretation and appropriation in that the secrets of the *Kathāmṛta*, like Ramakrishna's early ecstasies and visions, offer very little self-interpretation, whereas the "hidden meanings" of the *Līlāprasaṅga* are explicitly interpretive. In the *Kathāmṛta*, and even in the *Līlāprasaṅga*, Ramakrishna confesses numerous times that he does not know what his own secret visions mean. Saradananda, on the other hand, believes that he does and does not hesitate to tell us—Ramakrishna is God. It is almost as if the secrets of the *Kathāmṛta* constituted a troubling dream-vision that the *Līlāprasaṅga* sought to interpret and, by so doing, transform its strange contents into something that could be more easily appropriated by the social and cultural worlds. What was reported as a private mystico-erotic experience was thus transformed into a publically acknowledged theological state. Ramakrishna the secret Tāntrika became Ramakrishna the hidden incarnation.

These, then, are what one might call the eight dimensions and the two primary levels of Ramakrishna's secret. But I am uncomfortable with such lists and numbers. They may be helpful, but they also tend to render concrete and clear what is in fact extraordinarily slippery. Ramakrishna's secret, after all, was and still is a very complex phenomenon. It appears, it reveals itself. And again it disappears, it is concealed. It is generated in mystical states, formed by psychological processes, nurtured by ritual, shaped by mythological and symbolic tradition, and expressed in ways that define social relationships. It carries hints of the highest flights of human experience, as well as scars of childhood and adolescent traumata. It is interpreted and changed in the process. And it lives on, frustrating the researcher with empty book stalls, tight-lipped hosts, and manuscripts that are preserved but cannot be found. The secret thief's chamber of the saint's vision still hides its secrets. Its contents can be guessed at but never adequately analyzed.

SEXUALITY AND MYSTICISM: REALIZING THE EROTIC

MANY OF RAMAKRISHNA'S mystical experiences were induced within erotic contexts, imagined or real. I believe that I have established this beyond a reasonable doubt. One could certainly challenge this or that conclusion of mine advanced over the course of the last five chapters; certainly many of my conclusions are speculative and open to debate. I would be the first to admit that. But *taken together* I believe that their combined weight adds up to a convincing argument for the "secret" erotic nature of Ramakrishna's mystical experiences. Given this sexual nature of Ramakrishna's secret, what are we to make of its specifically religious or mystical dimensions? Was Ramakrishna's secret nothing more than the result of repressed libidinal energies, hopelessly distorted and displaced through years of absent and dying fathers, sexually aggressive mothers, and abusive bosses? Certainly such events deeply influenced the symbolic form of Ramakrishna's visions and the specific contexts in which he experienced ecstasy and trance, but they say little about the content or object of the Paramahaṁsa's mystical experiences. Ramakrishna himself did not believe that the specific path automatically defined the goal. In his own words, the house can be entered through a variety of entrances, even through the latrine. This is to say, not that the house can be reduced to nothing more than a frame for the latrine, but that the house exists in its own right and can be entered through numerous routes, *even* through experiences that might strike our socialized emotions as disgusting. As I have tried to show, in Tantra the mystical lies beyond the social and its categories of the pure and the good. It is embodied, not by a moral code or a social judgment, but by a naked goddess standing on an ithyphallic corpse. It is by nature a scandalous, "dirty" thing.

In a sense I have taken Ramakrishna's metaphor of the dirty latrine and extended it to justify my own approach to the house of mystical experience. Consequently, I have insisted both on the *radical* human context of Ramakrishna's mystical experiences and on the specifically religious nature of their content or object. My method follows from this basic dialectical conviction. But what have I accomplished with such a method? More specifically, what does it mean to say that Ramakrishna's mystical experiences were "erotic," that in the very midst of an ecstatic state, supposedly "without even the smell of lust," Ramakrishna's foot, quite independently of Ramakrishna himself, found its way into the genitals of another human being? Surely we must ask with M why Ramakrishna's hair stands on end when he thinks about little Naran (KA 3.263), or smile when Ramakrishna brags that "I've never slept with a woman, even in a dream (KA 4.240)—so infatuated with boys, we might ask, what need did he have of women? But putting aside such doubts and smiles, we are still left with a very serious question: How were Ramakrishna's homosexual desires related to his mysticism? That is, how did Ramakrishna's sexual experiences and his mystical states come together to produce what I have called the erotic?

The Erotic Shaping the Mystical: The Child, the Female Lover, the Handmaid, and the Mother

RAMAKRISHNA'S HOMOSEXUAL TENDENCIES certainly determined the specific manner in which he appropriated the symbols of his religious universe. Such a universe was dominated by the "states" of two major symbolic worlds: Tantra and the Bengali Vaiṣṇava tradition. Whereas the symbolism of Tantra focused on the Hero and the Child (and to a much lesser extent, on the Female Servant of the goddess), the Vaiṣṇava tradition focused primarily on the "sweet" or erotic mood of Rādhā and, to lesser degrees, on the friendly identity of Rādhā's Girlfriend and on the mother state of Yaśoda, Kṛṣṇa's mother. I have concentrated on Tantra with its child and hero states because I believe the conflicted manner in which Ramakrishna deals with them reveals more about his secret than the rather straightforward homoerotic imagery of the Vaiṣṇava tradition. Tantra, after all, insists that the male practitioner become a Hero in relationship to the goddess, and that he engage her in some sort of sexual "intercourse"; for a homoerotic saint like Ramakrishna, such a symbolic equation can lead to serious conflict and emotional pain. Granted, in the end Tantra allows the male practitioner to assume the allegedly sexless nature of the Child, or even the feminine role of the goddess's Female Servant, but the Hero remains as *the* Tantric ideal.[3] And even when the female servant and child states are granted, they are given to the saint in specifically sexual contexts: Ramakrishna assumes the female servant state to deal with the sexual advances of his temple boss, Mathur, and of his wife, Sharada, and discovers that, even when he is a Child, the goddess in numerous women insists on relating to him in provocatively sexual ways. The Vaiṣṇava tradition, on the other hand, encourages the male aspirant to take on different feminine identities in relationship to a male god, be they a Mother of a divine child, an attending Girlfriend, or a Lover of the blue god. Its symbolic world thus poses no problem for a homoerotic saint; indeed, it offers great promise.[4] It is no accident, then, that Ramakrishna rejected the Hero and opted instead to become a Child, the sexless being, a cross-dressed Handmaid,[5] a Mother doting on her children,or Rādhā, the longing woman: in all four states he could avoid, theoretically at least, any sexual contact with a woman. In the states of Rādhā, the Handmaid, and the Mother, moreover, he could actually engage other males in erotic and quasi-erotic relationships, and do this through symbolic roles that his culture not only considered legitimate but also deemed sacred. Ramakrishna's homosexual tendencies, in other words, deeply influenced, indeed determined, the manner in which he created his own self-defined "states" out of the symbols of his inherited religious traditions. His homosexual desires, if you will, created the symbolic contours and shape of his mysticism.

Cultural Ambivalence and Ramakrishna's Self-Understanding

Different members of the saint's culture evaluated these religious roles, and perhaps their implied homosexual messages, differently. Whereas some, mostly male renouncers, saw in Ramakrishna's child state a mark of enlightenment and an almost feminist attitude toward the other gender, a group of Tantric women saw in it only a sign of immaturity and a certain "shortcoming" or fault: he had failed to become a Hero. The saint's assumption of the Rādhā mood evoked an equally ambivalent response. Narendra, for example, found it particularly annoying, if not downright embarrassing, and often attacked the Vaiṣṇava practice of a man imitating the gestures and mannerisms of a woman as emasculating and ridiculous (LP 5.12.3.11).[6] Others, the lonely and elderly Gangamata, for example, saw in Ramakrishna's Rādhā state hints of divinity. The effeminate Handmaid was no less problematic. Mathur may have found it especially attractive, commenting on the loveliness of the "woman" he supposedly did not recognize as his own temple priest, but others bitterly criticized the saint for his cross-dressing habits. As for Ramakrishna the Mother, some again found the state edifying, others proclaimed it bizarre. *Strange* is a word that can be found in M's text whenever the mood is mentioned. Despite the fact that its religious traditions often encouraged and even idealized such actions and feelings, then, the culture remained ambivalent at best about its own homoerotic saint.

How did the saint personally experience all of this? How aware was he of the homoerotic roots of his mysticism? Was he as conflicted over his homosexual desires as his culture seems to have been? I have argued throughout the study that the saint was not fully aware of this part of his secret: he almost kills himself in an act of symbolic castration; he falls into prolonged unconscious states when he is "kidnapped" by the Rāvaṇa-like Mathur and when he is abandoned by Tota Puri; he goes into semiconscious states to extend his foot into the laps of boys; he is incapable of deciphering the homoerotic images that consistently appear in his visions and language; he cannot stop himself from ecstatically worshiping the penises of boys; and he suffers from various digestive and anal conditions that are symbolically linked to his sexual past. All of these things suggest to me that Ramakrishna was not fully aware of his own homosexual desires. In some sense, they were a "secret" even to him. I must immediately add, however, that it does seem that, as the saint progressed in age, he became more and more accepting and conscious of this aspect of his secret. He may have attempted suicide for his anxious desires at twenty, but he shows no signs of shame for trying to "enter" Narendra in his late forties. Perhaps, then, the problem of the saint's self-consciousness can be resolved by plotting the signs of shame and unconsciousness in his early years and the marks of acceptance, awareness, and integration in his later, more mature years. Certainly such a development would fit well into the biographical pattern I have sketched here, with Ramakrishna's early anxiety and shame transformed through what I have called the Change and the saint's consequent descent into the forms of man. From this perspective, Ramakrishna's resolution of his psychosexual crisis would coincide with the full realization of his own "descending" divinity and the public's acknowledgment of his unusually powerful charisma.

Despite the misgivings of his own culture, then, Ramakrishna eventually learned to accept his homosexual desires as an important aspect of his descending energies. In his relationships with his boy disciples, the saint found joy, pleasure, and religious insight. Mythologically speaking, it was these homoerotic relationships that brought about the descent of God. The same, however, cannot be said for the "traumatic" experiences that defined his relationships to such people as Mathur, Tota Puri, and the Bhairavī. Days of unconsciousness at Mathur's residence, a six-month catatonic state related to Tota's departure, and the terror Ramakrishna attached to his experiences with the Bhairavī can hardly be considered normal. From Ramakrishna's perspective, at least, something was clearly going wrong.

On the Sanity of Madness

IN SHORT, THERE SEEMS TO BE little question about whether some of Ramakrishna's behavior and states were at times pathological, or in the terms of his own culture, mad (*unmāda*). The meaning of this madness and its relationship to Ramakrishna's mysticism, his homosexual tendencies, and the abusive dimensions of his past, however, are far from clear. We are simply not yet in a position to pass any definitive conclusions.

I think we can, however, make at least one observation that will stand up to any future discoveries: if Ramakrishna was mad, he was mad in a particularly healing way. Such a blend of madness and healing sanctity is by no means uncommon in Hinduism,[7] in Bengali religion,[8] or for that matter in the history of religions in general. Much like the shaman figure of so many primal cultures, the saint seems to have worked through his early initiatory psychosomatic illnesses and resolved his emotional, religious, and symbolic crises in a fashion that the culture found both convincing and meaningful. He thus resolved in a dramatic and magnified fashion the crises and conflicts that lay at the center of his culture's symbolic world. Because of this, he became a "wounded healer," capable of leading others, who no doubt shared many of the same crises and problems, to similar, if less pronounced, realizations and resolutions: "And he is hailed as Master and Teacher by all, because he interprets their own lives, and speaks the words that already they were struggling to express."[9] So great was his culture's gratitude and admiration that it bestowed on him its highest honor. In mythological language, he was declared to be an "incarnation," a god come down to earth to save Hindu society from its nineteenth-century spin into cultural chaos. If Ramakrishna was mad, then, his was a madness that his contemporaries often found to be strangely healing, emotionally beautiful, and religiously powerful. In the terms of the culture, it was a "divine madness" (*divyonmāda*).

The Erotic as the Mystical: The Dialectics of the Personal Symbol

BUT CLEARLY, however one chooses to evaluate the nature of Ramakrishna's ecstasies and sexual tendencies, it was not simply a matter of Ramakrishna's homosexual desires informing the symbolic shape of his mysticism, for the homoerotic energies themselves, freed from the usual socialized routes by the "shameful" nature of their unacceptable objects, were able to transform themselves, almost alchemically, until their dark natures began to glitter with the gold of the mystical. The same cultural world that had once given Ramakrishna shame now declared him a god. These homoerotic energies, in other words, not only shaped the symbolism of Ramakrishna's mysticism; they *were* his mysticism. Let me be very clear: without the conflicted energies of the saint's homosexual desires, there would have been no Kālī's sword, no unconscious Handmaid, no conflict between the Mother and the Lover, no Child, no Rādhā, no living *liṅgam,* no naked paramahaṁsa boys, no Jesus state, no love-body, no sex with the Self, no Change and descent into the forms of man, no ecstatically extended feet, no closing and opening doors, no symbolic visions, no *bhāva,* and no *samādhi.* In effect, there would have been no "Ramakrishna."

The erotic, then, *was* Ramakrishna. It defined the shape of his symbolic identities, lit up his shining visions, informed his Tantric teachings, and excited his famous ecstasies. The very pores of his body shook with its pleasure and power. The erotic, moreover, constituted both the central problem of the saint's life and its own eventual answer. It almost destroyed the man, and it eventually deified him. But how was all of this accomplished? What, if anything, can we say about this process of transformation? To get at this central question, I want to adopt the dialectical hermeneutics of Gananath Obeyesekere, who in his book, *The Work of Culture,* picks up the path Ricoeur traced in his *Freud and Philosophy*[10] and attempts a synthesis of Freud's psychoanalytic program and more recent work in anthropology and the history of religions. Obeyesekere sums up Ricoeur's thesis well:

> Freudianism, Ricoeur argues, essentially deals with the archaic substrate of a symbolic form in a regressive movement. Yet implicit in Freud's theory of sublimation is the *progressive* transformation of infantile and archaic motivations into art, religion, and public culture. Progression and regression are dialectical movements that may be found in such elemental

> expressions as dreams and fantasy, and in more complex ways in numinous religious symbols. . . . *A progressive movement of unconscious thoughts involves the transformation of the archaic motivations of childhood into symbols that look forward to the resolution of conflict and beyond that into the nature of the sacred or numinous.* This double movement of symbols permits the theoretical reconciliation of the Freudian hermeneutics as illusion which has to be deciphered in terms of archaic motivations, with the phenomenology of religion of Leenhardt, Eliade, and others, for whom the symbol must be deciphered as a "revelation of the sacred."[11]

Building on this program, Obeyesekere writes of what he calls "personal symbols," which we have seen him define as "cultural symbols that are related to individual motivation and make sense only in relation to the life history of the individual."[12] Such symbols carry general meanings for the culture at large but can only be properly deciphered by interpreting them in the light of biographical patterns and the intimate details of the individual's psychic life. When we look at these at once public and private symbols, sometimes we find only "symptoms," one-way signs that suggest a neurosis fixated on an unresolved crisis. But sometimes, in exceptional cases, we find genuine two-way "symbols" that function *both* as symptoms, harkening back to the original crisis, *and* as numinous symbols, pointing to a resolution of the crisis, greater meaning, and what Obeyesekere calls "a radical transformation of one's being."[13] Obeyesekere identifies Ramakrishna as one of those "exceptional cases" in which the symptom became a symbol and turned a crisis into an experience of the sacred: "Ramakrishna's Hinduism permits the progressive development of the personal symbol. . . . To Ramakrishna his own mother is mother Kali who is *the* Mother and the guiding principle of cosmic creativity. Through Kali, Ramakrishna has achieved trance and knowledge of a radically different order from the others, and he can progress to the heart of a specifically Hindu reality that is essentially salvific."[14] What Ramakrishna achieved (and did *not* achieve) "through Kali" is precisely what this present study has been all about. Through the black goddess and her mystico-erotic *śakti,* the saint worked through his originally "shameful" homosexual desires (chapter 1), defined his relationship to women and the world (chapter 2), rediscovered his originally suspect desires in a world of delight (chapter 3), created an intimate family of disciples, and eventually became a god (chapter 4). Such accomplishments did much more than simply legitimate a socially suspect homosexual tendency—they *transformed* the attraction itself, gave it a specifically sacred dimension, and so allowed it to burst forth into rapture, vision, and song: "A progressive movement of unconscious thoughts involves the transformation of the archaic motivations of childhood into symbols that look forward to the resolution of conflict and beyond that into the nature of the sacred or numinous."[15] In effect, Ramakrishna took the "anxious energies" of his early sexual crisis, a crisis for which he almost killed himself, and "turned them around the corner," where they revealed their essentially mystical natures. In Obeyesekere's terms, he took what were regressive symptoms and, through Kālī and her Tantric world, converted them into progressive symbols, into genuine experiences of a sacred, mystical realm.

The change was a radical one. Having once attempted to castrate himself symbolically with Kālī's sword for feeling "a strange sensation," he now compares his love for his male disciples to a mystical phallus. With a stray glance or a mere brush of bodies, Ramakrishna now finds himself "dissolved in the Undivided," uniting with his beloved Narendra in the thousand-petaled lotus floating in Ramakrishna's own subtle body, interestingly enough, in the head. Ramakrishna is now an *ūrdhvaretā,* one whose erotic energies have "turned up" away from the genitals and into the head.[16] He has become, as he claimed, a mystical phallus aroused into ecstasy "by the slightest things" (KA 2.49).[17] The lopped off, castrated head swinging in Kālī's hand has become Śiva's phallus, bold and sure in its erection, "thrust straight up from the underworld," till, as a phallic stem, it unites with its vagina-like lotus in the very same head Ramakrishna once threatened to cut off.

Here, then, is where I would locate the meaning of Ramakrishna's *eros—both* in his obvious infatuation with his boy disciples, an infatuation somehow connected with the archaic "regressive" motivations of his own personal history that struggled for legitimacy in a culture that considered them shameful, *and* in a "progressive," essentially mystical, order of rapture and vision, the realm of the sacred and the numinous. By a deft use of religious symbolism, Ramakrishna was able to use his homosexual desires as the driving, shaping force of his mystical life: what was once a crisis became the secret, not only of his mystical and charismatic success, but of his very divinity. Kālī's iconographic form was the primary symbolic focus of this transformation, of this dialectical movement back and forth between the regressive and the progressive. Her sword, her motherly and sexual features, her upside-down erotic posture, her gracious yet shocking feet, her lolling tongue—empowered with all their historical associations, seeming contradictions, and poetic ambiguities—would turn a lonely young man despairing of his life into a charismatic religious leader surrounded by some of Calcutta's most talented men, young and old.

The Erotic into the Mystical: Sublimation or Realization?

BUT AGAIN, even given this dialectical nature of Ramakrishna's personal symbols, *how* was this change affected? How do we get from the sexual to the mystical, from the shame of a despairing young man to the divine confidence of a virtual god? *Sublimation* is much too weak a word for what has happened. "Libidinal energies" have not been "sublimated" in a transformation that never quite escapes its materialistic origins; rather, a mystico-erotic energy called *śakti* has been "awakened," revealing to Ramakrishna that "She herself has become everything." The body and the entire physical world are now experienced for *what they have been all along,* the body of the goddess, physically, literally divine. Such an experience is more a "re-cognition" or a "realization" than a "making sublime," for the erotic in the life of Ramakrishna is not so much a product of some psychological or biological process as it is a realization of an ever-present, if usually unconscious, reality.

Such an observation admittedly refuses to answer the question of dynamics—be they socially, psychologically, or biologically defined—and instead turns to the specifically religious, even ontological, dimensions of the saint's world as the true locus of meaning. I make no apologies here. I have not attempted a study of the problem of sublimation. I have, however, offered an "ontological critique" of the traditional model and its answers, insisting that such answers are woefully inadequate as long as they assume a materialistic understanding of sexual energies that in effect reduces the mystical, in the words of Jacques Lacan, "to questions of fucking."[18] In short, I have posed the question of "sublimation" and criticized some of the traditional answers but have not answered the question myself. Certainly it is one aspect of Ramakrishna's secret that I have failed to reveal.

But perhaps I have failed to reveal this aspect of the secret simply because it fell outside the purview of my own particular questions and the methodological "paths" they sent me down. Here again my own methods seem much closer to those of Kakar's "mystics of psychoanalysis" than to the more traditional, and more reductionistic, methods of the classical theorists. Consider, for example, the speculations of one such mystic of psychoanalysis, Jacques Lacan. Commenting on the bridal mysticism of Saint Teresa of Avila and her famous mystico-erotic "transverberation,"[19] in which she moaned in intense pleasure and pain as a fiery seraph plunged a flame-tipped arrow deep within her again and again, Lacan writes: "You only have to go and look at Bernini's statue in Rome [his 'Teresa in Ecstasy'] to understand immediately that she's coming, there is no doubt about it." "And what is her *jouissance*, her *coming* from?" Lacan asks.[20] This, it seems to me, is as important a question as any, and I doubt very much that questions of pathology or the dynamics of psycho-social processes, however crucial such issues might be, have anything to do with its answer. It is simply a different type of question. Lacan was clear enough about his own answer to where Teresa was "coming from." He rejected the notion that the mystical can be reduced to sexuality and instead speculated that such ecstatic experiences of "a *jouissance* which goes beyond" issue forth from our own ontological ground: "Might not this *jouissance* which one experiences and knows nothing of, be that which puts us on the path of ex-istence?"[21]

And how should we answer the question? Ramakrishna in *samādhi*, not unlike Bernini's "Teresa in Ecstasy," is obviously "coming." But "what is his *jouissance*, his *coming* from?" From the fury of his own repressed "libidinal energies"? Or from the ontological ground of existence itself? To put it a bit differently, was Ramakrishna "sublimating" sexual energies into admittedly powerful but nevertheless perfectly "natural" states? Or was he "realizing" the erotic divinity in his own cosmic body? What *are* we to make of this man established in *samādhi*, his hair standing on end, his eyes squinting in pleasure, his foot in the lap of a boy? Everything depends upon our ontological understanding of human sexuality. Everything depends upon where we think he is "coming from." For my part, I have respected the religious world of Tantra and have chosen to interpret Ramakrishna's mystico-erotic experiences within that universe. I would argue, then, that the saint's experiences were "coming from" the ontological ground of his Tantric world, and that this "coming" was as much a realization of a divine *eros* as it was a sublimation of sexual energies. I would insist, moreover, that such a realization be understood on its own terms, as a genuine religious experience, and neither be reduced to the mechanics of our own making nor be effaced by a condemnation dictated by our own morals. In short, I think Lacan had the right question *and* the right answer.

Oddly enough, Ramakrishna himself rejected his own Tantric world and questioned its most basic dictum—that human sexuality and mystical experience are intimately related, if not identical, on some deep energetic level. He thus lacked the hermeneutical key with which to interpret his oddly placed foot, his disconcerting attraction for boys, and the contents of his strange dream-like visions. Unable to interpret them for himself, Ramakrishna asked others to explain his visions and "strange sensations" for him. His disciples did their best, and I have done mine with the interpretive techniques of Tantra and psychoanalysis. I have not argued that these two perspectives are identical. Clearly, tensions have emerged, and real differences. However sophisticated Tāntrikas might be in their ontological understandings of human sexuality, I think it is clear now that they are not always conscious of the latent meanings of their own symbols and rituals, at least in the same way that a psychoanalytically trained observer might be. After all, it is one thing to note the sexual symbolism of a flower, to compose texts filled with hidden (and not so hidden) sexual images and expressions, and to engage in rituals designed to capitalize on the energetic identity of sexual and mystical forces. It is quite another to analyze castration themes in Tantric iconography, to point out the oedipal and incestuous elements of Tantric ritual, to demonstrate the manner in which Hindu culture "splits" the male experience of woman into a pure Mother and a sexy Lover, or to suggest that a person's experience of Tantric ritual and symbolism is always shaped by the particularities of his or her sexual history. Tantra and psychoanalysis, then, might share common characteristics, but they nevertheless remain distinct in the levels and nature of their understandings. The Ramakrishna that I have uncovered in this study powerfully demonstrates this basic distinction between the two worldviews, for this greatest of the Tantric mystics, with all his visions and ecstatic states, nevertheless remained quite unaware of the latent or "hidden" themes that structured much of his own experience.

But still, after all this, perhaps I have left myself too open to the Baul charge of only having "rubbed my touchstone" against the lotus: "Who is this man, a dealer and expert in gold, who has entered the flowered garden? He rubs his touchstone against the lotus. Oh, the fun! Oh, the fun!"[22] Perhaps I have attempted to understand what were exquisite and delicate experiences, feminine flowers, with clumsy categories and unfeeling tools, hard masculine reasons. No doubt, Ramakrishna, who uttered half the *Kathāmṛta* "with a smile," would laugh at me and my touchstone. But I have tried anyway, knowing that when all is said and done, Ramakrishna's secret must remain a secret, his to experience, ours to ponder and to interpret from afar.

APPENDIX: SOME HISTORICAL AND TEXTUAL ASPECTS OF RAMAKRISHNA'S "SECRET TALK"

THE PRESENT STUDY has attempted to uncover and interpret the secret Tantric connection between the mystical and the erotic in the life and teachings of Ramakrishna. Since my general thesis that this secret has been passed down to us through a complicated social process of revealing and concealing was originally generated through a textual analysis of M's *Kathāmṛta,* it is essential that I state clearly my understanding of the history of this text and my theory regarding its structure, especially as it relates to the saint's *guhya kathā* or "secret talk."

ORIGIN OF THE TERM "SECRET TALK"

WE HAVE ALREADY SEEN that it was Ram Chandra Datta who first used the expression "secret talk" in print to express a certain quality or characteristic of the saint's life and teachings. "We have revealed many secret things [*guhya kathā*]," he wrote in 1890 in the introduction to his biography of the saint (JV [5], 3). It is quite possible that M got the expression from Datta, as Datta's biography appeared a full fourteen years before M uses the same expression for the first time in the second volume of his *Kathāmṛta* (1904). I think it is just as likely, though, that both Datta and M had no trouble remembering Ramakrishna's own use of the term and incorporated it directly into their writings independently of one another. The nature and content of Ramakrishna's secret talk were not characteristics of the saint's discourse that two such careful observers could easily overlook. The dramatic manner in which the saint often announced his secret talk, moreover, no doubt also added a certain weight to it, as if to hint to his recording disciples that *here* was something they should write down. The origin of the term, then, most likely stems back to Ramakrishna himself.

THE TEXT'S PREHISTORY AND EVOLUTION: AN IMAGINAL CREATION

ALTHOUGH I HAVE analyzed many of the "secret things" contained in Datta's biography, the focus has remained on the "secret talk" of M's *Kathāmṛta* and its cycles of occultation and revelation. But M's *Kathāmṛta* was by no means the first attempt to record the sayings and teachings of Ramakrishna. In actual fact, it was quite late. The history of recording Ramakrishna's personality, sayings, and teachings begins with a series of articles and collections of *ukti* or "sayings" that began to appear in Calcutta's English and Bengali newspapers in the 1870s. These early collections contain no "secret talk" but restrict themselves to metaphysical expositions, edifying tales, and folksy moral precepts. They are more impersonal, disembodied reflections of nineteenth-century Bengali religious discourse than graphic crystallizations of a mystic's soul and its inner life.

But with the appearance of M's first volume of the *Kathāmṛta* in 1902, we are on different ground, moving in a different world. The skeleton-like *ukti* have been embellished, artfully embedded in dramatic scenes enacted on the reader's mental stage. M supplies dates, the stage, the cast, and, at times, what he considers to be the plot. We are told who smiles, who frowns, who laughs, and when. Ramakrishna's admirers are present, but so are his detractors.

The text's evolution helps to explain its intimate character. On April 23, 1886, toward the end of Ramakrishna's life, Girish Ghosh, a well-known playwright, pressed M to show him the diaries in which M had been faithfully recording conversations Ramakrishna had had with his disciples and visitors for the last four years. M refused (KA 2.242). Those diaries, from which M was to write his *Kathāmṛta,* are still intact and, unfortunately, still off limits to questioning minds, be they of pious playwrights or curious scholars, hence what I can say about them is both limited and tentative. I am aware of only one living person who has had the opportunity to study them in detail, Swami Prabhananda of the Ramakrishna Order. What follows is based on a few photographs that he was kind enough to show me.

The diaries consist of approximately 850 small (4″ × 6″) pages, loosely bound by M himself into four "books," each of which is paginated both separately and serially (for example, page 96 of book four may be page 762 of the collection). The text itself consists of cryptic jottings in Bengali and English, using initials (e.g., "P" for *Paramahaṁsa*) to facilitate writing. Huge inner margins reduce the already small text to even smaller proportions. One thing is immediately clear from even a brief encounter with the diaries—the *Kathāmṛta* is not a verbatim recording of Ramakrishna's conversations, as is often implied or claimed. Rather, the *Kathāmṛta* is a spiritual or imaginal creation lovingly "meditated" into existence from the briefest jottings over a period of some fifty years (1882–1932). M himself is very clear: "I would carry the nectar-like words of Thakur in my memory and would record them briefly in the diary on returning home. The book written out from these notes appeared much later. On every scene I had meditated a thousand times. I would recreate, relive those moments by his grace. When I did not feel satisfied with my descriptions I would plunge myself into meditation on Thakur. Then the correct image would rise before my mind's eye in a bright, real living form."[1]

Perhaps, then, the best metaphor to describe the *Kathāmṛta*'s evolution is not the tape-recorded interview, which after all is a bit anachronistic, but the historical play. Given this genre's popularity in nineteenth-century Calcutta, Ramakrishna's enthusiasm for the theater, and the presence of a famous playwright (Girish Ghosh) among the disciples, the metaphor seems an apt one. Other factors, both historical and literary, add yet more weight to the theater metaphor. Girish's Star Theatre and his plays make numerous appearances in M's volumes, adding prestige and a certain theatrical air to the text. This same Star Theatre, moreover, would become the place of one of the earliest public proclamations of Ramakrishna's divinity, that of Ram Chandra Datta in 1892.[2] Finally, even the text's appearance (with speakers, dates, stage descriptions, and moods all described) suggests a play script.

But the biographical and theological justifications for a theatrical model are even stronger. Ramakrishna, drawing on a long and complex Vaiṣṇava tradition of religious "play-acting,"[3] often would admit that he saw no difference between the true and the imitation.[4] For him at least, artistic creation and reality were interchangeable. Just as an actor after acting a woman's part for some time takes on the gestures and moods of a woman, so too, if one thinks of God long enough, one obtains God's very "being" (*sattā*) (KA 5.118). Acting and imitation, in other words, can lead to reality. And reality is really just an act, a huge play in which God acts all the parts.[5] It is also clear that, much like an actor editing his own recorded performance, Ramakrishna knew that M was recording his teachings and actions and often stopped to correct M's record or emphasize some important point.[6] M's text, then, can be read as a play that was written to capture its audience with a vision of a man whose acts revealed reality and whose reality was expressed through acts.

The Cycles and Their Secrets

But if the *Kathāmṛta* is a play, its five volumes or "acts" are arranged in a most curious manner. As I have pointed out already, M's five volumes defy any linear chronological sequence, that is, they overlap one another in cycles, each volume beginning anew with 1882, the year M first met Ramakrishna, and ending in 1886, the year of Ramakrishna's death.[7] No one has been able to offer any good reason why M arranged them in such a way. R. K. Das Gupta raises the issue in 1986 and offers his explanation: "Why Mahendranath covers all the years between 1882 and 1886 in all the five volumes and why he did not arrange the conversations in a chronological order from February 1882 to April 1886 it is difficult to say. . . . Perhaps he perceived some progression in the circle, some blooming of a consciousness in the disciples. . . . and above all some significant changes in the temper of the Master himself and wanted to show that progression in each volume to make it viable as a divine story."[8] Das Gupta, apparently not impressed by this progressive circle, goes on to suggest that no harm would be done if the dates were rearranged chronologically, something the Mission's publishing wing, Udbodhan, had done already in its one-volume 1986 edition when Das Gupta published his article that same year. As should be apparent by now, I do not share Das Gupta's indifference to the text's ordering. As helpful and handy as the one-volume Udbodhan edition may be, it is not the original*Kathāmṛta*—M's structuring of the text has been seriously violated. To transform M's five-act cyclical play into a one-act linear drama is an understandable and perhaps even legitimate move for a publishing house interested in disseminating Ramakrishna's religious message, but it is an unforgivable sin for the scholar interested in textual analysis. How could such an obvious and seemingly illogical characteristic of the text be without significance? As we have seen, it is in fact very significant.

Volume 1 appeared in 1902 and volume 2 in 1904. Three years later, in 1907, M published his own reworking of these first two volumes in an English version, *The Gospel of Sri Ramakrishna*.[9] It was this material, no doubt, that M felt was most accessible and acceptable to his audience, be they Bengali or Western. *There is not a single occurrence of the term "secret talk" anywhere in volume 1 or in the 1907 English edition and only one occurrence in a section heading in volume 2.* This silence is broken, however, in 1908 with the appearance of volume 3, which contains six, relatively innocuous, occurrences of the term. Just two years later, in 1910, volume 4 appeared with eight, more than any other volume. Volume 4 was to be the last published during M's life. Volume 5 did not appear until twenty-two years later in 1932, shortly after M's death. It contains three occurrences of the term. By this time, M was running out of material, a fact evident by the shortened nature of the scenes (many only a few pages long) and the brevity of the volume (running to only 153 pages, half the length of volume 4).

There is, indeed, then, "some progression in the circle,"[10] as Das Gupta sensed, but not the sort of progression Das Gupta had in mind. That which progresses through the five volumes is not "the temper of the Master" nor "a blooming of consciousness in the disciples" but rather M's audacity in revealing those secret dimensions of Ramakrishna that he had held back in the earlier volumes. Consequently, what we see is an initial concealing of the secret (volumes 1 and 2), a few hints (volume 3), a full-blown confession (volume 4), and an anticlimactic supplementary volume (volume 5). The "secret" of M's play, it seems, is to be found in act 4.

I have gone back and checked most of the occurrences of Ramakrishna's secret talk that occur in volume 4 with a first edition of the same volume. The Udbodhan edition mentioned above shows no tampering with the content of the text, although, as we have seen, it does violate the original form: the secret is intact, but it is now scattered through some twelve-hundred pages of text instead of being more or less concentrated in the last hundred pages of volume 4. Nikhilananda's 1942 English edition, however, is another story. Nikhilananda has violated both the form and the content of M's *Kathāmṛta,* arranging the scenes in a linear sequence (forty-four years before the Udbodhan edition) and ingeniously mistranslating (or omitting) almost every single secret. I find it remarkable that what M insisted on publishing in 1910, Nikhilananda refused to publish in 1942. Keeping in mind M's own act of concealment in his 1907 English edition, however, it appears that it was the intended audience as much as the year that determined how much of the secret was to be revealed. "English-speaking readers," it was felt, simply could not handle Tantra, while the Bengalis could. Calcutta beat out New York.

Summing up, we might say that the *Kathāmṛta's* general history can be understood as a relative silence followed by a gradual revealing and then concealing of a secret. The text's prehistory is characterized by numerous collections of sayings, most of which concentrate on moral precepts, doctrinal issues, and Ramakrishna's famous universalism. With the exception of Datta's *Jīvanavṛttānta,* the *Kathāmṛta's* prehistory can be characterized as one of impersonal discourse and a certain silence in regard to Ramakrishna's more intimate dimensions. Disembodied "sayings" (*ukti*) rather than deeply personal "visions" (*darśana*) or intimate "conversations" (*kathā*) dominate the texts. With the appearance of the *Kathāmṛta* in the early years of the twentieth century, however, this silence is broken as M gradually, and perhaps reluctantly, reveals aspects of Ramakrishna's secret to his Bengali readers. But once haltingly revealed, Ramakrishna's secret was again soon concealed, this time in Nikhilananda's English translation of 1942, *The Gospel of Sri Ramakrishna.*

DEFINING THE "SECRET TALK" PASSAGES

THERE IS A PROBLEM with listing all the occurrences of Ramakrishna's secret talk. It involves an issue of classification: precisely what passages are we to classify as secret talk? Only those passages in which the term *guhya kathā* occurs? If so, do we want to make a distinction between those passages in which Ramakrishna is recorded as using the term and those passages in which M uses the term? Or shall we broaden the category a bit and also list all of those passages in which Ramakrishna relates something to his disciples in secret but does not use the term *guhya kathā?* Or what about those passages in which the expression "secret talk" is not used but M uncovers a "secret meaning"[11] or a "secret interpretation"[12] in Ramakrishna's discourse? Or what about those passages that do not use the adjective "secret" but are clearly related to Ramakrishna's secret,[13] or are even alternate descriptions of events that are elsewhere described within the saint's secret talk?[14]

For the sake of clarity and conciseness, I have categorized as secret talk only those passages in which the term *guhya kathā* occurs. I have made no distinction between M's use of the term and Ramakrishna's in my counting of the eighteen occurrences. I adopt such a definition of Ramakrishna's secret talk for the sake of theoretical precision. I should immediately add, however, that including "secret meanings" and "secret interpretations," or even passages that clearly imply a secret but do not use the term, would not substantially change my basic argument. The pattern of relatively silent early volumes and explicitly revealing later volumes would hold, regardless of how loosely or tightly we define the saint's secret talk. Here, then, are the eighteen occurrences of the term "secret talk" as they appear by volume:

Volume 2 (1904): There is not a single occurrence of Ramakrishna's secret talk anywhere in volume 1 (1902). The first occurrence of the term occurs very late in volume 2 (KA 2.205), and then only in a section heading. It is M's expression. The subsection that follows records a conversation between Ramakrishna and M on the possible incarnational status of Ramakrishna, his relationship to Caitanya (a previous incarnation), and the Tantric category of *śakti.* From the very beginning, then, the secret involves at least two elements: Ramakrishna the incarnation and the role of Tantra in such an incarnation.

Volume 3 (1908): Unlike volumes 1 and 2, there are numerous secrets in volume 3, most of them dealing with Ramakrishna's status as an incarnation of God. There are, however, Tantric secrets here as well. The six secrets of volume three include: the love-body passage (KA 3.20–22); the thief's door vision (KA 3.33); a vision of Saccidānanda declaring from within Ramakrishna's body that it incarnates from age to age (KA 3.121); a section identifying Jesus, Caitanya, and Ramakrishna as "one person" (KA 3.210–212); a lengthy passage describing Ramakrishna's visions of the man of sin and the bearded Muslim (KA 3.140–142); and a passage on the hidden comings and goings of the incarnation (KA 3.251).

Volume 4 (1910): Four out of the seven secrets of the first two volumes concern Ramakrishna's incarnational status. In volume 4, the passages begin to emphasize the Tantric aspects of the secret. The eight occurrences include: a philosophical exposition on the mystical nature of *brahman* and the dialectic of the eternal and the play (*nitya-līlā*) in the incarnation (KA 4.44); a long passage describing, among other things, the cosmic love-making of Śiva and Śakti (KA 4.56–57); a discussion of the role of *śakti* in the incarnation's descent (KA 4.101); a vision of Śiva (KA 4.220);[15] a description of the Change that occurred after he dislocated his hand (KA 4.227); a long section on the Tantric experiences of the saint, including secret descriptions of how Kṛṣṇa worshiped Rādhā's "cosmic vagina" (*brahmayoni*) and Ramakrishna's inability to stop himself from worshiping the penises of boys (KA 4.232); the cunnilingus vision (KA 4.238); and the fog of bliss vision (KA 4.259).

Note carefully that the page numbers of these last five secrets all occur in the last one hundred pages of volume 4. If we add to those listed above passages not technically listed as "secret talk" but nevertheless obviously related to Ramakrishna's secret, these last one hundred pages become even more significant. Within them, for example, we encounter: an ecstatic (and laughing) Ramakrishna fondling the penis of a naked visionary paramahaṁsa boy (KA 4.231); Ramakrishna's confessed desire to kiss and embrace the boy Purna (KA 4.271); a description of how Ramakrishna dislocated his left hand while he was trying to erotically engage the divine Jagannath on his way to defecate (KA 4.227); theological reflections on the nature of the incarnation and his *liṅgam*-like love for his disciples (KA 4.193); a scene in which Ramakrishna cannot defecate because he falls into *samādhi* watching Mishra take off his Western pants to reveal an ochre loincloth underneath (KA 4.277); and a self-description of how the saint's ecstatic states used to possess him like ghosts until he finally could expel them out through his bowels (KA 4.232). Clearly it is here, toward the very end of volume 4, that M spilled the secrets of his diaries. I suspect that in 1910, when he published these particular secrets, M believed that this fourth volume would be his last.

Volume 5 (1932): Volume 5 adds little to the amazing list of volume 4. Ramakrishna describes how he circumambulated the "seat of bliss" (a woman's lap) to conquer lust (KA 5.25), gives M some general instructions on the renunciation of lover-and-gold, and explains the details of some mystical techniques, which M unfortunately refuses to share with us (KA 5.96), and returns again to "the mystery of the divine incarnation" and his own experience of the Change (KA 5.122), but not much more.[16] By this time, M had told all he was going to tell.

Concluding Comments: Continuing the Search

We have seen throughout the eighteen passages, and indeed throughout this study, that Ramakrishna's secret possessed two major elements: Ramakrishna the Tāntrika and Ramakrishna the incarnation. We have seen both dimensions embodied in Ramakrishna's foot, that sexually charged organ that became the focus of the earliest speculations on Ramakrishna's divine nature. We also saw this dual secret in the vision of Jagannath, that erotic experience of God in which Ramakrishna dislocated his hand. It was because of this experience, the saint tells us, that he learned to love God "in the forms of man," that is, in the forms of his boy disciples, many of whom would later declare their Master to be the new incarnation of the age. An aborted Tantric experience, a Change, and a declared descent—they were all related.

I have concentrated primarily on the Tantric aspect of the secret because I believe it was more important in forming how Ramakrishna felt about himself and his world. This does not mean, however, that I think the incarnational aspect is not important. If we were to continue to follow Ramakrishna's secret, we would see this incarnational aspect greatly emphasized and its Tantric elements deemphasized or simply denied. Certainly Saradananda's *Līlāprasaṅga* and its "hidden meanings" have inherited the dual secret, but they have also changed it into a more respectable, socially acceptable truth. That which is "hidden" in Saradananda's text has little to do with ithyphallic boys or vagina-shaped lotuses, for now the secret is a theological secret: Ramakrishna was God, that king of the world who came "in secret" (*guptabhāve*). If we were to pursue our secrets further, it would be here, in the secret king and the mythology of the incarnation.

NOTES

Introduction

1. "Paramahaṁsa" or "supreme swan" is a title commonly given to a Vedantic sage and carries numerous symbolic meanings. Such a sage, for example, is said to be able to discriminate between the reality of *brahman* and the illusion of the world, just as the mythical swan (*haṁsa*) is said to be able to separate milk from water with its tongue.

2. Meaning vol. 5, p. 105.

3. The title is a long compound that can be broken down as follows: *Śrī-śrī-rāmakṛṣṇa-kathā-amṛta* or "The Nectar [*amṛta*] of the (Twice-)Blessed [*śrīśrī*] Ramakrishna's Talk [*kathā*]." I am using the Kathamrita Bhaban five-volume set: Mahendranath Gupta, *Śrīśrīrāmakṛṣṇakathāmṛta,* 31st ed. (Calcutta: Kathamrita Bhaban, 1987).

4. Except volume 4. It begins in 1883.

5. See the appendix for an extended discussion of these cycles and their relationship to the secret.

6. And even in volumes 4 and 5, M did not always reveal the contents of Ramakrishna's secret talk. Consider, for example, KA 4.232: "I performed many Tantric rituals under the bel tree. I sat on a seat of skulls and again on a seat of ———." What M held back is impossible to say, as the diaries from which he edited the *Kathāmṛta* are off-limits to scholars.

7. I am aware of only one other full English translation of the *Kathāmṛta,* Malcolm D. McLean's "A Translation of the *Śrī-Śrī-Rāmakṛṣṇa-Kathāmṛta* with Explanatory Notes and Critical Introduction" (Ph.D. diss., Otago University, 1983).

8. Timothy Jensen makes some insightful comments on Ramakrishna's split vocation in his "Madness, Yearning, and Play: The Life of Śrī Rāmakṛṣṇa" (Ph.D. diss., University of Chicago, 1976).

9. The title, a long compound, can be broken down as follows: *Śrī-śrī-rāmakṛṣṇa-līlā-prasaṅga* or "On the [*prasaṅga*] Divine Play [*līlā*] of the (Twice-) Blessed Ramakrishna." I will reference it as LP, followed by the part, chapter, and paragraph numbers. When the English translation (GM) paragraph numbers diverge from the Bengali text, I will note the English reference in parentheses.

10. Quoted in Narasingha P. Sil, "Vivekānanda's Rāmakṛṣṇa: An Untold

Story of Mythmaking and Propaganda," *Numen* 40 (1993): 50; italics in original.

11. KA 1.136; 1.187; 3.130; 4.28; 4.61.

12. There was also a third group, the *rasaddāra* or "suppliers" (KA 4.283), who provided Ramakrishna with his material needs.

13. KA 3.125; 4.164; 4.202 et al.

14. Note that Ramakrishna is not sure: he "thinks" he saw M in the visionary crowd.

15. See also KA 3.104; 3.280; 4.239; 4.283.

16. Dharm Pal Gupta, *Life of M. and Sri Sri Ramakrishna Kathamrita* (Chandigarh: Sri Ma Trust, 1988), 288; see also pp. 308–311 for an insightful refutation of this view.

17. Graveyards are considered auspicious in Tantric practice (LP 2.4.16).

18. For a discussion of the Dakshineshwar image and temple grounds, see Elizabeth U. Harding, *Kali: The Black Goddess of Dakshineswar* (York Beach, Maine: Nicolas-Hayes, 1993).

19. Steven T. Katz, "Language, Epistemology, and Mysticism" in Katz, ed., *Mysticism and Philosophical Analysis* (London: Oxford University Press, 1978), 26.

20. Ibid., 62–63.

21. Frederick Streng, "Mystical Awareness and Language" in *Philosophical Analysis,* 166.

22. Edmund Colledge, O. S. A., and Bernard McGinn, *Meister Eckhart* (New York: Paulist Press, 1981), 198.

23. Michael A. Sells, "Apophasis in Plotinus: A Critical Approach," *Harvard Theological Review* 78, nos. 3–4 (1985): 53.

24. Ibid., 64.

25. Robert K. C. Forman, ed., *The Problem of Pure Consciousness: Mysticism and Philosophy* (London: Oxford University Press, 1990), 13.

26. See especially, Louis Bouyer, "Mysticism: An Essay on the History of the Word," in *Understanding Mysticism,* ed. Richard Woods (Garden City, N.Y.: Doubleday, 1980), 42–55.

27. For a discussion of the term's etymology, see Max Müller, *The Upaniṣads* (New York: Dover, 1962), 1:lxxix–lxxxiv; and Paul Deussen, *The Philosophy of the Upanishads* (New York: Dover, 1966), 10–15.

28. See Deussen, *Philosophy,* 10–15.

29. See his *Mystical Languages of Unsaying* (Chicago: University of Chicago Press, 1994).

30. Moshe Idel and Bernard McGinn, eds., *Mystical Union and Monotheistic Faith: An Ecumenical Dialogue* (New York: Macmillan, 1989), 186.

31. See also KA 4.15 and TP, no. 168.

32. See also LP 5.8.2 where Ramakrishna speaks of a special "memory nerve" that develops after twelve years of celibacy. With such a nerve, the intellect develops and can comprehend God.

33. Colm Luibheid and Paul Rorem, trans., *Pseudo-Dionysius: The Complete Works* (New York: Paulist Press, 1987), 82, 84.

34. See, for example, KA 3.30. The term is *sarvadharmasamanvaya.*

35. Ramakrishna does use the expression *samanvaya* or "synthesis," but only rarely (KA 5.65).

36. See also KA 5.21; 5.39; 5.82; 5.162; 5.204.

37. Cf. KA 1.48; 5.34.

38. See also LP 5.8.2.19.

39. KA 2.250; 3.272 et al. See also LP 5.6.2.8; 5.12.3.11.

40. Quoted in Sil, "Untold Story," 46.

41. Narendra was a "lion among men" (LP 5.12.3.11).

42. Such apparel is a clear mark of luxury (GSR, 1021, n. 1).

43. KA 3.41; 5.67; 5.84.

44. Gopinath Kaviraj, *Tāntrika Sādhanā o Siddhānta* (Bardhaman: Bardhaman University, 1983), 1.

45. Douglas Renfrew Brooks has recently given us two fine textual studies of Śrī Vidyā Tantrism in south India and has promised a third, anthropological study of Śrī Vidyā ritual practice, but such "southern" works have been the exception. See Brooks, *The Secret of the Three Cities: An Introduction to Hindu Śākta Tantrism* (Chicago: University of Chicago Press, 1990), and *Auspicious Wisdom: The Texts and Traditions of Śrīvidyā Śākta Tantrism in South India* (Albany: State University of New York Press, 1992).

46. "*Jāgrata Naramuṇḍa: Ekṭi Cyāleñj,*" *Ājkāl* (Calcutta), 5 March, 1990.

47. June McDaniel's study of madness in the colorful vernacular biographies of Bengali Śākta saints, *The Madness of the Saints: Ecstatic Religion in Bengal* (Chicago: University of Chicago, 1989), and Sudhir Kakar's analyses of his memorable Tantric informants in *Shamans, Mystics and Doctors: A Psychological Inquiry into India and Its Healing Traditions* (Delhi: Oxford University Press, 1986), are two notable exceptions.

48. Douglas Renfrew Brooks, "Encountering the Hindu 'Other': Tantrism and the Brahmans of South India," *Journal of the American Academy of Religion* 60, no. 3 (1992): 414.

49. I am quite aware that the text itself is "bipolar" in that it was generated "within" or "between" a human relationship defined by two living individuals, M and Ramakrishna. Ideally, then, a proper interpretation of the text would require a study, not only of Ramakrishna as he is represented in the text, but also of M as the author of that representation. I can only confess that I have not attempted such an ideal study here and will restrict myself to the Ramakrishna side of the text.

50. Rahul Peter Das argues for a similar approach when he describes Tantric phenomena as "parts of real and very material life, subject to all its influences and developments, and not to be separated from the humans who form and are formed by them—humans who are characterized by unpredictability, inconsistence, desultoriness, and all the other traits that so frustrate psychologists and sociologists" ("Problematic Aspects of the Sexual Rituals of the Bauls of Bengal," *Journal of the American Oriental Society* 112, no. 3 [1992]: 422).

51. Brooks, *Secret*, ix.

52. See, for example: Sanjukta Gupta, Dirk Jan Hoens and Teun Goudriaan, *Hindu Tantrism* (Leiden: E. J. Brill, 1979), 5–9; André Padoux, "Tantrism: An Overview" and "Hindu Tantrism," in *Encyclopedia of Religion*, ed. Mircea Eliade, vol. 14 (New York: Macmillan, 1987); and Brooks, *Secret*, 55–72.

53. The italics in each of these five characteristic quotes are my own.

54. For two excellent discussions of this dialectic between Brahmanical notions of purity and the Tantric ideal of power, see Alexis Sanderson, "Purity and Power among the Brahmans of Kashmir," in *The Category of the Person: Anthropology, Philosophy, History,* ed. Michael Carrithers, Steven Collins, Steven Lukes (New York: Cambridge University Press, 1985), 190–216; and Brooks, *Auspicious Wisdom,* pt. 2, "Interpreting Tantric Ritual."

55. JU, 70–71, is a good example of this phenomenon.

56. KA 1.247; 3.31; 4.28; 1.214; 4.208; 5.51.

57. Paul Ricoeur, *The Symbolism of Evil,* trans. Emerson Buchanan (Boston: Beacon Press, 1967), 348.

58. Gananath Obeyesekere, *The Work of Culture: Symbolic Transformations in Psychoanalysis and Anthropology* (Chicago: University of Chicago Press, 1990), 24.

59. See Stanley N. Kurtz, *All the Mothers Are One: Hindu India and the Cultural Reshaping of Psychoanalysis* (New York: Columbia University Press, 1992).

60. Mircea Eliade, *Myths, Dreams and Mysteries* (New York: Harper & Row, 1975), 13.

61. Melford E. Spiro, *Oedipus in the Trobriands* (Chicago: University of Chicago Press, 1982), 143.

62. Obeyesekere, *Work of Culture,* 52.

63. M distinguishes between Ramakrishna "established in *samādhi*" (*samādhistha*) and Ramakrishna "in ecstasy" (*bhāve*) or "established in ecstasy" (*bhāvāviṣṭha*) by the level of absorption. When Ramakrishna is in *samādhi,* his body becomes motionless, his eyes and lips are parted slightly in pleasure, his lips are sealed in a smile. In *bhāva,* on the other hand, he can move, even dance, and his lips are free to talk, even if his speech is garbled in its ecstatic drunkenness.

64. Sudhir Kakar, *The Analyst and the Mystic: Psychoanalytic Reflections on Religion and Mysticism* (Chicago: University of Chicago Press, 1991), 9.

65. Ibid., 26–27.

66. Ibid., 5.

67. Ibid., 27.

68. Ibid., 27.

69. Romain Rolland, *The Life of Ramakrishna,* 12th ed. (Calcutta: Advaita Ashrama, 1986), 216, n. 1.

70. KA 1.62–63; 1.76; 4.115; 5.108.

71. See KA 3.243; 4.115; 5.29.

72. Kakar has noted this "very sketchy and indeed barely existing theory of sublimation" in the Freudian corpus in his review of *The Work of Culture* by Gananath Obeyeskere in *History of Religions* 32, no. 3 (February 1993): 309.

73. Kakar, *The Inner World: A Psycho-analytic Study of Childhood and Society in India* (Delhi: Oxford University Press, 1988), 28.

74. Kakar, *Inner World,* 29.

CHAPTER 1

1. Christopher Isherwood, *Ramakrishna and His Disciples* (New York: Simon and Schuster, 1970), 6.

2. Shashibhushan Dasgupta, *Bhārater Śakti-sādhanā o Śākta Sāhitya* (Calcutta: Sahitya Samsad, 1985), 234.

3. Nathan Leonard and Clinton Seely, *Grace and Mercy in Her Wild Hair: Selected Poems to the Mother Goddess, Rāmprasad Sen* (Boulder, Colo.: Great Eastern Book Company, 1982), no. 32.

4. The blackness of night is sometimes associated with an ontological formlessness: "Haladhari used to dwell on form during the day and on the formless during the night" (KA 2.52).

5. Nathan and Seely, *Grace and Mercy,* no. 53.

6. Rachel Fell McDermott has compared Kālī's skirt of human hands to an American "mini-skirt" (Rachel Fell McDermott, "Kālī's Tongue: Historical Reinterpretations of the Blood-lusting Goddess" [paper presented at the Mid-Atlantic Regional Conference of the American Academy of Religion, Barnard College, New York, March 21, 1991], 8). *Bikini* might be an even better word.

7. Bipinchandra Pal, *Saint Bijayakrishna Goswami* (Calcutta: Bipinchandra Pal Institute, 1964), 29–30. Given what we know about the saint's fear of women and his pronounced homosexual tendencies, I doubt seriously that Ramakrishna ever practiced this technique. But that matters little, for the report, accurate or no, was recorded and preserved within the culture and as such represents an assumed connection between the phallus and the head.

8. KA 4.112; 4.195.

9. Jadunath Sinha, *The Cult of Shakti: Rama Prasada's Devotional Songs* (Calcutta: Jadunath Sinha Foundation, 1981), no. 251, no. 220.

10. Dasgupta, *Bhārater Śakti-sādhanā,* 224.

11. Ibid., 273; see also ibid., 214. I have followed a different transliteration scheme here (*kālo* for *kāla*) to catch the rhyme.

12. See JU, 48–49, for a similar realization in Ramakrishna's life.

13. Max Müller, *Rāmakṛṣṇa: His Life and Sayings* (London: Longmans, Green, and Co., 1898), 24.

14. Rolland, *Life of Ramakrishna,* 21, n. 1. Dhan Gopal Mukherji opts for a very similar approach in his *The Face of Silence* (1926; London: Servire, 1973). Rejecting the supposedly dry and boring "Rama Krishna history" for the more exciting and spiritual "Rama Krishna legend" (ibid., 12), Mukherji goes on to write a poetic account that is entertaining but unfortunately riddled with serious historical errors. To give just one minor example, Mukherji states that Ramakrishna's chosen wife lived in a village four hundred miles away (ibid., 32), when in fact she lived just down the road! Many of his mistakes are no doubt simply the result of a lack of correct information (or a map). Others—e.g., his emphasis on Ramakrishna's Vedantic training and his consequent failure to even mention the saint's Tantric practices—can be attributed to a single mistaken assumption, his belief that "the chroniclers" (the monks and followers of the Ramakrishna Order) are more important than "the chronicle" (the historical documents) in reconstructing the saint's life and teachings (ibid., 7).

15. Kakar, *The Mystic and the Analyst,* 7.

16. Chatterjee becomes "Bhattacarrya" in some contexts.

17. *Life of Sri Ramakrishna* (Calcutta: Advaita Ashrama, 1983), 28–29.

18. Narasingha P. Sil. *Rāmakṛṣṇa Paramahaṁsa: A Psychological Profile* (Leiden: E. J. Brill, 1991), 35.

19. For a longer version, see KA 4.45.

20. See JV (5), 2, n., for Datta's account.

21. There is something of a controversy over the source and temporal origin of the name "Ramakrishna." Swami Prabhananda, however, using family charts and a temple document, has convincingly shown that it was Kshudiram, Ramakrishna's own father, who gave the name "Ramakrishna" to the young boy at birth (see Swami Prabhananda, "Who Gave the Name?" *The Vedanta Kesari,* March 1987, 107–112). Since the name "Gadadhar" was used in the village but was virtually unknown at the temple precincts of Calcutta, I will use "Gadadhar" only for these early village scenes and then gradually switch to "Ramakrishna" as the scene shifts to the temple.

22. *Life of Sri Ramakrishna,* 13.

23. Datta does not even mention the event in his *Jīvanavṛttānta.*

24. *Life of Sri Ramakrishna,* 17.

25. Jensen, "Madness, Yearning, and Play," 62, 85.

26. *Life of Sri Ramakrishna,* 15.

27. Cf. LP 1.7.6.

28. "When I was ten and living back in the village, this state (the state of *samādhi*) occurred. While I was walking through a field, I saw something and on account of it fell down unconscious" (KA 5.25). This passage might be construed as "secret talk" since it occurs, with another specifically Tantric passage, below the occurrence of the term *guhya kathā.*

29. *Life of Sri Ramakrishna,* 21.

30. Jensen, "Madness, Yearning, and Play," 73, n. 4. See also Sil, *Rāmakṛṣṇa Paramahaṁsa,* 27.

31. *Life of Sri Ramakrishna,* 22.

32. Ibid., 27.

33. Ibid., 29.

34. Sil, *Rāmakṛṣṇa Paramahaṁsa,* 28.

35. *Life of Sri Ramakrishna,* 27.

36. Ibid., 27.

37. Ibid., 6.

38. Jensen, "Madness, Yearning, and Play," 66.

39. Ibid., 53.

40. Ibid., 56.

41. The *Life of Sri Ramakrishna* calls it "heretical" (38).

42. Sil, *Rāmakṛṣṇa Paramahaṁsa,* 118.

43. See ibid., 28, and JU, 45–48, for similar descriptions.

44. *Decapitate* may seem too strong a word here, but we must remember that Kālī's sacrificial sword was used to decapitate sacrificial goats and that self-decapitation was allegedly used by the goddess's devotees to show their profound devotion (Kinsley, *Hindu Goddesses: Visions of the Divine Feminine in the Hindu Religious Tradition* [Delhi: Motilal Banarsidass, 1987], 145).

45. There is no sword in either the JV or the JU. I am following Saradananda here because there are numerous passages in the *Kathāmṛta* that suggest a simi-

lar, if not identical, incident. Although by no means beyond questioning, the tradition is just too strong to ignore.

46. The expression is M's (KA 1.175). But see PDU, 14.

47. The expression "black *bhāva*" is mine.

48. See also JV(5), 56; KA 3.244; 4.113; 5.207.

49. KA 2.160; 2.163; 3.4; 4.9.

50. KA 5.2; 5.21; 5.82; 5.204.

51. Its presence, on the other hand, frees one from the necessity of a guru (PRU, 3–4).

52. KA 1.94; 4.66; 4.205; 5.34; 5.104; 5.126; 5.211; 5.212.

53. KA 2.18; 2.44; 2.90; 4.17.

54. Ramakrishna's "some Purāṇa or another" may refer to a passage in the *Padma Purāṇa* (6.272.165–167), which Robert P. Goldman eloquently discusses in his "Transsexualism, Gender, and Anxiety in Traditional India," *Journal of the American Oriental Society* 113, no. 3 (1993): 389; see also 383–384.

55. KA 2.48; 2.73–74.

56. KA 2.110; 5.108.

57. Cf. KA 2.49.

58. KA 2.49; 2.110.

59. See also KA 5.81.

60. Cf. K 2.129. M, guessing his reader's thoughts, is quick to explain what Ramakrishna meant: "If he would have looked at the boy any longer, the Master would have become lost in ecstasy" (KA 2.121). Nikhilananda, *fearing* his reader's thoughts, completely omits Ramakrishna's words and instead puts M's gloss in Ramakrishna's mouth: "I should have been overwhelmed with ecstasy if he had stayed here a little longer" (GSR, 556).

61. But Ramakrishna wants nothing to do with pictures of women (KA 4.263).

62. It was only the homoerotic that lit up the memory. Sexual desire for a woman, what the saint called lover-and-gold, only leads to forgetfulness (KA 3.143; 3.144; 4.66; 4.263).

63. See also KA 5.116.

64. The human being, for example, is described as the puppet of God (KA 3.61).

65. Cf. KA 3.136.

66. KA 3.133; 5.24.

67. For a similar passage, see KA 4.204.

68. LP 4.4.52 (GM 4.4.47).

69. I am aware of only one exception: LP 3.1.24.

70. Ramakrishna also threatened to drown himself (KA 1.168–169).

71. I treat the knife passages in the order that best suits the flow of my argument.

72. KA 4.212; Cf. 3.130. *Where* the sandalwood is rubbed on Purna's body is a legitimate question, since in KA 4.232 Ramakrishna tells M, in secret, that he used to worship the "little cocks" (*dhana*) of boys with sandal-paste and flowers.

73. Cf. KA 4.217–218.

74. "Scoot closer" was a common request of Ramakrishna's (cf. KA 3.99; 3.209).

75. It should be pointed out here that this day was "split" by M to conceal this secret confession. The afternoon conversation of the day was recorded in the very first volume (1902), whereas the morning session, when the confession occurred, was kept for the fourth (1910). Again, this is a good example of the "cyclical" effect that I have analyzed above.

76. Psychoanalytically trained students of Hindu culture have tended to see such symbolic self-castrations as productive of a "negative Oedipus complex" in which the boy, instead of renouncing his desires for the mother and identifying with the father (the "normal" outcome of Freud's Oedipus complex), ends up identifying with the mother by renouncing his masculine identity through a symbolic castration (see, for example, G. Morris Carstairs, *The Twice-Born: A Study of a Community of High-Caste Hindus* [Bloomington: Indiana University Press, 1967], 160–169; Sudhir Kakar, *Inner World*, 102, 133–135; Gananath Obeyesekere, *The Cult of the Goddess Pattini* [Chicago: University of Chicago Press, 1984], 474–480; and A. K. Ramanujan, "The Indian Oedipus," in *Oedipus: A Folklore Casebook*, ed. Lowell Edmunds and Alan Dundes [New York: Garland, 1983], 234–261; for an important alternative reading, see Kurtz, *All the Mothers Are One*, chap. 6, "The Durga Complex"). This in turn creates a marked homosexual tendency in the boy, who now experiences himself in some sense as a woman. Kakar adds another level to the theory by suggesting that the self-castration also functions to help the boy avoid the powerful advances of the sexually aggressive mother, who, more or less deprived of an adequate sexual relationship with her husband, focuses all of her libidinal energies on the male child: "to identify with one's mother means to sacrifice one's masculinity to her in order to escape sexual excitation and the threat it poses to the boy's fragile ego" (Kakar, *Inner World*, 102). We might thus identify at least three dimensions of Ramakrishna's experience of Kāli's sword: (1) my theory that the sword was aimed at the symbolic phallus in order to end the tormenting shame the saint felt for his homosexual desires; (2) the traditional psychoanalytic reading of self-castration in Hindu mythology as productive of a "negative Oedipus complex" that in turn results in marked homosexual tendencies; and (3) Kakar's maternal seduction theory, in which the sword is invoked as a defense against the sexually aggressive mother. If we put the first two together, we could read Ramakrishna's attempted self-decapitation as an ironic act that at once attempted to "cut off" the "strange sensation" of his homosexual desires and yet at the same time reinforced those desires by more or less cementing a feminine gender identity. Kakar's maternal seduction theory is important as well since, as we will see below, evidence exists to suggest that Ramakrishna, both as a boy and later as an adult, experienced a number of older women as dangerously aggressive mothers: in his own words, their "maternal affection" (*vātsalya*) was in fact a sexual "deception" (*tācchalya*).

77. Obeyesekere, *Work of Culture*, 24.

78. Sumit Sarkar, "The Kathamrita as Text: Towards an Understanding of Ramakrishna Paramahamsa," *Occasional Papers on History and Society* 12 (New Delhi: Nehru Memorial Museum and Library, 1985), 103.

79. For an intelligent and balanced treatment of homosexuality in Hinduism in general, see Arvind Sharma's "Homosexuality and Hinduism," in *Homosexuality and World Religions*, ed. Arlene Swidler (Valley Forge, Pa.: Trinity Press, 1993), 47–80.

80. They apparently feared that Narendra would not marry (LP 5.8.3).

81. KA 3.98; 4.143.

82. KA 3.179; 4.234.

83. Cf. KA 3.180.

84. The phrase "loving the boys" is *chokarāder bhālavāsā*. See also KA 3.180.

85. Sarkar, "Kathamrita as Text," 103.

86. "I said to Kedar, 'Nothing will happen if your mind dwells on lover-and-gold.' I wanted to pass my hand over his breast, but I could not. It was all knotted up inside. I couldn't enter a room that smelled of feces" (KA 4.230).

87. KA 3.176; 3.184; 4.68.

88. KA 3.176; 3.184; 4.163; 5.145. Cf. also LP 5.7.13.

89. KA 3.89; 3.176; 4.263; 5.114 et al.

90. Numerous scholars have commented on the symbolic equivalence between semen and milk in Indian culture (see especially Wendy Doniger O'Flaherty, *Women, Androgynes, and Other Mythical Beasts* [Chicago: University of Chicago Press, 1980], and John Stratton Hawley, *Krishna: The Butter Thief* [Princeton: Princeton University Press, 1983]). In the *Kathāmṛta* the equation appears here, in the milk of the boys, and in such passages as that in which Ramakrishna explains how a yogī can suck milk through his penis (KA 2.80), effectively reversing the flow of "semen" and turning the practitioner into an *ūrdhvaretā*, a man "whose semen in turned up."

91. KA 4.109. Whose body is allowed to touch whose reveals a great deal about Ramakrishna. For example, whereas he had no problem with all the caressing, massaging, and bathing going on between himself and his boy disciples, Ramakrishna condemned the "rubbing of bodies" that occurs between a husband and wife in bed—it produces too much "heat" (KA 4.214).

92. Obeyesekere, *Work of Culture*, 219–225.

93. Isherwood, *Ramakrishna and His Disciples*, 1.

CHAPTER 2

1. KA 3.137 glosses the phrase "at that time" as "at the time of *sādhana*."

2. Walter G. Neevel, Jr., "The Transformation of Sri Ramakrishna," in *Hinduism: New Essays in the History of Religions*, ed. Bardwell L. Smith (Leiden: E. J. Brill, 1976), 76. For similar, if differently argued, views, see Heinrich Zimmer, *Philosophies of India*, ed. Joseph Campbell (Princeton: Princeton University Press, 1974), 560–594; and M. D. McLean, "Ramakrishna: The Greatest of the Saktas of Bengal?" in *Memorial Festschrift for Ian Kesarcodi-Watson*, ed. P. Bilamoria and P. Fenner (Delhi: Indian Books Centre, 1988), 151–172. Although it has been effectively silenced within the tradition, such a Tantric reading is certainly not new in the Bengali literature. As early as 1897, for example, Satyacharan Mitra stated emphatically: "Although Ramakrishna Paramahaṁsa also practiced the *sādhanas* of various other traditions, the tradition of Tantra was his pre-eminent tradition. . . . Ramakrishna Paramahaṁsa was a fierce Tāntrika"

(JU, 72). More recently, the great scholar of Bengali religion, Shashibhushan Dasgupta, has written of Ramakrishna as the "culmination" (*pariṇati*) of the Śākta Tantra tradition in Bengal and has commented on the clear discrepancy that exists between such a reading and the more traditional (and problematic) "Vedantic" interpretations of the Ramakrishna Order (*Bhārater Śakti-sādhanā,* 275–276, 262).

3. Neevel, "Transformation," 93.

4. Ibid., 98.

5. In KA 2.141, when the subject of Tantra is raised, Ramakrishna began to "make fun" (*rahasya karā*) of it. The "secret" (*rahasya*) thus became a nervous "joke" (*rahasya*).

6. It could also mean "The Lover is (actually one's own) Mother," as Ramakrishna's story, which immediately precedes the comment, seems to suggest. Is Sarkar agreeing with the saint's story? Or is he gently disagreeing with it?

7. Of the Sanskrit text.

8. See also Sinha, *Cult of Shakti,* nos. 277, 302, 305.

9. Quoted by Woodroffe in Vimalananda's KS, 42, n. 2.

10. Sinha, *Cult of Shakti,* nos. 277, 301, 302.

11. Ibid., no. 278.

12. Ibid., nos. 278, 299, 300, 303, 305, 307.

13. Bengali commentary on KT 1.6.

14. Woodroffe in Vimalananda's KS, 42, n. 2.

15. Of the Sanskrit text.

16. John Woodroffe, *Principles of Tantra: The Tantra-Tattva of Śrīyukta Śiva Candra Vidyārṇava Bhattacārya Mahodya,* part I (1913; Madras: Ganesh and Company, 1986), 47, n. 2.

17. The same triple order again can be seen in KA 4.175; 5.67; 5.84.

18. JV(5), "Introduction," 3.

19. Cf. PU, 33–34.

20. JV(5), "Introduction," 2.

21. JV(5), "Introduction," 3.

22. Cf. LP 2.13.20 and 2.13.9.

23. Ramakrishna extolled what he called "grit" (*roka*) in the religious life: KA 1.45; 2.35; 4.83.

24. Cf. Jensen, "Madness, Yearning, and Play," 114.

25. The word for "mud" (*karddama*) can also mean "slime" or "sin."

26. Cf. also KA 4.73 and JV(5), 25.

27. See also JV(5), 21.

28. While the KA and JV note simply that Ramakrishna used a piece of cloth as a tail (KA 2.193; 3.111; 4.175; JV[5], 42), the LP claims that his coccyx actually grew an inch (LP 2.8.8).

29. The fact that Datta refers to a Śākta state (Ramakrishna fanning the goddess) and a Vaiṣṇava state (Ramakrishna as the "girlfriend" of Gangamata) as the *same* state is important, because it demonstrates convincingly that what the texts call the handmaid state is in fact a conflation of two different religious identities, the Śākta state of the Female Servant of the goddess (*dāsī-bhāva*) and the Vaiṣṇava state of the Girlfriend of Rādhā (*sakhī-bhāva*). This confusion is

compounded by the fact that Datta and Saradananda both commonly use the term *sakhī* to describe both the Śākta and Vaiṣṇava states. M is more careful to distinguish the two, hence he often uses the expression *dāsī* to describe the Śākta state (KA 2.49–50; 2.155), but he too sometimes conflates the identities (KA 2.154–155; 3.83). Since I am interested in analyzing the texts' understanding of these states and the texts themselves consistently conflate these two roles, my analysis of "the Handmaid" will treat the two as a single psychological identity, despite the fact that they issue from two historically distinct religious traditions.

30. The tone of KA 3.83 suggests a certain anxious necessity in Ramakrishna's becoming a Handmaid: "I used to say over and over, 'I am a Female Servant of the Blissful Mother!'"

31. Given the handmaiden context of the event in Datta's account, the famous scene of Ramakrishna spitting on the expensive shawl that Mathur had given him (JV[5], 48) may hint at Ramakrishna's rejection, not of the world, but of Mathur's sexual advances that were implied in such a gift.

32. JV(5), 48; LP 2.14.8. Mitra confirms this strong tradition (JU, 154).

33. Cited in Swami Chetananda, *They Lived with God: Life Stories of Some Devotees of Sri Ramakrishna* (St. Louis: Vedanta Society of St. Louis, 1989), 29. I am indebted to Narasingha Sil for pointing this passage out to me.

In *samādhi*, Ramakrishna saw the great bird Jatayu attacking Rāvaṇa's/Mathur's carriage in an attempt to rescue him as Sītā. This is an especially clear example of how Ramakrishna's ecstatic experiences and visions functioned as "defenses" against intolerable external circumstances.

34. Rādhā and Sītā are sometimes connected in Ramakrishna's memory, perhaps evidence of this early Vaiṣṇava period in which he practiced "according to the Purāṇas." See, for example, KA 2.192: "Many days I was in the state of Śiva and Parvatī. Again, for many days I was in the state of Rādhā and Kṛṣṇa! At other times I was in the state of Sītā and Rāma! In the state of Rādhā I used to cry, 'Kṛṣṇa! Kṛṣṇa!' and in the state of Sītā I used to cry, 'Rāma! Rāma!'" Note that all of these states were defined by a basic sexual polarity, with Ramakrishna always as the woman. The sectarian marks might change, but the erotic, bipolar structure of the experience remains constant.

35. Nikhilananda omits the word *vagina* (GSR, 346).

36. Such wordplays are not at all uncommon in the visions and teachings of Ramakrishna. See, for example, LP 5.9.1; 5.7.30; KA 1.94; 3.225; 3.256; 4.43; 5.87; 5.119.

37. Mitra too has the women rubbing Ramakrishna's body with oil (JU, 154).

38. The last line is particularly puzzling. Were these *meye* ("girls" or "women") Mathur's daughters, or were they Mathur's well-known lovers? The word *meye* is often used in the texts to refer to adult, sexually active women (see, for example, PU, 22, 28).

39. The Bengali expression is *kona rakama bhāva.*

40. The Bengali expression is *kona prakāra bhāvodaya.*

41. "The public" (*sādhāraṇa*) appears numerous times in Datta's text, always as those who are incapable of understanding the deep secrets of Ramakrishna's life (See JV[5], 33, 37, 50).

42. See also LP 3.6.6 for Mathur attracted to Gadadhar's boyishness and beauty.

43. LP 2.7.5; JV (5), 38.

44. KA 3.68; 4.35; 4.77; 4.144.

45. Quoted in the Bengali commentary to KT 1.19.

46. See JU, 74–81, for a more detailed version of these events.

47. LP 3.4.20 (GM 3.4.11).

48. The JV locates Ramakrishna's marriage much earlier, shortly after his move to Calcutta but still before the First Vision. Ramakrishna was sixteen at the time, and Sharada was eight (JV[5], 17). I discuss the marriage here because of the strong tradition that Ramakrishna was married as a means to cure his madness, which did not seem to set in until after the First Vision.

49. Rolland, *Life of Ramakrishna*, 41.

50. For more on this, see below, chapter 4, p. 225.

51. Cf. JV(5), 29.

52. Cf. KA 3.122; JV(5), 51; TP, no. 119; and LP 2.20.21.

53. Ramakrishna got this typology from the Tantras (cf. KS 4).

54. But he does suggest it. In JV(5), 32, Datta writes that Ramakrishna performed the Tantric practices "by means of" (*dvāra*) the Bhairavī, an expression that would suggest actual intercourse.

55. Wendy Doniger, foreword in Edward C. Dimock, Jr., *The Place of the Hidden Moon: Erotic Mysticism in the Vaiṣṇava-sahajiyā Cult of Bengal* (Chicago: University of Chicago Press, 1989), xiii.

56. The skeptical quote marks are my own. But see TS, 99–100.

57. See KA 4.232 for Ramakrishna being "forced" (cf. LP 2.11.7) and KA 3.24 for his descriptions of the Tantric rituals he performed as "very strange" and "not for the flippant."

58. KA 1.143; 1.195; 3.5; 3.59; 5.220.

59. KA 1.222; 2.15.

60. In his typical style, Saradananda cleans things up by claiming that this same Achalananda never drank too much and always behaved properly (LP 4.2.20)!

61. KA 2.143; 5.180.

62. JV(5), 31; LP 4.2.20–21; KA 2.131; 2.134.

63. There are passages in which a *mūdra*-like grain or rice dish is consumed (KA 3.141), but it is difficult to tell whether the ritual of the Five M's is implied in such cases.

64. For a list of different grain and rice dishes used as *mūdra*, see SM, 610–611.

65. "Vaishnavacharan followed the path of the Kartābhajās" (KA 5.180).

66. I suspect, but cannot prove, that these "women" were in fact Hijras, a religious sect of surgically emasculated men who perform various ritual functions in Indian society and sometimes engage in homosexual prostitution. For a sensitive study of this sect, see Serena Nanda, *Neither Man nor Woman: The Hijras of India* (Belmont, Calif.: Wadsworth, 1990).

67. For a fuller account of these Kartābhajā stages (and a fourth level), see KA 3.21; TS, 41–43.

68. The italics are in the Bengali as bold.

69. Italics are in the Bengali as bold. See also KA 3.138; 4.283.

70. Cf. KA 4.8.

71. "I saw with my own eyes God dwelling in the vagina! I saw God in the intercourse of a dog and a bitch" (KA 3.33). This vision is preceded by the bold-print phrase: *"Listen! I'm telling you something very secret!"*

72. Nikhilananda tones this down considerably by translating "wet their faces in" (*mukha jubare thāke*) as "revel in" (GSR, 1013).

73. The Bengali commentator says that "there is a special secret meaning of this in the *sādhana* of the Hero," but he will not tell us what it is (KT, 49). He is almost certainly referring to the Tantric practice of drinking the "flower of the vagina" (*yonipuṣpa*) or the menstrual fluids to increase the energy and power of the Tantric practitioner (see J. A. Schoterman, *Yonitantra* [New Delhi: Manohar, 1980], 28–32).

74. Quoted in Schoterman, *Yonitantra*, 14.

75. Quoted in ibid., 27.

76. For lotuses and their symbolic associations, see KA 2.16; 2.37; 2.54; 4.147; 4.192; 5.83.

77. The word that the Tāntrika uses here (*yonirūpa*), lit. "in the shape of the vagina," is the same term that Ramakrishna uses to describe the "vaginal shape" of the lotuses in KA 4.238.

78. I might note here that he also associated flowers with prostitutes (TP, no. 258).

79. The Bhairavī sometimes used other women to train her young disciple (LP 2.11.8; 2.11.10).

80. See, for example, Bholanath Bhattacharya, "Some Aspects of the Esoteric Cults of Consort Worship in Bengal: A Field Survey Report," *Folklore* (Calcutta) 18 (1977): 392.

81. The verb in question is *ramaṇa karā*, literally "to do [sexual] delight." There is also no mention of the shape of the lotuses in the GSR. See LP 2.11.20 for a similar censoring.

82. "Each and every woman is a form of Śakti" (KA 3.28; cf. also KA 2.232).

83. KA 3.24; 3.112.

84. See, for example, KA 2.143.

85. KA 2.8; 3.112.

86. KA 1.209; 2.8; 2.143; 5.105.

87. KA 1.181;1.221; 5.109; 5.141; 5.200.

88. The perfect wife has little lust or anger, sleeps little, gives body rubs to her husband, is affectionate, compassionate, devoted and shy, and does not spend a lot of money so that her husband will not have to work hard and can have more time for religious exercises (KA 5.141).

89. KA 1.113; 2.233.

90. Nikhilananda omits this tidbit of gossip (GSR, 284).

91. LP 4.2.40 tells us that his birthname was Rajkumar.

92. Although this event probably took place well after Ramakrishna's *sādhana* period, I will look at it here, since its themes fit in so well with those of the present chapter.

93. See LP 3.4.21–26 and LP 2.20.

94. LP 2.20.9 (GM 2.20.8).

95. KA 2.154–155; LP 3.4.12. But see LP 2.20.16, which claims it was over a year.

96. The expression "one-sixteenth" refers to the *anna,* a small monetary unit, sixteen of which make up one *rupee,* the basic unit or "dollar" of the Indian monetary system.

97. LP 3.4.14 (GM 3.4.23).

98. LP 3.4.13 (GM 3.4.22).

99. LP 3.4.14 (GM 3.4.23).

100. Ramakrishna may have been inspired to perform such a ritual by Gauri, a local Tāntrika who was known to have performed the same ritual with his wife (LP 4.1.32).

101. This entire scene occurs in chapter 16 of Datta's text, JV(5), 59–62; cf. JU, 72–73.

102. See also KA 2.62 on the "fear of lust" (*kāmer bhaya*) that exists in a worldly life.

103. KA 5.140–141; the italics are in the Bengali as bold. Nikhilananda bowdlerizes the phrase "I saw that her breasts were Mother's breasts, that her vagina was Mother's vagina" (GSR, 701).

104. Compare also KA 2.155.

105. KA 2.232; 4.203.

106. KA 1.114; 2.106; 2.110; 3.232–233 et al.

107. See, for example, the story about King Janaka's fear (KA 5.55).

108. KA 2.97; 2.200 et al.

109. Nikhilananda omits the phrase "shitting, pissing" (GSR, 418). Cf. also KA 4.77.

110. *Mātṛyoniṁ paritajya viharet sarvayoniṣu* (quoted by Woodroffe in KS, verse 11).

111. Ramakrishna's rejection of Tantra is itself couched in Tantric terminology and assumes a knowledge of the Tantras. After all, his famous (if usually untranslated) phrase *sarvayoni mātṛyoni* ("every vagina is Mother's vagina") draws on the Tantric prohibition against ritual intercourse with a *mātṛyoni,* that is, with a woman who has borne a child (see, e.g., YT 2.5).

112. See also KA 4.32 for another version.

113. Kakar, *The Analyst and the Mystic,* 26–27.

114. See also JV(5), 16, for Datta's gloss on *chidra* as the "holes" of a woman's body.

115. See KA 2.166 et al.

116. Keshab Sen was his usual target here. See KA 2.166; 5.49.

117. See, for example, KA 2.35; 2.192; 3.161; 4.3.

118. Cf. KA 4.43.

119. Sudhir Kakar first developed the theme in his *Inner World,* chap. 3.

120. See also KA 2.88 and LP 3.8.35.

121. The first italics are in the Bengali as bold, the second are mine. Cf. 4.164; 4.221–22.

122. See KA 3.100 for a similar scene with the boy Narayan.

Chapter 3

1. Quoted by Smrititirtha in his commentary on the KT, 30–31.
2. Quoted in Dasgupta, *Bhārater Śakti-sādhanā*, 210–211.
3. Ibid., 70.
4. Woodroffe in the KS, 44, n. 5.
5. Smrititirtha's Bengali commentary to the KT, 31.
6. Ibid., 31.
7. Woodroffe notes the discrepancy in Vimalananda's KS, 52.
8. Rachel Fell McDermott, "Evidence for the Transformation of the Goddess Kālī: Kamalākānta Bhaṭṭācārya and the Bengali Śākta Padāvalī Tradition" (Ph.D. diss., Harvard University, 1993), 108.
9. See SM, 492–495, for other traditional interpretations.
10. See also LP 3.8.45, n. 1.
11. Chapatis are flat doughy "pancakes" used like bread with the meals.
12. The initials are in the Bengali as bold. See also LP 3.8.18.
13. The fact that Saradananda records perhaps a dozen scenes in which it takes Ramakrishna "three days" to accomplish this or that tends to undermine the credibility of such "three days."
14. Jensen, "Madness, Yearning, and Play," 119–120.
15. LP 3.4.1; 3.3.
16. Both the translator and the biographer seem to be aware of the contradiction. Jagananda correctly glosses *bhāvamukha* to mean "the threshold of relative consciousness" (GM 2.21.7) and Saradananda describes the state as that "world which is both dual and nondual" (LP 2.17.1).
17. The italics are in the Bengali as bold.
18. The word I translate as "little cock" is *dhana*, a slang word for the penis, which literally means "treasure," as in our own "family jewels." It is a crude word. My Bengali tutor had to whisper its meanings to me. It is used especially to refer to "the penis of a small boy" (see *dhona* (=*dhana*), in Jnanendramohan Das, ed., *Bāṇālā Bhāṣāra Abhidhāna* [Calcutta: Sahitya Samsad, 1971], 1119). I am indebted to Malcolm McLean for this dictionary reference.
19. In one Tantric ritual, after the male partner has rubbed the *yoni* or "vagina" of his Śakti with sandal-paste, the Śakti then rubs her partner's *liṅgam* or "penis" with sandal-paste (YT 2.9). Ramakrishna may have been enacting the female role of this Tantric ritual.
20. Given that this act is connected in the text to the Bhairavī, it is possible, but not necessary, that it occurred before the arrival of Tota. It is important here to keep in mind that the Bhairavī stayed on with Ramakrishna for years and was still at the temple during, and even after, Tota's departure.
21. Nikhilananda omits the phrase "And a little pearl would come out!" (GSR, 491). I am indebted to Narasingha Sil for his interpretation of the pearl as a ball of seminal fluid.
22. Saradananda contradicts himself here. In one passage, he states clearly that the Ramawat babas came after the paramahaṁsas, who came shortly after Ramakrishna's Vedantic practices (LP 4.2.10). In another passage (LP 4.2.24), however, he suggests a very different chronology, with the Ramawat babas com-

ing first, followed by the Vaiṣṇavas, the Tāntrikas, and finally the paramahaṁsas. This latter chronology, which contradicts Saradananda's hierarchical scheme of the *sādhanas,* is very close to what I have called the "*Kathāmṛta* version" of the *sādhanas* (the Ramawat babas and the Vaiṣṇavas, both of whom worship forms of Viṣṇu, fit nicely into the "practices according to the Purāṇas," the Tāntrikas replicate the "practices according to the Tantras," and the paramahaṁsas come with the "practices according to the Vedas").

23. See KA 2.132 for the only *Kathāmṛta* passage.

24. Could this be the same vision of the command to "Remain in *bhāvamukha*" discussed above (LP 2.8.17)? It does strongly resemble the earlier bearded-man vision.

25. KA 3.141; 3.46. I treat both of these visions in some detail below, in chapter 5, pp. 267–269.

26. See also JV(5), 66.

27. See also KA 3.28.

28. Saradananda is drawing heavily on KA 3.28–29.

29. See also LP 4.4.39.

30. See also KA 3.28.

31. See KA 3.31.

32. Quoted in Sil, "Untold Story," 46.

33. KA 4.167; 4.135.

34. Datta saw something similar happening (TS, 10).

35. KA 1.61; 2.19; PU, 14; PRU, 2; TS, 74–75; TP, no. 29.

36. See Pravrajika Atmaprana, *Sri Ramakrishna's Dakshineswar* (New Delhi: Ramakrishna Sarada Mission, 1986), 19–22.

37. Translating the Bengali expression *majār kuṭi* or "mansion/hut of fun" is rather tricky since the term *kuṭi* can mean either a simple, mud and straw "hut" or an elaborate stone "mansion" where a rich man carries on his business. I originally opted for "hut," but I have since concluded that, because Mathur's own *kuṭhi* (=*kuṭi*) or "mansion" occupied such an important place in Ramakrishna's lived experience, "mansion" is the better translation, at least here, where we are translating the expression *as it was used and understood by Ramakrishna*. Even if the term *kuṭi* may indeed have meant "hut" in its original literary context (a poetic duel between Ramprasad and Aju Gosai), it is extremely unlikely that Ramakrishna could have uttered the expression without immediately associating it with the *kuṭhi* in which he lived for some sixteen years—his boss's temple "mansion." For a brief discussion of this "mansion of fun" in Bengali literature and Ramakrishna's own use of the expression, see my "Kālī's Child" (diss.), chapter 3, "The Hut's History: From Poetic Sarcasm to the Joke of the World."

38. KA 1.105; 1.152; 1.209.

39. The expressions are *anuloma* and *viloma,* literally, "with the hair" and "against the hair."

40. For a very similar reading of Vedānta, see Datta's "hidden meaning" in his TS, 84.

41. KA 1.100; 2.73.

42. For some sayings related to this theme, see, for example, TP, nos. 12–17.

43. This is an entirely traditional vision. Consider, for example, the following passage from the *Gandharva Tantra* (36.29): "Know that the animate and inanimate world is filled with Śiva and Śakti" (quoted in SM, 339, n. 4).

44. See also TP, nos. 12–17.

45. KA 1.247; 2.193; 2.221; 3.55; 3.175; 3.219; 4.146; 4.147; 5.113; 5.188.

46. Cf. KA 4.77, where Ramakrishna declares that "Ma herself has become everything."

47. Cf. TP, no. 235; PDU, 18.

48. Compare KA 5.68 for the equally ambiguous gender of the goddess.

49. Cf. PRU, 11.

50. Cf. also KA 2.237.

51. KA 3.68.

52. For other images, see KA 1.177; 4.176.

53. This expression is M's.

54. This expression is M's.

55. See, for example, PRU, 24.

56. Betty Heimann, *The Significance of Prefixes in Sanskrit Philosophical Terminology* (Royal Asiatic Society, 1951).

57. Interestingly, the word *bhāva* can also be used to refer to a person's sexual orientation or intention. For example, in JV(5), 49, Ramakrishna's implied intention to join Mathur and his wife in bed and Mathur's desire to lie down with Ramakrishna are both described as *bhāvas*.

58. See also TP, nos. 83, 128, 149.

59. See TS, 83.

60. Note the primacy of the wife in these states. See also TP, no. 150.

61. KA 2.110; 5.52.

62. KA 2.111; 4.6; 5.61.

63. KA 2.179; 3.246.

64. KA 2.96–97; 2.221; 3.56; 5.113; 4.209.

65. The expression "spiritual senses" is foreign to Ramakrishna but not, I believe, to his beliefs about the love-body. I use it here as a comparative analogue to the spiritual senses of the Christian mystics, such as Origen and Augustine, as analyzed by Bernard McGinn (*The Foundations of Mysticism: Origins of the Fifth Century* [New York: Crossroad, 1991], 121ff).

66. KA 1.36; 3.135; 4.201.

67. It is likely that the saint got the phrase from a certain Mr. Ghosh (KA 1.215).

68. See TS, 85, for a similar erotic engendering of *brahman*.

69. In an obscure passage, Ramakrishna speaks of a similar erotic "delight" (*prīti*). This delight exists in the human body and somehow leads to the realization that, "he who (knows) himself knows the Lord and he who loves himself loves the Lord. . . . " (PDU, 18). At this point the text, literally broken off the page, is missing.

70. The word for "hole" (*chidra*) used here is used elsewhere to refer to the

anus of a woman's body (JV[5], 16; cf. KA 4.201). Does the feminized male Tāntrika enjoy "sex with the self" in this "hole" as well?

CHAPTER 4

1. Wendy O'Flaherty, trans., *The Rig Veda* (New York: Penguin, 1981), 30–31.
2. Sinha, *Cult of Shakti*, no. 176; emended slightly.
3. Ibid., no. 4; emended slightly.
4. Sinha, *Cult of Shakti*, no. 93; emended slightly.
5. See also no. 111.
6. Sinha, *Cult of Shakti*, nos. 19, 25, 33, 53, 151, 152, 168, 210, 215 et al.
7. LP 4.4.52 (GM 4.4.47).
8. See also LP 5.2.6.
9. See also KA 1.219; 4.258.
10. Quoted in Brajendranath Bandyapadhyaya and Sajanikanta Das, eds., *Samasāmayika Dṛṣtite Śrīrāmakṛṣṇa Paramahaṁsa* (Calcutta: General Printers and Publishers: 1984), 1.
11. Quoted in ibid.
12. Pratap Chandra Mozoomdar, "Sri Ramakrishna Paramahamsa," in *Commemorative Souvenir*, ed. Swami Lokesvarananda (Calcutta: Ramakrishna Mission Institute of Culture, 1987), 53.
13. Ibid., 54, 57, 58.
14. See the chapter title to LP 5.2.
15. Note that here Saradananda explicitly connects "social work" and the influence of "Western learning and ways." This seemingly obvious truth will be hotly denied by later writers.
16. *The Life of Swami Vivekananda by His Eastern and Western Disciples* (Mayavati: Advaita Ashrama, 1989), vii.
17. LP 5.3.8 (GM 5.3.7).
18. Narendra got the term from "Abercrombi and the English philosophers."
19. The "body" (*aṅga*) is a rather safe term to explain the object of Ramakrishna's foot, despite the fact that the term can also mean "limb" and in another passage (LP 1.4.8) is used to describe Śiva's phallus. In any case, the "body" (usually *gā*) is used a number of times in the early volumes of the *Kathāmṛta*. In the later volumes, however, the term is sometimes replaced by a more precise one, the "lap" (*kola*). It is quite possible that Ramakrishna's foot was placed in Narendra's lap or even on his "limb" here, although this cannot be established with any certainty.
20. *The Complete Works of Swami Vivekananda* (Calcutta: Advaita Ashrama, 1989), 8:263–264.
21. LP 5.5.15 (GM 5.5.14).
22. LP 5.5.9 (GM 5.5.8).
23. LP 5.5.10 (GM 5.5.9).
24. LP 2.4.20; 2.8.28; 3.2.43 et al.
25. Neevel refers to something very similar in his "The Transformation of Śrī Rāmakrishna."
26. See also KA 5.114.

27. KA 4.63; 5.107.
28. See also KA 3.69; 4.64.
29. See KA 3.21–22; LP 2.13.27; and LP 2.13.25.
30. According to my tentative count, the number of passages are as follows: volume 1 (zero); volume 2 (two); volume 3 (three); volume 4 (nine); volume 5 (two).
31. See also LP 4.1.29.
32. See also LP 4.1.37.
33. KA 2.192; 4.75; 4.80.
34. Datta misreads the passage as referring to the desexualized nature of the "final state."
35. See also KA 4.164; 5.180.
36. See also KA 4.80.
37. Cf. KA 2.192.
38. Cf. KA 5.116 and KA 3.107, where the Mother becomes the only actress.
39. See also KA 2.142.
40. KA 4.199. Note that this passage occurs in volume 4.
41. Cf. KA 1.192; 4.207.
42. Cf. KA 5.128 for a very similar scene and set of questions.
43. KA 3.181; 5.28 et al.
44. Nikhilananda omits M's question (GSR, 273).
45. See also KA 5.62.
46. For a good example of this argument, see SM, 212–227.
47. Again, note the volume.
48. KA 2.136; 2.7; 4.227; PU, 42.
49. This might help explain why Ramakrishna often objected to women taking part in the singing and dancing (KA 3.98).
50. Quoted in Sil, *Rāmakṛṣṇa Paramahaṁsa,* 108.
51. For another scene, see LP 5.7.16.
52. See also KA 2.154; 5.140 and PU, 35.
53. KA 1.211; 2.162; 4.258.
54. As do Rakhal and Niranjan (KA 4.100).
55. KA 3.224; 4.98.
56. See also KA 2.58.
57. This passage is bowdlerized by Nikhilananda (GSR, 905).
58. See KA 2.82; 4.45; 4.239; 4.283; LP 2.APP.26.
59. See also KA 3.183.
60. The English word *sinful* is actually incorporated directly into the Bengali text.
61. Without denying the possible Hindu roots of Girish's theology, I would nevertheless insist on the predominantly Christian origins of this idea as it was presented by M in the *Kathāmṛta.* When M, for example, comments that some considered Ramakrishna's final sufferings to be a "Crucifixion" in which Ramakrishna "sacrificed his body for the sake of the devotees" (KA 3.249), it is very clear that M does not have Indian gurus in mind as his theological models.

CHAPTER 5

1. It is no accident this passage occurs in volume 4.

2. KA 1.247; 3.31; 4.28; 1.214; 4.208; 5.51; TP, no. 273.

3. McDermott, "Kālī's Tongue," 8.

4. For a detailed and entertaining discussion of this anomaly, see Richard Shweder and Usha Menon, "The Story of Kali's 'Shame' and the Authority of 'Original Texts': Or, Tales that You Can Find in the Puranas Which Aren't Really There" (unpublished manuscript).

5. I am deeply indebted here to the work of David Kinsley, whose *The Sword and the Flute* first set out a general, and I think generally correct, historical understanding of Kālī, at least as she has been worshiped in Bengal. Rachel Fell McDermott, in her "Evidence for the Transformation of the Goddess Kālī," has recently revised and deepened Kinsley's original insights into the "sweetening" of Kālī through a profound study of the Kālī *bhakta* and poet Kamalākānta.

6. KA 1.235; 1.236; 4.267.

7. Wendy Doniger O'Flaherty, *Tales of Sex and Violence: Folklore, Sacrifice, and Danger in the Jaiminīya Brāhmaṇa* (Delhi: Motilal Banarsidass, 1987), 101–103.

8. *Muṇḍaka Upaniṣad* 1.2.4.

9. *Sauptika Parva* 8.65–68.

10. *Devī-Māhātmya* 7.9 (I am using the edition of Swami Jagadishwarananda, ed. and trans., *Devi Mahatmyam* [Madras: Sri Ramakrishna Math, 1953]; the translation is mine).

11. Ibid., 8.62.

12. See, for example, Nityananda's commentary on the KT, 31.

13. Usha Menon and Richard A. Shweder, "Kali's Tongue: Cultural Psychology and the Power of 'Shame' in Orissa, India," in *Culture and the Emotions*, eds. Hazel Markus and Shinobu Kitayama (Washington, D.C.: American Psychological Association, 1994), 241–284.

14. F. A. Marglin, *Wives of the God-King* (New York: Oxford University Press, 1985), 214–215, cited in Shweder and Menon, "The Story of Kali's 'Shame.'"

15. Menon and Shweder, "Kali's Tongue," 271.

16. Ibid., 278.

17. See also LP 5.7.30.

18. The LP lists 5.13.1–3 as appendixes and does not provide paragraph numbers. I am thus following the numbering system from the GM but translating from the Bengali of the LP.

19. According to Datta, Ramakrishna addressed the question to Debendra (JV[4], 146).

20. See also LP 2.INTRO.5 and Vivekananda's *Collected Works*, 7: 207–208.

21. See KA 3.274 and 5.155 for M's version of the event.

22. KA 2.110 and KA 3.94.

23. Saradananda, probably drawing on Datta's account, mentions this scene in LP 2.8.23.

24. Note that this tradition is not revealed until the very last volume.

25. See, e.g., the myth of the demon Āḍi in Wendy O'Flaherty's *Hindu Myths* (Middlesex, England: Penguin Books, 1984), 257.

26. André Padoux, *Vāc: The Concept of the Word in Selected Hindu Tantras,* trans. Jacques Gontier (Albany: State University of New York Press, 1990), 61, n. 71.

27. *The Theistic Quarterly Review,* October–December 1879, 32–39; reprint in Swami Lokesvarananda, *Commemorative Souvenir,* 53–61 (page references are to reprint edition).

28. Ibid., 62.

29. Müller, *Rāmakṛṣṇa: His Life and Sayings,* 64.

30. See, for example, M. D. McLean, "Women as Aspects of the Mother Goddess in India: A Case Study of Ramakrishna," *Religion* 19 (1989): 13–25.

31. This process begins in the last entries of M's diaries, where the brother monks reflect back on Ramakrishna's teachings on *kāma-kāñcana,* "lust-and-gold" (KA 1.259).

32. Preface, Udbodhan edition of KA (1985), v.

33. The saint was particularly incensed by the fact that some of his male disciples actually did the grocery shopping for their wives (KA 4.109).

34. KA 1.111; 1.189; 2.231; 2.232; 3.124.

35. See KA 2.262 for Narendra's adoption of the same list.

36. KA 2.232; 4.272.

37. Sarkar, "Kathamrita as Text," 100.

38. KA 2.199; 2.229; 3.143; 3.245; 4.92.

39. KA 1.19; 1.153; 2.88; 3.155.

40. KA 1.57–58; 1.70; 3.154; 4.237.

41. KA 3.19; 5.109.

42. KA 1.71; 3.245; 4.203; 4.272; 5.144.

43. KA 2.99; 5.126.

44. KA 2.201; 3.131; 2.168.

45. KA 2.168; 3.143. Cf. KA 1.132; 2.62; LP 3.4.17. This bit of bitterness may have been the result of one of Ramakrishna's experiences with his own wife: "I wanted to go somewhere once. I asked my wife about it and she said no, so I didn't go. A little while later, I thought, 'Geez! I'm no householder, I'm a renouncer of lover-and-gold, and that's that!' Worldly men don't know just how much they are under the control of their wives!" (KA 4.202; cf. TP, nos. 187, 192).

46. KA 1.178; 2.61–62. Hari is possessed but by an actual witch who lives in a tree (KA 3.30).

47. KA 2.202; 3.193; 4.31; 4.36; 4.38; 4.57–58; 5.98; 5.183; 5.221; TP, no. 42.

48. KA 1.85; 2.227; 4.142. For other fecal images, see KA 2.21; 5.200; PU, 1–2.

49. KA 4.68; 5.43.

50. KA 1.143; 1.195; 3.5; 3.59; 5.220; PU, 11; PRU, 21; TP, no. 229.

51. KA 5.52; PRU, 8.

52. KA 1.57–58; 5.30.

53. KA 1.208–209; 2.88; 2.227. Cf. KA 1.209; 3.59; PRU, 18–19.

54. KA 1.154; 1.89; 1.96; 1.131. Cf. PU, 28.

55. KA 5.16; 5.29. See also PRU, 7, 9.

56. KA 2.61–62; 1.153; 1.176; 5.52.

57. Cf. KA 1.153.

58. See also KA 1.173; 2.97; 2.249; 3.67; 4.31; 4.38; 5.168.

59. This phrase refers back to an oft-repeated scene in Ramakrishna's life in which he took some money (*ṭākā*) and some clay (*māṭi*), weighed their natures in his hands, decided that they were basically the same thing, and threw them both away in an act of "discriminating" (*viveka*) renunciation.

60. KA 4.28; 4.61.

61. KA 1.111; 1.187; 2.261; 2.264; 3.266.

62. Cf. TP, no. 220.

63. KA 5.34. See PU, 26, and TP, nos. 189, 254–255, for a slightly different typology.

64. Sarkar, "Kathamrita as Text," 101, 104.

65. KA 2.80; Sinha, *Cult of Shakti,* no. 206.

66. It is worth pointing out that the Bauls allegedly practice a secret ritual in which they consume the four "moons" of feces, urine, menstrual blood, and semen (Das, "Problematic Aspects," 417–418), the very same four substances that Ramakrishna mentions here. This might help explain why the saint mentions only four essences, despite the fact that he said there were five.

67. KA 1.61; 2.19 et al.

68. There are others, for example, his curious inability to defecate within the city limits of Kashi when he was staying there with Mathur on pilgrimage (LP 4.3.18). Was this somehow connected to Mathur's presence?

69. The term *cora* and its cognates often imply theft, secrecy, or an illicit "criminal" sexuality. Kṛṣṇa, for example, is described as a *cora* who secretly "steals" the hearts of the milkmaids. These sexual meanings are important for the present passage, since Ramakrishna associates the vision, at least as it appears in the text, with graphic sexuality: *immediately* after he relates it, he describes another in which he saw God dwelling in the canine vagina of a bitch in the heat of intercourse. (I am indebted to Narasingha Sil for pointing this out to me.)

70. Much of what follows was inspired by my personal conversations with Sarah Caldwell, whose exploration of the role of sexual abuse in the worship of Bhagavati-Kali in Kerala inspired me to take another look at the saint through this perspective (see her "O Terrifying Mother: Mudiyettu Ritual Theater of Kerala, South India"]Ph.D. diss., University of California at Berkeley, forthcoming[).

71. J. Moussaieff Masson's provocative piece, "The Psychology of the Ascetic" (*Journal of Asian Studies* 35, no. 4 [August 1976]), in which he argues that "*all* ascetics suffered massive traumas in their childhood" (623; emphasis his), has focused much of the debate. As will become clear below, I agree with Masson that trauma can set up the psychological conditions necessary for certain types of religious experience, but I object both to the dogmatic, universalizing rhetoric of his claim and the ontological reductionism that it implies.

72. If we were to pursue this topic, we would have to be very clear about what we meant by "sexual abuse" by identifying such markers as age and power differences, the presence of coercion or threat, the breakdown of bodily

and psychological integrity, and the betrayal of trust, among others. We would also have to address the troubling issue of whether "sexual abuse" in New York is "sexual abuse" in Calcutta. Do cultural assumptions and religious structures (ritual, symbol, myth, etc.) alter the nature and meaning of a particular act?

73. The reliability of memories related to early sexual abuse has become a particularly thorny issue recently, especially with the charges of Masson that Freud deliberately suppressed his earlier trust in the victims' stories for the tenuous, but politically feasible, thesis that these stories were in fact fantasies (*The Assault on Truth: Freud's Suppression of the Seduction Theory* [New York: Harper Perennial, 1992]) and the growing awareness that false memories are sometimes manufactured in the recovery process (see, e.g., Michael D. Yapko, *Suggestions of Abuse: True and False Memories of Childhood Sexual Trauma* [New York: Simon & Schuster, 1994]). When discussing a case such as Ramakrishna's, for which we *only* have texts, I think it is important that we keep both perspectives in tension: although it is quite possible that I have manufactured "textual memories" through my selective methods and their particular interpretive techniques, it is equally possible that the texts accurately record the saint remembering, through the symbolic discourses of vision, ritual, and myth, early scenes of what we have come to call "sexual abuse."

74. Sil, *Rāmakṛṣṇa Paramahaṁsa*, chaps. 2 and 3.

75. See my review of his *Rāmakṛṣṇa Paramahaṁsa: A Psychological Profile* in *The Journal of Religion* 73, no. 3 (July 1993): 447–449.

76. Judith Lewis Herman, *Trauma and Recovery* (New York: Basic Books, 1992), 96.

77. These are all common symptoms discussed in the literature: Dante Cicchetti and Vicki Carlson, eds., *Child Treatment: Theory and Research on the Causes and Consequences of Child Abuse and Neglect* (Cambridge: Cambridge University Press, 1989); Herman, *Trauma and Recovery;* John N. Briere, *Child Abuse Trauma: Theory and Treatment of the Lasting Effects* (Thousand Oaks, Calif.: Sage, 1992); Oliver C. S. Tzen el al., *Theories of Child Abuse and Neglect: Differential Perspectives, Summaries, and Evaluations* (New York: Praeger, 1991).

78. Jensen, "Madness, Yearning, and Play," 93.

79. Since the time of Janet and Freud, we have known that individuals who have suffered some type of abuse often enter altered states of consciousness, especially under conditions that remind them of the earlier traumatic experience. Today such reactions are discussed as a possible component of "post-traumatic stress disorder."

80. Adults who have not actively integrated their memories of abuse into their conscious selves often reenact their childhood experiences by becoming abusers themselves. For an engaging account of just such a process in the life of a successful American male, see Richard Berendzen and Laura Palmer, *Come Here: A Man Overcomes the Tragic Aftermath of Childhood Sexual Abuse* (New York: Random House, 1993).

81. Swami Purnatmananda, ed., *Smṛtir Ālaya Svāmījī* (Calcutta: Udbodhan Kārjalay, 1991), 250. I am indebted to Narasingha Sil for pointing out this passage to me. The translation is his.

82. See, for example, YT, 14.

83. Masson, "Psychology of the Ascetic," 623.

84. It is also worth pointing out that the advent of his childhood ecstasies are traditionally, and explicitly, connected to the terminal illness and death of his father.

85. I think it is important that we not naively read each and every ecstatic state of Ramakrishna as an example of "*samādhi*" or even as "mystical." Context and emotional content are both crucial here. Whereas some such states seem to have been painful reactions or "escapes" from intolerable situations, others were clearly spontaneous and joyful. That is not to say, however, that these two types of states are unrelated. On the contrary, it seems quite possible that the former "defensive" reactions provided Ramakrishna with consciousness-altering techniques that he later developed into a visionary art of joyful colors and integrating emotional tones.

86. KA 3.33; 3.141; 4.109. Cf. also LP 3.2.31.

EPILOGUE

1. The italics are in the Bengali as bold.

2. The open empty field is also a place of sexual temptation in at least one of the saint's sayings (TP, no. 257).

CONCLUSION

1. M, however, did finally give in to Girish, promising the playwright post-mortem access to the diaries: "When I die, you will get them."

2. See, for example, KA 2.205; 3.121; 3.251; 4.101; 4.227. See also KA 2.143; 3.179.

3. Hence Ramakrishna must "forget the mantras and the Tantras" before he becomes "like a boy" before the goddess (JU, 45).

4. Consider, for example, the Vaiṣṇava Sakhi-bhava or "handmaid state" sect, about which Serena Nanda has recently written. Male devotees of this sect take on feminine identities and "engage in sexual acts with men as acts of devotion" (Nanda, *Neither Man nor Woman*, 21).

5. Recall that the handmaid state, as it is discussed in the texts, is in fact a conflation of two different states, the Śākta state of the Female Servant of the goddess (*dāsī*) and the Vaiṣṇava state of the Girlfriend of Rādhā (*sakhī*).

6. Such criticisms can still be heard. The Bengali anthropologist Manisha Roy, for example, charges much the same thing in her book on Bengali women. Describing the Vaiṣṇava tradition as overemotional and socially irresponsible, she blames it for "intellectual decline and the emasculation of national life in pre-British Bengal" (*Bengali Women* [Chicago: University of Chicago Press, 1975], 4). Narendra, no doubt, would have agreed with her.

7. See, for example, David Kinsley, "'Through the Looking Glass': Divine Madness in the Hindu Religious Tradition," *History of Religions* 13, no. 4 (May 1974): 270–305. Carl Olson discusses Ramakrishna's madness in this specifically Hindu context in his *The Mysterious Play of Kālī: An Interpretive Study of Rāmakrishna* (Atlanta: Scholars Press, 1990), chap. 4.

8. See especially June McDaniel, *Madness of the Saints.*

9. Sister Nivedita, *Kali the Mother* (Calcutta: Advaita Ashrama, 1986), 45.

10. Paul Ricoeur, *Freud and Philosophy: An Essay on Interpretation* (New Haven: Yale University Press, 1970).

11. Obeyesekere, *Work of Culture,* xviii, 17; second italics mine.

12. Ibid., 24.

13. Ibid.

14. Ibid., 21.

15. Obeyesekere, *Work of Culture,* 17.

16. See, for example, KA 4.85.

17. The context is interesting: "the slightest thing" Ramakrishna is referring to is his worship of a fourteen-year-old girl.

18. Jacques Lacan, "God and the Jouissance of Woman," in *Feminine Sexuality: Jacques Lacan and the École Freudienne,* edited by Juliet Mitchell and Jacqueline Rose and translated by Jacqueline Rose (New York: W. W. Norton & Company, 1985), 147.

19. *The Book of Her Life* in *The Collected Works of St. Teresa of Avila,* trans. Kieran Kavanaugh and Otilio Rodriquez (Washington, D.C.: ICS Publications, 1976), 1: 193–194.

20. Lacan, "God and the Jouissance," 147.

21. Ibid. It would be interesting to compare Lacan's notion of *jouissance* with the Hindu category of *ānanda* or "ontological bliss."

22. Quoted in Shashibhushan Dasgupta, *Obscure Religious Cults* (Calcutta: Firma KLM, 1976), 159.

APPENDIX

1. Swami Deshikananda, *M. the Apostle and the Evangelist,* 2d ed. (no publication information given), 1:422, cited in Gupta, *The Life of M,* 247.

2. He published this historically important lecture as the first volume of his *Rāmacandrer Vaktṛtāvalī: "Rāmakṛṣṇa Paramahaṁsa Avatāra ki nā?"* (Calcutta: Star Theatre, 1892).

3. For a fine study of the Vaiṣṇava tradition of religious "play-acting," see David L. Haberman's *Acting as a Way of Salvation: A Study of Rāgānugā Bhakti Sādhana* (Oxford: Oxford University Press, 1988).

4. KA 2.122; 4.76.

5. KA 4.76; 5.116. Cf. PDU, 13, and PRU, 10.

6. See B. Dey, "The Story of the Kathamrita," in *Sri Sri Ramakrishna Kathamrita Centenary Memorial,* ed. D. P. Gupta and D. K. Sengupta (Chandigarh: Sri Sri Kathamrita Peeth, 1982), 144.

7. Again, volume 4 is the exception: it begins in 1883. In his appendixes M also records a number of dates after Ramakrishna's passing away and even includes five scenes dated in 1881, well before he met Ramakrishna in February 1882.

8. Das Gupta, "Religious Classic," in Lokesvarananda, *Commemorative Souvenir,* 97–98.

9. M [Mahendranath Gupta], *Gospel of Sri Ramakrishna* (Madras: Brahmavadin Office, 1907).

10. Das Gupta, "Religious Classic," in Lokesvarananda, *Commemorative Souvenir,* 98.

11. See, for example, KA 5.147 and KA 3.179.

12. See, for example, KA 4.34–35.

13. See, for example, KA 4.271.

14. Take, for example, the cunnilingus vision of KA 4.238, which is clearly preceded by the expression "very secret talk." Two other shorter and less explicit versions occur in KA 3.138 and KA 4.283, neither of which are described as "secret talk."

15. The expression here is *guhya darśanakathā.*

16. Volume five also includes a repetition of KA 3.121 in one of its numerous appendixes (KA 5.182).

WORKS CITED

Bengali and Sanskrit Texts

Bandyapadhyaya, Brajendranath, and Sajanikanta Das, eds. *Samasāmayika Dṛṣṭite Śrīrāmakṛṣṇa Paramahaṁsa.* Calcutta: General Printers and Publishers, 1984.

Bhattacarya, Satyanarayan. *Rāmaprasāda: Jivanī o Saṁgraha.* Calcutta: Granthamal, 1975.

Das, Jnanendramohan, ed. *Bāṇālā Bhāṣāra Abhidhāna.* Calcutta: Sahitya Samsad, 1971.

Das, Jyotirlal, trans. and ed. *Yoni Tantra.* Calcutta: Nababharat, 1981.

Dasgupta, Shashibhushan. *Bhārater Śakti-sādhanā o Śākta Sāhitya.* Calcutta: Sahitya Samsad, 1985.

Datta, Ram Chandra. *Rāmacandrer Vaktṛtāvalī, Prathama Vaktṛtā: "Rāmakṛṣṇa Paramahaṁsa Avatāra ki nā?"* Calcutta: Star Theatre, 1892.

———. *Śrīśrīrāmakṛṣṇa Paramahaṁsadever Jīvanavṛttānta.* 4th ed., Calcutta: Jogodyan, Kakurgachi, n.d.

———. *Śrīśrīrāmakṛṣṇa Paramahaṁsadever Jīvanavṛttānta.* 5th ed. Calcutta: Jogodyan, Kakurgachi, 1935.

———. *Śrīśrīrāmakṛṣṇa Paramahaṁsadever Jīvanavṛttānta.* 7th ed. Calcutta: Jogodyan, Kakurgachi, 1950.

———. *Tattvaprakāśikā.* 2d ed. Calcutta: Kakurgachi Jogodyan, 1891.

———. *Tattvasāra.* 1885. Edited by Apurbakumar Mukhopadhyaya. Calcutta: Shashadhar Prakashani, 1983.

Datta, Suresh Chandra. *Paramahaṁsa Rāmakṛṣṇer Ukti.* Calcutta: Jogendra Nath Basu, 1884.

Gitaratna, Sacchidananda. *Paramahaṁsadever Ukti.* Calcutta: Saccidananda Gitaratna, 1892.

Gupta, Mahendranath [M]. *Śrīśrīrāmakṛṣṇakathāmṛta.* 31st ed. Calcutta: Kathamrita Bhaban, 1987.

———. *Śrīśrīrāmakṛṣṇakathāmṛta.* 2 vols. Calcutta: Udbodhan Karjalay, 1986.

Jagadishwarananda, Swami, trans. *Devi Mahatmyam.* Madras: Sri Ramakrishna Math, 1953.

"Jāgrata Naramuṇḍa: Ekṭi Cyāleñj." *Ājkāl* (Calcutta), 5 March 1990.
Kaviraj, Gopinath. *Paramārtha Prasaṅge, Prathama Khaṇḍa.* Calcutta: Sri Jagadishwar Pal, 1984.
———. *Tāntrika Sādhanā o Siddhānta.* Bardhaman: Bardhaman University, 1983.
Mitra, Satyachara. *Śrī Śrī Rāmakṛṣṇa Paramahaṁsa—Jīvana o Upadeśa.* Calcutta: Great Indian Press, 1897.
Muṇḍaka Upaniṣad. In *Śrīśaṅkaragranthāvaliḥ,* edited by V. Sadanand. Vol. 8. Madras: Samata Books, 1983.
Purnatmananda, Swami, ed. *Smṛtir Ālaya Svāmījī.* Calcutta: Udbodhan Karjalay, 1991.
Rāmaprasāda Sener Granthāvalī. Calcutta: Basumati, n.d.
Ray, Amarendranath, ed. *Śākta Padāvalī.* Calcutta: Calcutta University, 1989.
Saradananda, Swami. *Śrīśrīrāmakṛṣṇa-Līlāprasaṅga.* Calcutta: Udbodhan Karjalay, 1986.
Sen, Girish Chandra. *Paramahaṁser Ukti (Dvitīya Saṁkhyā) evaṁ Saṁkṣipta Jīvana.* Calcutta: Ramasarbashwa Bhattacarya, 1887.
Smrititirtha, Srinityananda, ed. *Kālī-Tantra.* Calcutta: Nababharat, 1982.
Vimalananda, Swami. *Karpūrādistotram.* Edited and translated by Arthur Avalon. Calcutta: Sanskrit Press Depository, 1922.

ENGLISH SOURCES

Atmaprana, Pravrajika. *Sri Ramakrishna's Dakshineswar.* New Delhi: Ramakrishna Sarada Mission, 1986.
Berendzen, Richard, and Laura Palmer. *Come Here: A Man Overcomes the Tragic Aftermath of Childhood Sexual Abuse.* New York: Random House, 1993.
Bhattacharya, Bholanath. "Some Aspects of the Esoteric Cults of Consort Worship in Bengal: A Field Survey Report." *Folklore* (Calcutta) 18 (1977): 310–324, 359–365, 385–397.
Briere, John N. *Child Abuse Trauma: Theory and Treatment of the Lasting Effects.* Thousand Oaks, Calif.: Sage, 1992.
Brooks, Douglas Renfrew. *Auspicious Wisdom: The Texts and Traditions of Śrīvidyā Śākta Tantrism in South India.* Albany: State University of New York Press, 1992.
———. "Encountering the Hindu 'Other': Tantrism and the Brahmans of South India." *Journal of the American Academy of Religion* 60, no. 3 (1992): 405–436.
———. *The Secret of the Three Cities: An Introduction to Hindu Śākta Tantrism.* Chicago: University of Chicago Press, 1990.
Caldwell, Sarah. "O Terrifying Mother: Mudiyettu Ritual Theater of Kerala, South India." Ph.D. diss., University of California at Berkeley, forthcoming.
Carstairs, G. Morris. *The Twice-Born: A Study of a Community of High-Caste Hindus.* Bloomington: Indiana University Press, 1967.
Chetananda, Swami. *They Lived with God: Life Stories of Some Devotees of Sri Ramakrishna.* St. Louis: Vedanta Society of St. Louis, 1989.
Cicchetti, Dante, and Vicki Carlson, eds., *Child Treatment: Theory and Research*

on the Causes and Consequences of Child Abuse and Neglect. Cambridge: Cambridge University Press, 1989.

Colledge, Edmund, O. S. A., and Bernard McGinn. *Meister Eckhart.* New York: Paulist Press, 1981.

The Complete Works of Swami Vivekananda. Calcutta: Advaita Ashrama, 1989.

Das, Rahul Peter. "Problematic Aspects of the Sexual Rituals of the Bauls of Bengal." *Journal of the American Oriental Society* 112, no. 3 (1992): 388–432.

Dasgupta, Shashibhushan. *Obscure Religious Cults.* Calcutta: Firma KLM, 1976.

Deussen, Paul. *The Philosophy of the Upanishads.* New York: Dover, 1966.

Dimock, Edward C., Jr. *The Place of the Hidden Moon: Erotic Mysticism in the Vaiṣṇava-sahajiyā Cult of Bengal.* With a new foreword by Wendy Doniger. Chicago: University of Chicago Press, 1989.

Eliade, Mircea. *Myths, Dreams and Mysteries.* New York: Harper & Row, 1975.

Forman, Robert K. C., ed. *The Problem of Pure Consciousness: Mysticism and Philosophy.* London: Oxford University Press, 1990.

Goldman, Robert P. "Transsexualism, Gender, and Anxiety in Traditional India." *Journal of the American Oriental Society* 113, no. 3 (1993): 374–401.

Gupta, D. P., and D. K. Sengupta, eds. *Sri Sri Ramakrishna Kathamrita Centenary Memorial.* Chandigarh: Sri Sri Kathamrita Peeth, 1982.

Gupta, Dharm Pal. *The Life of M. and Sri Sri Ramakrishna Kathamrita.* Chandigarh: Sri Ma Trust, 1988.

Gupta, Sanjukta, Dirk Jan Hoens, and Teun Goudriaan. *Hindu Tantrism.* Leiden: E. J. Brill, 1979.

Haberman, David L. *Acting as a Way of Salvation: A Study of Rāgānugā Bhakti Sādhana.* Oxford: Oxford University Press, 1988.

Harding, Elizabeth U. *Kali: The Black Goddess of Dakshineswar.* York Beach, Maine: Nicolas-Hayes, 1993.

Hawley, John Stratton. *Krishna: The Butter Thief.* Princeton: Princeton University Press, 1983.

Heimann, Betty. *The Significance of Prefixes in Sanskrit Philosophical Terminology.* Royal Asiatic Society, 1951.

Herman, Judith Lewis. *Trauma and Recovery.* New York: Basic Books, 1992.

Idel, Moshe, with Bernard McGinn, eds. *Mystical Union and Monotheistic Faith: An Ecumenical Dialogue.* New York: Macmillan, 1989.

Isherwood, Christopher. *Ramakrishna and His Disciples.* New York: Simon and Schuster, 1970.

Jagananda, Swami, trans. *The Great Master.* 5th ed. Mylapore: Sri Ramakrishna Math, 1978.

Jensen, Timothy. "Madness, Yearning, and Play: The Life of Śrī Rāmakṛṣṇa." Ph.D. diss., University of Chicago, 1976.

Kakar, Sudhir. *The Analyst and the Mystic: Psychoanalytic Reflections on Religion and Mysticism.* Chicago: University of Chicago Press, 1991.

———. *The Inner World: A Psycho-analytic Study of Childhood and Society in India.* Delhi: Oxford University Press, 1981.

———. Review of *The Work of Culture,* by Gananath Obeyesekere. In *History of Religions* 32, no. 3 (February 1993): 308–309.

———. *Shamans, Mystics and Doctors: A Psychological Inquiry into India and Its Healing Traditions.* Delhi: Oxford University Press, 1986.

Katz, Steven T., ed. *Mysticism and Philosophical Analysis.* London: Oxford University Press, 1978.

Kavanaugh, Kieran, and Otilio Rodriquez, trans. *The Collected Works of St. Teresa of Avila.* Vol. 1. Washington, D.C.: ICS Publications, 1976.

Kinsley, David. 1987. *Hindu Goddesses: Visions of the Divine Feminine in the Hindu Religious Tradition.* Delhi: Motilal Banarsidass, 1987.

———. *The Sword and the Flute: Kālī and Kṛṣṇa, Dark Visions of the Terrible and the Sublime in Hindu Mythology.* Berkeley: University of California Press, 1975.

———. "'Through the Looking Glass': Divine Madness in the Hindu Religious Tradition." *History of Religions* 13, no. 4 (May 1974): 270–305.

Kripal, Jeffrey J. "Kālī's Child: The Mystical and the Erotic in the Life and Teachings of Ramakrishna Paramahaṁsa." Ph.D. diss., University of Chicago, 1993.

———. "Kālī's Tongue and Ramakrishna: 'Biting the Tongue' of the Tantric Tradition," *History of Religions* 34, no. 2 (November 1994): 152–189.

———. "Ramakrishna's Foot: Mystical Homoeroticism in the *Kathāmṛta.*" In *Religion, Homosexuality and Literature,* ed. Michael L. Stemmeler and José Ignacio Cabezón, 31–74. Gay Men's Issues in Religious Studies Series, vol. 3. Las Colinas, Texas: Monument Press, 1992.

———. "Revealing and Concealing the Secret: A Textual History of Mahendranath Gupta's *Śrīśrīrāmakṛṣṇakathāmṛta.*" In *Calcutta, Bangladesh, and Bengal Studies,* ed. Clinton B. Seely, 245–252. Lansing: Michigan State University Press, 1991.

———. 1993. Review of *Rāmakṛṣṇa Paramahaṁsa: A Psychological Profile* by Narasingha P. Sil. *The Journal of Religion* 73, no. 3 (July 1993): 447–449.

Kurtz, Stanley N. *All the Mothers Are One: Hindu India and the Cultural Reshaping of Psychoanalysis.* New York: Columbia University Press, 1992.

Lacan, Jacques. "God and the Jouissance of Woman." In *Feminine Sexuality: Jacques Lacan and the École Freudienne,* ed. Juliet Mitchell and Jacqueline Rose, trans. Jacqueline Rose. New York: W. W. Norton & Company, 1985.

Life of Sri Ramakrishna. Calcutta: Advaita Ashrama, 1983.

The Life of Swami Vivekananda by His Eastern and Western Disciples. Mayavati: Advaita Ashrama, 1989.

Lokesvarananda, Swami, ed. *Commemorative Souvenir: 150th Birth Anniversary of Sri Ramakrishna Centenary of the Ramakrishna Order and 49th Foundation-Day of the Ramakrishna Mission Institute of Culture.* Calcutta: Ramakrishna Mission Institute of Culture, 1987.

Luibheid, Colm, and Paul Rorem, trans. *Pseudo-Dionysius: The Complete Works.* New York: Paulist Press, 1987.

M [Mahendranath Gupta]. *Gospel of Sri Ramakrishna.* Madras: Brahmavadin Office, 1907.

Marglin, F. A. *Wives of the God-King.* New York: Oxford University Press, 1985.

Masson, J. Moussaieff. *The Assault on Truth: Freud's Suppression of the Seduction Theory.* New York: Harper Perennial, 1992.

———. "The Psychology of the Ascetic." *Journal of Asian Studies* 35, no. 4 (August 1976): 611–625.
McDaniel, June. *The Madness of the Saints: Ecstatic Religion in Bengal.* Chicago: University of Chicago Press, 1989.
McDermott, Rachel Fell. "Evidence for the Transformation of the Goddess Kālī: Kamalākānta Bhaṭṭācārya and the Bengali Śākta Padāvalī Tradition." Ph.D. diss., Harvard University, 1993.
———. "Kālī's Tongue: Historical Re-interpretations of the Blood-lusting Goddess." Paper delivered at the Mid-Atlantic Regional Conference of the American Academy of Religion, Barnard College, New York, March 21, 1991.
McGinn, Bernard. *The Foundations of Mysticism: Origins to the Fifth Century.* New York: Crossroad, 1991.
McLean, Malcolm. "Ramakrishna: The Greatest of the Saktas of Bengal?" In *Memorial Festschrift for Ian Kesarcodi-Watson,* ed. P. Bilamoria and P. Fenner, 151–172. Delhi: Indian Books Centre, 1988.
———. "A translation of the *Śrī-Śrī-Rāmakṛṣṇa-Kathāmṛta* with Explanatory Notes and Critical Introduction." Ph.D. diss., Otago University, 1983.
———. 1989. "Women as Aspects of the Mother Goddess in India: A Case Study of Ramakrishna." *Religion* 19 (January 1989): 13–25.
Menon, Usha, and Richard A. Shweder. "Kali's Tongue: Cultural Psychology and the Power of 'Shame' in Orissa, India." In *Culture and the Emotions,* edited by Hazel Markus and Shinobu Kitayama. Washington, D.C.: American Psychological Association, 1994.
Mukerji, Dhan Gopal. *The Face of Silence.* London: Servire, 1973.
Müller, F. Max. *Rāmakṛṣṇa: His Life and Sayings.* London: Longmans, Green, and Co., 1898.
———. *The Upaniṣads. Vol. 1.* New York: Dover, 1962.
Nanda, Serena. *Neither Man nor Woman: The Hijras of India.* Belmont, Calif.: Wadsworth, 1990.
Nathan, Leonard, and Clinton Seely. *Grace and Mercy in Her Wild Hair: Selected Poems to the Mother Goddess, Rāmprasad Sen.* Boulder, Colo.: Great Eastern Book Company, 1982.
Neevel, Walter G., Jr. "The Transformation of Sri Ramakrishna." In *Hinduism: New Essays in the History of Religions,* edited by Bardwell L. Smith, 53–97. Leiden: E. J. Brill, 1976.
Nikhilananda, Swami, trans. *The Gospel of Sri Ramakrishna.* New York: Ramakrishna-Vivekananda Center, 1984.
Nivedita, Sister. *Kali the Mother.* Calcutta: Advaita Ashrama, 1986.
Obeyesekere, Gananath. *The Cult of the Goddess Pattini.* Chicago: University of Chicago Press, 1984.
———. *The Work of Culture: Symbolic Transformations in Psychoanalysis and Anthropology.* Chicago: University of Chicago Press, 1990.
O'Flaherty, Wendy Doniger. *Hindu Myths.* Middlesex, England: Penguin Books, 1984.

———. *Tales of Sex and Violence: Folklore, Sacrifice, and Danger in the Jaiminīya Brāhmaṇa.* Delhi: Motilal Banarsidass, 1987.

———. *Women, Androgynes, and Other Mythical Beasts.* Chicago: University of Chicago Press, 1980.

Olson, Carl. *The Mysterious Play of Kālī: An Interpretive Study of Rāmakrishna.* Atlanta: Scholars Press, 1990.

Padoux, André. 1987. "Hindu Tantrism." In *Encyclopedia of Religion,* ed. Mircea Eliade, 14:272–280. New York: Macmillan and Co.

———. 1987. "Tantrism: An Overview." In *Encyclopedia of Religion,* ed. Mircea Eliade, 14:272–274. New York: Macmillan and Co.

———. 1990. *Vāc: The Concept of the Word in Selected Hindu Tantras,* trans. Jacques Gontier. Albany: State University of New York Press.

Pal, Bipinchandra. *Saint Bijayakrishna Goswami.* Calcutta: Bipinchandra Pal Institute, 1964.

Prabhananda, Swami. "Who Gave the Name Ramakrishna and When?" *Vedanta Kesari* (March 1987): 107–112.

Ramanujan, A. K. "The Indian Oedipus." In *Oedipus: A Folklore Casebook,* edited by Lowell Edmunds and Alan Dundes. New York: Garland, 1983.

Ricoeur, Paul. *Freud and Philosophy: An Essay on Interpretation.* New Haven: Yale University Press, 1970.

———. *The Symbolism of Evil,* trans. Emerson Buchanan. Boston: Beacon Press, 1967.

Rolland, Romain. *The Life of Ramakrishna.* 12th ed. Calcutta: Advaita Ashrama, 1986.

Roy, Manisha. *Bengali Women.* Chicago: University of Chicago Press, 1975.

Sanderson, Alexis. "Purity and Power among the Brahmans of Kashmir." In *The Category of the Person: Anthropology, Philosophy, History,* ed. Michael Carrithers, Steven Collins, and Steven Lukes, 190–216. New York: Cambridge, 1985.

Sarkar, Sumit. "The Kathamrita as Text: Towards an Understanding of Ramakrishna Paramahamsa." *Occasional Papers on History and Society* 12. New Delhi: Nehru Memorial Museum and Library, 1985.

Schoterman, J. A. *The Yonitantra.* New Delhi: Manohar, 1980.

Sells, Michael A. "Apophasis in Plotinus: A Critical Approach." *Harvard Theological Review* 78, nos. 3–4 (1985): 47–65.

———. *Mystical Languages of Unsaying.* Chicago: University of Chicago Press, 1994.

Shweder, Richard, and Usha Menon, "The Story of Kali's 'Shame' and the Authority of 'Original Texts': Or, Tales that You Can Find in the Puranas which Aren't Really There." Unpublished manuscript, University of Chicago.

Sil, Narasingha P. *Rāmakṛṣṇa Paramahaṁsa: A Psychological Profile.* Leiden: E. J. Brill, 1991.

———. 1993. "Vivekānanda's Rāmakṛṣṇa: An Untold Story of Mythmaking and Propaganda." *Numen* 40 (1993): 38–62.

Sinha, Jadunath. *The Cult of Shakti: Rama Prasada's Devotional Songs.* Calcutta: Jadunath Sinha Foundation, 1981.

Spiro, Melford E. *Oedipus in the Trobriands.* Chicago: University of Chicago Press, 1982.

Swidler, Arlene, ed. *Homosexuality and World Religions.* Valley Forge, Pa.: Trinity Press, 1993.

Tzen, Oliver C. S., et al. *Theories of Child Abuse and Neglect: Differential Perspectives, Summaries, and Evaluations.* New York: Praeger, 1991.

Woodroffe, John. *Principles of Tantra: The Tantra-Tattva of Śrīyukta Śiva Candra Vidyārṇava Bhattacārya Mahodya,* Part I (1913; Madras: Ganesh and Company, 1986).

Woods, Richard. *Understanding Mysticism.* Garden City: Doubleday & Company, 1980.

Yapko, Michael D. *Suggestions of Abuse: True and False Memories of Childhood Sexual Trauma.* New York: Simon & Schuster, 1994.

Zimmer, Heinrich. *Philosophies of India.* Edited by Joseph Campbell. Princeton: Princeton University Press, 1974.

INDEX

I have ignored diacritical marks in alphabetizing terms. I have not indexed the subject "Ramakrishna" and have only lightly indexed the terms "Tantra," "mystical," and "erotic." The entire book, after all, is about this individual and these themes.

knower (*jñānī*)
  boring, 186
  grammar of, 187–188
  and mat of deception, 177, 178
  transcended by mystic, 185, 186–187
Komartoli, 51
Krishnamayi, 126
Kṛṣṇa
  and cross-dressing, 26
  -fiṣṇa nonsense, 26
  and homoeroticism, 52, 66, 81, 261–262
  as incarnation, 227
  and Kālī, 47, 51–52, 63, 83–84, 181
  and milkmaids, 27, 56, 58, 64–65, 66, 112, 116, 154, 167, 190–191, 358n. 69
  and Nārāyāṇa, 228
  nipples of, 233
  passionate-, 132
  and Rādhā, 66, 68, 81, 92, 96, 113, 181, 190, 194, 236, 237, 261, 334
  Ramakrishna as, 56, 58, 116, 219, 298
  and states, 190
  temple, 14
  as thief, 358n. 69
  See also Gopāla state; Rādhā
Kshudiram, 54–57, 360n. 84
kuṇḍalinī, 44, 51, 96, 128, 288
Kurtz, Stanley, xvi, 38

Lacan, Jacques, 40–41, 325–327
Lachmibai, 122
landlords, 102
language
  and body, 37
  and gender, 25–27, 181, 183, 194, 234
  and mysticism, 17–19, 187–189
  and transliteration, xix–xx
lap
  of boy, 1, 2, 36
  distribution of term (*kola*), 354n. 19
  of Dr. Sarkar, 239–240
  of Mother, 138–139
  of naked woman, 120
  of Ramakrishna, 141, 191
  as "seat of bliss," 138, 335, 337n. 6
latrine of the house, 32, 287–290, 297, 302–306, 314, 317
Latu, 274
left
  as feminine, 235
  -footed, 201
  -handed rituals, 50, 102, 117–119
  side, 48
lightning, 191
liṅgam
  censorship of term, 29, 231
  and conception, 55
  cosmic, 110
  and love for disciples, 230–231, 241
  and phallic love, 230–231, 335
  stem of lotus as, 128
  temples, 14
  worship of living-, 159–163, 196, 231, 241, 299, 301, 312, 322, 351n. 19
  See also penis
lion, 26, 66
Long-Tongue, 247–248, 251
lotus
  and *cakras*, 44, 128, 236–238
  and Kālī's feet, 204
  thousand-petaled, 44, 96, 114, 237, 324
  as vagina, 45, 127–130, 138, 195, 204, 231, 237, 271, 275, 289, 327–328, 349n. 77
love-body, 192–197, 199, 322
Lover
  Bhairavī as, 115–116
  body of, 137–139
  and Child, 123–125, 133–136
  as dirty, 289
  as flip side of Mother, 35–36, 102, 115–116, 130, 133–136, 142–143, 168, 277–278, 312, 322, 327
  and householder, 130–132
  and "lover-and-gold," 277–287
  Mother as, 85, 87–90, 120
  and sexual abuse, 300
  See also Hero; Mother; Tantra
lover-and-gold, 44, 82, 127, 207, 259, 277–287, 335, 357n. 31
lust (*kāma*)
  avoidance of, 207, 233–235
  and *bhakti*, 189–192
  in bowdlerization of "lover-and-gold," 357n. 31
  and householders, 13
  and *prema*, 196
  and *tamas*, 72
  turning around corner, 195, 223
  and woman as lover (*kāminī*), 280–281

M. *See* Gupta, Mahendranath
mā, 48, 88

madness
  accusations of, 78–79, 110, 122, 209, 210–211, 213, 265–266, 297
  and childhood, 57–58
  divine, 321
  and family, 54, 55
  and Hanuman state, 103
  and incarnation, 241
  indigenous understandings of, 78–79, 206–207, 213, 241, 265, 297, 321
  as *mahābhāva*, 113
  marriage to cure, 78–79, 111–112
  Mathur causing, 112, 175
  and nudity, 101, 107, 161, 299
  pathology and method, 40, 45, 213, 241
  public anger over, 110, 122
  and *sādhana*, 94, 95, 101–102, 181
  from sexual abuse, 175, 298–299
  from sexual continence, 78–79, 111–112, 121, 122
madya. *See* Five M's
Mahabhārata, 248
maithuna. *See* Five M's
Mallik, Jadu, 211
Mallik, Ram, 59
Mallik, Shambhucharan, 168
maṁsa. *See* Five M's
Manindra, 235
mansion
  of fun, 18, 26, 174, 176–179, 182, 185, 191, 196, 200, 352n. 37
  Mathur's, 175–176
Marglin, Frédérique, 250
marriage, 78–79, 111–112, 134
Masson, Jeffrey Mousaieff, 303, 358n. 71
materialism, 38, 112
Mathur Babu
  affairs of, 299–300, 347n. 38
  attracted to Ramakrishna, 60–61
  and Bhairavī, 115, 219, 224, 314
  causing madness, 112, 175
  and cross-dressing, 92–93, 103–104, 105, 300
  death of, 175
  "making" Ramakrishna, 113, 219, 223, 255
  mansion of, 175–176
  and pilgrimage, 166–167
  protecting Ramakrishna, 110
  and Ramakrishna as girl, 97, 103–104
  as Rāvaṇa, 104–107, 320, 347n. 33
  and sexual abuse, 2, 19, 92–93, 105–107, 112, 175–176, 265, 299–300, 303, 314, 317, 318–319, 320, 321
  staging temptation scenes, 121–122
  and Tantric practices, 112, 134
McGinn, Bernard, 21
meat. *See* Five M's
memory
  and homoerotic, 343n. 62
  nerve, 67, 338n. 32
  and psychosexual conflict, 86, 359n. 73
  Ramakrishna's, 293, 297
  and texts, 71, 91, 94–95, 100, 298, 359n. 73
Menon, Usha, 250–252
menstruation. *See* blood, menstrual
milana, 114
milk, 2, 82–83, 138, 177–178, 180, 187, 189, 345n. 90. *See also* semen
milkmaids. *See* Kṛṣṇa
Mishra, P. C., 250–251, 293–296, 335
misogyny
  denial of, 10, 278–281
  genesis of, 141
  nature of, 32, 285–287
  and teachings, 281–285
  See also disgust; fear; lover-and-gold
Mitra, Satyacharan, 63
Mitra, Surendra, 209
money, 126, 358n. 59. *See also* lover-and-gold
monism
  and dualism, 146, 182
  theistic, 93, 110
Mother
  and Christianity, 169–170
  as flip side of Lover, 35–36, 102, 115–116, 130, 133–136, 142–143, 168, 277–278, 312, 322, 327
  as girl, 48, 49, 102, 126
  homoerotic nature of, 52, 141–142, 191, 220–222, 301, 318–320
  as Lover, 85, 87–90, 120–121
  as sexually aggressive, 140–142, 300–301, 303, 344n. 76
  and states, 190
  as "strange," 141, 319–320
  and temptation scenes, 120–125
  vagina of, 89–90
  See also Child; lover-and-gold; *mā*
Mozoomdar, Pratap Chandra, 206–207, 278
mūdra. *See* Five M's